Intelligent Tutoring System

Changing Role of ICT in Education

Noushad Husain

SHIPRA

ISBN: 978-81-7541-686-4

First Published in India in 2013

Intelligent Tutoring System: Changing Role of ICT in Education

Published by:
SHIPRA PUBLICATIONS
H.O.: LG 18-19, Pankaj Central Market, I.P. Ext.,
Patparganj, Delhi 110092, Ph. 22235152, 22236152
Br. Off.: 4617/18, Main Ansari Road, Daryaganj,
New Delhi 110002; Ph.9650028065, 9810522367
Email: info@shiprapublications.com
Website: www.shiprapublications.com

The Author Gratefully Acknowledges His
Indebtedness To
God
For His Mercy

Dedicated to My Beloved
Father **Zakir Husain** and
Mother **Aishya Begum**
Who Taught me the First Word

Preface

In the conventional teaching format, instruction is viewed as a process of transmission. In this viewpoint, ideas and thoughts are communicated in the sense that meaning is packaged into words and "sent" to another who unpacks the meaning from the sentences. Here the learner is like a sponge. This passive view of learning is one of the major causes of turning students into memorizers and poor problem-solvers. There is now a general conviction that this traditional way of expository teaching is not optimal for teaching and training students that the market requires and who need deep, flexible and transferable knowledge. This need has led to new pedagogical philosophies in which constructivism is the key item.

According to the constructivist theory, knowledge is being actively constructed by the individual and knowing is an adaptive process, which organises the individual's experiential world. Constructivism claims that individuals interpret and construct the world in their own way. Thus, learning is an individual process manipulating and interpreting the surrounding world. In the extreme, this view implies that reality is constructed by each individual. The implication for teaching is to focus on student learning, not on teaching, and on the actions of learners rather than those of teachers. The primary target of this strategy is supporting a process of construction for individual students.

One of the basic assumptions of constructivism is that knowledge cannot be objectively defined and statically represented (as it is in conventional student models). Instead, it is individually constructed from what learners do in their experiential worlds. By means of acting in a world, learners assimilate new concepts to their previously constructed cognitive structures or modify their cognitive structures to accommodate interpretations of the new experiences. It follows that knowing and doing cannot be separated and that the activity and context of an experience become an integral part of the meaning of that experience. Therefore, the focus is on the process by which knowledge is constructed rather than on target domain knowledge to be acquired. The constructivist school of learning suggests that learners construct personal knowledge from the learning experience itself as stated in. Thus, learning can be seen as an active process and knowledge cannot be received from outside or from someone else. Learners should be allowed to construct knowledge rather than being given knowledge through instructions. Furthermore, constructivists emphasise situated learning, which sees learning as contextual and suggests strategies promoting multi-contextual learning to make sure that learners can apply the information broadly.

Emerging of a knowledge society and growing demands for highly skilled and educated labor, force claim for changing traditional teaching and learning processes. One way of changes is related with an integration of various kinds of computer-based learning systems as supplements to conventional teaching methods. Research has shown that the appropriate use of computer technology can catalyze the paradigmatic shift in both content and pedagogy that is at the heart of education reform in the 21st century. If designed and implemented properly, computer-supported education can promote the acquisition of the knowledge and skills that will empower students for lifelong learning. Computers have become an invaluable asset to students and instructors in the educational process. The increase in availability of computers and network technology in the classroom has led to further use of these technologies by both instructors and students.

In computer science, 'Artificial Intelligence' is an important subject and refers to that category of research which tried to give computers some abilities like a human brain, such as speech recognition, image understanding and recognition, synthesizing, analyzing and decision making. The introduction of Artificial Intelligence techniques and Expert Systems technology to CAI systems gave rise to Intelligent Tutoring Systems (ITSs), i.e., intelligent tutors that can model the learner's understanding of a topic and adapt the instruction accordingly. An ITS is a learning system that is capable to analyze learners knowledge from their performances on exercises or tests so that the system can provide appropriate learning contents to individual learner. Intelligent Tutoring Systems is one of the artificial intelligence techniques that can simulate the human tutor in delivering courses. Intelligent Tutoring Systems (ITS) provide the benefits of one-on-one instruction in an automatic way and cost effectively, keeping in mind their multidisciplinary nature.

This book has been mainly prepared to serve the purpose of students, pupil-teachers, teachers and teacher educators for developing a better understanding about Intelligent Tutoring System (ITS).

I hope that after reading the book, the readers will be able to understand the concept about Artificial Intelligence (AI), Expert System (ES), Intelligent Tutoring System (ITS), etc. and they will understand the role of Intelligent Tutoring System (ITS) in education. The chapter namely "Role of Computers in Education" provides valuable discussion about why computers should be used in teaching-learning process. It gives a valuable insight about role of computers in education. The chapter "Artificial Intelligence" gives a clear understanding about the concept of intelligence, artificial intelligence and various disciplines related to artificial intelligence. Comparison between artificial intelligence and natural intelligence and problem solving through artificial intelligence is also discusses in this chapter. The chapter namely "Expert Systems" explains the concepts of expert system and architecture of expert system so that readers can understand the concepts easily. Learning theories as a basis for intelligent tutoring system is discussed in the chapter namely "Learning Theories and Intelligent Tutoring System". An effort has been made to enable the teachers that they develop intelligent tutoring system according to the need of their students in their subject. For this purpose the chapters namely–"Intelligent Tutoring System" and "Development of Intelligent Tutoring System (ITS)" are written and I am sure that that they develop an insight amongst the readers that how to develop an Intelligent Tutoring System with the help of existing tools and techniques.

The chapters "Mobile Learning and Intelligent Tutoring System", "Collaborative Inquiry Tutors" and "Intelligent Tutoring System and Online Learning" cover up the issues that help the users to understand how Intelligent Tutoring System will be helpful for online learning. These chapters show that intelligent tutoring systems are helpful for collaborative inquiry among learners. Several recent issues are raised in these chapters.

The book consists of 16 chapters with a long reference of index. An outstanding feature of this book is that it has been written in an easily understanding and simple language. An effort has been made to clear the different concepts with the help of flowchart and diagrams.

The present book provides an understanding about AI, Expert System and Intelligent Tutoring System (ITS). The chapter contains three main sections. The first provides an over view of Artificial Intelligence (AI). The second section provides the knowledge about expert systems. The third section provides an understanding about Intelligent Tutoring System (ITS) and addresses several issues concerning ITS.

I will be grateful to the students and teachers, if they offer me their valuable suggestions and comments about this book.

First of all I thank a lot of my indebtedness to "God for his mercy" because without the mercy of God the present work could not be completed. He gave me direction, knowledge, support and patience to complete this book.

I would also like to show my gratitude towards all those authors and publishers whose works have been consulted, quoted and abstracted to make the book up-to-date and interesting.

An effort has been made to coordinate several existing research information with personal experiences, understanding and desire. I remember with great gratitude all those great scholars who have influenced my thoughts with their masterly writings. Whatever worthwhile in this book couldn't have been brought to publication without the cooperation, advise, guidance and assistance of many of my well wishers.

With great pleasure, I express my grateful thanks to my father Mr. Zakir

Husain and mother Mrs. Aishya Begum, wife Razda Khan and brother Shahab Husain and other family members for their encouragement and staunch support. At the time of completing this work when I felt mentally tired, the children and my family members given me emotional and moral support and boost up me. I am grateful to my family for emboldening me in my task.

In the end I am grateful to Mr. D. Kumar, Shipra Publications for publishing this book within the shortest time with accuracy and style.

Lastly, I offer this book to all those who join me in making computers a worthy tool in the teaching-learning process.

Dr. Noushad Husain

Contents

List of Figures and Tables

Figures

Tables

1

Role of Computers in Education

Education systems around the world face formidable challenges that are taxing conventional strategies. Fresh approaches are needed to address persistent problems of the past and provide students with an education appropriate to the needs of a modern, information-based global economy. Now, after more than two decades of unfulfilled promises to revolutionize education, computer and communication technologies are finally able to offer opportunities to significantly improve teaching and learning.

Education and learning are among the most important of all human activities and always have been the principal means of creating productive and sustainable societies. With globalization and the increasingly dominant role that information and knowledge play in all economies, providing quality education is becoming ever more important. At the same time, the emergence of information and knowledge as core assets for development and economic growth is widening the gap between the rich and the poor. The gap is growing between those who have access to and can manage modern information and knowledge systems and those who lack the access and ability to actively participate in the information age. As shown in various gender and ICT use studies, this gap is particularly pronounced for women of developing countries, and strategies must be created to address the gender as well as the digital divide (Hafkin and Taggart, 2001).

Quality education is fundamental to successfully addressing development problems and bridging the information gap. Recognizing the fundamental link between education and development is easy. Creating systems that provide quality education for all, even when demand outstrips human and capital resources, is an extremely difficult challenge. Yes there is an urgent need to provide education that goes beyond teaching basic literacy and numeracy skills. Education must help to build higher-order cognitive abilities, strengthen processes of inquiry, enable collaborative problem solving, and prepare people to compete in global markets and become productive members of democracies. No single solution exists to address these immense challenges. New approaches and strategies for change are needed, and computers, mediated communication, and related educational technologies are an important part of these approaches and strategies.

When used effectively and integrated into schools, computers can improve teaching and learning, strengthen teacher professional development, support broad educational reform, enhance school-community partnerships, and improve school management.

Improving Educational Access, Equity and Quality

Over the last three decades, much international donor funding for education focused on the critical issues of strengthening basic education with an emphasis on increasing educational access and equity. These investments contributed to significant increases in school enrollments for both boys and girls in most countries, especially at the primary level. However, growth in enrollments among boys and girls generally has not been matched by improvements in the quality of education provided most students. In many cases, educational quality actually has eroded as the numbers of students increased without corresponding increases in supporting educational resources.

Labour markets and our global society increasingly demand more from school graduates than just basic skills. Education in the 21st century must continue to do what it has been doing to educate students and much more.

Investments to increase educational opportunities will pay dividends in terms of meaningful development only if students learn useful, realworld skills, gain appropriate knowledge, develop higher cognitive abilities, and are able to work collaboratively across cultures and languages. Unfortunately, many schools provide students with grossly inadequate literacy and numeracy skills, and higher level thinking skills are often not taught at all (World Bank 1999).

For many nations, meeting educational needs is complicated by limited financial, material, and human resources, the accelerating demand for education at all levels, and persistent poverty and equity concerns. These problems result in a massive challenge for education. As Wadi Haddad (1998) states, "Business as usual will not meet the challenge. Linear projections will not do. It is time for a radical rethinking of education."

Rethinking Education and Technology's Role

For many nations, the basic ways of organizing and practicing education have changed very little over the last century or so. Continued efforts are needed to modernize content, increase school resources, enhance teacher training, and improve access and equity. As a result of globalization, however, a new paradigm is evolving in the educational arena and changing how teaching is delivered and learning is processed. To begin, learning is no longer confined to the physical school building or the classroom but can take place anytime and anywhere, such as in computer labs and via the radio, television, or Internet. Additionally, the role of the teacher as sole provider of knowledge is also evolving to that of a facilitator and tutor. Lastly, learning materials are greatly expanding, and textbooks and some audiovisual aids are being supplemented by a plethora of multimedia materials in print, audio, video, and digital form. Through the power of networking, boundaries for learning are disappearing as both teachers and students are able to communicate, plan lessons, execute projects, share work, and forge new friendships and understanding across school districts, states, and countries. Computers and multimedia technologies in schools now offer potential learning opportunities and solutions that were not readily available before.

Critical Educational Issues

No single change or reform can possibly address all educational challenges, but information and communication technology can address a broad range of changes and improvements. Some areas in which the appropriate use of computers in education might make an important difference are:

Learner-Centered Education: Teachers must take on new roles as facilitators who empower students to question, experiment, collaborate, inquire, and construct knowledge and understanding.

Higher-Order Cognitive Skills: New curricula, teaching practices, and pedagogies are needed that enable students to develop and refine critical thinking skills.

Enabling Reflective Learning and Creative Expression: Educators need to create learning environments that enable students to acquire and use information that helps them understand their world and experiences and, eventually, generate new information and knowledge.

Lifelong Learning: Learning has to take place before, during, and after formal education, beyond the classroom, and through a variety of means.

Active Inquiry, Research and Analysis: Students must learn to formulate critical questions, identify, acquire, and organize information from different sources, and analyze and make judgments about collected information.

Collaborative, Project-Based Learning: Students must be able to work cooperatively in groups, on projects that cross disciplines, constructing knowledge using a variety of both electronic and print research and reference materials, just as problems are solved in real-world and work situations.

Technological Literacy: Digital technologies have penetrated most work environments, so the lack of technical literacy and skills is a serious handicap in modern economies.

Educational/Real World Relevance: Education must provide information, skills, and experiences that are relevant to the world in which students will live and work.

Individualized Instruction: Differences in individual knowledge, learning abilities, and styles are not usually accommodated in traditional classrooms. As a result, students often demonstrate lower retention rates, poor performance, a dependence on rote learning, and a lack of enthusiasm. Current learning models show that individualized, project-based instruction can reverse these negative effects and contribute to greater student and teacher satisfaction.

Can Computers in School Improve Learning?

Soon after the first personal computers appeared more than two decades ago, grand claims were made about how they, and related educational technologies, would accelerate learning, bring education to those without them, improve teaching conditions, enhance school and classroom management, encourage needed changes in pedagogy, and enrich and individualize learning. In short, computers would revolutionize education. After many promising experiments, numerous failures and near failures, and a few notable successes, it is clear that the promised revolution has not occurred.

Computer Technologies as Educational Tools

Computers are often viewed as tools that can be used to achieve diverse educational ends similar to the way that textbooks, laboratory equipment, curricula, or other educational technologies can be used to enhance education. This perspective of computers as tools is only partly correct. The limited view of computers as single-purpose and single-user tools often results in computers being treated as just another piece of equipment and not as an integral part of teaching and learning. One result of this narrow view of computer technologies and education is that computer use may be restricted to select groups of students, often those in computer science classes and those who pursue a narrow set of training activities such as word processing and computer programming. In fact, computer technologies can be thought of as boxes comprised of multiple intelligent tools that take on new functions and enable new results to suit the needs of different users. As Herbert Kohl (1996) explains, computers more closely approximate the functioning of the mind than any other device.

> Like the mind, [computers are open] to new use, new configurations and rules, new means of representation, and always new applications. In addition, computers are adept at crossing boundaries. Photos, words, sounds, and so on are all common objects that can be organized, manipulated, and joined to one another with the same general technique, but in unlimited combinations. This mobility has provided previously unimagined power to the mind to think globally and develop unanticipated connections or contrasts. [Computers] can (and most likely will) lead to new ways of telling stories, developing narratives, recording history, and organizing experience. The computer is unique, both a tool and an extension of the mind.

Changing the way we think about computers as tools is fundamental to our understanding of their potential impact on education and to determining how to integrate computer technologies into all aspects of education effectively.

Seeing computer technologies as multi-use and multi-user tools affects how we consider using them and how we evaluate their effect on learning outcomes and improving educational quality. Studies and evaluations of computer education programmes often seek to uncover significant causal relationships between single uses of computers and individual changes in student learning and behaviour. The very nature of learning and education, and the characteristics of computer technologies generally makes such studies ineffective. It is not surprising, therefore, that results from these studies are rarely conclusive. Research, monitoring, and evaluation studies should be designed to combine a mix of qualitative and quantitative methods that examine computers' diverse array of effects on learning, teaching, and broad educational goals.

Models of Computer Use in Education

Because computer technologies are not single-use or single-user tools, they can be used to improve education in many ways. When considering potential use of computers in education, it is helpful to create a few models of good use to guide decision making and stimulate creative applications. Designing, planning, and implementing new programmes and projects without models or examples are extremely difficult. Kohl (1996) describes this difficulty as the "paradox of large-scale innovation." According to Kohl, "[w]ithout models, people are left anxious and directionless, innovation fades, and things remain unchanged." On the other hand, the slapdash use of models can perpetuate poor practices, constrain the use of computers in schools, and inhibit innovation.

Two Common Approaches: Two contrasting approaches are often used to describe how computers can be used in education. One is based on how computer systems are actually installed in schools. This physical or structural approach results in two general types of school computer arrangements: stand-alone computers and networked systems. Similarly, physical models of computer use can be based on how computers are deployed in schools, either in classrooms or computer labs. The primary benefit of applying physical models when designing school computer projects is that their clear technical focus makes planning easier. However, using physical models to design school computer programmes can result in technology issues directing the project rather than educational needs determining how technology should be used.

An outcome approach is the second and more appropriate way of determining how computers can be used to achieve specific objectives and solve problems. To achieve real and lasting benefits for students and teachers, it is essential that genuine, clearly articulated educational needs—not the technology—be the foundation and driving force of computers-in-schools initiatives. It is important to realize that the best computers-in-school initiatives involve a mix of all the areas of focus this model describes. Therefore, the model should not be seen as a set of independent separate units but as an interrelated whole.

Computers Improved Students' Learning

The potential for computers to significantly enhance learning and teaching are the most important reasons for introducing computers into schools and integrating them into all aspects of education. For this reason, improving student learning is the core of this model and is supported by the four other areas. The many ways in which computers can be used to enhance learning share one fundamental principle—"individualized activity" (Osin 1998)—that makes them different from all other educational technologies.

Unlike other types of educational technologies, computers enable individuals to have unique, interactive learning experiences. When mixed with communication technologies, they provide high levels of interactivity, some of which occur between users and the software they are running. For example, a student using a spreadsheet to apply mathematics principles quickly can see how a graph changes when the variables in an equation are changed. The student decides which variables to change, and the computer responds by displaying a new graph. The student and the computer are interacting at an individual level. Even when groups of learners work collaboratively with the spreadsheet, the user has both an individual and a group experience.

At another level, learners can engage in interactive educational games, which are designed to help them learn deductive and inductive reasoning as they solve entertaining problems. Each time learners apply logic to solve the problem with their own and game-based information, the scenario changes. This combination of "moves" by the learner creates a unique response from the computer that can test the student's thinking and logic skills. Through a process of repetition and increasingly more difficult problems, participants learn logical reasoning and sharpen their skills. The better the learning software or the exercises using basic applications, the more individualized and enriching the interactivity.

Research shows that individualized instruction accelerates and intensifies learning. When instruction conforms to a student's learning style, as well as his/her existing knowledge, rate of processing information, unique needs, and innate abilities, the student masters content and skills more quickly and completely, and learning is more enjoyable and rewarding. Computers can make learning individualized and interactive and enables students to discover patterns of information, experiment with and explore new forms of expression, and pursue questions and ideas. This capability of computers, when coupled with communications technologies, allows learning to become a dynamic social process within and beyond classrooms and schools. Networks of computers in schools, nations, and around the world can link students to diverse sources of information and perspectives that extend the horizons of study and catalyze collaborative learning.

Models of Use of Computers in Education

Computers can improve teaching and learning in six principal ways.

1. Computer-Assisted Learning (CAL)

In this category of use, also called computer-aided instruction (CAI), computer-aided learning (CAL), and computer-based training (CBT), computers are used to tutor students by providing programmed instructions and information. Students respond to a series of questions, usually in a multiple choice or true and false format. At its less sophisticated level, CAI is used for drill and practice to aid in memorization and self-assessment, most commonly to support math and foreign language learning. More sophisticated forms of CAL strengthen logical thinking and problem-solving skills by guiding students through progressively difficult scenarios. These applications often require learners to combine new information from the programme with existing knowledge to attain new knowledge and solve problems.

Research shows that when used to support and reinforce quality conventional teaching, CAL can result in improved learning outcomes. Students benefit from CAL by learning at their own speed and cognitive level, and they experience less anxiety when making and correcting errors. CAL tutorial and problem-solving applications also enable students to learn and master new skills independently. However, CAL can have a negative effect on learning if used as a substitute for teacher-facilitated learning (ETS 1998).

CAL also can supplement and bolster the quality of instruction when teachers are poorly trained or inexperienced, as in areas where lack of adequate teacher training results in teachers with both a poor command of the subject matter and effective teaching practices. When used in such situations, as it was in a rural school in Grenada, CAL for math and English education resulted in significant learning gains and a rise in test scores. Grenada marked the beginnings of measuring the quantitative impact of CAL technologies on language learning. Due to a breakdown of the main server and lack of ability to provide for maintenance, the programme came to an early end. As a result, there was a substantial drop in test scores, indicating the technology indeed was making a difference, and its re-introduction into the schools was necessary (Bosch 1994).

Learning Impacts: Two critical lessons emerge from nearly two decades of experience with CAL, as illustrated by the results of an ETS study of the effects of computers on student achievement in math. First, as with all tools, the quality of results is often more strongly linked to how teachers use CAL than with the applications themselves. Second, greater impact is achieved when learning problems and student needs direct decision making about what CAL technologies are used and how. Additional educational benefits emerge when students and teachers create their own CAL applications. This builds high-level technical capacity, results in CAL tools being tailored to specific teacher-and student-defined needs, increases integration of computer use into school curricula, and strengthens feelings of ownership of computer systems.

2. Simulation and Exploration

Using conventional teaching approaches, teachers usually find large, natural, mathematical, economic, or social systems difficult to clearly explain or demonstrate. Similarly, the time and difficulty of performing complex mathematical equations and graphical functions often prevents teachers and students from fully exploring and understanding complex principles. Computer simulations, a sophisticated form of CAL, make it possible for students to experience and experiment with a variety of biological, scientific, weather, mechanical, business, mathematical, social, and political phenomena with less risk, cost, and time than has ever been possible. More important, however, computer simulations make it possible for students to quickly grasp complex concepts and apply their understanding. In the absence of computer simulations, students usually learn the behaviour of complex systems passively through general descriptions and definitions of system elements and primary governing rules. However, because most complex systems involve several levels of positive and negative feedback and intricate interrelationships, general descriptions and basic rules are incapable of conveying much understanding.

Learning Impact: Computer simulation allows students to observe the behaviour of complex systems and interact with key variables to derive basic principles and make predictions about the consequences of changes in such systems. A simulation of an ecosystem can enable students to comprehend quickly the delicate balance between species and the impact that shifts in the population of one species can have on the entire system. In a matter of a few minutes, several seasons or lifetimes can be simulated as variables are changed and monitored and predications made and verified. As students interact with a simulation, they develop and sharpen their cognitive skills and begin to construct mental models and new understandings of the complex world around them. There are a variety of educational simulation games for teaching physics, chemistry, biology, environmental studies, math, political science, economics, history, and geography.

As with other types of CAL applications, it is possible for students to construct their own simulations by defining the elements of a system and the rules that govern how they interact and function. Through such exercises, students attain new levels of understanding, they often cross disciplinary boundaries, and skills are reinforced and made relevant. The process of developing a simulation often requires students to work in collaborative teams, carry out detailed research in different fields, and address numerous problems and challenges. These and other educational benefits contribute greatly to creating a quality learning experience.

3. Research and Analysis

Living and working in knowledge-rich societies demands new abilities. Individuals should be able to formulate critical questions, identify, acquire, organize, and summarize information from diverse sources, and analyze and make judgments about the results. Learning and perfecting these skills requires that research and analysis activities be integrated into learning across disciplines and throughout schools. In addition to the practical benefits of developing critical workplace skills, learning that involves research and analysis fosters development of higher-order cognitive abilities and is more enjoyable than rote learning. Research and analysis are powerful learning processes through which students actively create their own understanding rather than simply acquiring information passively from teachers.

Computer technologies are not required to enable students to engage in challenging and productive research and analysis experiences. However, these technologies can remove or lessen barriers to quality research and analysis, making the process easier and less frustrating. Technology also can lower the costs of research and analysis and lead to more sophisticated and rewarding results. In all research and analysis activities, there are practical trade-offs between labour and intellectual activities. When students spend time and effort physically seeking information, less time is spent in higher-order activities such as reading and thinking about their topic, formulating new questions, or exploring possible relationships and patterns. Computers also can shift the balance between labour and learning in favour of higher value activities and contribute greatly to producing quality results.

Digital Libraries: In some situations, computers and reference CD ROMs, electronic journals and periodicals, and communication tools can provide affordable access to current research and reference resources that cannot be obtained from conventional libraries and paper-based systems. It is unlikely that most countries can afford to establish and maintain conventional libraries in the hundreds of thousands of schools that have none. This, coupled with the long-term social costs of students not having access to reference material or the opportunities to learn to research and analyze, makes computer mediated research very cost-effective.

Conventional libraries are the principal sources of information for most student research in developed countries. Most schools in the developing world, especially those in rural or poorly served areas, do not have a library. Even a modest school library, with only a few thousand volumes, a handful of periodicals, desks, shelves, and supplies, can be prohibitively expensive to set up and maintain. For a fraction of the cost, it is possible to create a robust electronic library consisting of one or two computers, and a variety of CD-ROMs that can provide access to current and detailed reference information, a collection of periodicals, and an assortment of literature. Access to the Internet, if possible, makes an electronic library global. Electronic reference libraries cannot replace conventional libraries, but they are superior to no library at all.

It is useful to note that the same tools that provide access to digital information can enable students to analyze and digest it, as well as create reports and papers that combine text, graphics, and images. With a link to the Internet, the universe of reference sources explodes, and it becomes possible for students to engage in collaborative research with students in others schools and countries. In short, greater educational benefits can be achieved, at lower cost, through computer-assisted research and analysis than with conventional manual approaches.

4. Computation and Production

Computers excel at manipulating information, performing complex calculations, graphing relationships, and accomplishing repetitive tasks. Many of the most important learning activities—reading, writing, mathematics, languages, mapping concepts and relationships, presenting information in useful ways, discovering relationships and patterns, and sharing understanding with others—can be enhanced significantly by the judicious and creative use of computers. While these benefits are being realized, students learn practical skills in using core computer applications.

5. Learning Networks and Computer-Mediated Communication

When computers are linked to create local networks in classrooms and schools, it becomes possible for users to communicate across the network and access common resources including hardware, software, references materials, and text and multimedia files. When many local networks in a city, country, or around the world are interconnected, as they are through the Internet, the range, diversity, and means of communication and access to information grows exponentially. Network learning, or the use of computers and networks for collaborative learning, research, and communication, is rapidly becoming one of the\ most potent means for applying computer technologies to improve education. As Neil Rudenstine (1997) explains, network learning…

> …enhances the vital process of "conversational" learning… People argue and debate, listen and react, and sometimes even discover common solutions to difficult problems. [Computer networks create] an array of new electronic forums for such conversational learning. Communication takes place at all hours, across distances, among people on campus, and beyond. Instructors can hold supplementary "electronic office hours" and moderate on-line discussion groups, unbounded by time or place. Students, even those who are reticent in the classroom, can put forward their hypotheses and invite their peers' reactions, or describe a problem they are struggling to solve and solicit suggestions from others.

Central to all learning networks, computermediated communication (CMC) uses a variety of software that enables synchronous and asynchronous communication. The most common tools include email, listservs, computer conferencing, online discussion forums, newsgroups, and chat rooms. CMC in its different forms enables people to share information, ask questions, make new friends, collaborate, and learn in ways unimaginable less than five years ago.

At a minimum, CMC can improve communication among administrators, teachers, and students within a school. Electronic mail, the single most common use of CMC systems, has been shown to lower overall communication costs while increasing the frequency and quality of communication. At its most robust, CMC enables users to engage in research and collaborative learning that would be impossible without this global system. CMC's effect on education and learning should not be underestimated, and teachers and students are only just starting to realize the benefits of this exciting use of computers in schools.

Learning Impact: Engaging students in learning networks through deliberate strategies with defined learning outcomes and assessment activities can achieve many of the elements of a quality education. Participating in learning networks requires students to be active and engaged learners, "following leads, distinguishing the substantial from the trivial, synthesizing insights drawn from different sources, and formulating new questions. Seated before the computer, a student is challenged to make something happen, to act or pursue, rather than merely react or absorb. Such an approach holds particular promise in an era when students, more than ever, will need to sustain the capacity for serious learning throughout their lives and careers." (Rudenstine 1997)

Nearly all the information provided to students during the course of their education is heavily filtered and processed by teachers, textbook authors, educational radio and television programmes, and curriculum guides. Therefore, it should be no surprise that students often lack the critical thinking and analytical skills needed to determine if the raw, unfiltered information that permeates the world outside the classroom is true or useful. The best way to learn these skills, as with all higher-order cognitive abilities, is through active and collaborative learning processes.

Combining learning networks with computer mediated communication and the Internet has the potential to radically change education in new ways. Geography and poverty have become less of a barrier to quality teaching and learning. Because of the democratic nature of the Internet, learning networks are enabling information and knowledge equity. Learning networks are one of the only viable strategies available to poorer countries and communities to address one of the world's newest forms of poverty, "the poverty of information and knowledge."

6. Artistic Expression and Creativity

Discussions about educational development and learning technologies rarely include consideration of artistic expression and creativity. Yet these two related but distinct concepts are vitally important to the ability of all communities and nations to survive and prosper. Creativity is critical to the success of some of the most important human endeavors, including education, learning, the social and natural sciences, business and commerce, governance and politics, entrepreneurism, and the arts. Creativity and its twin, innovation, may be humankind's best hopes for addressing the many challenges we face, and sustainable development and global democracy would be all the more difficult to achieve without the possibility of human creativity.

Whether education and schooling can teach creativity or induce artistic expression is debated. However, education either can foster and nurture creativity and provide productive outlets and training to refine and direct artistic talent, or it can stifle these precious human qualities. Computers can be a powerful means of fostering, enabling, and sharpening creativity, as well as providing a whole new set of outlets for it. The computer industry, and especially the Internet, is considered one of most creativity-demanding fields of work. Core activities, including software development, chip engineering, marketing, web site design, and the redefinition of commerce, both demand and enable creativity.

Learning Impact: Computers enable and enhance creativity in four ways:

- First, computers and the different new media that have sprung from this technology are providing new mediums of artistic expression that have expanded definitions of art and music.
- Computer technologies, especially the Internet, are providing new ways to produce, publish, and distribute literature and poetry, making it possible for nearly anyone to share his or her art, writing, music, and poetry with a global audience.
- Computer programming, which demands and cultivates creativity, is one of the fastest growing areas of employment.
- At a more practical level, computers have become a primary means for graphic artists, designers, architects, and a whole new breed of web site designers to create and publish images, develop new products, and design buildings.

It is well known that academic achievement can be enhanced through participation in creative and artistic programmes. In the US, research shows that students participating in music education score an average of 10 per cent higher on Scholastic Aptitude Tests (SATs) than those who do not. Many classroom teachers have discovered that positive changes in behaviour, performance, and attitudes toward learning occur when artistic and creative activities are integrated into academic studies. Computer technologies provide new opportunities to capitalize on the mutually reinforcing relationships between creative and academic achievement while helping students strengthen, refine, and direct innate abilities. Creative writing programmes, for example, that use the combined power of computers and the Internet demonstrate the positive effects of mixing the creative, computational, and publishing capability of these technologies.

Role of Computers in Education

Computers have changed the way we work, be it any profession. Therefore, it is only but natural the role of computers in education has been given a lot of prominence in the recent years. Computers play a vital role in every field. They aid industrial processes; they find applications in medicine; they are the heart of the software industry; they play a vital role in education. The uses of computers in education are manifold. Here, we shall discuss the important facets of the role of computers in education. The computer technology has a deep impact on education. Computer education forms a part of the school and college curricula, as it is important for every individual today, to have the basic knowledge of computers. The advantages of computers in education include an efficient storage and rendition of information, quick information processing and very importantly the saving of paper.

Computer teaching plays a key role in the modern systems of education. Students find it easier to refer to the Internet than searching for information in fat reference books. The process of learning has gone beyond learning from prescribed textbooks. Today, aspirers can satiate their thirst for knowledge by means of the Internet. It is easier to store information on computers than maintaining hand-written notes. Online education has revolutionized the education industry. The computer technology has made the dream of distance learning, a reality. Education is no more limited to classrooms. It has reached far and wide thanks to the computer technology. Physically distant locations have come close to each other only due to computer networking.

Computers facilitate an efficient storage and effective presentation of information. Presentation software like PowerPoint and animation software like Flash and others can be of great help to the teachers while delivering information. Computers can turn out being a brilliant aid in teaching. Computers facilitate an audio-visual representation of information, thus making the process of learning interactive and interesting. Computer-aided teaching adds a fun element to education. Internet can play an important role in education. As it is an enormous information base, it can be harnessed for the retrieval of information on a wide variety of subjects. The Internet can be used to refer to information on various subjects to be taught to the students.

Moreover, computers facilitate an electronic format for storage of information, thereby saving paper. Homework and test assignments submitted as soft copies save paper. Electronically erasable memory devices can be used repeatedly. They offer a robust storage of data and reliable data retrieval. The computer technology thus eases the process of learning. A life without computers would seem almost unimaginable for many. The importance of computers is evident today and having the perfect know-how of computers can only propel one's career in the right direction. Today, computers are a part of almost every industry. They are no more limited to the software industry. They are widely used in networking, information access, data storage and the processing of information. So why not introduce computers early in education? Introducing computers early in education lays the foundation of most of the major competitive careers. Computers play a significant role in one's personal and professional life.

Computers are used extensively in the field of education from kindergarten to college. Computers are often viewed as an effective tool for teaching many topics and lessons. Some view computers as a productive educational tool while others view them as a hindrance to education and social networking.

Computers play a significant role in education. They store information without wasting paper. Computers can also be a great teaching aid. Lessons become interactive and more dynamic when students use computers.

Benefits of Computers in Education

Computers offer students a wide range of advantages. They facilitate Internet information searches. Instead of spending lots of time leafing through thick, heavy reference books, students can use the Internet to find information. Also, it is easier to store information on computers than it is to maintain handwritten notes. Computers make audiovisual representations of information possible. In that way, the process of learning becomes interactive and more interesting.

Computer-Based Presentations: More and more teachers make use of computer technology in their teaching. By using PowerPoint applications, a teacher can encapsulate a lesson in a colourful, dynamic presentation that many students find more interesting than a lecture.

Distance Learning: Thanks to computers, online education is now possible. Online education has revolutionized the education industry. Education is no longer just limited to a classroom setting. It has reached far and wide with the use of computer technology. Different people, from remote locations, are able to share educational experiences because of computer networking.

Computers are used in education for a variety of purposes. Students benefit from using them as tools and resources for gathering information. Teachers use them as tools as well, to help gather student achievement data, or compile teaching activities and resources for their students. Computers are essential tools for productive and successful students. Additionally, the teaching profession benefits tremendously from the use of computers as diagnostic tools and sources of shared information among professionals.

Function: Student use of computers in education has increased dramatically over the last few decades. Students of all ages use computers for looking up research materials, producing media and multi-media projects and presentations, as well as classic tasks such as word processing. Teachers use computers to process grades, analyze and input student achievement data, collaborate with peers, network with each other, and communicate information to their students. Many schools in developing nations do not have access to computers and their achievement data reflects their absence. Computers serve a vital need in the education field for the dissemination and absorption of vast amounts of information between large numbers of people.

Features: Students in schools where technology is prevalent and easily accessible have access to classes in technology, business, graphic design and many others. These classes wouldn't be possible without computers and them open doors to different career and education paths that might not be pursued without early experience in these fields. Elementary students use computers to get familiar with basic computer skills, such as word processing, that will serve them throughout their education and into adulthood. Educators use computer technology with speech software to aid in teaching second languages and assist with reading comprehension. Many school districts analyze student achievement data using computers to input and process test scores and grade reports.

Considerations: The World Wide Web has computerized everything from telephones to television. In order to gain a competitive edge, today's students must familiarize themselves with computer skills and implementation. Many advanced teaching degree programmes include a course in technology curriculum and instruction. It's essential for both students and teachers to be comfortable and familiar with using computers to gather and distribute information. It has also been argued that modern students simply will not maintain interest in a classroom that does not incorporate the use of computer technology, whether it be Powerpoint presentations, multi-media websites for class information, or web forums to share content and ideas. Computers have become so much a part of our every day lives that education can no longer keep the interest of those who use computers for entertainment or information outside of school.

Effects: Computers benefit students by providing quick access to information and skill sets that might take much longer to acquire using traditional methods. Students do not need to be ignorant of their areas of strength or needed improvement with easy access to grades and achievement information. Educators use computers to quickly and easily input grades and student data into programmes that will compute percentages and scores accurately and consistently. Weighting grades is no longer a question of mathematical accuracy on the part of the teacher, but correct input so that the computer can do its job correctly in calculating scores. Student achievement increases with timely and accurate feedback provided through the use of computer networking and web based grading programmes.

Benefits: Teachers also benefit from access to thousands of resources for improving and diversifying curriculum with a World Wide Web of teachers that share presentations, reproducible worksheets, activities and ideas. Computers have made a well-rounded and diverse education available to those in remote areas with networking software and programmes. When barriers to communication disappear, the possibilities for education are endless.

Computers are used in a variety of settings within the educational field. They can be used by guidance counselors, administrators, web masters, library media specialists, students, teachers, clerical workers and food service employees for many different reasons. Computers lend an organizational hand to schools, and they also improve productivity in several areas. For these reasons, computer technology has become an essential part of the educational system.

Clerical Staff: Educational clerical staff members use computers to store and maintain student records at both the district and the building level. Because student information needs to be readily accessible at all times, computers provide the means for teachers, parents and other school personnel to communicate and share information easily. Schools can use SIS (School Information Systems) databases to track student attendance, progress and personal or health information. These records can often be imported into other educational departments and areas; for example, some school library cataloging software can upload student records from the district's SIS, which makes it much more manageable to input large amounts of student data.

Guidance Counselors and Social Workers: Guidance counselors and school social workers use computer technology to communicate with teachers and parents, and they also use technology to keep and monitor student records. Additionally, counselors use computers to monitor student academic transcripts and grades as well as report information to necessary authorities or departments.

Administrators: School administrators at both the building and the district levels use computers to communicate electronically with other staff members and parents, and they also use computers to generate letters and documents for parents, send automated phone calls to parents or staff (weekly announcements or school cancellations) and report data to their state departments of education. School administrators also use computers to administer computer-based standardized tests to students and to monitor and track student assessment data.

Building and District Webmasters: Computers are also used in schools in order to maintain websites. Many school have building-level web masters, while a few also employ district-level web masters to maintain school and teacher websites. (In many schools, individual teachers are also required to maintain their own websites.) School web masters upload important documents to electronic document files, update calendars and important school information and provide helpful links to parents and teachers.

School Library Media Specialists: School library media specialists use computer technology to catalog books and keep student checkout records. Additionally, many school libraries maintain websites that serve as portals for their student populations. The portals allow students and teachers to access subscription-based resources including databases and encyclopedias. School librarians are often able to upload and maintain school library OPACs (online public access catalogs) that students and parents can utilize to search for books and resources at home.

Teachers: Teachers use computers for a variety of reasons. They use computers to keep electronic grade books; maintain and update personal websites to share information with families; communicate with other teachers, parents and administrators and use software to create classroom newsletters. Teachers also use computers to access information, engage in video conferencing, research various topics and create and update lesson plans. Teachers use computers to design personalized web-based learning programmes for students, and they also allow teachers to design assignment requirements and web quests for student use. Finally, teachers can use computer technology to generate and utilize electronic testing for their students.

Students: In school settings, students use computers to learn both with and from technology. Computers enable students to research a variety of subjects, create projects to demonstrate learning and sort and synthesize information. Students can also use computers to view assignment guidelines and requirements at home and communicate with teachers about assignments. Some students use computers to blog about what they've learned or communicate with other students around the world.

Advantages of Computers

The interactive nature of computers in instruction underlies most of their advantages. As an active mode of instruction, they require learner participation. Specific advantages are the following:

- Simply allowing students to learn at their own pace produces significant time savings over conventional classroom instruction. Computer-based instruction allows students some control over the rate and sequence of their learning (individualization).
- High speed personalized responses to learner actions yield a high rate of reinforcement.
- The patient, personal manner that can be programmed provides a more positive affective climate, especially for slower learners. Mistakes, which are inevitable, are not exposed to peers and therefore are not embarrassing.
- Computer-assisted instruction is effective with special learners-at-risk students, students with diverse ethnic backgrounds and disabled students because their special needs can be accommodated instruction proceeds at an appropriate pace.
- Colour, music, animation, sound and animated graphics can add realism and appeal to drill exercises, laboratory activities, and simulations and so on.
- The record keeping ability of the computer makes individualized instruction feasible; individual prescriptions can be prepared for all students (particularly mainstreamed special students) and their progress can be monitored.

- Computers can provide coverage of a growing knowledge base associated with the information explosion. They can manage all types of information: text, graphic, audio and video. More information is put easily at the teacher's disposal. Computers also provide a broad diversity of learning experiences. These learning experiences can utilize a variety of instructional methods and can be at the level of basic instruction, remedial or enrichment.
- The computer provides reliable and consistent instruction from learner to learner, regardless of the teacher or trainer, the time of the day or the location.
- Computer-based instruction can improve efficiency and effectiveness. Effectiveness refers to improved learner achievement, whereas efficiency means achieving objectives in less time or at lower cost. Efficiency is very important and is becoming increasingly important in educational settings.
- One serendipitous effect of working with computers is that they literally force us to communicate with them in an orderly and logical way. The computer user must learn to communicate with explicit, exact instructions and responses. Any departure from precision is rejected by the computer.
- Computer users learn keyboarding or typing skills. Now very young children as well as adults are developing these skills in order to communicate with computers.
- With the advent of easy-to-use authoring systems, some teachers can develop their own customized computer-based learning programmes.

Characteristics of Computers as Instructional Tool/Assistant

Casey (1997) lists characteristics and advantages of computers as instructional tools and assistants in the classroom:

- Computers are motivating and fun. They make things happen.
- Computers with good software can be highly interactive as opposed to books, tapes, films, radio or television. The user controls what happens.
- Computers are non-judgmental and they have infinite patience.
- Computers with hypermedia can explain concepts in a more interesting, visual or animated manner.
- Computers can simulate situations which are too complex, dangerous or costly to do in the classroom. Chemical reaction, ecosystems, apace travels and the like can safely be explored.
- Children can create reports and research for their peers by using hyper-studio and other authoring systems. Real-word learning occurs in problem-solving and the creation of these materials.
- Through telecommunication, computers bring the resources of the

world into the classroom and allow students in one classroom to communicate with others anywhere in the world.

Computers Promotes Individualized Teaching and Learning

Since 1920's researchers have been looking for different ways to utilise teaching machines, auto-instructors and, later on, computers in instruction. Despite that, computers are only seldom used systematically in teaching. There exist many reasons for that, such as unawareness of human learning, the complexity of the design process of computer-aided instruction (CAI) applications, and the fast development of computer technology, which has caused problems since CAI materials designed for certain computer configurations become obsolete in a few years. In the early days of computer-aided instruction there was a dream that human teachers will someday be replaced by computers. This dream is nowadays rejected because it has become clear that computers are not capable to take care of the role of a human teacher since, firstly, human contact is very important and, secondly, human-like features, such as heuristical problem solving and concluding, should progress extremely within computers, which hardly happens in near future. Therefore, human teachers will keep on teaching, maybe not the way they have always taught but using computers as tools.

Computer-aided instruction can be defined concisely as a teaching method in which a student interacts with a specialised computer application designed to instruct certain skills and knowledge. A more extensive definition includes the use of computers in all study tasks, such as students using computer applications as tools (e.g., text processors, spreadsheet calculators), teachers preparing lesson materials (e.g., lecture notes, presentation materials, software demonstrations, CAI applications), or school administration personnel organizing educational administration on computers (e.g., curriculum design, student files). Depending on the situation, several abbreviations can be used, such as CAI (computer-aided/assisted instruction), CAL (computer-aided/assisted learning), CBE (computer-based education), CBI (computer-based instruction), CBT (computer-based training), and CMI (computer-managed instruction). These abbreviations have different shades of meaning, though they all refer to use of computers in education. This study concentrates on CAI in its concise meaning, that is, the use of computer applications in instruction.

CAI is considered to be based on Pressey's teaching machines dating back to the 1920's. According to Sloffer (1996), these teaching machines presented questions or problems to students who had to respond by writing an answer or pressing a certain button. Students were informed about the correctness of the answer and occasionally given the explanation why it was right or wrong. An account of responses was often kept. In the 1950's Skinner introduced his version of a teaching machine and programmed instruction which were based on his theory of operant conditioning. According to Li (1996), programmed instruction had important long-term effects on the evolution of educational technology;

namely, it had a strong influence on the development of systems approach, and it introduced the early ideas of individualisation of instruction. A decade later teaching machines were considered to be obsolete since researchers perceived that as a teaching tool the machines are not as important as the programmes. The concept of CAI was introduced in the 1960's.

Two important projects in the history of CAI are PLATO (Programmed Logic for Automatic Teaching Operations) and TICCIT (Timeshared Interactive Computer-Controlled Information Television). These two projects were competing with each other to become the national automated instruction system in United States of America. Even though both of them were based on mainframe computers, the rest of the technical solutions differed a lot from each other. Neither of them became predominant since the expected fall in installation and utilisation costs did not happen. Nevertheless, both of them served as a basis for other instructional systems.

The built-in educational properties are the essence of CAI applications. These properties include clearly stated learning aims, methods to reach these aims, and testing whether these aims are achieved. In addition, CAI applications support and guide students' proceeding in a CAI application. These properties separate CAI applications from other computer applications, such as multi- and hypermedia applications and expert systems, which all have been used for instructional purposes. Since the educational properties are usually missing from these other applications, the instructional use of them differs noticeable from the use of CAI applications. Thus, CAI applications can be used as tutors, while the other computer applications can be considered as tools.

Traditionally teaching has been a situation in which a teacher talks in front of students. Teaching this way is strongly teacher-centered but many times it has been the only possibility. Reasons for that could have been the lack of teaching materials, teachers, classrooms, etc. Also the earlier learning theories assumed that students are like empty baskets and teacher's task is to fill them with information. These kind of theories are not valid anymore because research has revealed that human learning is more complicated. This observation has affected the teacher's role in instruction.

Researchers of human learning have presented lists of educational or instructional tasks, which should provide the necessary conditions for learning. These tasks are good to remember while designing instruction and selecting appropriate media. As an example, Gagné and Briggs (1974) have presented the following nine instructional events:

1. *Gaining attention* means that students' interests in teaching subject are awakened. This can be done, for example, with questions or demonstrations.
2. *Informing the learner of the objective* gives students the learning aim. This phase is not necessary if the aim is obvious.

3. *Stimulating recall of prerequisite learned capabilities* helps students to combine their prior knowledge to new information. Stimulation can be done asking recall questions.
4. *Presenting the stimulus material* is closely connected to the learning aim. It is necessary that stimuli must support students to reach the aim.
5. *Providing learning guidance* is an event in which students are guided to the direction of the correct answer or performance. The form of learning guidance can be, for example, questions or hints proposed during instruction.
6. *Eliciting the performance* means that students show what they know or are able to demonstrate their skills.
7. *Providing feedback* is telling students the correctness of their performance. In some cases this is not necessary if there exists 'automatic' feedback, such as in throwing darts the result is immediately clear.
8. *Assessing performance* focuses on the reliability and validity of students' performance. A couple of appropriate questions that force students to apply their new knowledge should convince the teacher that students' performance is valid.
9. *Enhancing retention and transfer* means systematic reviews and practicing of skills.

A teacher does not have to strictly follow these steps described above. A better result is often achieved when these steps have been used to form a fluently proceeding, well-adjusted unity in which these demands have been taken into account.

Within instruction, teachers are responsible of the totality. They decide what to teach and how to teach, and they take care of the needed material. It is assumed that teachers apply some learning theory while designing the lessons. This is something that computers cannot do by themselves. Furthermore, teachers are human beings with their gestures, expressions and intelligence. They are able to think, to make heuristic conclusions and use body language. For example, students easily see if teachers are motivated and interested in topic they are teaching. That is likely to increase students' motivation and improve learning results. Likewise, teachers are able to react to students' behaviour, for example, when they seem to be confused or have problems.

Computers have no human properties which is the most important reason why they cannot replace human teachers. Instead, computers should be used as tools in instruction because they have many valuable properties, such as availability in a sense that they are cheap, relatively high speed, tirelessness, large memory capacity, and ability to animate graphics. It would be wise to use these properties whenever it is appropriate.

One of the strongest advantages of computers is their ability to present animated graphics. According to Kiser (1987), this unique feature permits designing of computer lessons that instruct in a way that static formats cannot. Richards and Fukuzawa (1989) have pointed out that seeing shapes, forms, and symbols manipulated in a concrete way is more effective than trying to visualise an abstract model in one's mind. Baek and Layne (1988) have reported that well-designed computer lessons with animation have improved student scores more than presentations with graphics and text or text alone. Since animation is a strong effect it must be used wisely. It overrules the main subject if it is used too much or in a wrong place.

Computers have a great memory capacity which can be used for storing large amounts of information. They are also fast in certain tasks. Rapidity is useful, for example, when searching information from diverse sources for writing an essay, or solving mathematical problems containing time-consuming routines.

Tirelessness is valuable, for example, when practicing vocabulary or similar tasks. Students can repeat difficult things as many times as needed. They are also able to study as long as they like and continue at their own pace. In classroom usage, proceeding with individual speed is valuable because students will not become frustrated studying at an appropriate speed for them.

Computers treat students equally ignoring their sex, colour and social class. There are no bad days for computers, that is, instruction is not depending on feelings or other human features. Furthermore, computers can be equipped with unusual peripherals, such as touch screens or special keyboards, to enable the usage for disabled students. For many seriously disabled persons a computer offers a possibility to communicate with other people and to study.

Tutoring System

With the emergence of computers in the past decades, computer technologies have been significantly changing the content and practice of education. The consequent applications of multimedia, simulation, computer-mediated communication and communities, and internet-based support for individual and distance learning all have the potential for revolutionary improvements in education [McArthur *et al.* 1993, Forbus and Feltovich 2001]. The affordable, individualized teaching and learning environments become possible for a large and diverse population of students under real-world constraints such as limited financial resources and insufficient numbers of qualified instructors. The concept of education has been far more than traditional school education and the population of students is being broadened from children to nearly all adults for the needs of lifelong learning.

Tutoring and learning are two dependent aspects in education. The goal of tutoring is to help learners acquire more knowledge as well as improve their learning abilities. Thus, the development of tutoring patterns serves learning needs eventually. In history, tutoring patterns have evolved from the traditional one-on-one method and classroom method to the modern *computer-assisted instruction* (CAI) and *intelligent tutoring systems* (ITS). Correspondingly, learning patterns have also developed from the traditional pure textbook and classroom learning to *multimedia learning, distance learning,* as well as *interactive learning environments* (ILEs). CAI and ITS originate from the application of computer software and artificial intelligence (especially for the latter) to education, so the corresponding tutoring systems can be summarized as software tutoring systems. Similarly, the non-traditional learning can be summarized as *e-learning* [Clark and Mayer 2002], which is implemented on computers (via CDROM, Internet, or Intranet) and is designed to support individual learning or organizational performance goals.

Software tutoring system is a contrary concept to the traditional human tutoring system. The course tutor (not a human tutor) in a software tutoring system cannot enjoy the powerful face-to-face communication channels with students available in a classroom setting. Thus the control over learners is relatively weaker than in the traditional tutoring, where it is the tutor who is charge of the contents, sequence and pace of instruction and learning. In the software tutoring systems, however, it is easy for a learner to lose learning interest and leave the computers without the consent from tutors. Therefore, in order to obtain better tutoring outcomes, a software tutoring system should emphasize engaging students in the learning process and be adaptive to each individual learner.

The goal of the early software tutoring systems was to build clever tutors able to communicate knowledge to the individual learners. Recent and emerging work focuses on the *learner control* over the learning process such as learner exploring, designing, constructing, and using adaptive systems as tools [Kay 2001]. The concept of learner control is relative to the terms of tutor control, system control, and programme control. When learners have the option to select the topics they want, control the sequence and pace at which they progress, and decide whether and how to use system-provided tools, the tutoring system can be said to offer learner control.

Learner control in tutoring systems is intuitively appealing, which embodies the subject and the objective of tutoring and learning. It can alleviate boredom, frustration, and anxiety of the learners because it enables learners to skip over materials they have previously learned or avoid materials they are not prepared to study [Steinberg 1977, Steinberg 1989]. It provides learners more autonomy. Although the benefits of learner control have not been explored thoroughly, the critical problem is no longer *whether* learner control should be applied to software tutoring systems but *how* to apply learner control strategies into software tutoring systems to maximize the learning benefits.

Software Tutoring Systems

The software tutoring systems are generally specific to situations where learners and tutors no longer have to meet like in the traditional classroom-based instruction. Similar to the definition of e-learning [Clark and Mayer 2002], a software tutoring system can be defined as a teaching and learning environment built on computers by way of CDROM, Internet, or Intranet with the following features: (1) include content relevant to the learning objective; (2) use instructional methods such as examples and practice to help learning; (3) use media elements such as words and pictures to deliver the content and methods; and (4) build new knowledge and skills to achieve individual learning goals or improve organizational performance.

The courses in software tutoring systems include both content (i.e., information) and instructional methods (i.e., techniques) helping people learn the content. They are digitized so they can be stored in electronic form, and delivered via computer using words in the form of spoken or printed text and pictures such as illustrations, photos, animation, or video. The purpose is to help individuals achieve educational goals or to help organizations build skills linked to improved job performance through training. The development of software tutoring systems has experienced three generations in rough and a variety of learner control strategies have been applied into each generation in different measures.

Tutoring has offered support to student learning and for improving student skills for many years. With continued emphasis on student academic performance and accountability, interest in tutoring programmes has resurfaced as a method to support students at risk for academic failure. Tutoring programmes, whether in school or out of school, volunteer or paid, are of interest to parents, educators, and researchers. The questions being asked about tutoring are:

- What types of tutoring programmes exist?
- What are the benefits of tutoring?
- What makes a tutoring programme successful?

Two Types of Tutoring Programme

While there are many different ways to structure tutoring programmes, two of the most common are volunteer and peer/cross-age tutoring programmes.

Volunteer Programmes: Volunteer tutoring programmes have been common in schools for many years; they typically involve an adult, who may be a parent, teacher, or other interested community member, paired with a student to work on academic skills. There are considerable data to support the effectiveness of volunteer tutoring (Potter *et al.*, 1999) and considerable information on the benefits volunteer tutoring programmes can offer. Students in volunteer tutoring programmes benefit academically, and they may also develop a more positive attitude toward the tutored subject matter (Powell, 1997).

Peer/Cross-Age Programmes: In peer and cross-age tutoring programmes, students help students. Peer tutoring programmes involve two students of the same age; cross-age tutoring programmes involve an older student tutoring a younger student. Traditionally, although these arrangements have involved a competent student helping a struggling student, there is evidence that this sort of arrangement is not essential. Tutors need not be experts. Both successful students and struggling students can gain from peer or cross-age tutoring relationships, and at-risk students may benefit significantly. According to Kalkowski, low-achieving students may "show impressive gains" from tutoring. Research indicates that peer-tutoring programmes have a positive effect on student learning and may have social and emotional benefits as well (Cohen *et al.*, 1982).

Computer-Assisted Instruction Systems

During the 1960s, educators were under considerable pressure to improve the quality of education as well as to educate a broader segment of society [Steinberg 1977]. Holt deplored the limitations of the widespread used lockstep instruction [Holt 1967]. Rapidly expanding community colleges had to accommodate increasingly numerous heterogeneous students. Teaching alternatives were sought at all levels and individualized instruction became a likely alternative. The application of computers to education made individualization even more feasible in terms of computer-assisted instruction (CAI, or computer-aided instruction). CAI systems were the first generation software tutoring systems. A CAI system presents a page of text or graphics, and puts up a different page depending upon the student's answer [Hefferman and Koedinger 2002]. Although the implementation approaches of CAI vary significantly, in which the computer plays the role of the tutor and communicates with the learner through human-computer interface in the form of text, graphics, multimedia, etc.

Model-Tracing Intelligent Tutoring Systems

Intelligent tutoring systems (ITS) are the earliest applications of artificial intelligence (AI) in education. Although ITS differ in a variety of ways. [McArthur *et al.* 1993, Kay 2001].

The learner interacts with the tutoring system via the *interaction module*, which may support natural language interaction or offer graphical interfaces. The *learner model* represents static beliefs about the learner and may stimulate the learner's reasoning, which is refined during interaction between learner and system. The *pedagogical module* determines the system's teaching actions, which draws upon the current state of the learner model and the domain expertise to teach individual learners. The *domain expertise* module enables the tutoring system to perform as an expert, which may be accessible by the learner in different ways such as glossary. The domain expertise module forms the heart of an ITS. The expertise system embeds sufficient knowledge of a particular topic area to provide "ideal" answers to questions, correct not only in the final result but in each of the smaller intermediate reasoning steps. The expertise system can also generate many different answer paths or goal structures. The detailed data structures generated in modeling expert reasoning permit ITS to explain their reasoning to learners at arbitrarily detailed levels [McArthur *et al.* 1993].

Some earlier ITS are model-tracing ITS. They are the second generation of software tutoring systems that allow the tutor to follow the line of reasoning of the learner [Hefferman and Koedinger 2002]. Like CAI systems before them, model-tracing ITS have attempted to implement traditional methods of learning and teaching exemplified by the one-on-one human tutoring interaction. In general, both CAI systems and model-tracing ITS are characterized as high *tutor control* and *short-answer* task format. Students learn by working a series of relatively brief questions, and the system plays the role of the task expert, controlling the selection of tutoring content, while the student responsible for answering them. The main differences between model-tracing ITS and CAI systems reflect engineering and psychological enhancements that permit model-tracing ITS to tutor in a *knowledge-based* fashion, enabling model-tracing ITS to teach in a much more detailed way than CAI systems.

Intelligent Tutoring Systems

Another less common tutoring format uses intelligent tutoring systems, a form of computer-assisted instruction (CAI). Since computers were introduced to classrooms, they have been used to help students practice skills. Intelligent tutoring systems (ITS) offer a new perspective on traditional CAI. Unlike traditional CAI, which allows students to drill on skills, ITS are intended to imitate human tutors. ITS determine the student's level of competence, begin instruction there, and adapt computer responses to student input. As a result, instruction is tailored to the individual learner. As technology continues to be integrated into educational initiatives, ITS may be increasingly useful as a part of a complete student support programme.

Benefits of Tutoring Programmes

Studies show that in tutoring sessions, tutor and tutee benefit academically, but they may profitgain in other ways as well. Tutoring sessions allow students to experience instructional support that is geared to their needs and provides opportunities for them to ask questions and practice skills that might not be available in regular classroom instruction. During tutoring sessions students are able to receive immediate praise appreciation and useful feedback. Additionally, students may develop a more positive attitude toward subject matter as a result of tutoring, and self-confidence and self-esteem may improve as students participate in tutoring programmes as tutors or tutees.

Characteristics of Effective Tutoring Programmes

Although each tutoring programme is different, effective programmes have some characteristics in common. Effective programmes:

- *Provide tutors a structured programme to follow.* A clear plan should be in place indicating what should take place during a tutoring session. This can be generic, allowing choice of materials and activities, or it can specify materials and procedures.
- *Maintain a high level of intensity in the tutoring programme.* Although there is no definitive standard, some studies indicate that programmes that are shorter in duration and higher in intensity are most effective.
- *Provide training for tutors on an ongoing basis.* According to Topping (2000), tutors should receive training in general tutoring skills as well as programme specific training. In addition, other sources indicate that it may be helpful to provide tutors with training on how to work with students.
- *Monitor tutoring sessions carefully.* Tutoring sessions should be monitored to allow for feedback and intervention when it is needed. Programmes may rely on a teacher or programme coordinator to provide monitoring, which may consist of techniques such as direct observation, self-referral, or session logs reviewed regularly (Topping, 2000).

Inquiry-Based Intelligent Tutoring Systems

Although CAI systems and model-tracing ITS permit learner control, most of interactions between learners and systems are tightly controlled by the software. The system selects the next task or problem, decides when the learner needs support and feedback in problem solving, and determines the information the learners receive. The learners can tailor information, for example, they may request more detailed explanations, but their behaviours are usually highly limited. Essentially, these systems focus on knowledge acquisition and knowledge review more than on knowledge construction, and are employing computer technologies to implement traditional tutor-centered teaching and learning such as one-on-one and drill-and-practice methods.

Another teaching and learning method, *inquiry-based* method (also described as student-centered, constructionist, constructivist, or discovery-based), has been deeply explored over the recent years and a transition towards inquiry-based instruction has begun. In [McArthur *et al.* 1993], systems that implement inquiry-based learning are collectively referred as *interactive learning environments* (ILEs). The ILEs have the following common characteristics:

- *Construction*: Students learn by constructing their own knowledge, not through lecture or organized drill and-practice.
- *Learner control:* The tutor is viewed only as a guide.
- *Individualization determined by the learner:* Learners receive unique

feedback and information as a function of their interaction with the environment built into the system instead of the tutor.

- *Rich feedback generated by the learner's interaction with the learning environment:* Fine-grained feedback arises from the learner's choices and actions rather than from discourse of the tutor.

Model-tracing ITS generally lack a good sense of interaction between learners and systems that may lie in the human tutoring as a dialog format. Based on model-tracing ITS and the features of ILEs, the third generation software tutoring systems have emerged which help learners to construct knowledge and tutor meta-cognitive processes. These inquiry-based ITS engage in *dialogs* with learners using multiple strategies. A learner's problem solving behaviour is the objective while the model tracing is the tool. The main difference between the first two generations and the third generation software tutoring systems is that the former is based on an "*instructionist*" approach to learning while the latter on a "*constructionist*" or "*constructivist*" approach to learning.

The classification of different generations of tutoring systems is not very strict. In fact, they have developed nearly in parallel. With the introduction of more complex tutoring and learning environments such as *collaborative learning*—a structured instructional interaction method among two or more learners to achieve a learning goal or complete an assignment [Panitz 1996], and *agent-based* tutoring systems—an agent is a computer system situated in some environment and capable of autonomous actions in this environment in order to meet its design objectives [Wooldridge 1999] which is often used in distributed tutoring systems, some researchers also classify the development of software tutoring systems into two generations, *solo-learning* (in form of individual) and *collaborative learning* (in form of small-group), from the perspective of learning. Thus the classification is becoming overlapped and obscured. Nevertheless, the most obvious fact is that more control is being given to the learner instead of the tutor in these systems.

2

Artificial Intelligence

Intelligence, as we understand it, refers to the ability to comprehend a given set of events, to analyze the results thereof and to use the knowledge thus gathered to interpret, predict or conceptualize other similar or dissimilar occurrences. There is a lot more at work here than mere comprehension and analysis. After all, even supposedly unintelligent beings such as plants can comprehend and analyze, if we go by Acharya Jagdish Chandra Bose's experiment which demonstrated that plants react in different fashions to different people, depending on their previous experiences with the person. But can we term them as intelligent? You'll be surprised, but yes, even they are intelligent, though in their own botanical fashion. For, the evolution of intelligence does not depend on the size or content of the brain but on necessity. Take for instance your pet dog. As Anton Pavlov had demonstrated, if a bell is rung regularly before your pet's lunchtime, a day will come when your pet would begin to salivate on the mere sound of the bell, regardless of the fact that there is no food on its plate. This is a simple form of association—the dog associates food with the sound of the bell. Since the evolution of the dog did not move in the same direction as of us humans, its (and most of the animal kingdom's, for that matter) intelligence is reflected towards meeting the more basic necessities—that of food and shelter.

So where did we humans go wrong (or right)? Surely we have evolved in a totally different fashion, food and shelter being only two of our several basic necessities? The trick lies in the word necessity. While weeds propagate in leaps and bounds and monkeys can leap while cheetahs can bound, us humans have no such inherent self-preservation module. We therefore, had to rely on other, external devices to save us from extinction. And as our reliance on such tools and devices grew, our intelligence too began to manifest itself towards that goal. We learned to assimilate complex information and to process it logically to develop more and more sophisticated scientific wizardry.

The second most important thing in the evolution of human intelligence was language. You see, we humans can speak, not merely communicate, but speak. With a rich vocabulary, we have words to express and explain almost anything under the sun. And this development of language leads to exchange of thoughts and ideas, which in turn lead to scientific thinking. For all other animals, communication has remained a collection of signals or a limited range of sounds which is definitely prohibitive so far as development of schools of thought is concerned.

The Nature of Intelligence

To understand "intelligent" systems, we must first attempt to understand the nature of intelligence. Theories of human intelligence abound but there is no consensus about what constitutes intelligence (Sternberg, R., 1987). This lack of a widely accepted definition of intelligence is an obstacle for AI researchers.

Based on a review of major models of human intelligence, Cook *et al.* (1988) conclude that the following ten factors are most pertinent to expert system research:

1. *Acquisition*: the ability to acquire new knowledge.
2. *Automatization*: the ability to refine procedures for dealing with a novel situation into an efficient functional form.
3. *Comprehension*: the ability to know, understand, cognize and deal with novel problems.
4. *Memory management*: the ability to represent knowledge in memory, to map knowledge on to that memory representation and to access the knowledge in memory.
5. *Metacontrol*: the ability to control various processes in intelligent behaviour.
6. *Numeric ability*: the ability to perform arithmetic operations.
7. *Reasoning*: the ability to use problem-solving knowledge.
8. *Social competence*: the ability to interact with and understand other people, machines or programmes.
9. *Verbal perception*: the ability to recognize natural language.
10. *Visual perception*: the ability to recognize visual images.

This is certainly a very useful list for its intended purpose; however, if we encountered a system exhibited these traits and no others, would we consider that system to be intelligent by human standards? Probably not. The reason is that our notion of human intelligence is quite likely determined by the entire gestalt of human existence—the fact that we are transient organic beings that possess five senses and feel as well as think. In short, computers lack these attributes.

What is Intelligence?

Individuals differ in their intellectual abilities and that humans differ from machines. The scientific study of intelligence attempts to describe and explain the mysteries of these differences and the structures and processes of these abilities. Intelligence is an intriguing concept in theory-building and research. As a human characteristic and a potential characteristic of machines, intelligence is a concept which captures the imaginations of philosophers, scientists and layperson alike. Numerous books and articles have been written on the topic of intelligence. Many theories of intelligence exist. Most of these theories propose to have implications for describing, explaining, predicting and intervening in human behaviour. Few, if any, of these theories have established a level of detail necessary for the construction of machine intelligence.

To be productive, individuals and machines must work hard, work long but most of all work smart. Working smart requires an understanding of intelligent behaviours. This practical concern with intelligent behaviours motivates much of the research concerned with it. As noted by Conger (1957):

> ....intelligence is not a thing in any tangible sense. We cannot see it, touch it or hear it. It is purely a hypothetical construct, a science fiction, like the concept of force in physics. We invent it because it helps us to explain and predict behaviour.

The hypothetical construct that intelligence is what intelligence tests measure is used most frequently to predict and intervene. For example, the intelligence test scores of mentally retarded individuals are used to predict the likelihood of their school failure and to intervene with an individualized special education programme. The basis for these predictions and interventions is the individual's performance on a standardized intelligence test which samples a range of behaviours considered to be "intelligent" by most people. Although the measurement-oriented approach to intelligence is useful for some purposes of psychology, education and training. It has limited impact on an understanding of the processes required for intelligent behaviour.

Disciplines such as philosophy, psychology, linguistics, anthropology and neuroscience offer varied approaches to the study of the processes of intelligence. Interdisciplinary researchers seeking to understand the processes of intelligence must explore questions of common interest such as:

- What are the similarities and differences between the processing of information by humans and machines?
- What problem solving processes do humans and machines use to act intelligently?

The process-oriented approaches to intelligence that are of primary interest to AI are called "information processing".

Intelligence as Operational Knowledge

We understand intelligence in terms of operational knowledge: knowledge that is represented implicitly or explicitly in such a way that it provides an agent with the ability to perform some tasks. More intelligent agents can cope with a broader set of tasks. Complete understanding of the world (and infinite computation power) would yield the ability to take the optimal decisions on all tasks. Conversely, the ability to respond correctly to any question regarding a particular environment is equivalent to complete understanding of that environment. Different agents may have incomparable intelligence (in the sense that one can do things that the other can't), so the whole notion of 'measuring' intelligence is tricky. We would consider a machine intelligent if it gave us the impression that it understands us and the world we live in. Since we mostly communicate with each other through visual and verbal means, machine vision and natural language understanding are two key aspects we expect from an intelligent machine.

Where Does the Knowledge Come From?

The knowledge that an agent exploits is either handed to it initially ("prior knowledge" obtained from another agent, the person who designed it, its ancestors, etc.) or learned. Even the prior knowledge is somehow acquired (e.g. through evolution, or from the learning done by other agents). Attempts to feed all our human knowledge directly to machines in order to obtain AI has failed because

- humans do not have complete explicit knowledge of their own operational knowledge (in fact most of our operational knowledge is not in a form that can be readily verbalized, it is hidden in our brain)
- explicit knowledge expressed by humans generally lacks a required description of associated uncertainty (our world is not well described by facts, it is better described by probabilistic relations)
- the engineering effort to build a coherent and computer-exploitable description of human knowledge is failing because of the sheer complexity of hand-crafting and maintaining the coherence of all the pieces of knowledge.

Hence it appears that we need learning algorithms for reaching AI. It does not mean that we should not use our knowledge of a particular domain when solving a particular task, since learning algorithms can combine prior knowledge and knowledge acquired from examples. Much of the literature in machine learning (especially concerning graphical models and domain-specific kernels) concentrates on incorporating prior knowledge in learning. This generally offers the best short-term payoff. On the other hand, it also distracts us from longer-term research on more generic methods that would realistically allow us to move closer towards AI. When a particular industrial application presents itself, one can (should) always inject a proper dose of engineering to exploit explicit and implicit human knowledge. However, when the objective is to progress in bold steps towards AI, we believe that research in more generic learning algorithms is a better investment, besides being more exciting, because of the potential leverage on a wider variety of tasks.

Intelligence as Information Processing

The information processing approach examines not only input and output but also explores memory and internal processing of information. These studies of cognitive functioning explore sensory processing, coding strategies and short-intermediate and long-intermediate memory. Experiments with human subjects attempt to determine how they receive, store and retrieve different kinds of information. This approach to intelligence enables comparisons of the processing of information by humans and by machines.

The information processing approach assumes a mechanistic model of intelligence. That is, it makes the assumption that humans are like machines or computers and that the processing of information in the human can be described and explained as if the human were a machine. The analogy of a computer allows for a simplified information handling machine-less complex than the brain and central nervous system. This simplification provides the possibility for clearer descriptions and explanations. Obviously, many critics of the information processing approach attack these mechanistic assumptions both in terms of their usefulness and implications for prediction and intervention. From the foundation of AI, the information processing approach has been an assumed model for description, explanation, prediction and intervention. AI founders Alan Newell and Herbert Simon note this relationship:

> ....the programmed computer and human problem solver are both species belonging to the genus "Information Processing System".

Intelligence is an "amalgam of many information processing and information representation abilities" according to AI assumptions (Winston & Brady, 1987). Nilsson (1980) emphasizes the relationship of AI research and information processing theory:

> AI has also embraced the larger scientific goal of constructing an information-processing theory of intelligence. If such a science of intelligence could be developed, it would guide the design of intelligent machines as well as explicate intelligent behaviour as it occurs in other animals.

Descriptions and explanations of how intelligence works require an analysis of the components and tasks in the processing of information. Predictions and intervention in AI are based on result of research related to each component. Interventions assert ways to improve the functioning of components such as long-term memory or ways to teach formal reasoning abilities.

Research and development using the information processing approach is not limited to the concept of intelligence but extends to the concepts of learning and instruction. For example, Gagne (1985) indicates the influence of information processing approaches on education and training:

> The information processing model of learning has important implications for an understanding of instruction. The stimulating conditions that are brought to bear on the learners are not viewed simply as stimuli to which they react. Instead, these external stimuli may be conceived as initiating, maintaining or otherwise supporting several different kinds of ongoing internal processes involved in learning, remembering and performing.

The interdisciplinary study of information processing by educators and trainers will result in a better understanding of how human and machine intelligence works and how symbolic processing contributes to intelligence and learning.

Intelligence as Symbolic Processing

Knowledge and information are represented as symbols in a computer programme. Symbolic processing emphasizes the importance of symbols in information processing. Symbols may represent words, concepts, objects, ideas or procedures. Symbolic processing is significantly different from numeric processing which focuses on numbers and data. The computer is capable of inputting or reading symbols, outputting or writing symbols, storing, copying and comparing symbols. A fundamental hypothesis of AI is that these symbols manipulating capabilities are those required to exhibit "intelligence" in both humans and machines (Fischler & Firschein, 1987).

AI is a field of research which seeks to solve the symbolic types of problems that experts presently can better solve. When computers were first developed, little distinction was made between intelligent or symbolic processing and unintelligent or numerical computer programmes (Carrico, Girard & Jones, 1989). Basic machine capabilities such as performing calculations were viewed as intelligent tasks. Solving a simple addition problem was considered machine "thinking" and an indication of intelligence. Over a long period, views on what an intelligent programme is have changed. Programmes must now solve real world problems of much greater complexity to be considered "intelligent".

Intelligence as Problem Solving Processes

Intelligence may be defined as "competency in problem solving", which is a type of general information and symbolic processing (Tennyson & Park, 1984). The study of human and machine intelligence leads to a clarification of how humans and computers solve specific problems. The complexity of the concept intelligence has resulted in the necessity of an operational definition. This definition narrows the construct of intelligence to a focus on problem solving processes. Gevarter (1985) indicates that:

> One way of viewing intelligent behaviour is as a problem solver. Many

> AI tasks can naturally be viewed this way and most AI programmes draw much of their strength from their problem solving components.

This ability to solve novel problems by successful behaviours is the problem-solving aspect of the concept "intelligence". Dede (1986) describes the focus of AI as:

> ....expert problem solving in complex, unstructured environments with multiple obstacles and no universal solution algorithm.

The AI method is to build computer programmes that simulate and demonstrate "intelligent" behaviours when solving ill-defined problems. These problem solving processes are those without algorithmic or a step by step solutions. Gevarter (1985) indicates that:

> The computer programmes with which AI is concerned are primarily symbolic processes involving complexity, uncertainty and ambiguity. These processes are usually those for which algorithmic solutions do not exist and search is required. Thus, AI deals with the types of problem solving and decision making that human begins continually face in dealing with the world.

If AI researchers and developers are able to construct an artificial model which functions "intelligently" and solve complex problems then this model has both theoretical and practical value for education and training.

As computer scientists enabled computers to accomplish many numerical and data processing tasks better than humans, tasks which were once thought to require intelligence became algorithmic, easily understood replicable, step-by-step procedures. Easily programmed tasks, then, would not be defined as intelligent machine behaviours. Tasks which people are able to perform, while machines are not, become the challenge for AI research. This changing definition of machine intelligence has resulted in a lack of consensus on clear distinctions between intelligent and non-intelligent behaviour. This confusion also results in a lack of consensus regarding the characteristics of an "intelligent" computer programme and the content of intelligence.

The Human-Machine Contrast

Human intelligence consists of fact, concepts, rules and heuristic knowledge. Facts and concepts can be thought of as structures that house symbols. Rules and heuristic knowledge can be thought of as manipulators of the symbols. Mental models are formed using facts, concepts, rules and heuristic knowledge in ever-changing arrays. Human thinking can be viewed in term of categories of thinking. These categories are cognitive, associative and philosophical. Human cognitive thinking involves the gathering of input data and the manipulation of symbols. The manipulation of symbols, take place through mental models. Machine thinking does an admirable emulation of the cognitive process. Both the human and machine are able to process input to reach decisions for action of project future events from that input.

Figure 2.1: Man-Machine Interaction

Associative thinking consists of the concepts of vertical and lateral thinking. According to deBono (1973) there are two basic thinking styles, vertical and lateral. Vertical or logical, thinking involves movement from state to state through a series of justified steps. Lateral thinking uses information not for its own sake, but for its side effects. Vertical thinking is selective and lateral thinking is generative. Human are able to think laterally and machine cannot. Lateral thinking is associative with creativity and the ability of the mind to be self-organizing and self-maximizing.

Maximally efficient problem-solving uses both vertical and lateral thinking to address and resolve problem situations. While machine systems are adequate for certain tasks, there is still room for improvement in their capability for this kind of reasoning. Philosophical thinking involves rhetorical query. It can encompass a patter-matching attempt such as, "Is there a correspondence between the breadth of a tree's branches and the breadth of its root system?, If so, is this correspondence consistent across species? What could I do with this information?". Philosophical thinking can also involve pondering one's existence. It is the realm of original thought and involves self-consciousness. At this time, philosophical thought is the sole domain of humans.

Human Reasoning

- They use specific rules, a priori rules
- They Use Heuristics—"rules of thumb"
- They use past experience—"cases"
- They use "Expectations"

From Intelligence to Artificial Intelligence

As man progressed up the ecological chain and gained a place of import, his thirst for knowledge was fuelled by his desire to create. You see, since eternity (read for the past five thousand years) human intelligence has been skewed towards creation—from the first stone clubs to the modern day skyscrapers. Combined with the genetic need of living beings to create their own replicas, this desire naturally progressed towards replicating his own image, not through reproduction alone but also through scientific gimmickry. And with the rapid development of computing and robotics in the past few decades, man today suddenly finds himself on the doorstep of his long cherished dream—to assemble a non-human device that can understand, analyze and interpret information and use the same to predict or conceptualize similar or dissimilar occurrences. In other words a device that is Artificially Intelligent.

What is Artificial Intelligence?

The phrase Artificial Intelligence, which was coined by John McCarthy three decades ago, evades a concise and formal definition to date. One representative definition is pivoted around the comparison of intelligence of computing machines with human beings. Another definition is concerned with the performance of machines which "historically have been judged to lie within the domain of intelligence". None of these definitions or the like has been universally accepted, perhaps because of their references to the word "intelligence", which at present is an abstract and immeasurable quantity. A better definition of artificial intelligence, therefore, calls for formalization of the term "intelligence". Psychologist and Cognitive theorists are of the opinion that intelligence helps in identifying the right piece of knowledge at the appropriate instances of decision making. The phrase "artificial intelligence" thus defined as the simulation of human intelligence on a machine, so as to make the machine efficient to identify and use their "Knowledge" at a given step of solving a problem. A system capable of planning and executing the right task at the right time is generally called rational. Thus, AI alternatively may be stated as a subject dealing with computational models that can think and act rationally 1, 2, 3, 4. A common question then naturally arises: Does rational thinking and acting include all possible characteristics of an intelligent system? If so, how does it represent behavioural intelligence such as machine learning, perception and planning? A little thinking, however, reveals that a system that can reason well must be a successful planner, as planning in many circumstances is part of a reasoning process. Further, a system can act rationally only after acquiring adequate knowledge from the real world. So, perception that stands for building up of knowledge from real world information is a prerequisite feature for rational actions. One step further thinking envisages that a machine without learning capability cannot possess perception. The rational action of an agent (actor), thus, calls for possession of all the elementary characteristics of intelligence. Relating artificial intelligence with the computational models capable of thinking and acting rationally, therefore, has a pragmatic significance.

Artificial Intelligence is a subdivision of Computer Science devoted to creating Computer software and hardware that attempts to produce results such as those produced by people. The concept of Artificial Intelligence and Commercial application that result from research in this area may change the way some organizations operate and are managed. AI is a dynamic and varying field.

Artificial Intelligence (AI) is a branch of Computer Science, which deals with helping machines find solutions to complex problems in a more human-like fashion. This generally involves borrowing characteristics from human intelligence and applying them as algorithms in a computer friendly way. A more or less flexible or efficient approach can be taken depending on the requirements established, which influences how artificial the intelligent behaviour appears. AI is generally associated with computer science but is has many important links with other fields, such as—Mathematics, Psychology, Cognition, Biology and Philosophy, among many others. Our ability to combine knowledge from all these fields will ultimately benefit our progress in the quest of creating an intelligent artificial being.

The main aim of Artificial Intelligence (AI) is to study how to build artificial systems that perform tasks normally performed by human beings. This concept was born in 1956 in the Darthmounth conference. From that moment on a lot of effort has been made and many goals have been achieved but unfortunately many failures as well. Today the AI is a very important discipline and it includes a number of well-recognized and mature areas: Expert Systems, Fuzzy Logic, Genetic Algorithms, Language Pro-cessing, Logic Programming, Planning and Scheduling, Neural Networks and Robotics.

Artificial Intelligence (AI)

Artificial intelligence can be viewed from a variety of perspectives.

From the perspective of intelligence

"*Artificial intelligence* is making machines "intelligent"—acting as we would expect people to act".

- The inability to distinguish computer responses from human responses is called the Turing test.
- Intelligence requires knowledge.
- Expert problem solving—restricting domain to allow including significant relevant knowledge.

From a research perspective, "A*rtificial intelligence* is the study of how to make computers do things, which at the moment, people do better" [Rich and Knight, 1991, p. 3].

- AI began in the early 1960s—the first attempts were game playing (checkers), theorem proving (a few simple theorems) and general problem solving (only very simple tasks)
- General problem solving was much more difficult than originally anticipated. Researchers were unable to tackle problems routinely handled by human experts.
- The name "artificial intelligence" came from the roots of the area of study.

From a **business** perspective AI is a set of very powerful tools, and methodologies for using those tools to solve business problems.

From a **programming** perspective, AI includes the study of symbolic programming, problem solving, and search.

- Typically AI programmes focus on symbols rather than numeric processing.
- Problem solving—achieve goals.
- Search—seldom access a solution directly. Search may include a variety of techniques.

Definitions of "Artificial Intelligence"

1. Simon, H.A. (1969)—"*Artificial intelligence (AI) is the capacity of a digital computer or computer-controlled robot device to perform tasks commonly associated with the higher intellectual processes characteristics of human, such as the ability to reason, discover meaning, generalize or learn from past experience. The term is also frequently applied to that branch of computer science concerned with the development of systems endowed with such capabilities.*"
2. Nilsson, Nils, J. (1971)—"*The goal of work in artificial intelligence is to build machines that perform tasks normally requiring human intelligence.*"
3. Slagle, James, R. (1971)—"*Research scientists in artificial intelligence try to get machines to exhibit behaviour that we call intelligent behaviour when we observe it in human beings.*"
4. Boden, M. (1977)—"By artificial intelligence I therefore mean the use of computer programmes and programming techniques to cast light on the principles of intelligence in general and human thought in particular."
5. Charniak and McDermott (1985) offered, "Artificial intelligence is the study of mental faculties through the use of computational models."
6. Schildt (1987) claimed, "An intelligent programme is one that exhibits behaviour similar to that of a human when confronted with a similar problem. It is not necessary that the programme actually solve, or attempt to solve, the problem in the same way that a human would."

7. Waterman (1986) offered that artificial intelligence was "the part of computer science concerned with developing intelligent computer programmes." This tautological statement offers no basis for designing an intelligent machine or programme.
8. Rich (1983) offered, "Artificial intelligence (AI) is the study of how to make computers do things at which, at the moment, people are better," which was echoed even as recently as 1999 by Lenat (in Moody, 1999). But this definition, if regarded statically, precludes the very existence of artificial intelligence. Once a computer programme exceeds the capabilities of a human, the programme is no longer in the domain of AI.
9. Russell (quoted in Ubiquity, 2004) offered, "An intelligent system is one whose expected utility is the highest that can be achieved by any system with the same computational limitations." But this definition appears to offer intelligence to a calculator, for there can be no higher expected utility than getting four as the right answer to two plus two. It might even extend to a pebble, sitting at equilibrium on a bottom of a pond, with no computational ability whatsoever. It is no wonder that we have not achieved our dreams when our efforts have been defined so poorly.

The majority of definitions of artificial intelligence proffered over decades have relied on comparisons to human behaviour. Staugaard (1987) attributed a definition to Marvin Minsky—"the science of making machines do things that would require intelligence if done by men"—and suggested that some people define AI as the "mechanization, or duplication, of the human thought process."

The Disciplines of Artificial Intelligence

The subject of artificial intelligence spans a wide horizon. It deals with the various kinds of knowledge representation schemes, different techniques of intelligent search, various methods for resolving uncertainty of data and knowledge, different schemes for automated machine learning and many others. Among the application areas of AI, we have Expert systems, Game-playing, and Theorem-proving, Natural language processing, Image recognition, Robotics and many others. The subject of artificial intelligence has been enriched with a wide discipline of knowledge from Philosophy, Psychology, Cognitive Science, Computer Science, Mathematics and Engineering. Thus in Figure 2.2, they have been referred to as the parent disciplines of AI. Figure 2.2 Reveals the Subject Area of AI and its Application Areas

The terms "Artificial" and "Intelligence" are plainly central concepts of AI. These concepts are not easily defined or described. The concept "Artificial"

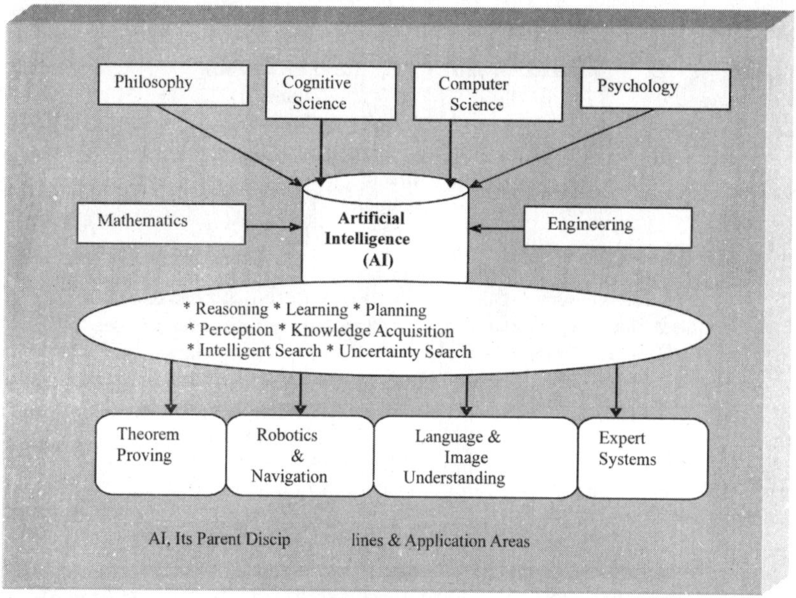

Figure 2.2: AI, Its Parent Disciplines and Application Areas

may be used in differing ways. For example, "artificial" light is a useful source for illumination that is similar to natural light but "artificial" flowers are only related to natural flowers in appearance (Sokolowski, 1988). Will the meaning of "artificial" in AI denote both usefulness and reality? Wenger (1987) defines AI as:

> ....the study of principles of computational intelligence as manifested in man-made systems.

Thus, AI may be operationally defined as studying computing machines and the concept of intelligence. Winston (1984) defines AI simply as "the study of ideas that enable the computer to be intelligent". These definitions imply that the terms artificial and computing systems are synonymous but fail to clarify the meaning of "intellig ence" (Figure 2.3).

If "intelligence" is operationally defined as "competence in problem solving", then this definition leads to an emphasis on problem-solving behaviours as demonstrated by either humans or computing machines. AI programmes exhibit behaviour which is normally identified with human intelligence but not traditionally identified with computers. For example, humans demonstrate intelligent behaviour when they consult one another or make effective decisions. If computers can be programmed to provide effective consultation and decision-making related to specific tasks such as medical diagnosis or to consult with human beings then their behaviour may be defined as "intelligent". An "intelligent" behaviour would be demonstrated by the

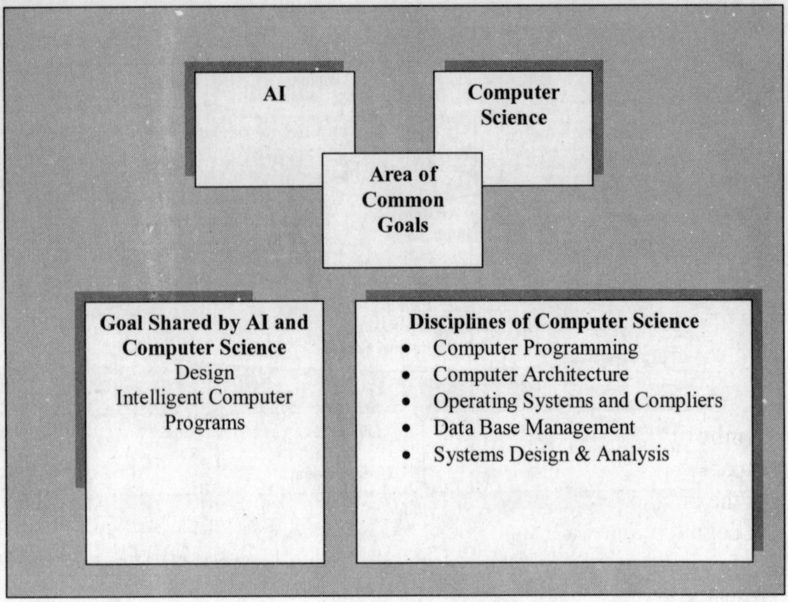

Figure 2.3: Relationship of AI and Computer Science

ability to solve novel problems. AI then becomes the process of finding or constructing solutions to problems through the use and study of computing systems.

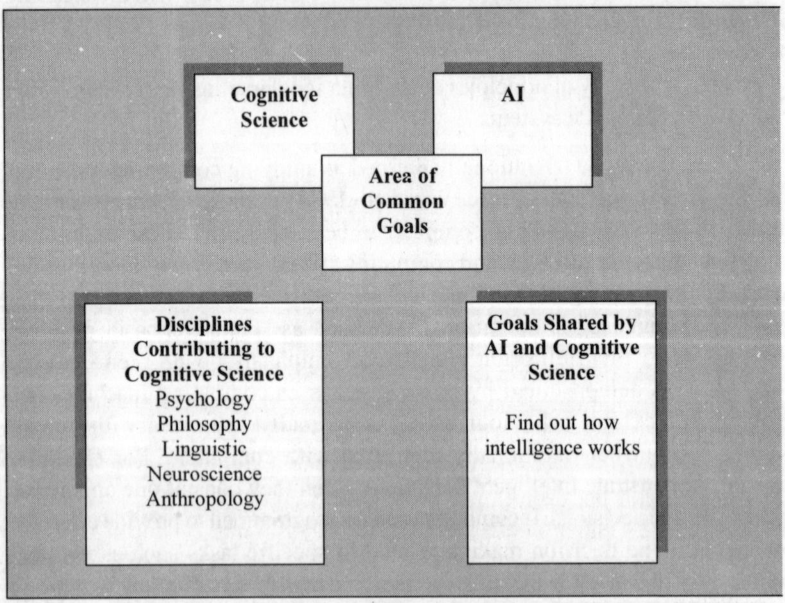

Figure 2.4: Relationship of AI and Cognitive Science

AI and Cognitive Science

Cognitive science investigates the detailed workings of intelligence and problem solving. Cognitive science has been defined as "the study of the principles by which intelligent entities interact with their environments" (Pylyshyn, 1987). The comparative study of intelligent entities includes both humans and machines. Cognitive scientists use these principles to devlop workable theories of human intelligence. Mishkoff (1985) indicates:

> As cognitive scientists determine the processes that produce human intelligence in a given situation, these processes my be programmed into a computer in an attempt to simulate that behaviour. This AI technique is called modeling or simulation.

Cognitive science is an analytic and rational approach to exploring the symbolic representation, information processing and computational capabilities of human intelligence as well as the structural and functional aspect of the brain. The nature and representation of knowledge are major concerns of cognitive science research. Cognitive science is a diverse, interdisciplinary field of study with boundaries which still require definition. Cognitive science research involves contributions from one or more of the following disciplines: psychology, philosophy, linguistics, neuroscience, anthropology and AI.

Cognitive science and AI are closely related and may one day merge (Pylyshyn, 1979). The borders between AI and cognitive science are particularly fuzzy and show considerable overlap. AI has been identified as one of the major disciplines of cognitive science. In a simplified analogy, cognitive science studies the architecture of the human mind while computer science studies the architecture of the computer. AI provides the linkage between cognitive science and computer science. Since the detailed processes of intelligent behaviour are unknown, AI research ahs come forth o assist cognitive science in clarifying these processes. Other disciplines of cognitive science contribute theories, research and valuable ideas to this endeavor but these theories and ideas have been too vague and incomplete to be stated in computational terms (Clancey, 1987). AI research may work in cognitive science or related disciplines. Cognitive science and AI both explore areas such as language, vision, models of human performance, learning and training. Applications of cognitive science include human-machine interface, teaching methods, communication techniques, prostheses for the handicapped and methodologies for exploring expertise (Pylyshyn, 1984). AI has a significant role in promoting cognitive science research and applications. Scientific research and the desire to know will lead to increasingly useful cognitive technologies and applications.

One major goal of AI emerges from the emphasis of cognitive science. Cognitive science pursues the goal of developing models of how intelligence works and how problems are solved. This goal involves the desire to understand the working of the brain and cognitive processing, to understand the principles of intelligent behaviour. Insight into the nature of mind can be gained through developing "intelligent" computer programmes. Computer programmes force precision and provide a test for computational models of cognition. AI may be described as an attempt to build computer programmes that can account for human cognition (Winograd & Flores, 1987). AI focuses cognitive science on the problems of removing this vagueness and designing working models of intelligence.

Models of Thinking from Cognitive Science

The field of cognitive science is defined as the interdisciplinary study of mind and intelligence, which attempts to further our understanding of intelligent activities and the nature of thought (Audi, 1995). The major contributing disciplines to the field include philosophy, psychology, computer science, linguistics, neuroscience, and anthropology. The intellectual foundation for the field originated in the mid-1950s when researchers in several fields worked on the development of theories of mind employing complex representations and computational procedures.

History of Cognitive Science

Initial attempts to understand thought processes and the mind are documented in the work of such ancient Greek philosophers as Plato and Aristotle. From these origins, the study of the mind was seen as strictly the purview of philosophers. In 1879, Wilhelm Wundt, a German philosopher and psychologist, established the first experimental psychology laboratory (Plucker, 1998). Considered to be the father of experimental psychology and the founder of modern psychology, Wundt pioneered in a systematic examination of mental operations, describing mental events in terms of both objectively measurable stimuli and responses and introspective accounts by subjects. Later psychological research laboratories were modeled after the one developed by Wundt.

By the early 1950s, both the logical positivism in vogue in the field of philosophy and behaviourist theory then prevalent in the field of psychology questioned the value of systematic inquiry into the operation of the mind (Thagard, 1996a). Behaviourists such as John Watson held the view that psychologists should only examine observable phenomena and should focus on conducting stimulus/response experiments. This brought an end (fortunately a temporary one) to the discussion of mental representations and the mind, particularly among psychologists.

Between the mid-1950s and the early 1970s, each of the contributing disciplines to the field of cognitive science moved away from logical positivist and behaviourist approaches. In 1956, George Miller demonstrated capacity limits in human thinking, including a limit of approximately seven items that can be held in short-term memory (Miller, 1956). Miller observed that people overcome this limitation in short-term memory by employing chunking, a process of recoding information into manageable groups. Thus, Miller posited the existence of mental representations, supporting the procedures people use to encode and decode chunks of information. A parallel development in the field of linguistics was the development by Noam Chomsky of a set of rules to explain human understanding of language (Chomsky, 1957). In this way, Chomsky rejected behaviourist claims that language is merely a learned habit.

The introduction of computers capable of manipulating information supported the process of theorizing about information in an abstract manner. Research in artificial intelligence by John McCarthy (1959), Marvin Minsky and Seymour Papert (1969), Allen Newell and Herbert Simon (1972), and others supported the premise that machines could process information and behave in a way that demonstrated intelligence. Through these and other developments in each of the underlying disciplines, the foundation was laid for cognitive science.

By 1985, the field of cognitive science was sufficiently accepted for a respected cognitive psychologist, Dr. Howard Gardner, to publish an overview of the history and development of the field. In his book, entitled The Mind's New Science: A History of the Cognitive Revolution, Gardner defines cognitive science as "a contemporary, empirically based effort to answer long-standing epistemological questions—particularly those concerned with the nature of knowledge, its components, its sources, its development, and its deployment" (Gardner, 1985). While some cognitive scientists study intelligent activities performed by both machines and people, Gardner and other cognitive scientists recommend that the domain of cognitive science focus on an examination and explanation of human ways of knowing. Three major approaches to modeling thinking have been developed in the field of cognitive science (Eliasmith, 1998).

Symbolicism or Classicism: Symbolicism, or what is now referred to as Classicism, employs symbolic processing to model thought processes. The work of Allen Newell and Herbert Simon (1972) represents an early attempt to model human problem solving using symbolic processing. The early research efforts of Noam Chomsky (1957) on syntactic structures, Marvin Minsky and Seymour Papert (1969) in artificial intelligence, Jerry Fodor on the language of thought (1975), and Zenon Pylyshyn (1973) on visual perception are all based on the use of symbolic processing to construct models of human behaviour.

Connectionism: The school of thought known as connectionism views thought processes as connections between nodes in a distributed network. Warren McCullough and Walter Pitts (1943) developed the first model of neural networks. D.O. Hebb (1949) conducted research in biological neural studies and is considered by many to be the father of cognitive psychobiology. In 1957, Frank Rosenblatt invented the Perceptron at the Cornell Aeronautical Laboratory (Rosenblatt, 1958). In 1960, Rosenblatt demonstrated learning by a machine when the Mark I Perceptron "learned" to recognize and identify optical patterns. However, after Minsky and Papert's analysis of the limitations of the Perceptron work (1969), most research in the area of connectionism ceased. In Parallel distributed processing: Explorations in the microstructure of cognition, Rumelhart and McClelland (1986) re-introduced connectionist computational models into cognitive science research after a hiatus of approximately fifteen years.

Dynamic Systems Theory: The theoretical approach referred to as dynamic (or dynamical) systems theory uses differential equations to describe a multidimensional space of potential thoughts and behaviours, traversed by a path of thinking followed by an agent under certain environmental and internal pressures. Some cognitive scientists view dynamic systems theory as a promising approach to modeling human thinking. In The Dynamical Hypothesis in Cognitive Science (van Gelder, 1998), Tim van Gelder presents the view that cognitive agents may well be dynamical systems rather than computational systems.

Critique of Cognitive Science

Connectionism and Cognitive Architecture: A Critical Analysis, Fodor and Pylyshyn (1988) argue that both connectionist and classical architectures posit the existence of representational mental states but only classical architectures offer a symbolic level of representation. According to their paper, a symbolic level of representation is necessary to support productive and systematic thought as well as symmetries exhibited by cognitive capacities that allow thoughts with semantically related contents to be tied together. Therefore, they argue that the architecture of the mind/brain is not connectionist on the cognitive level.

However, Minsky (1990) believes that the schism between symbolic and connectionist approaches is wrong and that multiple representations are needed to model intelligent behaviour. In his paper Logical vs. Analogical or Symbolic vs. Connectionist or Neat vs. Scruffy, Minsky argues that "to solve really hard problems, we'll have to use several different representations. This is because each particular kind of data-structure has its own virtues and deficiencies, and none by itself seems adequate for all the different functions involved with what we call 'common sense'" (Minsky, 1990). In Society of Mind, Minsky discusses the meaning of meaning and states that "the secret of what something means lies in how it connects to other things we know. That's why it's almost always wrong to seek the 'real meaning' of anything. A thing with just one meaning has scarcely any meaning at all" (Minsky, 1985). Therefore, Minsky suggests that "in order to get around these constraints, we must develop systems that combine the expressiveness and procedural versatility of symbolic systems with the fuzziness and adaptiveness of connectionist representations. (Minsky, 1990). According to Minsky, researchers have been attempting to oversimplify their models of thinking. Minsky now believes that "to solve typical real-world commonsense problems, a mind must have at least several different kinds of knowledge. First, we need to represent goals: what is the problem to be solved. Then the system must also possess adequate knowledge about the domain or context in which that problem occurs. Finally, the system must know what kinds of reasoning are applicable in that area. Superimposed on all of this, our systems must have management schemes that can operate different representations and procedures in parallel" (Minsky, 1990).

Gardner (1985) lists several different issues raised by critics of cognitive science:

- There have been many models of human cognition, including the switchboard, the hydraulic pump, and the hologram. Many critics believe that it is a mistake to consider human beings to be systems that process information. Such critics are skeptical of the computer providing any better model for human cognition than previous failed models (Gardner, 1985).
- Anthropologists contend that historical and cultural factors affect human cognition and are not included in computational models (Gardner, 1985).
- Some critics believe that cognitive science cannot succeed unless the field addresses factors such as affect, history, and context, which impact human thinking (Gardner, 1985).
- Behaviourists criticize the representational view and believe that the focus should be on observable behaviours and neurological structures (Gardner, 1985).
- The interdisciplinary approach adopted by cognitive scientists is seen by some critics as an ineffective way to advance the research effort. These critics recommend that each discipline clarify its own individual approach rather than expending energy on trying to work with members of other disciplines (Gardner, 1985).
- Neuroscientists believe that mental representations are unnecessary since the brain provides its own model. Therefore, we can use ordinary language and the nervous system itself, without the need for an intermediary model of the thinking process (Gardner, 1985).
- At the same time, major disagreement exists about the applicability of brain science to cognitive science (Gardner, 1985).
- Philosophers Hubert Dreyfus and John Searle, though they vehemently disagree with each other on other points (Dreyfus, 1999) argue that the claim that human minds work by representation and computation is fundamentally wrong.

AI and Computer Science

Computer science is a field of study for individuals committed to the design of computer systems, software development and computational research. It is the study of how computers work and how computer programmes should be constructed. Computer scientists investigate the theories and principles that govern the ability to create, store, modify and manipulate information. Computer science research and development explores topics such as system analysis programme design, coding, data representation and design of operating systems (Hopper & Mandell, 1984). The emphasis in computer science is on mathematics and computation as a basis for developing machine techniques.

The computer science and mathematics approach to AI is frequently differentiated from the cognitive science and psychological approach. These alternative perspectives are not necessarily antagonistic but conflicts of perspective and ownership of AI are noted in many books and articles (Pylyshyn, 1987). For example, some computer scientists and AI researchers consider AI to be merely a branch of topic of computer science. The perspective of the AI computer scientists is that computer programmes need not replicate human approaches to problem solving except when this replication is useful. These computer programmes do not attempt to imitate or model humans but instead capitalize on the rapid data processing capabilities of the machine. This perspective allows programmes to maximize the superiority of the computer over humans in areas such as memory. The cognitive science perspective, by contrast, views human approaches to problem solving as the appropriate and more powerful cognitive model for AI science. AI as a part of computer science explores the range of tasks in which computers can assist humans.

A major goal of AI shared with computer science is to make computers more useful and applicable across a wider range of human endeavor. These useful computer programmes which incorporate AI concepts and techniques are changing the role of computers in our lives (Winston, 1984). AI advances computer science research by enhancing computer programming methods. The innovative applications resulting from AI research complement traditional computer programming. For example, AI languages and techniques are becoming required topics of computer science study. These AI languages and techniques will merge with computer science techniques to become commonplace. The by-products of this AI research and development include object-oriented languages, visual interfaces, windows, pop-up menus, icons and mouse input devices (Rauch-Hindin, 1988). AI challenges the limits of computer science and technology because AI programmes that model intelligence must be "massive and complex" (Winston & Brady, 1987). The problems of AI are difficult and interesting for computer scientists. Research in AI expands computer science by exploring ideas and methodologies of computational intelligence.

Why Artificial Intelligence

It is a well-known fact that human brain is more sophisticated and highly advanced with respect to intelligence. From the ancient times man has tried to conquer the natural forces because of his superior position amongst all the living beings. Such basic human behaviours as touching, smelling, hearing and seeing are the result of eons of evolutionary development. The origins of these behaviours lie deep in our physiology and we don't understand very well how they work. These are processes we have in common with the animal world. The thought patterns that differentiate us from the animals, however, are quite new. They are at the top of our thinking mechanisms. Thinking processes needed for such subjects as mathematics, Science, Literature and Logic are relatively recent acquisitions. It is these that artificial intelligence (i.e. expert systems) handles the easiest. For example, logic is a human invention but it is really "artificial"—it is not a natural product of human evolution.

Computers are fundamentally well suited to performing mechanical computations, using fixed programmed rules. This allows artificial machines to perform simple monotonous tasks efficiently and reliably, which humans are ill suited to. For more complex problems, things get more difficult. Unlike humans, computers have trouble understanding specific situations and adapting to new situations. Artificial intelligence aims to improve machine behaviour in tackling such complex tasks. Together with this, much of AI research is allowing us to understand our intelligent behaviour. Humans have an interesting approach to problem solving, based on abstract thought, high level deliberative reasoning and pattern recognition. Artificial intelligence can help us to understand this process by recreating it, then potentially enabling us to enhance it beyond our current capabilities.

Approaches to AI

Initially, researchers thought that creating an AI would be simply writing programmes for each and every function of intelligence performs. As they went on with this task, they realized that this approach was too shallow. Even simple functions like face recognition, special sense, pattern recognition and language comprehension were beyond their programming skills.

They understood that to create an AI, they must delve deeper into natural intelligence first. They tried to understand how cognition, comprehension, decision-making happen in the human mind. They had to understand what understanding really means! Some went into the study of the brain and tried to understand how the network of neurons creates the mind. Thus, researchers branched into different approaches, but they had the same goal of creating intelligent machines. Let us introduce ourselves to some of the main approaches to artificial intelligence. They are divided into two main lines of thought, the bottom up and the top down approach:

Neural Networks: This is the bottom up approach. It basically aims at mimicking the structure and functioning of the human brain, to create intelligent behaviour. Researchers are attempting to build a silicon-based electronic network that is modeled on the working and form of the human brain! Our brain is a network of billions of neurons, each connected with the other.

At an individual level, a neuron has very little intelligence, in the sense that it operates by a simple set of rules, conducting electric signals through its network. However, the combined network of all these neurons creates intelligent behaviour that is unrivaled and unsurpassed. So these researchers created network of electronic analogues of a neuron, based on Boolean logic. Memory was recognized to be an electronic signal pattern in a closed neural network.

How the human brain works is, it learns to realize patterns and remembers them. Similarly, the neural networks developed have the ability to learn patterns and remember. This approach has its limitations due to the scale and complexity of developing an exact replica of a human brain, as the neurons number in billions! Currently, through simulation techniques, people create virtual neural networks. This approach has not been able to achieve the ultimate goal but there is a very positive progress in the field. The progress in the development of parallel computing will aid it in the future.

Expert Systems: This is the top down approach. Instead of starting at the base level of neurons, by taking advantage of the phenomenal computational power of the modern computers, followers of the expert systems approach are designing intelligent machines that solve problems by deductive logic. It is like the dialectic approach in philosophy.

This is an intensive approach as opposed to the extensive approach in neural networks. As the name expert systems suggest, these are machines devoted to solving problems in very specific niche areas. They have total expertise in a specific domain of human thought. Their tools are like those of a detective or sleuth. They are programmed to use statistical analysis and data mining to solve problems. They arrive at a decision through a logical flow developed by answering yes-no questions. Chess computers like Fritz and its successors that beat chess grandmaster Kasparov are examples of expert systems. Chess is known as the drosophila or experimental specimen of artificial intelligence.

Applications of Artificial Intelligence

Artificial Intelligence in the form of expert systems and neural networks has applications in every field of human endeavor. They combine precision and computational power with pure logic, to solve problems and reduce error in operation. Already, robot expert systems are taking over many jobs in industries that are dangerous for or beyond human ability. Some of the applications divided by domains are as follows:

1. *Heavy Industries and Space:* Robotics and cybernetics have taken a leap combined with artificially intelligent expert systems. An entire manufacturing process is now totally automated, controlled and maintained by a computer system in car manufacture, machine tool production, computer

chip production and almost every high-tech process. They carry out dangerous tasks like handling hazardous radioactive materials. Robotic pilots carry out complex maneuvering techniques of unmanned spacecrafts sent in space. Japan is the leading country in the world in terms of robotics research and use.

2. *Finance:* Banks use intelligent software applications to screen and analyze financial data. Softwares that can predict trends in the stock market have been created which have been known to beat humans in predictive power.

3. *Computer Science:* Researchers in quest of artificial intelligence have created spin offs like dynamic programming, object oriented programming, symbolic programming, intelligent storage management systems and many more such tools. The primary goal of creating an artificial intelligence still remains a distant dream but people are getting an idea of the ultimate path which could lead to it.

4. *Aviation:* Air lines use expert systems in planes to monitor atmospheric conditions and system status. The plane can be put on auto pilot once a course is set for the destination.

5. *Weather Forecast:* Neural networks are used for predicting weather conditions. Previous data is fed to a neural network which learns the pattern and uses that knowledge to predict weather patterns.

6. *Swarm Intelligence:* This is an approach to, as well as application of artificial intelligence similar to a neural network. Here, programmers study how intelligence emerges in natural systems like swarms of bees even though on an individual level, a bee just follows simple rules. They study relationships in nature like the prey-predator relationships that give an insight into how intelligence emerges in a swarm or collection from simple rules at an individual level. They develop intelligent systems by creating agent programmes that mimic the behaviour of these natural systems.

7. *Education:* Now AI is used in education to increase the quality of education. AI can be use in teaching-learning process. It can be use to develop intelligent computer programmes that can instruct students in an intelligent way.

Branches of AI

Artificial Intelligence (AI) is a branch of computer science which tries to give "intelligence to machines". But the concept of intelligence itself is debatable, and making these machines without life "intelligent" is something near to impossible. But we can say safely that AI aims at producing intelligent behaviour from machines. What is the difference between having intelligence and having intelligent behaviour? You can exhibit intelligent behaviour in a narrow field for some time without really being intelligent. For example a computer playing chess at the master level does not even know that it is playing chess. But for the outsider the view is that it is intelligent like a master. Also we need only this intelligent behaviour for many practical purposes.

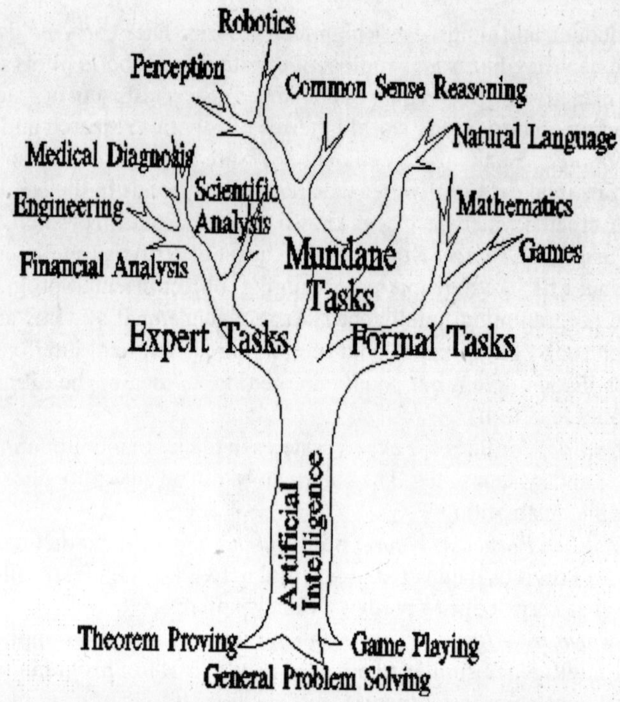

Figure 2.5: The Domains of Artificial Intelligence

AI uses ideas from diverse branches of knowledge like computer science, economics, biology, social sciences, mathematics and even grammar. It has also diverse applications in many areas of life. That is, it is an interdisciplinary subject which takes ideas from almost all fields of knowledge and has applications in many diverse areas of life. Some of the branches of AI are discussed below. This in no way is a complete list.

(1) *Game Playing:* Playing a game like checkers, chess or go, requires a lot of intelligence for a human being and so these tasks were one of the earliest attractions of AI. Samuel wrote a programme playing checkers in the 60s and many people contributed to the theory of game playing. Finally when a computer could beat the then world champion in a chess game, that was considered a victory of machine over man even though it was not so. Currently there are well known algorithms for game playing and game playing is considered falling into the domain of algorithms than AI.

(2) *Automatic Theorem Proving:* Mathematicians are believed to be super intelligent creatures and so in its early childhood AI tried to show intelligence by creating machines capable of proving theorems by themselves. By having some basic assumptions and rules, they tried to prove theorems by combining these rules, getting new assumptions and so on. Gelernters Geometry Theorem Prover was a typical example. Later it was realized that the intelligence of

human experts in this area is not easily imitable and the use of common sense and knowledge about mathematics was needed to prove theorems. Currently not many developments are taking place in this area.

(3) *Natural Language Processing (NLP):* Languages like English, French or Malayalam which are used by men are called natural languages. The language we speak is often context sensitive. "Did you shoot the tiger?", has different meanings when asked to a hunter and a photographer. Also our language is incomplete. Natural language processing deals with understanding this language using knowledge about the grammar rules and context. This has a wide variety of applications and is a field of active research. Also translation between these languages is studied in AI.

(4) *Vision, Speech Recognition and Similar Areas:* Seeing an animal and recognizing it as a cat is child play but a difficult task for computers. Modern AI programmes focuses on recognizing objects and persons and behaviour based on vision. This has many applications in robot navigation, crime detection, and military operations and so on.

(5) *Expert Systems:* A "knowledge engineer" interviews experts in a certain domain and tries to embody their knowledge in a computer programme for carrying out some task. How well this works depends on whether the intellectual mechanisms required for the task are within the present state of AI. When this turned out not to be so, there were many disappointing results. One of the first expert systems was MYCIN in 1974, which diagnosed bacterial infections of the blood and suggested treatments. It did better than medical students or practicing doctors, provided its limitations were observed. Namely, its ontology included bacteria, symptoms, and treatments and did not include patients, doctors, hospitals, death, recovery, and events occurring in time. Its interactions depended on a single patient being considered. Since the experts consulted by the knowledge engineers knew about patients, doctors, death, recovery, etc., it is clear that the knowledge engineers forced what the experts told them into a predetermined framework. In the present state of AI, this has to be true. The usefulness of current expert systems depends on their users having common sense.

Human experts are rare, costly and perishing. If we spend a large sum and train a person as a neurologist, the maximum we can expect is 30-40 years of service. And we cannot take a copy of the neurologist. So if we can train a computer to have the same expertise or to be precise expert behaviour at least in a narrow field the utility is high. Expert systems deal with extracting expertise and porting it to computers. That is creating software that can exhibit expert behaviour. This field has undergone explosive growth in the last few years.

(6) *Neural Networks:* Animal brain is composed of neurons and performs computations (thinking) by passing signals between these networks of neurons. Why not imitate this and evolve intelligence? Neural networks began from this foundation. They are capable of learning, adapting and predicting. Putting

in simple language, a neural network is a collection of computation units (real or virtually created), which are interconnected and cooperates for computation. Neural networks have applications in control systems, speech and natural language processing, vision and many other fields.

(7) *Logical AI:* What a programme knows about the world in general the facts of the specific situation in which it must act, and its goals are all represented by sentences of some mathematical logical language. The programme decides what to do by inferring that certain actions are appropriate for achieving its goals. The first article proposing this was (McCarthy, 1959). (McCarthy, 1989) is a more recent summary. (McCarthy, 1996) lists some of the concepts involved in logical AI.

(8) *Search:* AI programmes often examine large numbers of possibilities, e.g. moves in a chess game or inferences by a theorem proving programme. Discoveries are continually made about how to do this more efficiently in various domains.

(9) *Pattern Recognition:* When a programme makes observations of some kind, it is often programmed to compare what it sees with a pattern. For example, a vision programme may try to match a pattern of eyes and a nose in a scene in order to find a face. More complex patterns, e.g. in a natural language text, in a chess position, or in the history of some event are also studied. These more complex patterns require quite different methods than do the simple patterns that have been studied the most.

(10) *Representation:* Facts about the world have to be represented in some way. Usually languages of mathematical logic are used.

(11) *Inference:* From some facts, others can be inferred. Mathematical logical deduction is adequate for some purposes, but new methods of *non-monotonic* inference have been added to logic since the 1970s. The simplest kind of non-monotonic reasoning is default reasoning in which a conclusion is to be inferred by default, but the conclusion can be withdrawn if there is evidence to the contrary. For example, when we hear of a bird, we man infer that it can fly, but this conclusion can be reversed when we hear that it is a penguin. It is the possibility that a conclusion may have to be withdrawn that constitutes the non-monotonic character of the reasoning. Ordinary logical reasoning is monotonic in that the set of conclusions that can the drawn from a set of premises is a monotonic increasing function of the premises. Circumscription is another form of non-monotonic reasoning.

(12) *Common Sense Knowledge and Reasoning:* This is the area in which AI is farthest from human-level, in spite of the fact that it has been an active research area since the 1950s. While there has been considerable progress, e.g. in developing systems of *non-monotonic reasoning* and theories of action, yet more new ideas are needed. The Cyc system contains a large but spotty collection of common sense facts.

(13) *Learning from Experience:* Programmes do that. The approaches to

AI based on *connectionism* and *neural nets* specialize in that. There is also learning of laws expressed in logic (Mitchell, 1997). Programmes can only learn what facts or behaviours their formalisms can represent and unfortunately learning systems are almost all based on very limited abilities to represent information.

(14) *Planning:* Planning programmes start with general facts about the world (especially facts about the effects of actions), facts about the particular situation and a statement of a goal. From these, they generate a strategy for achieving the goal. In the most common cases, the strategy is just a sequence of actions.

(15) *Epistemology:* This is a study of the kinds of knowledge that are required for solving problems in the world.

(16) *Ontology:* Ontology is the study of the kinds of things that exist. In AI, the programmes and sentences deal with various kinds of objects, and we study what these kinds are and what their basic properties are. Emphasis on ontology begins in the 1990s.

(17) *Heuristics:* A heuristic is a way of trying to discover something or an idea imbedded in a programme. The term is used variously in AI. *Heuristic functions* are used in some approaches to search to measure how far a node in a search tree seems to be from a goal. *Heuristic predicates* that compare two nodes in a search tree to see if one is better than the other, i.e. constitutes an advance toward the goal, may be more useful.

(18) *Genetic Programming:* Genetic programming is a technique for getting programmes to solve a task by mating random Lisp programmes and selecting fittest in millions of generations. It is being developed by John Koza's group and here's a tutorial.

(19) *Computer Vision:* The world is composed of three-dimensional objects but the inputs to the human eye and computers' TV cameras are two dimensional. Some useful programmes can work solely in two dimensions but full computer vision requires partial three-dimensional information that is not just a set of two-dimensional views. At present there are only limited ways of representing three-dimensional information directly and they are not as good as what humans evidently use.

Artificial Intelligence Techniques

The main aim of Artificial Intelligence (AI) is to study how to build artificial systems that perform tasks normally performed by human beings (Nilsson, 1971). This concept was born in 1956 in the Darthmounth conference. From that moment on a lot of effort has been made and many goals have been achieved but unfortunately many failures as well. Today the AI is a very important discipline and it includes a number of well-recognized and mature areas: Expert Systems, Fuzzy Logic, Genetic Algorithms, Language Processing, Logic Programming, Planning and Scheduling, Neural Networks and

Robotics. Within these fields, our work focuses on *AI planning and scheduling (AIP & S)* and *expert systems* techniques.

AI Planning Techniques

These techniques have been applied to solve complex problems in domains such as robotics, logistics or satellites. The new Virtual Learning Environments also provide an interesting field for AI researchers. In this domain they can experiment with their automatic problem solving algorithms, or develop and design new techniques in this discipline. Then, the educational investigators can use this new kind of tools and methods that could aid them to detect, reason, and solve (automatically) deficiencies observed in their initial learning designs. Again, one of the areas of AI most suitable to be applied within this context is the Automated Planning and Scheduling. The combination of both tools can perfectly handle temporal reasoning and resource consumption, together with some quality criteria (usually centered on time or resource application).

In this context, a *planner* solves a concrete problem by finding a sequence of actions that transform an initial state into a final state. In a learning environment, an initial state can be described by the student's previous knowledge, the resources that a course (set of learning activities that are performed by the students) uses and the time period when they are available. A final state, or a goal, would be that the students are able to apply critical thinking to a specific subject.

In order for a planner to solve a problem, it is needed (1) to specify the domain that is composed of a set of operators that allow the planner to go from a defined initial state to a state in which a set of goals is fulfilled, and (2) to describe the initial and goal states. There are several planning techniques, among them we have chosen a total order planner. This generates solutions that are sequences of total ordered actions. The basic structure is a tree where nodes are plans or states, and edges can be actions or state transactions.

AI Scheduling Techniques

A schedule*r* organizes activities along the time line by taking into account the resources available. Many procedures used in this area of scheduling systems come from the Operational Research (OP) and the Constraint Programming (CP). This last discipline has been applied to the different scheduling problems with very good results, i.e. the Job Shop Scheduling Problem (JSSP) (Holland, 1998). These JSSP methods can be easily generalized and applied into a learning environment. In this case, instead of machines and jobs, there are students, teachers and learning units in courses.

In the application displayed is made in a natural way taking into account that each learning unit can be considered as an operation that needs to be processed during a period of time, for a given student (machine) and under the supervision of an educator. The course also must have a limited duration (deadline) and an instructor can only manage a limited number of students (each teacher is a resource with a total resource capacity given by the number of students he is able to advise).

In addition, it is necessary to know the initial and end time of each learning unit task considering precedence constraints among them. Also, it is mandatory to impose a course deadline (its total duration) and the resources (number of teachers) that are available. Furthermore, it is needed to establish other variables imposed by the problem conditions: number of learners, learning activities duration, course length, etc.

Once all these data have been recorded, it is up to the educator or the pedagogical responsible to establish the best way to distribute the number of hours and their contents among the different units in order to assure the quality of the educative process. This business can be done automatically by applying planning and scheduling techniques. The results will be a plan, or a set of plans, if a solution exists for a given deadline. A plan can be seen as a sequence of learning activities (operator applications) with a specific duration that must be accomplished from the initial state to a state where the goals are reached, under the teacher supervision, with the resources available.

Finally, it is appropriate to emphasize the possibility of compiling the information of the student interactions with the system throughout the time. This information can be used as a feedback in order to reschedule the whole course or to change the time assigned for a specific task. This way allows a better course adaptation to both: the student characteristics and the available time.

Artificial Intelligence and Problem Solving

How can a computer system be programmed to perform intelligently? This question drives the empirical and engineering research in a field called artificial intelligence (AI). The simplest definition of AI is that, *"Artificial intelligence is the study of mental faculties through the use of computational models."* One of the main objectives of AI is to design and development of computer systems that can solve the same kinds of activities that we deem intelligent (e.g., solving a math problem like a human being, understanding natural language etc.). In addition, AI techniques can include inductive and deductive reasoning processes that allow a system to access its own database to derive novel (i.e., not programmed) answers to learner's queries. Cognitive psychology also provides part of the answer to the question of how to get a computer to behave intelligently by examining issues related to the representation and organization of knowledge types in human memory. Research in this area provides detailed structural specifications for implementation in intelligent computer programmes. Cognitive psychology also addresses the nature of errors, a critical feature in the design of intelligent systems to assist learners during the learning process.

Procedural and Declarative Knowledge

Our mind/body "knows" a great deal of information. As Figure 2.6 suggests, this can be divided into two main categories: procedural and declarative.

Declarative knowledge can be divided into two categories: episodic and semantic.

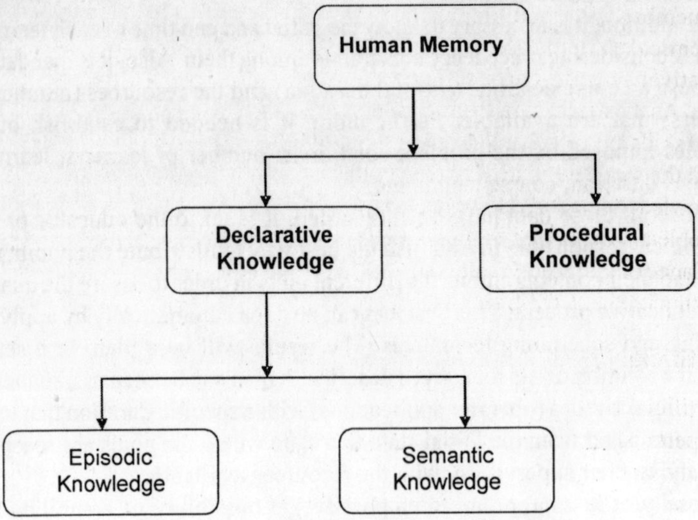

Figure 2.6: A Model of Human Memory

Procedural Knowledge

Procedural knowledge is knowledge about how to do things, it is often kinesthetic. Our mind/body has mastered many different physical procedures for accomplishing tasks. For example, when you were a young child, you did not know how to tie your shoes. Now, you tie your shoes without conscious effort. You have mastered this skill; it is stored in your mind/body.

Declarative Knowledge

Declarative knowledge is concerned with the facts that we know. We have memorized a great many facts or pieces of information. For example, you know the alphabet, some telephone numbers, addresses, names of people, dates and, so on. Such declarative knowledge is important to problem solving.

People often differentiate between procedural and declarative knowledge by calling the former "know how" and the later "know what". Our "know how" and our "know what" (knowledge) work together as we solve problems and accomplish tasks.

Declarative knowledge can be divided into two categories:

Episodic Declarative Knowledge: This type of knowledge is concrete. The knowledge is established when an episode or unusual event occurs. (Think of this as one trial learning) [Episodic]. Declarative knowledge is very personal intimately tied to specify episodes or settings such as: one's wedding; or a particular nice vacation event. Almost any "first time, memorable event" has a reasonable chance of becoming part of our "Episodic Declarative Knowledge."

Semantic Declarative Knowledge: Semantic declarative knowledge is more abstract. It tends to be symbolic and context free. You probably do not remember when you first learned the alphabet, the counting numbers or the chemical formula (H_2O) for water. Semantic declarative memories are relatively easy to create through study and they are easy to forget.

As the diagram in figure 2.6 suggests, these three categories of knowledge and skills are closely related. In essence, both the concepts and theory category and the strategies category are components of the declarative and procedural knowledge category. However, from a problem solving point of view, it is useful. Problem solving makes use of all three categories of knowledge. The specific balance of knowledge that is needed for problems in a particular domain varies both with the domain and with the person working to solve a problem.

Artificial Intelligence and Intelligent Behaviour

Artificial intelligence (AI) is a term that encompasses many definitions. Most experts agree that AI is concerned with two basic ideas. First, it involves studying the thought processes of humans; second, it deals with representing those processes via machines (computers, robots and so on). One well publicized definition of AI is "behaviour by a machine that, if performed by a human being, would be called intelligent". The three objectives of artificial intelligence are (1) to make machines smarter, (2) to understand what intelligence is and (3) to make machines more useful. What is the meaning of the term 'intelligent behaviour'? Several capabilities are considered to be signs of intelligence:

- Learning or understanding from experiences
- Making sense of ambiguous or contradictory messages
- Responding quickly and successfully to a new situation
- Using reasoning to solve problems and direct actions effectively
- Dealing with complex situations
- Understanding and inferring in ordinary, rational ways
- Applying knowledge to manipulate the environment
- Recognizing the relative importance of different elements in a situation

Although AI's ultimate goal is to build machines that will mimic human intelligence, current intelligent systems found in commercial AI products are far from exhibiting any significant intelligence.

Knowledge and AI

AI is frequently associated with the concept of knowledge. The computer cannot have experiences or study and learn as the human mind can but it can use knowledge given to it by human experts. Such knowledge consists of facts, concepts, theories, heuristics methods, procedures and relationships.

The collection of knowledge related to a problem to be used in an intelligent system is organized and stored in what we call a knowledge base and it is specific to a problem.

Comparing Artificial Intelligence (AI) and Natural Intelligence (NI)

The potential value of AI can be better understood by contrasting it with natural (human) intelligence. AI has several commercial advantages over natural intelligence:

- *AI is more permanent:* Natural intelligence is perishable from a commercial standpoint because workers mat take knowledge with them when they leave their place of employment or they may forget their knowledge. AI, however, is permanent as long as the computer systems and programmes remain unchanged.
- *AI can be less expensive than natural intelligence:* There are many circumstances in which developing or buying an intelligent system costs less than having human beings carry out the same tasks.
- *AI is consistent and through:* Natural intelligence is erratic because people are erratic, they may not perform consistently.
- *AI can be documented:* Decisions made by a computer can be easily documented by tracing the activities of the system. Natural intelligence is difficult to document.
- AI offers ease of duplication and dissemination: Transferring a body of knowledge from person to another usually requires a lengthy process of apprenticeship. Some expertise can never be duplicated completely. Knowledge embodied in a computer system can be copied and easily moved to another computer, anywhere and any time.

Problem Solving through 'Natural Intelligence'

Now let us see that if a human being has to face a problem then how he solve the problem through various steps, because to understand the functioning of the AI technique, it is important to understand these logical problem solving steps.

The above flowchart shows the problem-solving steps involved in human problem-solving procedure. The working of artificial intelligence is similarly as the process mentioned above to solve complex problems. The computer can be programmed to solve complex and logical problems. It can also be programmed to mimic various forms of human behaviour.

A General Strategy for Problem Solving

Here is general six steps strategy that we can follow in attempting to solve almost any problem. This can also be shown through the above flow chart given in Figure 2.7:

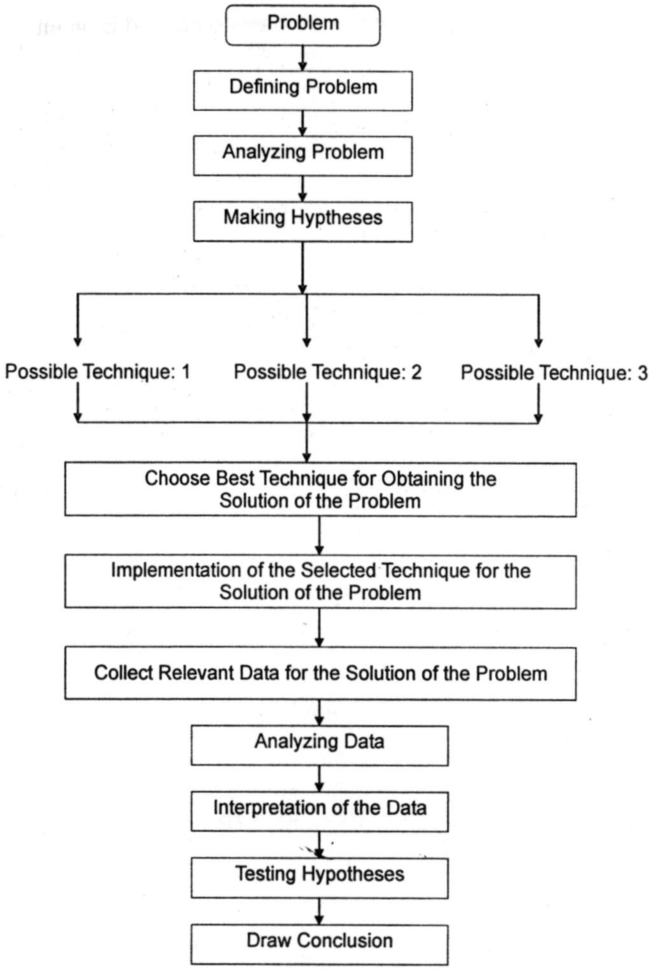

Figure 2.7: Steps Involved in Human Problem Solving

Six Steps Involved in Problem Solving

Step 1: Understand the Problem: Among other things, this includes working toward having a clearly defined problem. You need an initial understanding of the given goal and resources. This requires knowledge of the domain of the problem.

Step 2: Determine a Plan of Action: This is a thinking activity. What resources will you use, how will you use them, in what order will you use them? Are the resources adequate to the task?

Step 3: Think Carefully About Possible Consequences of Carrying Out Your Plan of Action: Place major emphasis on trying to anticipate undesirable outcomes. What new problems will be created? You may decide to stop working on the problem or return to step-1 as a consequence of this thinking.

Step 4: Carry Out Your Plan of Action: Do so in a thoughtful manner. This thinking may lead you to the conclusion that you need to return to one of the earlier steps. It is this reflective thinking that leads to increased expertise.

Step 5: Check to see if the desired goal has been achieved by carrying out your plan of action. For this purpose do one of the following:

- If the problem has been solved, go to step 6.
- If the problem has not been solved and you are willing to devote more time and energy to it, make use of the knowledge and experience you have gained as you return to step 1 or step 2.
- Make a decision to stop working on the problem. This might be a temporary or a permanent decision. Keep in mind that the problem you are working on may not be solvable, or it may be beyond your current capabilities and resources.

Step 6: Do a careful analysis of the steps you have carried out and the results you have achieved to see if you have created new, additional problems that need to be addressed. Reflect on what you have learned by solving the problem. Think about how your increased knowledge and skills can be used in other problem-solving situations.

Problem Solving through "Artificial Intelligence"

The problem is solved through "Natural Intelligence" is shown above. But when it is solved through "Artificial intelligence", the following major components of AI is used to solve the problem (Dubey, A. and Rathod, M.B.)

Major Components of Artificial Intelligence

AI system has four major components, namely—

- Knowledge Representation (KR)
- Heuristic Search (HS)
- AI Programming Language and Tools (AIPLT)
- AI Hardware (AIH)

Knowledge Representation

A knowledge representation system should possess the following characteristics:

- The representation scheme should have a set of well-defined syntax and semantics.
- The knowledge representation scheme should have a good expressive capacity.
- The representation must be efficient.

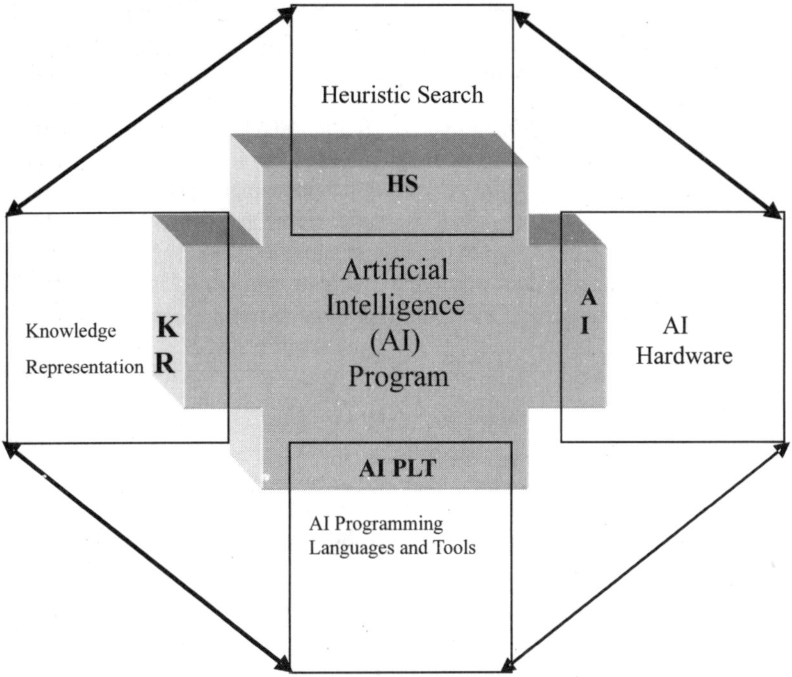

Figure 2.8: A Complete Model of Problem Solving through Artificial Intelligence (AI)

Heuristic Search

A heuristic is a technique that improves the efficiency of a search process. Using good heuristics we can hope to get good solutions to hard problems in less time.

AI Programming Languages and Tools

Now a day we have specified languages and programmes for data processing and scientific applications. Similarly specialized languages and tools are used for AI programming. AI languages provide the basic functions for AI programming and tools for the right environment.

(i) *Artificial Intelligence (AI) Tools:* Expert system tools help in constructing prototypes at rapid speed without compromising on the basic characteristics. In all expert system tools the knowledge base is empty and the domain expert himself or in conjunction with the knowledge engineer fills up the knowledge base. An expert system tool provides the following:

(a) Powerful editors, menus and graphical interfaces.
(b) Right environment for the expert to communicate with it.
(c) Provide facilities for communicating with the external environment.

(d) Helps in maintaining the system and historical database.
(e) Provide facilities for variety of knowledge representation.
(f) The experts methodology for handling uncertainty.

(ii) *Artificial Intelligence (AI) Programming Languages:* An AI programming language (LISP) developed by John Mc Cathy in late 1950s. LISP (List Processing) is a symbolic processing language that represents information in lists and manipulates. In LISP, the basic elements are treated as symbols irrespective of whether they are numeric or alpha numeric. Another important programming language used in solving problems through AI is PROLOG. The syntax and semantics of PROLOG are very close to formal logic.

AI Hardware

The AI hardware means the type of machines used in dealing with problems through AI intelligence. Earlier most of the AI programmes in India were implemented on Von Neumann machines only.

Search Algorithms in Artificial Intelligence

Some well-known search algorithms are:

- Generate and Test
- Hill Climbing
- Heuristic Search
- Means and Ends analysis

(a) *Generate and Test Approach:* This approach concerns the generation of the state-space from a known starting state (root) of the problem and continues expanding the reasoning space until the goal node or the terminal state is reached. In fact after generation of each and every state, the generated node is compared with the known goal state. When the goal is found, the algorithm terminates. In case there exist multiple paths leading to the goal, then the path having the smallest distance from the root is preferred. The basic strategy used in this search is only generation of states and their testing for goals but it does not allow filtering of states.

(b) *Hill Climbing Approach:* Under this approach, one has to first generate a starting state and measure the total cost for reaching the goal from the given starting state. Let this cost be f. While f = a predefined utility value and the goal is not reached, new nodes are generated as children of the current node. However, in case all the neighborhood nodes (states) yield an identical value of f and the goal is not included in the set of these nodes, the search algorithm is trapped at a hillock or local extrema. One way to overcome this problem is to select randomly a new starting state and then continue the above search process. While proving trigonometric identities, we often use Hill Climbing, perhaps unknowingly.

(c) *Heuristic Search:* Classically heuristics means rule of thumb. In heuristic search, we generally use one or more heuristic functions to determine the better candidate states among a set of legal states that could be generated from a known state. The heuristic function, in other words, measures the fitness of the candidate states. The better the selection of the states, the fewer will be the number of intermediate states for reaching the goal. However, the most difficult task in heuristic search problems is the selection of the heuristic functions. One has to select them intuitively, so that in most cases hopefully it would be able to prune the search space correctly.

(d) *Means and Ends Analysis:* This method of search attempts to reduce the gap between the current state and the goal state. One simple way to explore this method is to measure the distance between the current state and the goal, and then apply an operator to the current state, so that the distance between the resulting state and the goal is reduced. In many mathematical theorem-proving processes, we use Means and Ends Analysis.

Key Researchers in the Field of AI

While many researchers have evolved AI into the field that it is today, we will attempt to discuss a small cross-section of those pioneers and their contributions.

Alan Turing: The British mathematician Alan Turing first introduced the idea that all human-solvable problems can be reduced to a set of algorithms. This opened the door to the idea that thought itself might be algorithmically reducible, and therefore machines could be programmed to mimic humans in thought and perhaps consciousness. In coming to this conclusion, Alan Turing created the Turing Machine, which could mimic the operation of any other computing machine. Later, Alan Turing proposed the Turing Test to provide the means to recognize machine intelligence.

John McCarthy: John McCarthy is not only one of the earliest AI researchers, but he continues his research today as a Hoover Institution Senior Fellow at Stanford University. He co-founded the MIT AI Laboratory, founded the Stanford AI Lab, and organized the first conference on AI in 1956 (Dartmouth Conference). His research has brought us the LISP language, considered the primary choice of symbolic AI software development today. Time-sharing computer systems, including the ability to mathematically prove the correctness of computer programmes, were an early invention of John McCarthy.

Marvin Minsky: Marvin Minsky has been one of the most prolific researchers in the field of AI as well as many others. He is currently the Toshiba Professor of Media Arts and Sciences at MIT where, with John McCarthy, he founded MIT's AI Lab in 1958. Marvin Minsky has written seminal papers in a variety of fields including neural networks, knowledge representation, and cognitive psychology. He created the AI concept of frames that modeled phenomena in cognition, language understanding, and visual perception.

Professor Minsky also built the first hardware neural network-learning machine and built the first LOGO turtle.

Arthur Samuel: Arthur Samuel (1901-1990) was an early pioneer in machine learning and artificial intelligence. He had a long and illustrious career as an educator and an engineer, and was known as being helpful and modest of his achievements. Samuel is most well known for his checkers-playing programme, developed in 1957. This was one of the first examples of an intelligent programme playing a complex game. Not only did the programme result in beating Samuel, it defeated the fourth-rated checkers player in the nation. Samuel's papers on machine learning are still noted as worthwhile reading.

Problems that Fall within the Scope of Artificial Intelligence

Medium or large scale of Artificial Intelligence applications usually requires very powerful computers with fast CPUs and lots of memory. Most of the Artificial Intelligence research and many Artificial Intelligence applications were implemented in Mainframes and big Mini computers. So the increased cost of computer might represent on of the problems to some extent, the scope of Artificial Intelligence.

Difficulty of Artificial Intelligence softwares: Artificial Intelligence programmes are incredibly complex. As a result, they take more time to develop and they are far more expensive. Software development tools such as improved Artificial Intelligence programming languages and expert system shells help speed up and simplify Artificial Intelligence software development but they are expensive and require some talent to use.

3

Expert Systems

Artificial Intelligence (AI) is a branch of computer science, which focuses on the development of computer systems to simulate the processes of problem solving and duplicate human brain functions. Expert systems (ES) are a category of programmes based on the theory and methods of artificial intelligence.

The first expert systems appeared in the late sixties. Today, they exist in many forms, from medical diagnosis to investment analysis and from counseling to production control. Due to the advances of the last decade, today's expert systems users can choose from dozens of commercial software packages. At present, we accept as routine such expert systems as weather forecasting, online mapping and driving directions, diagnostic systems for automotive repair shops, and so on.

Many large corporations use expert systems in their business. The list of the companies using expert systems technology is long and varied: NASA, HP, Lockheed, Boing, DaimlerChrysler AG, various power, gas and oil stations, etc.

Expert systems tend to be more effective than other computer based applications, because they:

- may combine the knowledge of many experts in a specific field,
- can store an unlimited amount of information, and works much faster, than a human,
- are available 24 hours a day, and can be used at a distance over a network,
- are able to explain their information requests and suggestions,
- can process client's uncertain responses and, by combining several pieces of uncertain information, may still be able to make strong recommendations,
- can accumulate the knowledge of high level employees for any company, which is especially useful when the company needs to fire them due to worsened market conditions.

Expert Systems

An expert system is a computer programme dedicated to solving problems and giving advice within a specialized area of knowledge. A good expert system can match the performance of a human specialist. The field of expert systems is the most advanced part of AI and expert systems are in wide commercial use. The basic components of an expert system are a "knowledge base" and an "inference engine. The information in the knowledge base is obtained by interviewing people who are expert in the area in question. The interviewer or "knowledge engineer" organizes the information elicited from the experts into a collection of rules, typically of "if-then" structure. Rules of this type are called "production rules". Knowledge-based expert systems enable computers to make decisions for solving complicated non-numerical problems. These expert systems consists of hundreds or thousands of "if-then" logic rules formulated with knowledge gleaned from leading authorities in a given field. The inference engine enables the expert system to draw deductions from the rules in the knowledge base. For example, if the knowledge base contains production rules "if X then Y" and "if Y then Z", the inference engine is able to deduce "if X then Z". The expert system might then query its user "is X true in the situation that we are considering? An important feature of expert systems is that they are able to work cooperatively with their human users, enabling a degree of human-computer symbiosis.

An expert system is a computer programme that employs human knowledge to solve problems that usually would require human intelligence. This kind of programmes represents the expertise knowledge, about a specific class of problems, as data or rules that can be called upon when needed. They can also provide some analysis of the problems and they can even recommend user actions in order to perform improvements and rectifications. Expert systems seem to arrive at conclusions using reasoning capabilities.

The Need for Expert Systems

Expert systems are necessitated by the limitations associated with conventional human decision-making processes, including:

1. Human expertise is very scarce.
2. Humans get tired from physical or mental workload.
3. Humans forget crucial details of a problem.
4. Humans are inconsistent in their day-to-day decisions.
5. Humans have limited working memory.
6. Humans are unable to comprehend large amounts of data quickly.
7. Humans are unable to retain large amounts of data in memory.
8. Humans are slow in recalling information stored in memory.
9. Humans are subject to deliberate or inadvertent bias in their actions.
10. Humans can deliberately avoid decision responsibilities.
11. Humans *lie, hide*, and *die.*

Coupled with these human limitations are the weaknesses inherent in conventional programming and traditional decision-support tools. Despite the mechanistic power of computers, they have certain limitations that impair their effectiveness in implementing human-like decision processes. Conventional programmes:

1. Are algorithmic in nature and depend only on raw machine power
2. Depend on facts that may be difficult to obtain
3. Do not make use of the effective heuristic approaches used by human experts
4. Are not easily adaptable to changing problem environments
5. Seek explicit and factual solutions that may not be possible

Knowledge in the Expert System

The knowledge the expert uses to solve a problem must be represented in a fashion that can be used to code into the computer and then be available for decision making by the expert system. There are various formal methods for representing knowledge and usually the characteristics of a particular problem will determine the appropriate representation techniques employed.

Knowledge bases can be represented by production rules. These rules consist of a condition or premise followed by an action or conclusion (IF condition...THEN action). Production rules permit the relationships that makeup the knowledge base to be broken down into manageable units. Having a knowledge base that consists of hundreds or thousands of rules can cause a problem with management and organization of the rules. Organizing rules and visualizing their interconnectedness can be accomplished through dependency networks. This method of knowledge representation is discussed later in this discussion under knowledge acquisition and representation.

During the consultation, the rule base is searched for conditions that can be satisfied by facts supplied by the user. This operation is performed by the inference engine. Once all of the conditions (i.e. IF parts of rules) of a rule are matched, the rule is executed and the appropriate conclusion is drawn. Based upon the conclusions drawn and the facts obtained during consultation, the inference mechanism determines which questions will be asked and in what order. There are various inferencing methods available to perform the tasks of searching, matching, and execution.

A distinctive characteristic of expert systems that distinguishes them from conventional programmes is their ability to utilize incomplete or incorrect data. Given only a partial data set, an expert is likely to have less than absolute certainty in his conclusion. The degree of certainty can be quantified in relative terms and included in the knowledge base. The certainty values are assigned by the expert during the knowledge acquisition phase of developing the system. By incorporating rules in the knowledge base with different certainty values, the system will be able to offer solutions to problems without a complete set of data. The capacity to deal with uncertainty is available in development software.

Components of Expert Systems

Expert systems consist of two main parts: the knowledge base and the inference engine. The knowledge base contains the expert system knowledge. This can be catalogued as: factual and heuristic. The factual one is that knowledge that is widely shared and it can be typically found in books, articles, journals, etc. The heuristic knowledge is more experiential and it is rarely discussed. This is the knowledge derived of good training, good judgment and plausible deduction in the field. These two kinds of knowledge are organized and represented as rules IF-THEN. The inference engine manipulates the information stored in the knowledge base in order to form a line of reasoning. This engine is built into programme modules according to the problem-solving designed method.

One of the most attractive features of expert systems is their capacity to review its consultations and provide the user with an explanation for how its conclusions were derived. The exposition function is basically a record of the reasoning process used by the expert to solve the problem. It provides for a better understanding of how the conclusion was reached and yields in the user greater confidence in the conclusion and the expert system.

Expert systems can afford many tasks: monitoring, design, control, simulation, learning support and information retrieval, among others. In this article one expert system is used as instruction system to monitoring the learning process of a group of students. The system detects mistakes and identifies the suitable solutions. In this way, the system facilitates the student's education and the correction of errors.

An expert system is composed by: (1) a knowledge base and (2) an inference engine. Figure 3.1 shows the components of expert systems.

(1) The Knowledge Base

Knowledge base is "a collection of facts, relationships and rules which embody current expertise in a particular area". In order to build a knowledge base, knowledge needs to be engineered. To do so, two factual operations are required: (i) knowledge acquisition and (ii) knowledge representation.

(i) *Knowledge Acquisition*: The relevant knowledge pertinent to a specific knowledge domain needs to be elicited from wherever it might be (i.e. human experts, records). The main ways of knowledge elicitation from human experts are based on: (a) explanation and (b) observation.

(a) *Explanation*: The human expert describes, in a very through way, how he performs a certain task.

(b) *Observation*: The human expert presents concrete examples of what he do offering material for rule induction. What is required from the artificial expert at this stage is the capability of storing the acquired knowledge for future use. To do so knowledge must be memorized. Memory represents the founding capacity on which a knowledge

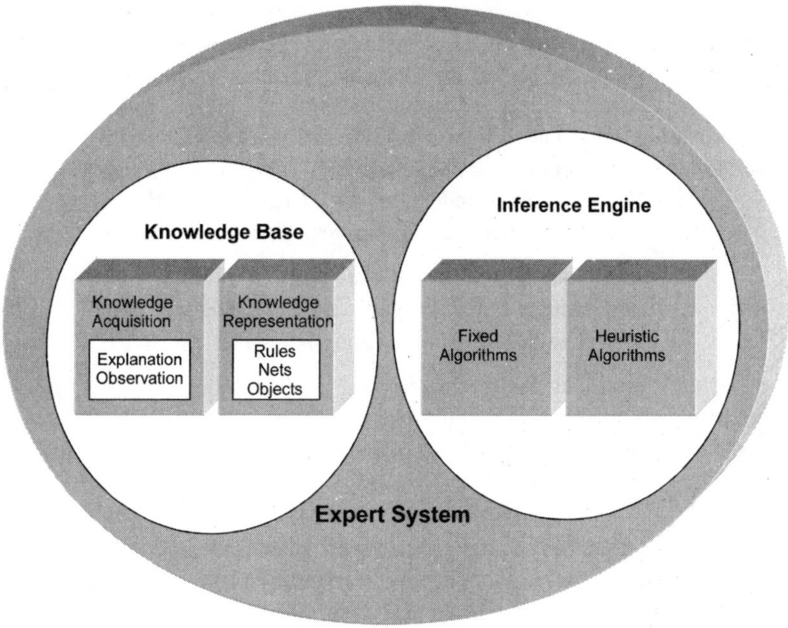

Figure 3.1: Components of Expert Systems

base is built. Without memory there is no knowledge base but memory, by itself, as a simple storage of data, is not sufficient to produce a knowledge base. What is required is an organized memory that allows for the quick and easy retrieval of what has been previously stored. To this purpose, knowledge needs to be represented in a way that fits the computer as a symbol manipulating machine. This exigency is fulfilled by the subsequent step in knowledge engineering.

(ii) *Knowledge Representation*: Knowledge representation consists in the symbolic way the acquired knowledge is expressed and structured in order to be dealt in a meaningful way by the machine. In an expert system, knowledge can be represented by: (1) rules, (2) nets, and (3) objects.

(a) *Rules*: Rules expressed generally in the if-then form (condition-action) meaning that whatever a certain situation(s) is encountered, a certain action is suggested (Rule based expert systems).
(b) *Nets*: Nets expressed in the form of nodes (containing evidence or hypotheses) and arcs (signifying casual linkages between nodes) (nets based expert system).
(c) *Objects*: Objects expressed in the form of attributes (properties that characterize the object) able to send and receive messages (interact).

Whatever the way of representing knowledge, what seems essential is the fact that knowledge needs to be "meaningful" to the artificial expert if problem solving tasks have to be performed. Past attempts, for instance in the artificial intelligence area of machine translation, failed because of lack of "understanding", on the part of the artificial translator, of the meaning of the text to be translated. Understanding and meaning are, clearly, in the minds of those who programme and those who use the artificial expert. Nevertheless, the artificial expert, in order to "behave intelligently", has to act as if it autonomously possessed a sufficient level of "understanding". To do so it needs to embody the capacity of mastery. In an expert system mastery should result in the ability to:

(i) Organize (classify, use taxonomies);
(ii) Evaluate (compare, discriminate, connect);
(iii) Explain (make clear the reasons underlying a certain advice/decision)

Mastery produces understanding and understanding "entails making inferences and results in the ability to make further inferences". This leads straight to the subsequent component of an expert system the inference engine.

(2) The Inference Engine

The knowledge acquired and represented is activated by symbols manipulators known as the inference engine. The inference engine is "the reasoning core of the system which infers logical conclusions from the knowledge base". Expert systems generally present a separation between the declarative knowledge (semantics) stored in the knowledge base and the procedural knowledge (syntactics) activated by the inference engine. This is said to promote flexibility (in terms of changes) and transparency (in terms of explanations). Clearly the correctness of the acquired knowledge and the effectiveness of its representation play, on the whole, a very important role and reserves have been expressed about "the strategy of complete separation of specific knowledge from general rule of inference". Nevertheless, what is here under focus are the capacities related to the process of making valid inferences and not the content of the statements to which the inference process is applied.

Interface Methods of Expert Systems

Expert systems present two kinds of inference methods based on the implementation of: (1) fixed algorithms, and (2) heuristic algorithms.

(1) *Fixed Algorithms*: The expert system solves problems executing a sequence of finite formally expressed steps. The capacity required by the system can be defined as consistency and it amounts to a correct linking and sequencing of statements according to the rules of logic.

(2) *Heuristic Algorithms*: The expert system tries to solve problems using plausible strategies that reduce (prune away) in a selective way the number of searches to be performed. Heuristics algorithms are implemented when the trap of combinational explosion is impending (i.e. when the number of possibilities to be investigated in order to solve the problem is enormous) or when the problem itself presents highly structured formalizable variations.

Expert Systems Characteristics

By definition, an expert system is a computer programme that simulates the thought process of a human expert to solve complex decision problems in a specific domain. The growth of expert systems is expected to continue for several years. With the continuing growth, many new and exciting applications will emerge. An expert system operates as an interactive system that responds to questions, asks for clarification, makes recommendations, and generally aids the decision-making process. Expert systems provide expert advice and guidance in a wide variety of activities, from computer diagnosis to delicate medical surgery.

Various definitions of expert systems have been offered by several authors. A general definition that is representative of the intended functions of expert systems is: *An expert system is an interactive computer-based decision tool that uses both facts and heuristics to solve difficult decision problems based on knowledge acquired from an expert.*

An expert system may be viewed as a computer simulation of a human expert. Expert systems are an emerging technology with many areas for potential applications. Past applications range from MYCIN, used in the medical field to diagnose infectious blood diseases, to XCON, used to configure computer systems. These expert systems have proven to be quite successful. Most applications of expert systems will fall into one of the following categories:

- Interpreting and identifying
- Predicting
- Diagnosing
- Designing
- Planning
- Monitoring
- Debugging and testing
- Instructing and training
- Controlling

Applications that are computational or deterministic in nature are not good candidates for expert systems. Traditional decision support systems such as spreadsheets are very mechanistic in the way they solve problems. They operate under mathematical and Boolean operators in their execution and arrive at one and only one static solution for a given set of data. Calculation-intensive applications with very exacting requirements are better handled by traditional decision support tools or conventional programming. The best application candidates for expert systems are those dealing with expert heuristics for solving problems. Conventional computer programmes are based on factual knowledge, an indisputable strength of computers. Humans, by contrast, solve problems on the basis of a mixture of factual and heuristic knowledge. Heuristic knowledge, composed of intuition, judgment, and logical inferences, is an indisputable strength of humans. Successful expert systems will be those that combine facts and heuristics and thus merge human knowledge with computer power in solving problems. To be effective, an expert system must focus on a particular problem domain, as discussed below-

Domain Specificity

Expert systems are typically very domain specific. For example, a diagnostic expert system for troubleshooting computers must actually perform all the necessary data manipulation as a human expert would. The developer of such a system must limit his or her scope of the system to just what is needed to solve the target problem. Special tools or programming languages are often needed to accomplish the specific objectives of the system.

Special Programming Languages

Expert systems are typically written in special programming languages. The use of languages like LISP and PROLOG in the development of an expert system simplifies the coding process. The major advantage of these languages, as compared to conventional programming languages, is the simplicity of the addition, elimination, or substitution of new rules and memory management capabilities. Some of the distinguishing characteristics of programming languages needed for expert systems work are:

- Efficient mix of integer and real variables
- Good memory-management procedures
- Extensive data-manipulation routines
- Incremental compilation
- Tagged memory architecture
- Optimization of the systems environment
- Efficient search procedures

Expert Systems are for Everyone

No matter which area of business one is engaged in, expert systems can fulfill the need for higher productivity and reliability of decisions. Everyone can find an application potential in the field of expert systems. Contrary to the belief that expert systems may pose a threat to job security, expert systems can actually help to create opportunities for new job areas. Presented below are some areas that hold promise for new job opportunities:

- Basic research
- Applied research
- Knowledge engineering
- Inference engine development
- Consulting (development and implementation)
- Training

- Sales and marketing
- Passive or active end user

An active user is one who directly uses expert systems consultations to obtain recommendations. A passive user is one who trusts the results obtained from expert systems and supports the implementation of those results.

Transition from Data Processing to Knowledge Processing

What data has been to the previous generations of computing, knowledge is to the present generation of computing. Expert systems represent a revolutionary transition from the traditional data processing to knowledge processing.

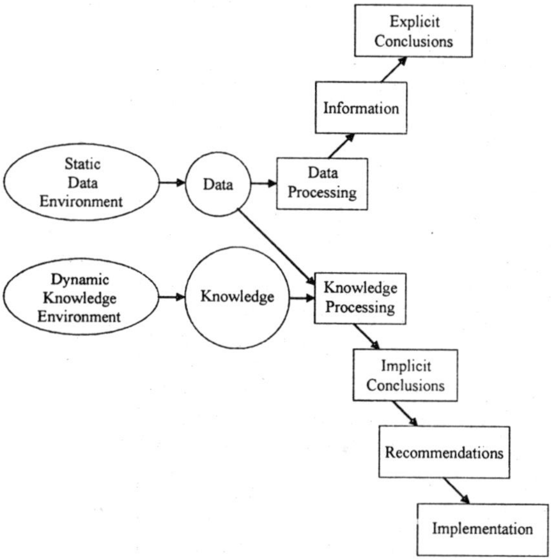

Figure 3.2: Data Processing versus Knowledge Processing

Figure 3.2 illustrates the relationships between the procedures for data processing and knowledge processing to make decisions. In traditional data processing the decision maker obtains the information generated and performs an explicit analysis of the information before making his or her decision. In an expert system knowledge is processed by using available data as the processing fuel. Conclusions are reached and recommendations are derived implicitly.

The expert system offers the recommendation to the decision maker, who makes the final decision and implements it as appropriate. Conventional data can now be manipulated to work with durable knowledge, which can be processed to generate timely information, which is then used to enhance human decisions.

Heuristic Reasoning: Human experts use a type of problem-solving technique called heuristic reasoning.

Commonly called rules of thumb or expert heuristics, it allows the expert to arrive at a good solution quickly and efficiently. Expert systems base their reasoning process on symbolic manipulation and heuristic inference procedures that closely match the human thinking process. Conventional programmes can only recognize numeric or alphabetic strings and manipulate them only in a preprogrammed manner.

Search Control Methods: All expert systems are search intensive. Many techniques have been employed to make these intensive searches more efficient. Branch and bound, pruning, depth-first search, and breadth-first search are some of the search techniques that have been explored. Because of the intensity of the search process, it is important that good search control strategies be used in the expert systems inference process.

Forward Chaining: This method involves checking the condition part of a rule to determine whether it is true or false. If the condition is true, then the action part of the rule is also true. This procedure continues until a solution is found or a dead end is reached. Forward chaining is commonly referred to as data-driven reasoning.

Backward Chaining: Backward chaining is the reverse of forward chaining. It is used to backtrack from a goal to the paths that lead to the goal. Backward chaining is very good when all outcomes are known and the number of possible outcomes is not large. In this case, a goal is specified and the expert system tries to determine what conditions are needed to arrive at the specified goal. Backward chaining is thus also called goal-driven.

User Interface: The initial development of an expert system is performed by the expert and the knowledge engineer. Unlike most conventional programmes, in which only programmers can make programme design decisions, the design of large expert systems is implemented through a team effort. A consideration of the needs of the end user is very important in designing the contents and user interface of expert systems.

Natural Language: The programming languages used for expert systems tend to operate in a manner similar to ordinary conversation. We usually state the premise of a problem in the form of a question, with actions being stated much as when we verbally answer the question, that is, in a "natural language" format. If, during or after a consultation, an expert system determines that a piece of its data or knowledge base is incorrect or is no longer applicable because the problem environment has changed, it should be able to update the knowledge base accordingly. This capability would allow the expert system to converse in a natural language format with either the developers or users.

Expert systems not only arrive at solutions or recommendations, but can give the user a level of confidence about the solution. In this manner, an expert system can handle both quantitative and qualitative factors when analyzing problems. This aspect is very important when we consider how inexact most input data are for day-to-day decision making. For example, the problems addressed by an expert system can have more than one solution or, in some cases, no definite solution at all. Yet the expert system can provide useful recommendations to the user just as a human consultant might do.

Explanations Facility in Expert Systems

One of the key characteristics of an expert system is the explanation facility. With this capability, an expert system can explain how it arrives at its conclusions. The user can ask questions dealing with the what, how, and why aspects of a problem. The expert system will then provide the user with a trace of the consultation process, pointing out the key reasoning paths followed during the consultation. Sometimes an expert system is required to solve other problems, possibly not directly related to the specific problem at hand, but whose solution will have an impact on the total problem-solving process. The explanation facility helps the expert system to clarify and justify why such a digression might be needed.

Data Uncertainties: Expert systems are capable of working with inexact data. An expert system allows the user to assign probabilities, certainty factors, or confidence levels to any or all input data. This feature closely represents how most problems are handled in the real world. An expert system can take all relevant factors into account and make a recommendation based on the best possible solution rather than the only exact solution.

Application Roadmap: The symbolic processing capabilities of AI technology lead to many potential applications in engineering and manufacturing. With the increasing sophistication of AI techniques, analysts are now able to use innovative methods to provide viable solutions to complex problems in everyday applications. Figure 3.3 presents a structural representation of the application paths for artificial intelligence and expert systems.

Symbolic Processing: Contrary to the practice in conventional programming, expert systems can manipulate objects symbolically to arrive at reasonable conclusions to a problem scenario.

Types of Expert Systems

Expert systems fall into a number of major categories (not exclusive) described below. There are many applications not covered and some manufacturers and vendors could fit in multiple categories but due to space limitations, they are only included in one.

(1) *Acquisition and interpretation of data:* These categories retrieve, analyze, filter and restore missed data as well as mine data, transform data in another format and so on.

(2) *Diagnosis and Abnormal Condition Management:* These categories recognize the condition of human health or the technical condition of complex industrial systems.

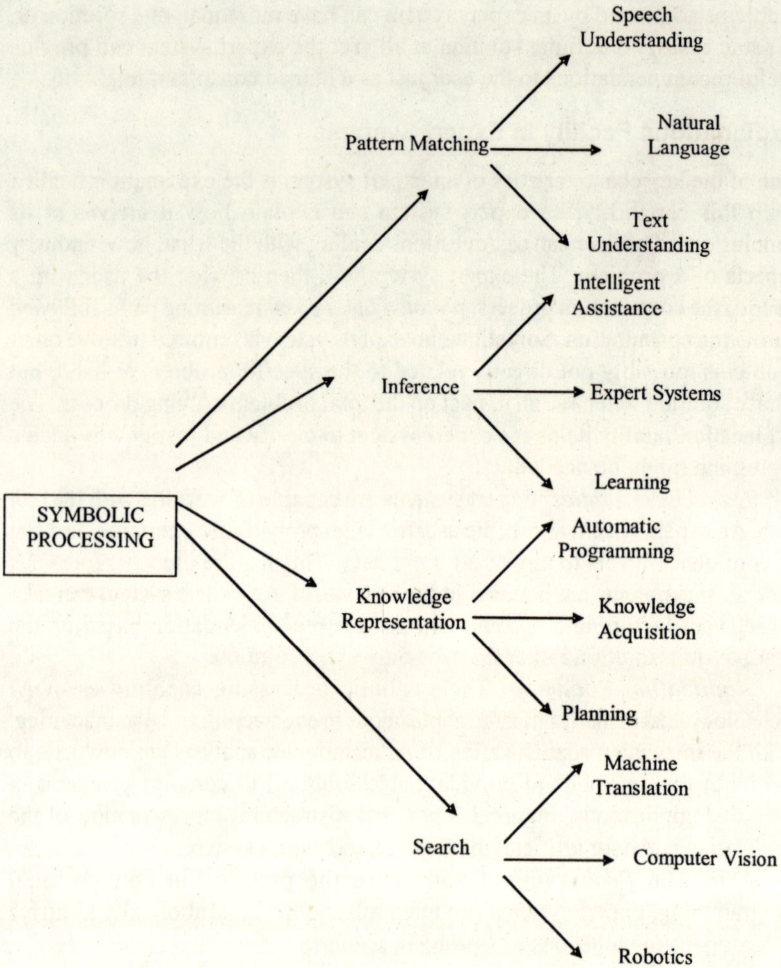

Figure 3.3: Application Roadmap for Expert Systems

(3) *Decision-making or decision support:* These categories include the following subcategories: Decision management, Decision optimization, Customer and Account management, Fraud management, Scoring and predictive modeling, Risk management, etc.

(4) *Design and management solutions:* After consideration of a large number of variable parameters for solving innovation tasks, it enables optimization of design and find the best management decisions.

(5) *Control and Monitoring:* These categories help monitor operation and control certain functions of machinery for heavy industry. Many corporations that developed Supervisory Control and Data Acquisition Systems (SCADA) used the expert systems for different control levels of industrial plants.

(6) *Prediction:* This category allows forecasting possible outcomes of observable situations. Here are weather forecasting, scoring and predictive modeling, risk management and other financial forecasting:

(7) *Marketing and trade management:* A key use of artificial intelligence is to determine marketing potential and business opportunities.

(8) *Human Resource Management Systems (HRMS):* The use of AI technology to find human technical talent.

(9) *e-Learning Systems (ELS):* Supply individual or group education and training for different disciplines on the basis of special tools. These learning tools and services allow learning faster and adapting quicker to the challenges of today's business world. ELS can include Learning Management Systems and Course Management systems.

Expert Systems Components

Generally, an expert system includes several key components:

- Data input/output
- Knowledge base or mathematical (logical models)
- Inference engine
- Explanation system
- Intellectual editor for the knowledge base,
- User interface

The main component of the expert system is knowledge base—an organized collection of facts, heuristics and other information on the subject of system's domain. An ES is built in a process known as knowledge engineering, during which knowledge about the domain is acquired from human experts and other sources. The part of the expert system that applies the knowledge to the problem's solving is called the inference engine. The explanation system explains the basis for the conclusion, reached by the expert system. The intellectual editor is a tool for correction, learning or self learning of the knowledge base. A friendly user interface enables inexperienced users to specify problems for the system to solve and to understand the system's conclusions.

Expert Systems Technologies

Expert systems technologies are typically based on the types of knowledge bases or mathematical (logical) models used for problem solving with the help of inference engines. Here are some examples of different types of technologies:

(1) *Model Based Reasoning*: Using a modeling environment to explore data, create algorithms, and create custom rules that offer early insights and competitive advantages.

In this field MATLAB®, Simulink®, Stateflow®, etc. (The Mathworks, Inc.) have become the fundamental tools for engineering and scientific work MATLAB integrates mathematical computing, visualization, and a powerful language to provide a flexible environment to explore data, create algorithms, and create custom tools that provide early insights and competitive advantages. Simulink is an interactive tool for modeling, simulating, and analyzing dynamic, multi-domain systems. Stateflow is an interactive design tool for modeling and simulating event-driven systems.

Opal-RT Technologies, Inc. specializes in new low-cost PC based tools for large-scale simulation, rapid control prototyping, and software or systems testing with hardware-in-the-loop.

(2) *Case-Based Reasoning (CBR)*: A CBR system compares the problem with previous cases, and then suggests the most successful course of action. Typically, in addition to manuali, built CBR systems, data mining methods also used.

(3) *Evolutionary Model Reasoning*: An evolutionary algorithm is a class of algorithms that finds approximate solutions to difficult-to-solve problems. They are inspired by mechanisms from biological evolution such as natural selection, mutation and recombination to find the best configuration for a specific system within specific constraints.

(4) *Stochastic Model Reasoning*: Bayesian Belief Network (BBN) uses a tree-based structure rather than logical "if-then", Bayesian systems iteratively use probabilities for finding any solutions.

The Netica APIs (Application Programme Interfaces) are a family of powerful Bayesian Network toolkits from the Norsys software corporation.. They enable the building of Bayesian belief networks and Influence Diagrams, do probabilistic inferencing, learning nets from data, modifying nets, and save and restore nets.

(5) *Fuzzy Logic Reasoning*: Fuzzy logic is the emulation of human reasoning on computers. The key concepts in fuzzy logic are the linguistic variable and membership function. A linguistic variable is a variable whose value is a word. (for example, the linguistic variable "temperature" might have the values: "normal", "high," "cold," "huge", "danger", "freezing," and so on). A membership function describes these linguistic values in terms of numerals. For example, to describe the word "cold", we can say, "If temperature is below 40 degrees, we can say it's definitely cold." The linguistic variables and their membership functions allow fuzzy logic to perform the imprecise, non-numerical reasoning performed in the same manner as humans.

(6) *Brain Simulation Reasoning*: Artificial Neural Networks (ANN) are named after the cells in the human brain, that include billions of neuron cells. ANN are formed from hundreds or thousands of simulated neurons connected together in much the same way as the brain's neurons. Neural networks are fast, tolerant of imperfect data, and do not need formulas or rules. ANN are good at pattern recognition, generalization, and trend prediction. Neural networks learn from experience, because they are trained by repeatedly reviewing examples. Each example includes both inputs (information you would use to make a decision) and outputs (the resulting decision, prediction, or response).

Neural Works Professional II/PLUS by Neural Ware Inc. is a comprehensive neural network technology platform that implements over 28 standard paradigms in an advanced model development workbench that is both integrated and extensible.

TRIZ systems (TRIZ is a Russian acronym for Theory of Inventive Problem Solving), that provides systematic methods for solving design and technological problems. This practical problem-solving paradigm was invented and developed by Genrich Altshuller, who discovered that technological systems evolve according to specific laws. TRIZ is rapidly gaining popularity with worldwide innovation communities by virtue of its success in guiding creative thinking and innovative product development.

Expert Systems Architecture

Figure 3.4 shows the most important modules that make up a rule-based expert system. The user interacts with the system through a *user interface* which may use menus, natural language or any other style of interaction). Then an *inference engine* is used to reason with both the *expert knowledge* (extracted from our friendly expert) and data specific to the particular problem being solved. The expert knowledge will typically be in the form of a set of IF-THEN rules. The *case specific data* includes both data provided by the user and partial conclusions (along with certainty measures) based on this data. In a simple forward chaining rule-based system the case specific data will be the elements in *working memory*.

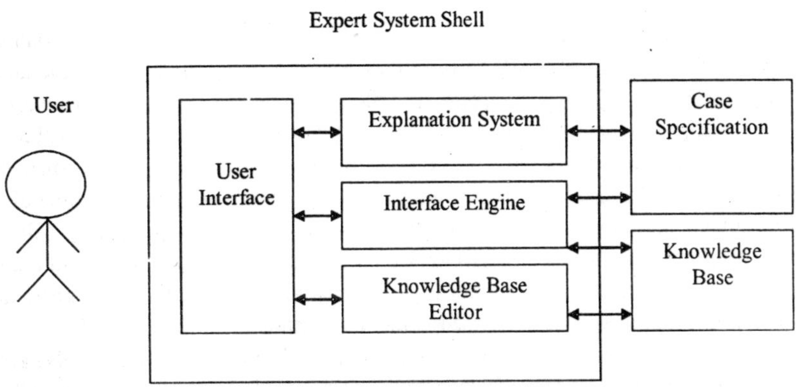

Figure 3.4: Rule Based Expert System

Almost all expert systems also have an *explanation subsystem*, which allows the programme to explain its reasoning to the user. Some systems also have a *knowledge base editor* which help the expert or knowledge engineer to easily update and check the knowledge base.

One important feature of expert systems is the way they (usually) separate domain specific knowledge from more general purpose reasoning and representation techniques. The general purpose bit is referred to as an *expert system shell*. As we see in the figure, the shell will provide the inference engine (and knowledge representation scheme), a user interface, an explanation system and sometimes a knowledge base editor. Given a new kind of problem to solve (say, car design), we can usually find a shell that provides the right sort of support for that problem, so all we need to do is provide the expert knowledge. There are numerous commercial expert system shells, each one appropriate for a slightly different range of problems. (Expert systems work in industry includes both writing expert system shells and writing expert systems using shells.) Using shells to write expert systems generally greatly reduces the cost and time of development.

Complex decisions involve intricate combination of factual and heuristic knowledge. In order for the computer to be able to retrieve and effectively use heuristic knowledge, the knowledge must be organized in an easily accessible format that distinguishes among data, knowledge, and control structures.

For this reason, expert systems are organized in three distinct levels:

1. *Knowledge base* consists of problem-solving rules, procedures, and intrinsic data relevant to the problem domain.
2. *Working memory* refers to task-specific data for the problem under consideration.
3. *Inference engine* is a generic control mechanism that applies the axiomatic knowledge in the knowledge base to the task-specific data to arrive at some solution or conclusion.

These three pieces may very well come from different sources. The inference engine, such as VP-Expert, may come from a commercial vendor. The knowledge base may be a specific diagnostic knowledge base compiled by a consulting firm, and the problem data may be supplied by the end user. A knowledge base is the nucleus of the expert system structure. A knowledge base is not a data base. The traditional data base environment deals with data that have a static relationship between the elements in the problem domain.

A knowledge base is created by knowledge engineers, who translate the knowledge of real human experts into rules and strategies. These rules and strategies can change depending on the prevailing problem scenario. The knowledge base provides the expert system with the capability to recommend directions for user inquiry. The system also instigates further investigation into areas that may be important to a certain line of reasoning but not apparent to the user.

The modularity of an expert system is an important distinguishing characteristic compared to a conventional computer programme. Modularity is affected in an expert system by the use of three distinct components, as shown in Figure 3.5.

With the increasing popularity of expert systems, many commercial

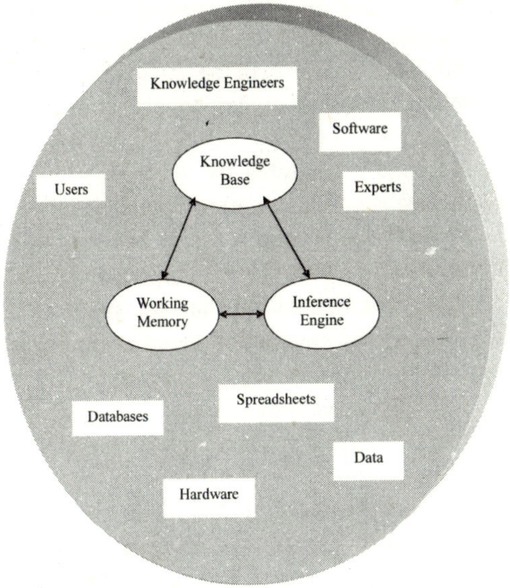

Figure 3.5: Experts System Organization and Operating Environment

inference engines are coming onto the market. A survey of selected commercial inference engines is presented in the Appendix at the end of this book. The development of a functional expert system usually centers around the organization of the knowledge base. A functional integration of expert systems components is shown in Figure 3.6.

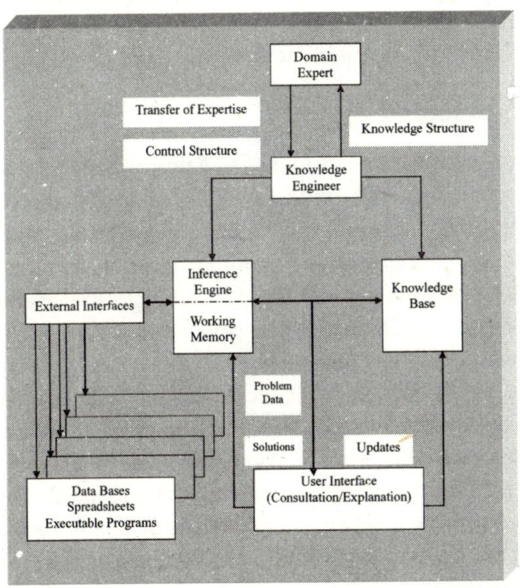

Figure 3.6: Integration of Expert Systems Components

A good expert system is expected to grow as it learns from user feedback. Feedback is incorporated into the knowledge base as appropriate to make the expert system smarter. The dynamism of the application environment for expert systems is based on the individual dynamism of the components. This can be classified as follows:

The knowledge base constitutes the problem-solving rules, facts, or intuition that a human expert might use in solving problems in a given problem domain. The knowledge base is usually stored in terms of if-then rules. The working memory represents relevant data for the current problem being solved. The inference engine is the control mechanism that organizes the problem data and searches through the knowledge base for applicable rules.

Most Dynamic–Working Memory: The contents of the working memory, sometimes called the data structure, changes with each problem situation. Consequently, it is the most dynamic component of an expert system, assuming, of course, that it is kept current.

Moderately Dynamic–Knowledge Base: The knowledge base need not change unless a new piece of information arises that indicates a change in the problem solution procedure. Changes in the knowledge base should be carefully evaluated before being implemented. In effect, changes should not be based on just one consultation experience. For example, a rule that is found to be irrelevant under one problem situation may turn out to be crucial in solving other problems.

Least Dynamic–Inference Engine: Because of the strict control and coding structure of an inference engine, changes are made only if absolutely necessary to correct a bug or enhance the inferential process. Commercial inference engines, in particular, change only at the discretion of the developer. Since frequent updates can be disruptive and costly to clients, most commercial software developers try to minimize the frequency of updates.

Applications of Expert Systems

The spectrum of applications of expert systems technology to industrial and commercial problems is so wide as to defy easy characterization. The applications find their way into most areas of knowledge work. They are as varied as helping salespersons sell modular factory-built homes to helping NASA plan the maintenance of a space shuttle in preparation for its next flight. Applications tend to cluster into seven major classes.

(1) *Diagnosis and Troubleshooting of Devices and Systems of All Kinds:* This class comprises systems that deduce faults and suggest corrective actions for a malfunctioning device or process. Medical diagnosis was one of the first knowledge areas to which ES technology was applied (for example, see Shortliffe 1976), but diagnosis of engineered systems quickly surpassed medical diagnosis. There are probably more diagnostic applications of ES than any other type. The diagnostic problem can be stated in the abstract as: given the evidence presenting itself, what is the underlying problem/reason/cause?

(2) *Planning and Scheduling:* Systems that fall into this class analyze a set of one or more potentially complex and interacting goals in order to determine a set of actions to achieve those goals, and/or provide a detailed temporal ordering of those actions, taking into account personnel, materiel, and other constraints. This class has great commercial potential, which has been recognized. Examples involve airline scheduling of flights, personnel, and gates; manufacturing job-shop scheduling; and manufacturing process planning.

(3) *Configuration of Manufactured Objects from Subassemblies:* Configuration, whereby a solution to a problem is synthesized from a given set of elements related by a set of constraints, is historically one of the most important of expert system applications. Configuration applications were pioneered by computer companies as a means of facilitating the manufacture of semi-custom minicomputers (McDermott 1981). The technique has found its way into use in many different industries, for example, modular home building, manufacturing, and other problems involving complex engineering design and manufacturing.

(4) *Financial Decision Making:* The financial services industry has been a vigorous user of expert system techniques. Advisory programmes have been created to assist bankers in determining whether to make loans to businesses and individuals. Insurance companies have used expert systems to assess the risk presented by the customer and to determine a price for the insurance. A typical application in the financial markets is in foreign exchange trading.

(5) *Knowledge Publishing:* This is a relatively new, but also potentially explosive area. The primary function of the expert system is to deliver knowledge that is relevant to the user's problem, in the context of the user's problem. The two most widely distributed expert systems in the world are in this category. The first is an advisor which counsels a user on appropriate grammatical usage in a text. The second is a tax advisor that accompanies a tax preparation programme and advises the user on tax strategy, tactics, and individual tax policy.

(6) *Process Monitoring and Control:* Systems falling in this class analyze real-time data from physical devices with the goal of noticing anomalies, predicting trends, and controlling for both optimality and failure correction. Examples of real-time systems that actively monitor processes can be found in the steel making and oil refining industries.

(7) *Design and Manufacturing:* These systems assist in the design of physical devices and processes, ranging from high-level conceptual design of abstract entities all the way to factory floor configuration of manufacturing processes.

Developing an Expert System

The power of an expert system is derived from the knowledge of the expert. The lack of computer skills should not inhibit anyone from using this tool in implementing their disease management programme. There are published procedures that one can follow to develop expert systems, although rigid adherence to these procedures is not necessarily a prerequisite for a successful development effort. Match your development technique with your own style of thinking and your resources and problem area.

Selecting the Problem

In this section we will discuss the development of expert systems in three parts:

- Selecting a problem
- Knowledge acquisition and representation
- Evaluation and adoption.

The most critical step in developing an expert system is identifying a suitable problem. Expert systems are best suited to problems that require experience, knowledge, judgement, and complex interactions to arrive at a solution.

One of the first tests to determine if a subject area is suitable for an expert system is whether the solution of the problem requires the knowledge and expertise of a human expert. For many situations a reasonably knowledgeable person with the correct information such as a production guide or a data base management system available can determine the solution without the help of an expert or an expert system. The abilities inherent in the expert system software may not be necessary to solve the problem.

Problems such as determining days-to-harvest limitations for a pesticide, or calculating infection periods may be better accomplished by using a production manual, or a conventional computer programme such as a spreadsheet or database manager. In addition, in crop areas where little is known about certain diseases the power of an expert system is really not necessary.

Cost of Development

Expert systems are expensive to develop. They require resources, expertise and time to build. It should be determined if the proposed expert system can be justified in terms of savings or other benefits it produces. Costs include software, hardware and personnel to do the work. A developer should ask if the problem to be solved justifies the investment of time and money. If current loss due to disease, whether it be due to reduced yield or quality, is great enough, then the successful implementation of an expert system may offset cost of development.

Sometimes there are other benefits in using expert systems which more than justify cost such as: reduced pesticide inputs, enhanced IPM training, effective delivery of IPM strategies not possible by any other delivery method and identification of gaps in knowledge to direct research programmes. Expert systems also have value in that they can make expertise available to decision makers when expert opinions are not available. An expert system can be available for the grower to use at any time of the day and it could be available to every grower in the state at the same time.

Knowledge Acquisition and Representation

After the problem has been selected, the knowledge acquisition phase of expert system development is begun. The task now is to have the knowledge which the expert uses to solve the problem displayed in a logical fashion so that it can be coded into the computer.

There are many discussions in the literature on the extraction of knowledge from domain experts. Most expert system developers suggest that a knowledge engineer (someone who is trained in the extraction of information from experts) extract the knowledge and design the expert system. In some cases, a knowledge engineer is needed to 'tease apart' highly compiled expert knowledge because the expert is too familiar with the area to break it into its logical components. There is also software available to help in self-knowledge engineering.

In the development of the PSAOC a different method of knowledge acquisition was undertaken. The domain experts were trained in knowledge acquisition and representation. After the domain experts had represented their knowledge in dependency networks (diagrams of the rules), the networks were given to programmers who coded it into the computer. The domain experts in this case were both the source of knowledge and the designers of the expert system. The most obvious advantage of this development method is that it is much less expensive to build expert systems if it is not necessary to support a knowledge engineer for the extraction and representation of knowledge. However, there is a more important advantage in using the domain experts as the knowledge engineers. Only the domain expert knows the extent of his knowledge, how he thinks about problems and what variables are important in the decision process. Rather than the knowledge engineer painfully extracting the information from the expert, the knowledge flows from the expert as he articulates from internal examination how he makes decisions. The domain expert becomes an active participant in the knowledge acquisition and representation process rather than a passive participant who is acted upon. The domain expert becomes more involved in the development of the expert system as he is challenged to represent on paper and then programme into the computer, the methods and processes by which he solves problems. In addition, domain experts can better communicate their logic to other domain experts; an important consideration where different domains overlap and there must be agreement among domains. Also, extension specialists who serve as the domain experts are more familiar with how the end users prefer to think about and solve problems. Their experience with the user clientele will help them to format the expert system in a manner that county agents or growers will best understand and utilize.

Tools for Development of Expert Systems

An expert system tool, or shell, is a software development environment containing the basic components of expert systems. Associated with a shell is a prescribed method for building applications by configuring and instantiating these components. Some of the generic components of a shell are shown in Figure 3.7 and described below. The core components of expert systems are the knowledge base and the reasoning engine.

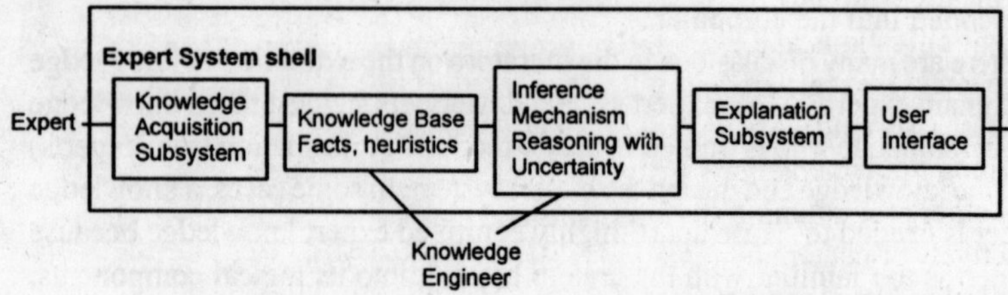

Figure 3.7: Basic Components of Expert System Tools

Knowledge Base: A store of factual and heuristic knowledge. An ES tool provides one or more knowledge representation schemes for expressing knowledge about the application domain. Some tools use both frames (objects) and IF-THEN rules. In PROLOG the knowledge is represented as logical statements.

Reasoning Engine: Inference mechanisms for manipulating the symbolic information and knowledge in the knowledge base is to form a line of reasoning in solving a problem. The inference mechanism can range from simple *modus ponens* backward chaining of IF-THEN rules to case-based reasoning.

Knowledge Acquisition Sub-system: A sub-system is to help experts in building knowledge bases. Collecting knowledge needed to solve problems and build the knowledge base continues to be the biggest bottleneck in building expert systems.

Explanation Sub-system: A subsystem that explains the system's actions. The explanation can range from how the final or intermediate solutions were arrived at to justifying the need for additional data.

User Interface: The means of communication with the user. The user interface is generally not a part of the ES technology, and was not given much attention in the past. However, it is now widely accepted that the user interface can make a critical difference in the perceived utility of a system regardless of the system's performance.

There are a number of different programming approaches, programming languages and development environment. Here are a few:

Programming Languages for Expert Systems

Almost every high level programming language ever created, and many lower languages, have been used to develop AI and ES applications. The most common seems to be: LISP, Prolog, C/C++ followed by Java. Here are some information on two programming languages Prolog and LISP, that were key to programming languages for Artificial Intelligence for the last two decades. Prolog is a full, industry-standard programming language, ideally suited to writing rules. Common Lisp is well suited to large programming projects, dynamic modifications and explorative programming.

In the 1980s several versions of Prolog came out, including Cogent Prolog, Turbo Prolog (Borland), Amzi! Prolog, and LPA. AMZI and LPA are medium-priced Prolog implementations with excellent integration with Delphi, Java, and many other programming environments and platforms. Another successful and attractively priced implementation is also available from Visual Prolog—from the Prolog Development Center (PDC), the successor of Turbo Prolog.

LPA (Logic Programming Associates Ltd) is developing world-class solutions for Artificial Intelligence, including state-of-the-art Prolog compilers, Chimera Agents, Flex Expert System Toolkit, WebFlex, and VisiRule.

Flex Expert System Toolkit: A powerful, hybrid expert system toolkit which offers frame-based representation with multiple inheritance and procedural attachment; interleaved forward and backward chaining rule-based reasoning; an automatic question and answering mechanism; employs an English-like Knowledge Specification Language (KSL), for specifying expertise; and has complete access to the underlying Prolog language.

WebFlex: WebFlex makes available Flex expert system programmes available on the Web supporting multiple asynchronous clients; allows customization of the presentation of questions and forms using the Flex KSL and/or HTML.

VisiRule: A powerful graphical tool, which lets draw decision charts, test and generate the code in terms of Flex and then publish on the Internet using WebFlex.

Franz. Inc.: Franz Inc. is currently the primary supplier of LISP development environment, created Allegro CL, a dynamic object-oriented development environment for Common Lisp/CLOS.

Shells: A shell is an expert system without a knowledge base. A shell furnishes the ES developer with the inference engine, user interface, and the explanation and knowledge acquisition facilities. All of this makes it unnecessary to rebuild the components for each new expert system.

CLIPS: CLIPS is a productive development and delivery expert system tool which provides a complete environment for the construction of rule and/or object based expert systems.

Using **Jess**, it is possible to develop Java software that has the capacity to "reason" using knowledge you supply in the form of declarative rules.

SDK and Environments: Using shells to write expert systems generally greatly reduces the cost and time of development (compared with writing the expert system from scratch). Software Development Kits (SDK) expand the capabilities of shells in various directions. Here are come examples of SDK and environments, all though most AI products provide an some form of environment.

G2 by Gensym Corporation is a graphical, object oriented software platform for rapidly building real-time expert system application.

GURU, product of Micro Data Base Systems, is a total system for developing applications that combine expert system and database technology.

The DX Solution Series product line, developed by Knowledge industries, consists of three components: DXpress, WIN-DX and API-DX.

Machine Learning Systems (MLS)

MLS are becoming an important part of the expert system environment. In contrast to performance systems that acquire knowledge from human experts, machine learning systems acquire knowledge automatically from examples, i.e., from source data. MLS are frequently used for learning neural network, knowledge bases, using inductive rule based algorithms, and evolution-based genetic algorithms, etc. MLS usually use data-driven, hypothesis-driven, and multi-strategy constructive induction.

Web-enabled Expert Systems

Here are some popular products and services:

EXSYS, Inc. is the first company providing the ability to run knowledge automation expert systems on the Web. Over the years, the EXSYS tools have been enhanced in many ways, but always with a focus on solving real-world problems through a practical easy-to-use development paradigm. Exsys CORVID is flagship "Knowledge Automation" paradigm resulting from a close examination of what is needed to build and field decision-making systems in today's Internet-oriented world. CORVID is designed to allow knowledgeable" experts" to develop and deploy powerful, interactive online advisory applications quickly and easily.

Amzi!Prolog has a server based Prolog implementations ideal for integration with the web.

Webcom, Inc. produces WebSource Configurator, an application that automates, simplifies, and accelerates a company's sales process. As a user responds to on-line questions about a product, WebSource Configurator, much like a good sales consultant, the software is adapting and preparing the next set of questions to specify the product.

Vanguard Software Corporation is developing the integrated software for management decision analysis, risk management, forecasting, optimization, and modeling. Vanguard Vista-Web-based survey tool that allows user to create, post, and track survey results online.

Conclusion: Although technical progress in the last decade has been satisfactory, as shown in examples above (far from complete), the number of widespread expert systems in use today is less than was expected. Now embedded expert systems tend to be more successful than advisory systems. The primary reason for the lower usage of expert system in advisory type roles is the very expensive procedures of retrieving knowledge in a short time. Developments in the machine learning systems could accelerate the number of new expert systems we see in the future.

Advantages and Disadvantages of Expert Systems

Advantages of Expert Systems

- *Permanence*—Expert systems do not forget but human experts may
- *Reproducibility*—Many copies of an expert system can be made, but training new human experts is time-consuming and expensive
- If there is a maze of rules (e.g. tax and auditing), then the expert system can "unravel" the maze
- *Efficiency*—can increase throughput and decrease personnel costs
    - Although expert systems are expensive to build and maintain, they are inexpensive to operate
    - Development and maintenance costs can be spread over many users
    - The overall cost can be quite reasonable when compared to expensive and scarce human experts
- *Cost savings*:
    - Wages—(elimination of a room full of clerks)
    - Other costs—(minimize loan loss)
- *Consistency*—With expert systems similar transactions handled in the same way. The system will make comparable recommendations for like situations. Humans are influenced by
    - recency effects (most recent information having a disproportionate impact on judgment)
    - primacy effects (early information dominates the judgment).
- *Documentation*—An expert system can provide permanent documentation of the decision process
- *Completeness*—An expert system can review all the transactions, a human expert can only review a sample
- *Timeliness*—Fraud and/or errors can be prevented. Information is available sooner for decision making
- *Breadth*—The knowledge of multiple human experts can be combined to give a system more breadth that a single person is likely to achieve
- *Reduce risk of doing business*
    - Consistency of decision making
    - Documentation
    - Achieve Expertise
- *Entry barriers*—Expert systems can help a firm create entry barriers for potential competitors

- Differentiation—In some cases, an expert system can differentiate a product or can be related to the focus of the firm (XCON)
- Computer programmes are best in those situations where there is a structure that is noted as previously existing or can be elicited

Disadvantages of Rule-Based Expert Systems

- *Common sense—In addition to a great deal of technical knowledge, human experts have common sense.* It is not yet known how to give expert systems common sense.
- *Creativity*—Human experts can respond creatively to unusual situations, expert systems cannot.
- *Learning*—Human experts automatically adapt to changing environments; expert systems must be explicitly updated. Case-based reasoning and neural networks are methods that can incorporate learning.
- *Sensory Experience*—Human experts have available to them a wide range of sensory experience; expert systems are currently dependent on symbolic input.
- *Degradation*—Expert systems are not good at recognizing when no answer exists or when the problem is outside their area of expertise.

Table 3.1: Expert System Terminology

Term	*Meaning*
Explanation Facility	That part of an expert system that explains how solutions were reached and justifies the steps used to reach them.
Metaknowledge	Knowledge in an expert system about how the system operates or reasons. More generally, knowledge about knowledge.
Problem Reformulation	Converting a problem stated in some arbitrary way to a form that lends itself to a fast, efficient solution.
Real-world Problem	A complex, practical problem whose solution is useful in some cost-effective way.
Robustness	That quality of a problem solver that permits a gradual degradation in performance when it is pushed to the limits of its scope of expertise or is given faulty, inconsistent or incomplete data or rules.
Scaling Problem	The difficulty associated with trying to apply problem-solving techniques developed for a simplified version of a problem to the actual problem itself.
Search Space	The set of all possible solutions to a problem.
Skill	The efficient and effective application of knowledge to produce solutions in some problem domain.

(*Contd.*)

Term	*Meaning*
Symbol	A string of characters that stands for some real-word concept.
Symbolic Reasoning	Problem solving based on the application of strategies and heuristics to manipulate symbols standing for problem concepts.
Toy Problem	An artificial problem such as a game or an unrealistic adaptation of a complex problem.
Artificial Intelligence	The part of computer science concerned with developing intelligent computer programs.
Domain Expert	A person who through years of training and experience has become extremely proficient at problem solving in a particular domain.
End-user	The person who uses the finished expert system; the person for whom the system was developed.

4

Computer Applications in Education

The history of computers is relatively short but even so their impact on society has been enormous. Nowadays, almost every facet of life has been influenced by this technology. For instance, twenty years ago, no one could have predicted that computers would have become so common place in the world of education. Now university, colleges and schools of all over the world are using computers in their teaching and administration.

From the earliest times when computers were commercially available, there were educational applications of computers. The earliest documented use of computers in education refers to the use of mainframe computers in the late 1950's (Oliver, 1986). In those early days, a large number of mainframe computers were to be found in some engineering and research departments of universities and tertiary institutions and they were used mainly for research and development programmes. By the mid-1960's, most colleges and universities and many larger schools used computer systems for administrative purposes (Bramble, Mason & Berg, 1985).

Computers in Teaching-learning Process

Historically the use of computers in teaching-learning process can be divided in three categories given below:

- Learning about computers
- Learning from the computers
- Learning with computers

Learning about Computers

During those years, one of the initial applications was to use educational computing as *an object of instruction*. Many courses were conducted so that learners could learn about the computers. One aspect stressed the explanation of computer structures and related electronic circuits, or in other words, the machine-level operation of the computer. In essence, the major aim was to promote learning about computer hardware. Another aspect emphasised software. This became popular after an important development in 1963 at Dartmouth College in the USA when a high-level computing language for "teaching" a computer to do specific tasks was invented (Dennis & Kanksy, 1984). The language was called BASIC (for **B**eginners **A**ll-purpose **S**ymbolic **I**nstruction **C**ode). The word beginners in the name of this language was significant, since one of its alleged merits was the ease with which it could be learned. This feature has caused BASIC to become overwhelmingly the most common language used at the pre-tertiary level in the teaching of programming. Since then, BASIC has become the resident language of most microcomputers as it was deemed to be particularly suited for beginners. Consequently, BASIC programming has often become part of the computer literacy programmes offered in schools.

Many other programming languages have been taught since then. They include FORTRAN, PASCAL, and PROLOG. These languages were initially taught at the tertiary level as they were only available on the mainframe computers. However, since the rapid development of microcomputer technology in the 1970's and in particular, the 1980's, they have often been part of the computer literacy and computer studies courses at the secondary as well as the tertiary levels.

Learning from the Computers

During the 1960's, one particular group of educators tried to integrate computers into the existing school curriculum in addition to the computer awareness courses. Their major aim was to programme computers so that learners could learn from the computers, in the same way that learners learn from teachers.

When computers were first introduced into the educational setting for general teaching and learning purposes, programmes were based mainly on behavioural theories. In particular, they were often modelled on "programmed instruction" (Taylor, 1980; Coburn, Kelman, Roberts, Snyder, Watt & Weiner, 1982; Maddison, 1983). This usage of computers has often been labelled Computer Assisted Instruction (CAI) or Computer Assisted Learning (CAL), probably because the ancillary tasks performed were similar to those that could be performed by (ideally) competent teaching assistants.

The focus of this strand of educational computing was on the teaching of various kinds of curriculum content with computers acting as tutors to the learners (Taylor, 1980). With this type of usage, the programme design often entailed a rigorous logical analysis of the subject matter, combined with a careful study of possible learning strategies. The results were then implemented through structured systems of programmed instruction that i) provided immediate feedback to the learners, ii) branched to the appropriate next lesson, and iii) kept meticulous records of student progress.

Back in the late 1950's and 1960's, significant potential was seen in CAI. As a result, many projects, for instance, PLATO and TICCIT, were undertaken at a number of tertiary institutions using mainframe computers to examine how computers might be used to enhance instruction (Bramble, Mason, & Berg, 1985; Oliver, 1986).

A number of benefits similar to those claimed for programmed instruction, were often ascribed to good CAI software. For example:

1. *One-to-one Interaction:* Computers could provide individual attention to the learners in a way not possible in traditional classrooms. It was often argued that one-to-one instruction provided by CAI, would result in (i) superior learning compared with the conventional classroom where students shared the teacher, and (ii) better interactive learning (compared with normally higher teacher-student ratios) (Telfer & Probert, 1986; Lockard, Abrams & Many, 1990).

2. *Immediate Feedback:* As a result of one-to-one interaction, the computer was able to provide immediate feedback to the learner and at a rate more frequent and desirable than was possible in a traditional classroom. Moreover, feedback could be tailored to reinforce learning. However, it should be noted that some researchers had suggested that immediate feedback might not be desirable for achieving optimal retention of learning (Rankin & Trapper, 1978).

3. *Small Logical Units:* As in programmed instruction, tasks could be broken down into small units hence providing opportunities for the learners to assimilate the sequences of a complex task in a hierarchical, logical step-by-step manner (Soulier, 1988).

4. *Individual Rate of Learning:* Students were able to work at their own speed and difficulty levels. Often the rate of learning could be either controlled by the learners or adjusted by computer programme based on the responses of the learners (Hofmeister, 1984; Mandell & Mandell, 1989).

5. *Overlearning:* The computer could be programmed to drill students in facts and lessons could be repeated until mastery learning was attained. Even after mastery, learning could be repeated so that overlearning which could lead to better retention over time, could be accomplished (Ryba, 1980). The unlimited patience of the computers was ideally suited for this purpose (Kinzer, Sherwood & Bransford, 1986)—particularly for students with learning difficulties (Au & Bruce, 1990).

6. *Freeing up Teachers' Time:* While the computers were doing most of the time-consuming tasks required of teachers, the teachers would then be able to devote their attention and time to other aspects of their teaching duties presumably to the benefit of the students.

7. *Comprehensive Student Records*: CAI could provide the means for keeping progressive records of student progress. A full profile might be kept of the student's strengths and weaknesses, allowing for individual remediation (or extension) programmes to be devised. The computer might also record the time taken by students to answer each question and/or complete each segment, thus helping to identify the areas that hinder student progress. Such an accurate picture of the progress of pupils through various instructional materials could help educators to formulate new curricula or remedial programmes (Hofmeister, 1984; Bitter & Camuse, 1988).

Some of the most common forms of CAI include: drill and practice, tutorial, simulation and dialogue (Coburn *et al*, 1982; Niemiec & Walberg, 1987). Drill and practice perhaps represents the most primitive form of CAI. Put simply, this is where the computer is used to take learners through a series of exercises. The learners can practise by responding to questions posed by the computer with the computer then analysing the answers and providing appropriate feedback to the learners. Drill and practice have developed over time into other modes such as tutorial, simulation and dialogue (Probert, 1985; Vockell & Schwartz, 1988). Tutorial software uses explanations, descriptions, illustrations and problems for concept development. Questioning and prompts are used widely in much the same way as a tutor would use them to help students gain an understanding of the subject material. Simulation CAI software is used to simulate real or imaginary situations, usually inviting students to make decisions based on information given. Many of the simulation software also incorporate games format to enhance motivation. Dialogue software are designed in such a way that it can be used to conduct the dialogue between the computer and the user. Many of the commonly available software consist of a mixture of these modes of computer assisted instruction.

Learning with Computers

Accompanying the advent and rapid development of microcomputer technology has been the production of highly user-friendly software that tends to place more emphasis on learner control the learning environment. Some software have been specifically developed to achieve this purpose, others are of a more general nature, e.g. word processor, database management programmes, spreadsheet, graphics programmes, telecommunication programmes, and adventure games etc.

When equipped with such capabilities, the computer then becomes a tool for students to learn with (Taylor, 1980) in contrast with learning about computers and learning from computers. In this new role, the computer is no longer restricted to specific subject matter, rather, it becomes a tool for students to explore and facilitate their own learning in an environment controlled by the students (Papert, 1980; Wills, 1984; Nolan & Ryba, 1984).

Four important issues lend support to the arguments that it is advantageous to use computer as a learning tool.

First, the learners can exercise more control over their learning environment. Second, the application of new general purpose software is not restricted to a particular subject and hence should facilitate the integration of computers across the entire curriculum irrespective subject areas. Third, computers can enhance learner access to information and learning. Fourth, computers can be used as objects by students to learn to think with, and even develop higher order thinking skills.

Types of Computer Based Learning Environments

Skinner, Pavlov, and Piaget all played important roles as founders of theories of learning. Skinner's and Pavlov's ideas about the way we learn things, based on the stimulus-response concept, were one source of inspiration for programmed learning or programmed instruction. Those theories have been used as the foundation for the design of the first generation of computer-based learning environments. Using this pedagogical model a huge industry of learning grew up during the early 1960s.

The First Generation: Programmed Learning

Computer Assisted Instruction systems (CAI) are a kind of interactive learning environment, based on programmed learning, which became common in the period from the mid of the 60s to the early 70s. Still, many projects are based on behaviouristic ideas (Broberg, 1997). This seems strange since these ideas and all what they stand for have been almost completely rejected in traditional classroom learning environments. At the same time, there is a very simple explanation: two of the major advantages with programmed learning are the possibility of self-administration of a course and the simplicity of implementing a computer-based learning environment with a behaviouristic control mechanism, (see Figure 4.1). Therefore, it is not hard to see the possibilities to make it serve as a basis for computer-based learning environments.

The Second Generation: Intelligent Tutoring Systems

Even if one can get positive results with regard to learning in the first generation of computer-based learning environments, there is much one can do to speed up the process of learning. One of the major drawbacks of the CAI environments is the lack of individualization. The learning situation is one-to-one, but all learners are still running through the course in the same order. Below, we present three examples of ideas that have been exploited in attempts to improve performance:

- multiple paths through the curriculum;
- present the material in different ways;
- analyze the errors that the learners do.

In the next generation of computer-based learning environments many of these ideas were implemented, by experimenting with implementation of intelligent behaviour in the computer systems—Intelligent Computer Assistant Instruction systems, (ICAI) and Intelligent Tutoring Systems (ITS) as they also were called. In 1973, Hartley and Sleeman outlined the basic requirements of ITS environments (Shute & Psotka, 1994):

- Knowledge of the domain (the expert model)

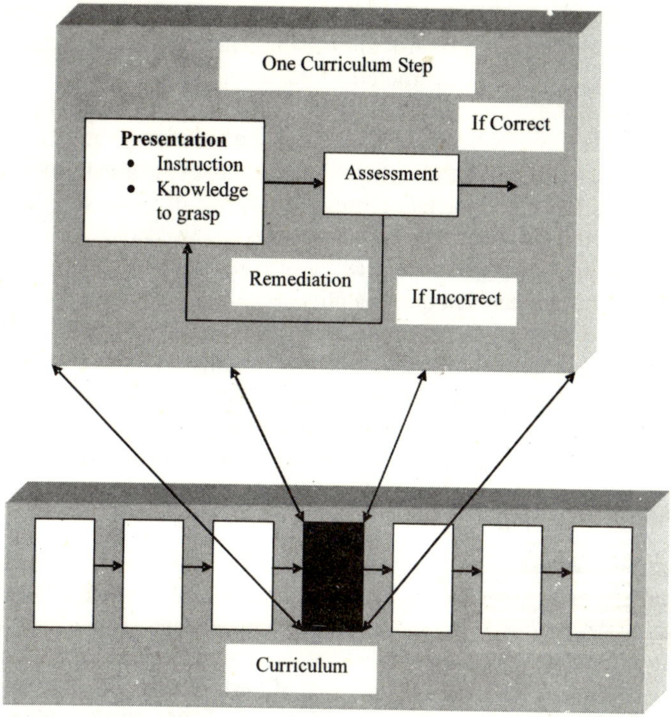

Figure 4.1: The Principle of the Behaviouristic Control Mechanism

- Knowledge of the learner (the student model)
- Knowledge of teaching strategies (tutor)

The above discussion indicates that there are major differences between ITS and its predecessor CAI: the ITS analyses the learner's erroneous behaviour and it models the learner's state of knowledge. The way the learners work with these ITS environments is quite similar to the way they worked with the CAI environments. The model of the learners, that is, what the learner knows and does not know and the model of how teachers act in different situations, are used by the system to accelerate the learning, an acceleration made possible by an individualization or adaptation to the learner's behaviour. A learner in such environments learns mainly by solving problems chosen by the tutor to promote efficient learning (Broberg, 1997).

The Third Generation: Cognitive Tools

The ITS approach has many good results to show, although it has also been criticized for a long period. Much of the criticism has concerned the possibilities to trace learners' state of knowledge. The cognitive tools approach to ILEs started as a strong criticism of ITS, attacking the student modelling approach, as well as the pedagogical basis. Cognitive tools are artefacts that amplify, support and unburden the user cognitively and have the ability to affect the task and the user's state of knowledge. The cognitive tools approach has its pedagogic base in constructivistic ideas of knowledge and learning, where the learners are considered to be active knowledge constructors.

What practical results are there, so far, in the area of computer-based cognitive tools supporting learning? According to Jonassen, not many of the tools constructed over the years, have been designed with the purpose of supporting learning. Although computer-based learning environments is and always has been an active area of research, it has not resulted in as many available products as one would wish. Due to this and the fact that cognitive tools is a rather new approach to computer-based learning environments there are not many cognitive tools for supporting the learning process. The examples of cognitive tools that the area presents vary in character. (Kommers, Jonassen, & Mayes, 1992), distinguish five categories of cognitive tools: semantic networking tools, expert systems, hypermedia, cooperative learning environments, and micro-worlds.

Semantic Networking

A semantic network is a representational scheme for concepts ordered hierarchically or by associations. The basic idea behind this category of tools is that by creating, processing and observing semantic nets (which many think are close to the way we actually store concepts), it is possible to learn. Concept-mapping is another term for this category of tools. Lanzing discusses many aspects of the use of concept-mapping (Lanzing, 1996), emphasizing those concept-mapping tools can be used in a variety of situations and for different kinds of knowledge work, of which learning is one.

Expert Systems

A term that is often used as a synonym for knowledge based systems. The representational scheme for knowledge that these systems use is commonly a form of rule-based representation; i.e. the database consist of *if-then* statements. As the name suggests, expert systems are commonly used to model the knowledge and behaviour of experts, e.g. systems for medical diagnose like MYCIN (Barr & Feigenbaum, 1982b). "Knowledge engineer" is a common term used for the category of persons working with constructing and maintaining the knowledge databases in an expert system. It is quite obvious that the kind of work that knowledge engineers do is a form of knowledge work. The idea of expert systems as cognitive tools for learning is to put learners on an equal footing with knowledge engineers, but the idea does not stop there. It also involves learners working with the knowledge database or the expert system, to extract and use the knowledge in it.

Hypermedia

Hypermedia is a form of media where documents have a non-linear structure, contrary to the basically linear structure that ordinary text documents have. The difference in structure between these two kinds of documents is mostly related to the kind of media. Janlert uses the term *medium-space* and *domain-space* to distinguish between structures that are related to the representational medium and the content respectively (Janlert, 1995). A hypermedium document consists of a number of nodes that can be viewed as containers storing information; these nodes are linked to other nodes, i.e. the document is a network of linked information. The link facility gives the opportunity to express relations between pieces of information. It is also via these links that most of the traversing of a hypermedia document is done. This usually implies that there are multiple ways of traversing the document and not a single path through it, as is normally the case with ordinary text documents. An additional perspective on hypermedia is that a hypermedium document can be viewed as a scheme for knowledge representation, with the nodes describing concepts and the links expressing relations between the concepts. This gives a representational scheme close to semantic nets and concept-mapping. Today, the WWW is the best known and established form of hypermedia.

The basic idea of hypertext as a cognitive tool is the assumption of a close mapping between the structure of the author's state of knowledge and the structure of the produced hypermedia document. Tool-use can involve constructing, processing and reading hypertext:

- when hypertext *authoring* is used to support learning it becomes very similar to semantic nets and concept-mapping;
- the document captures the learner's understanding of the topic as a concretization of the personal knowledge creation process;
- when *processing* of hypertext (the learners add links, for instance) is used to support learning, it should give positive effects of active reading;
- learning is believed to be better promoted by *reading* preproduced hypermedia documents than ordinary linear documents, Egan *et al.* carried out an experiment that strengthens this hypothesis. This presupposes that the reading environment supports the reader in overcoming the specific problems that readers of hypermedia documents face (McKnight, Dillon, & Richardson, 1993).

Hypermedia is a rather complex concept. In hypermedia literature such as (Conklin, 1987; McKnight *et al.*, 1993; Nielsen, 1995; Woodhead, 1990), many more aspects of hypermedia systems are discussed.

Micro-worlds

Micro-worlds can be viewed as dynamical models of both concrete and abstract concepts from the real world. Many take micro-world to be a synonym for cognitive tool for learning. The idea of micro-worlds is to offer an environment that would be inaccessible for the learner in the normal case, for economical or safety reasons, or for some other reason. Micro-worlds typically involve simulation, manipulation and testing of hypotheses, but the *creation* of micro-worlds is also important.

Co-operative Learning Environments

Learning is both an individual and a social activity. Co-operative learning environments are focused on the social and group aspects of learning. In a co-operative learning environment, the learners are together with other learners when they work with information. Working together with other learners has positive effects on the learning\ outcome. The activities in these environments are similar to those in individual environments: creating, processing and observing. In an environment where several individuals perform something together, there are distances between individuals. Bridging these distances is important for a fruitful collaboration. Computers connected into a network offer good opportunities for bridging distances between individuals.

Piaget and Interactive Learning Environment (ILE)

In Piaget's theory, learning is explained in terms of interaction with the environment and the learning is driven by our innate tendency to have a balance in the way we represent it and the way it actually is. Therefore, Piaget's role in the area of interactive learning environments is mostly related to learning environments with a pedagogical model based on learning by simulation, and manipulation of micro-worlds. Papert's programming language LOGO is an example of a computer-based learning environment based on Piaget's theories about cognitive development (Hoyles & Noss, 1992; Papert, 1980).

5

Computer Assisted Instruction (CAI)

Charles Babbage (early 1800s) is typically credited with being the first to envision a multi-purpose computer. He dreamed of creating an all-purpose machine, which he called the "Analytic Engine". However, because of the technological constraints of the time, he was never able to build his dream, although he did succeed in building a "Difference Engine", an automatic (mechanical) means of calculating logarithm tables. The notion of using "Intelligent Machines" for teaching purposes can be traced back to 1926 when Pressey built an instructional machine teeming with multiple choice questions and answer submitted by the teacher. It delivered questions, accepted learner's responses, and then provided immediate feedback to each earner. While the above system (Pressey's instructional machine) was definitely clever for its time, it could not be construed as intelligent as it was mechanically set with pre-specified questions and answers. So, although it was inflexible, this system did incorporate contemporary learning theories and pedagogical strategies into its design.

General-purpose digital computers arose in the mid 1990s, paving the way for truly (artificially) intelligent machines. Basically, these computers consisted of a numerical central processor, whose mechanism was electronic, not mechanical and based on a binary not decimal system. They were also characterized by having a built-in ability to make logical decisions and a built-in device for easy storage and manipulation of data. During this period of computer infancy, Alan Turing (1912-1954, British Mathematician and Logician) provided a major link between these modern, digital computing systems and thinking. He described a computing system capable of not only "number crunching" but symbolic manipulation as well. He also developed what is now known as the "Turing Test", a means of determining a machine's intelligence. We'll now review what led to the development of "intelligent" computerized instruction.

Programmed Instruction (PI) and Computer-Assisted Instruction (CAI)

In the early 1960s, programmed instruction (PI) was educationally fashionable. The kind of pedagogy related to any structured, goal-oriented instruction. PI required the programme designer to specify input and output in terms of entering skills and terminal behaviours of the learner. In performing a task analysis, the designer determined the sub-problems or component behaviours as well as their relationships. As learners were led through the problems in the curriculum, overt (external) responses were obtained at every step, incorrect responses were immediately corrected and learners were always informed of their solution accuracy before moving on to some other content area. Most supporters of the PI technology strongly believed that it would enhance learning, particularly for low aptitude individuals. In general, PI refers to any instructional methodology that utilizes a systematic approach to problem decomposition and teaching.

Brief History of Programmed Instruction (PI)

The antecedents to 20th century PI are not well defined. The rhetoricians of democratic Athens in 400 B.C. and later the catechumens of the middle ages, approached an early counterpart to the small steps, sequential instruction and question-and-answer pattern of 20th century programmed instruction. Their teaching procedures included the determination of subsequent instruction as a result of the user's answers to the questions. PI, however, is basically a 20th century phenomenon. In its current forms, its history comprises only 30 years. However, significant contributions were made by Sidney L. Pressey as early as 1915 in his efforts at the Ohio State University to build a simple machine for testing comprehension of material that had been taught. These crude machines presented multiple-choice questions to users while providing immediate knowledge of their results. It is important to note that these early teaching machines represent what Pressey called adjunct auto-instruction i.e. the use of test questions presented after conventional instruction. This means that the machines were not integrated into the instructional material; rather, they were added to (or adjunct to) traditional instruction (usually text), much the same as adjunct questions.

Skinner's Linear Programming

Modern PI is normally associated with B.F. Skinner, the Harvard behavioural psychologist. While, there were a number of programmed precursors to skinner's method of programming, it was his influence, which created the PI phenomenon of the 1950's and 1960's. His involvement is usually traced to his famous 1954 professional address, "The Science of Learning and the Art of Learning", in which he decried the traditional classroom instruction as being too aversive, too large, too negative and improperly sequenced. His solution to these problems was linear programmed instruction. Unlike Pressey's "adjunct" programming, designed to supplement regular course study, Skinner's linear teaching programmes were designed to replace traditional course of study i.e. to function as an instructor for users with no prior knowledge of a subject. Skinner's PI required the user to construct an answer by filling in a blank with the correct response, rather than to select one of four options as correct as in Pressey's machine. Filling in a blank is a recall type of learning because the user has to recall the answer from memory rather than merely recognize it as in multiple choice. After filling in the blank, the user compares his or her answer with the correct one.

The characteristics were designed by Skinner to overcome the classroom limitations stated above. Specifically, users learn without aversive threats, they work one step at a time, from simple to hard, they work at their own pace and they are frequently reinforced for their responses. Skinner's ideas regarding PI may not have been taken very seriously had it not been for the acute shortage of teachers in the 1950's. This situation forced many educators to consider using PI as an alternative teaching method. The use of PI grew until the early 1960's, when low quality programmes flooded the educational market and gave many educators a negative impression of PI that lasted until the early 1970's. The most frequent complaints against the Skinnerian form of linear programming were that it was boring and monotonous; especially for capable users and that the level of learning being supported was rote and meaningless.

Crowder's Intrinsic Programme

Norman A. Crowder, a contemporary of Skinner, was working independently for the armed services on programmed instruction. He felt that a programme was a form of communication between a programmer and a user. Like any communication, the programme must be directed to the individual. Unlike Skinner, Crowder was not working from a psychological perspective, but from a communications point of view. In an intrinsic or branching programme, each frame presents more text than the average linear frame. After reading, the user responds to an adjunct question, usually in a multiple option format. Unlike Pressey's auto-instructional approach, which provides only confirmation of the correctness or incorrectness of that response, branching style optional choices lead users to optional forms of feedback, most of which is corrective. If the user makes a correct response, the programme asserts the reasons why he or she was correct and moves on to new content. If an incorrect response is made, the programme, at the very least, informs the user that an error was made and then branches the user back to the previous frame for another try.

The primary purpose of feedback is to determine whether the communication was successful, in order that corrective steps be taken. Depending upon the complexity of the error committed, the programme may initiate a remedial sequence of instruction, a practice designed to eliminate the learning deficiency. Branching instruction adapts the sequence of the programme to a limited degree to fit the prior learning and processing capabilities of the user. The term intrinsic refers to the fact that all programme options are intrinsic to the programme and therefore, not dependent on any external programming device. The approach is especially adapted to machine presentation, which provides for greater level of adaptability. Branching texts tend to be large and confusing, especially when users try to access them in a manual way.

The primary difference between Skinner's conception of programming and Crowder's is in the function of the response. To skinner, learning results from making the correct response. Contrary to this response orientation, Crowder believed that learning results from the realignment of the user's knowledge structure and that the response is simply a means for controlling the programme or machine. The large chunks of information need to be assimilated and integrated with what the user already knows. The response, he believed, tests the level of integration. This type of programming benefits the higher ability user, who is more capable of higher-level integration of ideas, more than it does the lower-ability user.

The computer-assisted instruction (CAI) in education effectively began in the late 1950s with the use of time-sharing computers, where communication was mainly through the mainframe computers. Hativa (1989, p. 81) suggested that ... *the computer-assisted instruction (CAI) systems designed for the same educational objectives may be based on entirely different concepts and methods of operations and may produce different students attitudes and achievements.* According to Atkinson and Wilson (1969), the three important factors that contribute heavily to the growth of computer-assisted instruction are:

- Development of programmed instruction;
- Mushrooming of electronic data processing;
- Increasing aid to education sectors.

Kulik's research in the 1980s was focused on the use of computer-mediated instruction and found positive research outcomes. The meta-analysis, conducted on 254 controlled evaluation studies showed positive learning effect of computerbased instruction (Kulik & Kulik, 1991). Kulik's meta-analysis studies were carried out when software tutorial programmes had limited options. Nevertheless, Kulik's work has influenced educationalists and developers of computer-based instruction authoring systems for the last two decades. In an interesting study into assessing the effects of simulations and higher order thinking technologies with over 13,000 fourth and eighth grade students, Wenglinsky found gains in students' mathematics scores (Schacter, 2003). Also, the higher order use of computers was affected positively on most students' academic achievements. According to Pudlowski (1995), the use of computers in the teaching process should be considered as a supplement to available methods of instruction, rather than the universal remedy for all of the deficiencies that occur in the computer-based education.

The three most common modes of CAI used in learning are:

- Tutorials;
- Drills and practices;
- Interactive simulations.

Advantages of CAI

Computer-assisted instruction plays a very important role in the modern education process and extensive research shows increasing evidence of the use of computers in the teaching-learning process. There is a body of evidence that computerassisted instruction, which focuses on higher-order learning in technical education, has been more effective than traditional instruction (Yaakub, 2001). It has been shown that computer-assisted instruction has many advantages in teachinglearning processes, including the following important elements:

- Learners can progress at their own rate and pace.
- Learners can have more individual considerations.
- Immediate feedback is available.
- Learner's response can be recorded.
- Visualisation is properly increased.
- Remedial teaching is eliminated and the problem of discontinuance of learning is avoided.
- A deeper analysis of transfer phenomena is permitted and facilitated.
- An opportunity for the introduction of more effective methods for testing in the teaching/learning process is provided.
- Qualitative and quantitative analysis of student achievements is facilitated.
- Access to supplementary material through links is provided.
- Several complex process and interactions can be explained in simple format.

However, comprehensive research is required to determine the best methodology to be applied to the design and development of computer-assisted instruction, as well as the efficiency of the teaching/learning processes based on this particular method of instruction (Patil, 2004).

Origin of Computer Assisted Instructions (CAI)

The roots of computer-assisted instruction can be traced back to programmed instruction (PI). Computer assisted instruction (CAI) is a natural outgrowth of the application of the principles of programmed instruction (PI). Some similarities between PI and CAI are that both have well-defined curricula and branching routines (intrinsic branching for PI, conditional branching for CAI). A major distinction between the two is that CAI is administered on a computer. As we know the main objective of programmed instruction is to provide individualized instruction to meet the special needs of individual learners. To accomplish this objective, it needs some efficient and flexible device that can store gigantic amount of organized information and use selected portion to meet the needs of individual learner. A computer is such a device, which can cater to the needs of individual learners by storing huge amount of information. It can process the information suiting to the needs of individual learner. It can serve to a great variety of educational needs, which range widely with respect to educational levels, subject matter, style of instruction and level of learning from simple drill-and-practice to problem solving. In short, we can say that CAI covers the whole educational spectrum and is gaining more recognition as an important and useful tool in the teaching of various subjects.

Programmed instruction represents a model of how instruction should occur. Nowhere is this model more consistently applied than in computer-assisted instruction (CAI). Even though PI and CAI were developing independently in the 1960's, the instructional sequences and techniques of the former were borrowed by the latter. While PI has declined in popularity, CAI is in big demand. Its continued development has been fueled by the explosion of microcomputers in the 1980's and 1990's. The visual and auditory embellishments afforded by the graphics and sound capabilities of microcomputers make the reinforcement of drill and practice programmes initially more desirable and the programmes are able to keep records on a user's performance but the fundamental instructional model is that of PI.

Another popular form of computer courseware is the tutorial mode, which replicates on the screen branching programmed instruction. The computer's programme presents some information followed by questions on the screen and based upon the response, branches the user to alternative parts of the programme. These programmes, like intrinsic PI, may confirm the correct response, remediate an incorrect one or move the user forward or backward in the programme stream. Also, a number of authoring systems are available to help computer courseware authors circumvent the need for computer language proficiency.

The computers have a vast potential for instruction in all educational environments ranging from schools to universities. They were considerably exploited towards this purpose under the name of Computer Aided/Assisted Instruction. Incorporation of advances in Artificial Intelligence (AI) have led to the development of Intelligent Tutoring Systems (ITS), also referred to as Intelligent Computer Assisted Instruction (ICAI). ICAI is currently a research area and looks at the problems in automating the teaching-learning process. In order to understand ICAI, let us consider briefly the nature of existing CAI/CAL system and some related issues.

Traditional CAI exploits the computer as a medium for—

- Presenting mostly stored and occasionally information in the form of text, graphics and animations to support individualized, self-learning through tutorial mode.
- Providing exercises, accepting student responses and providing feedback regarding the correctness of the responses
- Providing simulated real experiences
- Offering administrative assistance

The normal CAI procedure presents some material to be learned, followed by a problem to be solved that represents a subset of the curriculum. Problem solution tests the learner's acquisition of the knowledge or skill being instructed at that time. The student's answer is compared to the correct answer, then the computer gives appropriate feedback. If the answer is correct, a new problem is selected and presented but if the student answers incorrectly, remediation is invoked that reviews the earlier material, presents simpler problems that graduate to the depth of the original material and so forth. Remediation usually requires some attempt to find the source of the error and to treat it specially. It can be seen in the model given in Figure 5.1.

Traditional Computer Assisted Learning Systems

The predecessors of Intelligent Tutoring Systems (ITS) were known previously as computer-assisted instructions or computer-aided learning systems. These traditional systems were developed to provide users with instructions in a particular area after which they were tested. Answers to questions, usually multiple-choice were used to direct the course of study. Users are presented with information after which a series of question are asked. If the user answers correctly, the next phase of instruction is entered. There may be a summary set of questions at the end of the instructions to judge how well the student has performed. If a user answers the questions incorrectly, the instructional material is presented again, perhaps in a slightly different format. If, after the material has been repeated, the student again answers incorrectly then remedial instructions may be presented. The flow of the instructions and the structure of the traditional computer assisted learning systems given in the flow chart in Figure 5.1.

Computer Assisted Instruction (CAI) and Computer Managed Instruction (CMI)

The technological revolution has a profound effect on education. Computer use in the classroom has grown at a phenomenal rate in the last several years. The relatively inexpensive cost of small but powerful computers on today's market has allowed schools to invest in these learning tools for use in the classroom. Computers provide individualized instruction and a sophisticated and accurate system of record keeping concerning that instruction. Use of the computer in the classroom can be divided into two main categories: Computer Assisted Instruction (CAI) and Computer Managed Instruction (CMI). CAI involves the presentation of material to the student, while CMI involves record keeping of the student's progress.

CAI involves the use of computers to present instruction to students. It is the interaction between a computer system and students, designed to help them learn new material or improve their knowledge of materials previously studied. The most widely accepted value of CAI is that it actively involves

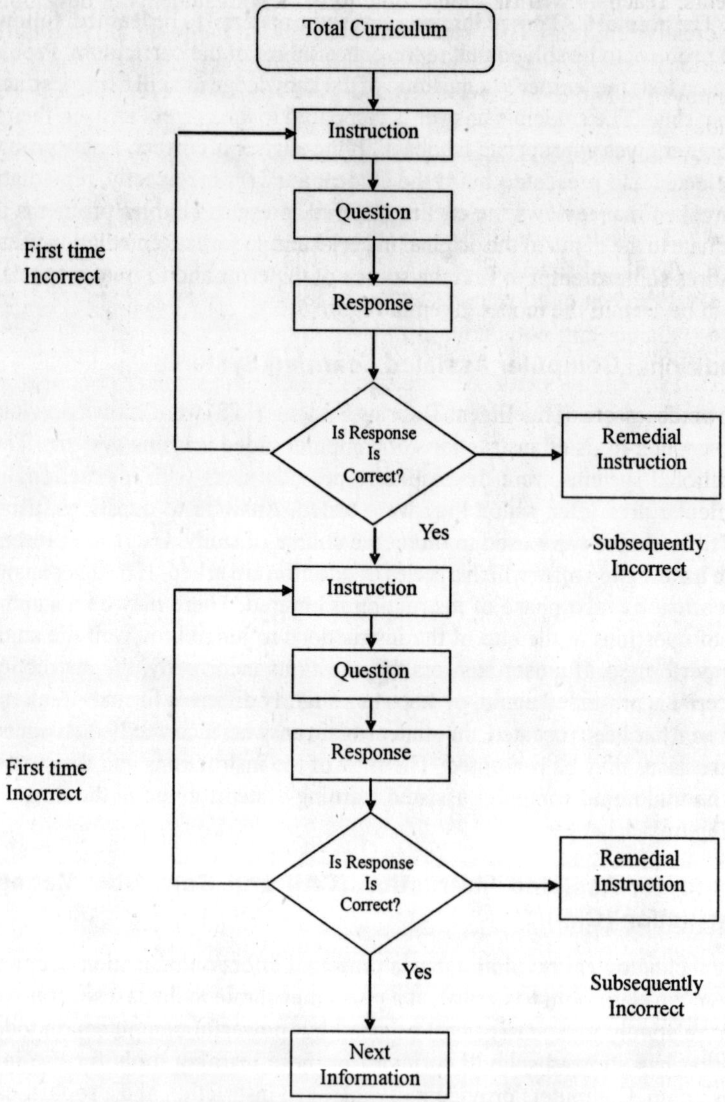

Figure 5.1: A Complete Structure of the Traditional Computer-Assisted Learning Systems

the individual in the learning process. Being a dynamic participant in the learning process facilitates learning. CAI allows the user to proceed at his/her own pace, which has strong implications for both the slow and gifted learner. Reinforcement of learning in such situations is immediate and systematized.

Using a computer in the teaching and learning environment allows teachers to devote his/her more time to the personal, human considerations of their students. Teachers will find more time to work with students in developing their creative abilities. The use of computers in CAI mode should result in an educational environment in which individuals learn more and their potential for innovative and creative professional work is more fully developed. CAI includes various modes of instruction. These modes are not mutually exclusive, however, and individual programmes can employ aspects of several modes at once. These modes include:

- Tutorial
- Drill and Practice
- Discover and Problem Solving
- Games and Simulations

Tutorial: In this mode, information is presented in small units or modules followed by a question. The student's response is analyzed by the computer and appropriate feedback is given. A complicated network of pathways or branches can be programmed. The more alternatives available to the computer, the more adaptive the tutorial can be to individual differences. In the tutorial mode, the computer initiates a self-paced dialogue related to the computer. Once a dialogue is established, the student will receive the instruction needed to continue progressing successfully through the material to be covered. If the computer should judge that the student has not mastered the material presented, the programme will branch either to content needed to re-teach the concept under consideration or to material aimed at presenting a prerequisite skill or concept. Normally, tutorial programmes offer instruction enhanced by graphics, animation and sound and a simple way of providing immediate feedback to students regarding their progress.

Using the computer in place of the conventional paper and pencil workbook drills has several advantages. One of the most important advantage is that computer offer "eye welcome" animation, colours, shapes and messages, reinforced by sound and interactivity.

Drill and Practice: Use of the computer for drill and practice purposes leads the student through a series of examples, problems or exercises to increase dexterity and fluency of a concept, rule or procedure which has already been taught to the student. The drill and practice mode facilitates memorization and/or improvement of the learner's performance within a specific skill area. The key is to reinforce constantly all correct responses. Drill refers to the repeating of facts, in written or oral form, for the purpose of increasing the speed and accuracy of recall. Drill and practice programmes provide a variety of questions and formats. The student is usually given several tries before the computer presents the correct answer. Several levels of difficulty can be available within the same drill and practice programme. Further, the student should receive feedback on the responses given and perhaps, at the end of the session, a summary report on overall performance.

When drill and practice programmes are carefully constructed and used as part of an overall programme, they can be well received and valuable. A computerized drill and practice package can offer a student a patient, tireless, nonjudgmental presenter of material with the ability to adjust the difficulty level as appropriate, based on pupil performance.

Discovery and Problem Solving: Discovery is general term to describe activities using an inductive approach to learning requiring problem solving. In this mode, the computer presents problems which the student solves, after trial and error. The aim of the discovery approach is the deeper understanding that results from grappling with a puzzling problem. A computer programme may lead a student to make discoveries about principles underlying the natural world. In using the discovery mode, the computer programme presents students with sources of information, stores data and provides facilities for information retrieval from a database. The instructor presents a basic problem and monitors the students' progress. The students make hypotheses, test guesses, develop principles and draw conclusions. Finding answers usually requires higher-level thinking skills such as—predicting, inferring and estimating. Problem-solving involves a student's ability to integrate what is learned with his/her existing knowledge base.

Games and Simulation: The three earlier modes of CAI—tutorial, drill and practice and discovery employ aspects of two techniques games and simulation. Games provide the opportunity for students to receive instruction in a motivating format. Educators have discovered that routine instruction can come alive when presented as a game. It increases student motivation, enthusiasm and attention. When applied to instructional tasks, gaming can be a highly motivating framework, especially for repetitious drills. Children learn not only the objective of the lesson but also how to follow directions while playing these games.

A simulation is a dynamic representation of a real object, situation or environment. It is a model or description of events and conditions that allows decisions to be made that affect outcomes. Computer simulations focus on cognitive strategies put the student in an active role, process input, makes decisions, monitor progress and coordinate efforts to reach a goal. Simulation and modeling show great promise as CAI tools. Well designed and carefully selected simulation programmes can be appropriate supplements to curricula. Simulations provide a medium of instruction that enables the student to act on more abstract and complex issues in ways that can facilitate learning. The computer in a simulation mode permits students to explore time and space, to dissect a frog, for example, in a simulated lab without killing the frog, or to investigate complex problems using instruments and methodologies which would be excessively costly or not possible at all without the computer.

There are many important advantages to computer simulations in the classroom. Many educators and researchers find that simulations have the following advantages:

- Simulations allow students to interpret data, understand concepts and develop inquiry skills through interaction with the model.
- Simulations motivate students by incorporating a degree of drama.
- Simulations provide insight into situations difficult or impossible to study in real life.
- Simulations can be less expensive than the lab equipment necessary for certain science experiments.
- Simulations can provide opportunities for more individualized learning experiences than would normally be available in the conventional classroom.
- Simulations can alter time; that is, the computer can speed up time in situations that would take too long to observe in reality.
- Simulations can slow down certain processes that, in a natural setting, may occur too quickly for students to observe.

Computer Managed Instruction

CMI refers to the use of a computer system to manage information about learner performance and the use of tools such as word processors, databases, spreadsheets, etc., to manage instruction. CMI helps teachers to manage instruction in a variety of ways, including computer-based testing, record keeping and prescription. Computer-based testing stores and files test items either by subject, objectives or level of difficulty. Scoring and analyzing the test can also be computerized. It is possible using these systems to get a breakdown of student response to particular items. Student scores on tests can be stored and updated each time a test is taken. In this “electronic grade book”, computers can prescribe a learning package for each student. CMI is an aid to teachers in making decisions. CMI programmes used for this purpose should be examined closely to determine if they emphasize a higher level of educational goals and a higher level of management. The validity and reliability of the tests should be considered as well as the structure of the programme for diagnosis and prescription.

CMI can bring about improvement in the educational environment by developing measurable learning objectives, prioritizing learning objectives, evaluating instructional materials and developing a system of recording students’ progress. CMI is considered an asset to teachers and administrators as a means of organizing and arranging instructional information. One should keep in mind, however, that whether the computer is used to assist teachers to manage instruction or by administrators to organize records, the compatibility of the system with the rest of the educational programme must be a high priority. CMI helps teachers to manage the classroom in the following ways:

- Computer Based Testing
- Computer Based Prescription
- Record Keeping

Computer Based Testing: Computers can be used to store and file banks of test items. The test items can be filed by subject, objective measured and/or level of difficulty. Items in the bank can be readily updated and modified, new items added and old items deleted with minimal effort. From the pool of test items, the instructor can choose the items to include on an examination or the computer can be programmed to select items based upon variables used to classify test items in each category. The computer also can be used to print out a copy of the test in as many different forms as desired or to administer the test to the student who is sitting at the computer. In the latter case, the computer can provide immediate feedback regarding right and wrong responses and keep a permanent record of the learner's achievement on the test.

Test scoring and analysis can be computerized by typing the student responses at the keyboard, by using mark-sense sheets during the test that can be read by the computer or by having the student take the test at the computer. The computer can display the number of students selecting each alternative as well as the raw scores and standard scores of each student. In addition, group data such as means and standard deviations can be calculated.

Computer Based Prescription: Based upon student data (background, interest, test scores, etc.) and instructor input (available materials, alternative sequences, time available, etc.), the computer can develop a learning prescription for each student. Often traditional instruction is lock-sep because the teacher cannot keep all the alternatives and each student's characteristics and background in mind. The computer with its extensive storage capacity can perform the countless manipulations necessary to assign instructional activities and learning materials based on a wide variety of decision parameters programmed into it.

Record Keeping: Records of student scores on tests can be stored by the computer. Then student record can be updated each time a test is taken. The computer serves as an 'electronic grade book'. At the end of the grading period, the scores can be manipulated (i.e. the lowest score can be dropped, the highest score doubled). The average is calculated, the final grade determined and the students' complete performance printed out by the computer.

Computers in the Curriculum

Computer applications in school administration affect the entire instructional information system at all the level. The results can be observed in both regular and special education. In general, computers can be used to gather information for planning instruction, providing a rich environment for hands-on student experience in learning a new concept, helping teachers to help students learn and analyzing data for instructional and administrative purposes. Computer technology has been a boon to special education because of the development of speech synthesis, speech recognition and modified keyboards. Revolutionary technology reads for visually impaired students, writes for paralyzed pupils, moves individuals with limited mobility and sometimes hears for deaf students. The computer contribution to individualized instruction is invaluable. Because the learning ability for disabled students differs drastically from individual to individual, self-paced learning, large bright letters, simple and clear instruction and positive reinforcement are essential. A word processor is a most helpful tool in school. With a word processor, it is easy to delete, add or move punctuation, words, sentences, paragraphs or pages anywhere in the text. In making revision easier, the word processor may encourage a student to revise more often and be more adventuresome.

It is obvious that today, more than ever, high quality hardware and software are available. Through planning and good organization, teachers can utilize computers to get maximum use of classroom time. The potential for the computer as an instructional tool for both teachers and students is likely to be limitless.

Using the Computer in School Subject Areas

In recent years, computer use in schools has changed dramatically. No longer do schools use computers to process administrative data only. Since the advent of the microcomputer, educators at all levels have begun to use computers as learning tools. This influx of computers has and will continue to have, a major impact on many aspects of teaching and the learning process. The following are some major applications of computers in different subject areas:

Use of Computer in Mathematics

- Drills and tutorials on basic arithmetic operations, problems on algebra, geometry, calculus, trigonometry, etc.
- Teaching coordinate systems, geometry, trigonometry, calculus, probability and statistics.
- Performing complex calculations, using programmes to solve equations, inverting matrices and plotting graphs.
- Printing out worksheets with randomly generated problems.
- Diagnosing specific skill deficiencies.
- Testing students, giving assignments, storing progress records and printing results.

Use of Computer in Language Arts

- Drills on tutorials on reading comprehension, vocabulary development and spelling (flashing words or dictation with speech synthesizers).

- Vocabulary development games, story generation and sentence completion activities.
- Making vocabulary activities such as crossword puzzles, hidden words, etc.
- Creative writing using word processing (students can write, revise and edit their composition on the computer, checking spelling and grammar).
- Testing students, giving assignments, storing progress records and printing results.

Use of Computer in Science

- Science drills and tutorials
- Simulations of scientific experiments or natural phenomena which could not otherwise occur in a classroom.
- Data analysis for scientific experiments.
- Searching through a database to find information or test hypotheses.
- Testing students, giving assignments, storing progress records and printing results.

Use of Computer in Social Sciences

- Social studies tutorials and drills.
- Simulations of historical events, geographical exploration, business operations, social conflict resolution and psychological experiments.
- Data analysis of experiments in the social sciences and building models in economics.
- Searching through a database to find information or test hypotheses.
- Testing students, giving assignments, storing progress records and printing results.

Use of Computer in Special Education

- Special tutorials and drills.
- Simulation of social events and scientific experiments.
- Remedial work for reading and language arts.
- Word processing with spelling checker.
- Modifying CAI programmes to suit slower learners.

Use of Computer in Foreign Languages/Bilingual Education (Including English as a Second Language)

- Tutorials and drills on vocabulary and grammar.
- Pronunciation and oral discrimination with a speech synthesizer.
- Word processing with spelling and grammar checker.
- Electronic bilingual dictionaries.
- Using computers to elicit conversation in the second language.

Use of Computer in Art

- Computer learning environments which allow students to explore screen graphics.
- Programming activities using screen graphics and graphics on printers and plotters.
- Graphic design utility programmes.
- Videodisc information retrieval systems for slide collections.

Use of Computer in Music

- Tutorials and drills on musical terminology and notation (with a sound generation unit).
- Computer learning environments which allow students to explore computer-generated music.
- Music synthesizers as tools for composers and music students.

Use of Computer in Health and Home Economics

- Using computer programmes for drug education.
- Simulation of body defense mechanism against microorganism.
- Preventive measures and scheduling vaccinations.
- Aspects of personal and public health.
- Utility programmes to determine recipe ingredient quantities and shopping lists.
- Analyzing nutritional content of meals and planning diets.
- Storing recipes and retrieving them as needed.
- Managing household budgets.

Use of Computer in Physical Education

- Recording sports performance and progress.
- Monitoring athletes' training.
- Evaluating physical parameter (body composition, percent body fat).
- Scoring fitness and fitness tests.
- Personalizing exercise programmes.
- Planning game strategy.

Use of Computer in Business Education

- Tutorials and drills on business related aspects.
- Simulations of actual business operations and procedures.
- Business application software, including word processor, databases, spreadsheet and accounting packages.

Use of Computer in Industrial Arts

- Tutorials for training on machine operation.
- Drills on various procedures.
- Utility programmes to determine materials specifications.

- Computer-aided design (CAD) and computer aided manufacturing.
- Computer installation and repair.

Limitations with CAI/CAL

In the traditional computer assisted learning systems, the instruction was not individualized to the learner's needs. The decisions about how to move through the lesson were script like, such as:

- If the current screen is read, proceed to the next screen, or
- If the current question is answered correctly, go on with the next question, or
- If the current picture is shown, proceed with next topic, or
- If the current task is done correctly, proceed with next topic; otherwise go back and show the current topic.

These actions were buried into the source code, meaning that any changes to some noticed disadvantage were impossible without the programmers. Analogously, the learner's abilities and previous knowledge were not taken into account; the same teaching material is presented to everybody in the same way and there is no difference between different classrooms. The required knowledge for learning some lesson in some domain is not the same even in one country itself (the north-south problems, country-town etc.) but CAI systems do not allow different approaches. Also those systems do not inspire or motivate the learners and they do not identify common or specific errors or misunderstandings. The common limitations with CAI are:

CAI provides only a rigid and restrictive environment for the interaction.

CAI basically presents pre-stored information or problems according to the pre-decided pedagogical control structure.

Computer has a very little ability to re-structure the material with respect to the student needs and cannot respond to situations not anticipated by the teachers, as it is not possible to store every type of information and every situation of teaching-learning process.

We could say that individually pieced instruction in computer programmes and frame-based computer-aided instruction comprised early attempts of using the computer in education. Even though these systems had some success for some types of learning, generally they did not prosper because their learning environments were too monotonous and simple and their ability to adapt was limited to branching between static screens. Recent technological advances in computer hardware, software and multimedia systems, by themselves have been insufficient to realize the dreams of a computer-driven revolution in educational practice. Significant benefits will start to accrue when computer-based technologies are systematically incorporated into a system of tools that support thinking and learning activities.

Is there an Intelligent Machine?

Unlike the computer a human teacher has the ability to restructure the information and thus handles new situations in a novel way. Even, if the computer is made to 'generate' responses in the form of information or logic or solution, the pedagogical decisions such as when to intervene in student's exploration, what would be the likely response of the student for a question posed to them are still to be taken by the author. The pedagogical decisions incorporated as decision rules in CAI are generally based upon empirical experience of the author, as the conventional CAI does not support the derivation of such decision rules based on pedagogical principles.

In order to facilitate the teachers to develop courseware without extensive knowledge of programming, a set of tools like authoring languages and authoring systems are available which reduce the programming time considerably. The development of sophisticated graphic software has enhanced the communication capabilities of the computer.

The above-discussed limitations of traditional computer-assisted learning systems were serious enough for researchers to explore the possibility of incorporating some of the artificial intelligence (AI) techniques into CAL. Thus the evolution of ICAI began. ICAI is intended to draw best from both traditional CAI and reactive learning environments and then to construct systems that emulate a real teacher working with an individual learner.

The necessity of human dimension in instruction cannot be overlooked and thus the realistic view of ICAI would be, to look at it as an assistant to the teacher, which can encourage the learner to learn and practice, arouse learner's curiosity through exploration and experimentation and offer advice and help whenever required. This would free the teacher from routine tasks and make him available for more creative work and for helping learners to overcome more difficult problems that are beyond the capability of ICAI. Incorporation of advances in Artificial Intelligence (AI) has led to the development of Intelligent Computer Assisted Instructions (ICAI) or Intelligent Tutoring System (ITS).

6

Artificial Intelligence and Education

How can artificial intelligence are used in the education. There are expert systems, simulations, computer assisted instruction and other technological adaptations in education. Many AI researchers have begun looking at public education with a new perspective as to how learning takes place in a society saturated with virtual reality, the Internet, video games and other such technologies. They are exploring the reformation of a system built on the three Rs. Many of these researchers are realizing that such an educational system may be ineffective in producing adults who will successfully use the technology of the future. They claim that the focus should be on a system that adapts media to serve the needs of the individual. Most believe, as David Sewell wrote in his book *New Tools for New Minds*, that technology is both a tool (a way to express skills) and a means to an end, the end being cognitive growth.

"Constructionism" is a theory of learning and a strategy for education. Constructionism is based on two different senses of construction. It is based on the idea that people learn by actively constructing new knowledge, not by having information "poured" into their heads. Moreover, constructionism asserts that people learn with particular effectiveness when they are engaged in "constructing" personally meaningful artifacts (such as computer programmes, animations or robots).

Background and Philosophy

Originally a mathematician, Seymour Papert worked on cognitive development with Jean Piaget in Geneva in 1958-1963 where he first began his work of using mathematics in the service of understanding how children think and learn. Moving to MIT in the 1960s, he worked with Marvin Minsky where he helped found the Artificial Intelligence Laboratory and invent the programming language LISP. He also helped invent a simpler form of LISP called LOGO, which he constructed to allow children to programme "turtles" to draw intricate geometrical figures. In 1985 he was one of the founders of the Media Arts and Sciences Programme and the MIT Media Laboratory and in 1988 he was named LEGO Professor of Learning Research, a chair created for him.

In his book *Mindstorms: Children, Computers and Powerful Ideas*, Papert wrote that he became interested in the way a relatively young computer culture was allowing psychologists to develop new ways to think about thinking. This in turn led to the belief that children could also benefit from the way in which computer models seemed able to give concrete form to areas of knowledge that had previously appeared so intangible and abstract. While psychologists use ideas from AI to build formal, scientific theories about mental processes, children use the same ideas in a more informal and personal way to think about themselves.

Using the programming language LOGO to programme a "turtle", Papert believed that it was possible to teach aspects of AI to children so that they, too, could think more concretely about mental processes. Children were held back in their education, Papert claimed, because they had a model of learning in which there was a right way and a wrong way to do something. But when programming a computer, the programmer almost never gets it right the first time. The question to ask about the programme is not whether it is right or wrong, but if it is fixable. If this way of looking at intellectual products were generalized, Papert proposed, learners might be less intimidated.

Papert wrote that when Piaget talked about the developing child, he was really talking about the development of knowledge. As a mathematician and Piagetian psychologist, Papert had been interested in studying computational models that would help him better understand the developmental process. He said that some studies in AI have tended to use deductive methods that would enable conclusions to be drawn from general principles while others draw on large pools of knowledge which can be used to solve problems. These approaches, he claimed, are static. The kind of questions Papert would ask need a dynamic model for how intellectual structures themselves could come into being and change, the kinds of models that are most relevant to education.

Papert said that the computer was a more powerful tool for intellectual development than other new technologies because it put the learner in a new relationship to a domain of knowledge, more active and self-directed. When children used the programming language LOGO to programme turtles, they were basically teaching the computer to think. To accomplish this, they have to think about thinking themselves, becoming epistemologists, someone who studies the theory of knowledge. Seen in this light, Papert stated, the computer is not just another powerful educational tool. The computer solves problems in such a way that the abstract and hard to grasp becomes concrete and transparent.

In his more recent book *The Children's Machine*, Papert notes that there is more involved in literacy that the ability to read. "Becoming literate," Papert asserts, means thinking differently than one did previously, seeing the world differently, and this suggests that there are many different literacies. Papert differentiates between literacy and "letteracy", thus reflecting the media used for the transmission of information and ideas. The mainstream education system addresses only one medium—the printed word.

Exploring new media will change children's relationships with knowledge, as well as to the present education system. Papert declares that children who grow up with the opportunity to explore the world with the latest technologies are less likely to sit quietly through anything even vaguely resembling the elementary-school curriculum. Papert's vision of reform as proposed in *Mindstorms* has yet to be realized. However, he is still hopeful that change will occur because of at least one aspect of technology—electronic communications.

Artificial Intelligence in Perspective

In the classical sense, there was a lot of initial groundwork that was laid that became the foundation for artificial intelligence from the time that Aristotle invented syllogistic logic up to the mid 20th century. In 1950 A.M. Touring published his book, *Computing Machinery and Intelligence* which established a test (Touring's Test) for determining intelligent behaviour in machines. Shortly after, in 1956 John McCarthy coined the term "artificial Intelligence" (AI) at the Dartmouth Conference. From that time forward the development of AI grew as each new innovation built upon its predecessors. Today we have a variety of applications that work alongside educators to increase understanding and retention in many different aspects of learning.

Artificial Intelligence and Education

Although the idea of intelligent machines is over hundred years old, research on artificial intelligence (Turning test) started in the 1950's with very ambitious goals. However in the 1970's it was found that desirable aims were not realized but the research was continued with more realistic goals mainly restricted to the research and implementation of new programme methods and tools. Besides, a new relationship of industrial and business institutions towards artificial intelligence resulted from the Japanese 5th generation project and achievements in the applications of the artificial intelligence in the expert systems areas. In this environment CAI has undergone transformation. The goal of researchers and designers of CAI systems was to design a curriculum, which may be included in well-prepared teaching materials and adapted to each individual student. Such CAI systems received the prefix intelligent, i.e. Intelligent Computer Assisted/Aided Instruction (ICAI) or Intelligent Tutoring systems (ITS). An intelligent CAI system should be able to present a rich domain knowledge (subject material), which the student should be able to use in a way, which is not defined in advance by the teacher. Besides, the instruction should pay attention to the student's abilities, weakness and preferred styles of learning.

Ad-hoc Frame Oriented CAI

First curricula had different forms and modality of use but all of them followed the same pedagogical paradigm. The student usually has to read the text followed by a question, which requires a short answer. After that, the computer tells him whether his answer is right or wrong. Sometimes his answers ask for repetition of some parts of the material, which the student must repeat and sometimes he is offered further text with new information. The process of learning is branched. The PLATO system distinguishes two kinds of branching.

In author initiated branching the author establishes error criteria while the students can always be directed back or asked for further explanation. The authors of courseware try to predict every wrong answer of the student and adapt further explanation and help to the student's specific purposes.

This branching is the first step towards individualization of instruction. Carbonell (1970) calls this CAI "ad-hoc frame oriented" CAI (AFO CAI) and points out its dependence on information modules which were prepared by the author. AFO CAI design is based on a stimulus-response (S-R) system.

Criticism of CAI

Carbonell (1970) and Rickel (1989) agree that the greatest difficulty in application of CAI lies in the representation of domain knowledge, in building student models and in student diagnosis. This knowledge consists of a canned presentation of the information to the student, canned problems with which to test his knowledge, canned answers and pre specified branches in the presentation based on a pre-remunerate set of possible responses. These systems were criticized for their lack of adaptation to the student. Their pre specified branches present them from adapting the presentation to the needs of the student. They also prevent them from handling unanticipated answers. And their pre specified answers leave them with no criteria for judging student responses other than as right or wrong.

Generative and Intelligent CAI

In most CAI systems of the AFO type the computer does little more than what a programmed textbook can do and one may wonder why the machine is used at all (Carbonell, 1970, p. 194). In contrast to the AFO approach in design and implementation of SCHOLAR tutorial systems Carbonell defines structure oriented information base as a network of facts, conceptions and procedures. Elements of this net are units, which define words and events in the form of a multilevel hierarchical information tree. Carbonell has made a remarkable advancement in designing a structure of CAI when he applied the ISO system to build mixed-initiative dialogue (student-tutor) in SCHOLAR. Mixed-initiative dialogue offers more sensitive and efficient systems and gives better conditions for individualized learning. Carbonell's work in this field is treated by Barr and Feigenbaum (1986) as a pioneer step and in their opinion it defined other types of CAI—intelligent CAI or knowledge based CAI. Besides the above mentioned, early use of the artificial intelligence techniques in CAI systems pointed out the possibilities of generating problems supported by a database with domain knowledge. These systems were called generative CAI. In these systems the problem is generated on the basis of the established rules or other suitable structures. Syntax and semantics of the problems are determined by the system, which gives more interesting possibilities of one ways of "mixing" problems. The system can direct and control the process of problem generation by establishing the difficulty and the field of interest and by trying to realize the individual abilities of the students. In the 1970's the second phase in the development of ICAI or ITS systems started with the following characteristics: building of the student model and student diagnosis and establishing and developing of the tutorial strategies. The intelligent tutoring systems should pass three tests of intelligence—

1. The subject matter or domain knowledge must be 'known' to the computer system well enough to enable it to draw inferences or solve problems.
2. The system must be able to deduce a learner's approximation of that knowledge.
3. The tutorial strategy must be intelligent as "instructor in the box" can, implement strategies to reduce the difference between expert and student (Burns and Capps, 1998).

There are at least three essential reasons why intelligent tutoring systems are confirmed as a good "test bed" in realization of the projects for artificial intelligence:

- Applications for wide spectrum of domain knowledge including artificial intelligence itself.
- Open for development because they can easily embody a spectrum of levels of "intelligence", without losing their effectiveness.
- Multifarious functions because it integrates various specific ways of thinking in problem solving area (What? Whom? and How?).

Computer-Aided/Assisted Instruction (CAI) systems were first developed by educational researchers and widely used during the 1950's and 1960's. Carbonell (1970) defined a second type of CAI, Intelligent Computer Aided Instruction (ICAI), initiated by computer scientist. The ICAI is the result of the merging of the three main domains, namely-Computer Science (AI), Education (CAI) and Psychology (Cognition). It aims to teach the individual student more effectively and adaptively than traditional CAI systems, by applying AI principles and techniques. Although there is no standard architecture for an ITS, four software components emerge from the literature as part of an ITS (Burns & Capps, 1988; Gott & Pokorny, 1987; Massey, 1986). Typical ICAI systems consist of four main components. For each component of the system, various AI techniques have been applied to improve the performance of the system.

AI Research

Areas of AI research can be divided into two major branches-science and engineering. The concern of AI science with theory building and understanding both human and machine intelligence may be differentiated from product directed concerns of building expert systems. However, AI science and engineering are not independent. Although, some conflicts of interest occur, AI science coexists with the AI engineering discipline (Wenger, 1987). The boundaries that define AI science and engineering will gradually shift as AI techniques which emerge from research laboratories become commonly accepted and used in applied settings and product development.

Research relies upon the scientific method to examine the information and to draw conclusions from the findings and facts. AI scientists are primarily concerned with studying problem solving and reasoning in the abstract. Many AI scientists explore problem solving through academic research programmes at major universities and laboratories (Harmon & King, 1985). These AI scientists seek general techniques for solving broad classes of problems. Scientific research in AI, like scientific research in general, focuses on hypothesis testing. The contribution of AI science is the exploration of theoretical issues in problem analysis, knowledge representation, reasoning methodologies and heuristic search strategies.

AI research occurs in numerous areas of computer and cognitive science. The role of research is to seek areas where knowledge is incomplete and to solve problems which need solutions. AI researchers seek to identify relevant knowledge and information related to human and machine problem-solving capabilities. For example, AI scientists study natural language processing, speech recognition, computer vision, robotics and automatic programming. AI engineering attempts to apply research findings in the development of useful "intelligent" computer programmes. AI engineers work with AI scientists to apply symbolic representation and symbolic inference procedures of real-world problems. According to Carrico, Girard and Jones (1989):

> ....AI can be considered a group of problem-solving techniques or tools that emulate human thought to help in increasing knowledge, processing productivity or making decisions.

Applications of AI research are of current commercial interest because of the success of several research projects. The success of expert systems in the commercial marketplace has lead to high interest in AI engineering. Transfer of expertise is a major area of research for both engineers and scientists. Some individuals working toward the transfer of expertise call themselves "knowledge engineers". Knowledge engineers use AI concepts and techniques. Knowledge engineers develop expert systems and intelligent computer assisted instruction (ICAI) systems through a systematic process of planning, designing, constructing and evaluating expert systems. Knowledge engineers focus on capturing and encoding knowledge, reasoning and expertise in problem solving areas that can be defined, organized and structured. Knowledge engineering processes assist individuals in analyzing and solving complex problems. Knowledge engineers use AI programming languages and expert systems development tools in the construction of prototypes and in working AI programmes. Expert systems development tools may be used in clarifying knowledge and developing products for education and training. Knowledge engineering will complement the research and development area of instructional design. Both processes seek to clarify expertise and to transfer that expertise to novices.

Transfer to expertise from humans to machines and back to other humans is a major goal of AI research and development. A major question pursued by AI scientists and knowledge engineers is "How can problem solving abilities and expertise be organized so that they can be used for consulting and teaching?" Figure 6.1 shows a transfer of expertise model which may be applied in the development of knowledge bases, expert systems and ICAI systems. As shown, domain expertise is captured in a knowledge base by the knowledge engineer. Then this knowledge base may be used as a source for either consultation through an expert system or teaching through an ICAI system.

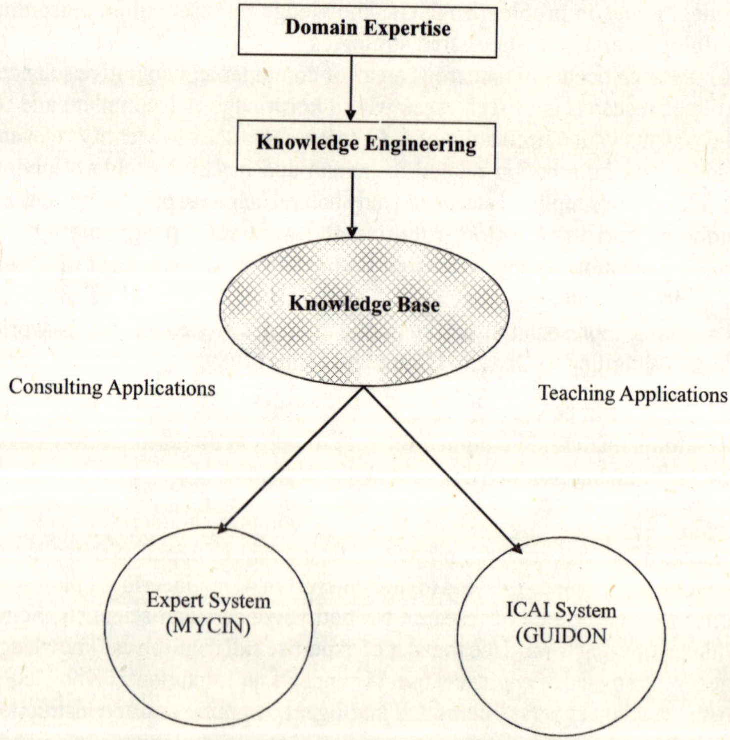

Figure 6.1: Transfer of Expertise

Techniques of Artificial Intelligence (AI) in Intelligent Computer-Assisted Instruction (ICAI)

(1) *Knowledge Representation Technique (KRT):* Early efforts to apply AI techniques in ICAI systems focused on the representation of the subject matter, which was implicitly encoded in the programme in early CAI systems. Various knowledge representation techniques, such as—semantic networks, rules and scripts have been applied. But the most important progress is to create an explicit and separate domain knowledge base. This development allows easy modification of the domain knowledge without reformulating the whole system.

(2) *Natural Language Generation Technique (NLGT):* Another AI technique, natural language generation plays a very important role in ICAI systems. Users can communicate with the system by asking a question and answering the question in a language they already know. SCHOLAR [Carbonell, 1970], SOPHIE [Brown *et al.*, 1982] and WHY [Stevens et., al., 1982] adapted natural language interaction. In addition, it can provide context-dependent tutoring (Woolf and Mc Donald, 1984).

(3) *Knowledge Status Analysis Technique (KSAT):* From the mid-1970's, ICAI systems focused on the analysis of the student's learning status. Generally well-defined expertise does not guarantee an expert teacher. Without exact knowledge about what the student knows and does not know for a giving problem, the system cannot provide adaptive instruction. Hence, AI techniques were used to evaluate the knowledge status of the student (Carbonell and Goldstein, 1977; Brown and Burton, 1978). This technique can be used effectively for deciding the next appropriate tutoring strategy by the tutoring module.

(4) *Expert's Pedagogical Knowledge Technique (EPKT):* Finally, AI techniques are applied to represent the expert's pedagogical knowledge. In traditional CAI systems, the tutoring strategy is procedurally hard-coded in the programme. It is structured as a branching programme; If the student answers 'A' then go to this section, if the student answers 'B' then move to the next section. If the system needs to contain all the possible answers from the student, the system may become very complex. Hence the system is expensive to build and hard to modify, because the system is greatly anticipated by the effort of a human author. A using AI techniques, such as instructional planning, the tutorial strategies can be represented explicitly and automatically.

Intelligent Tutoring System (ITS)

The most general way to describe ITS, is to say that it is the application of AI to the education. During the several last decades the penetration of computers essentially influenced the architectures of the so-called 'intelligent tutoring' systems. It is fashionable recently to mark sophisticated software systems with this attribute. The definition of *intelligence* is context dependent and we will not deal with the phenomenon of intelligence. The aim of this paragraph is to present several definitions of the ITSs.

- 'ITSs are computer software systems that seek to mimic the methods and dialog of natural human tutors, to generate instructional interactions in real time and on demand, as required by individual students. Implementations of ITSs incorporate computational mechanisms and knowledge representations in the fields of artificial intelligence, computational linguistics, and cognitive science.'
- 'Broadly defined, an intelligent tutoring system is educational software containing an artificial intelligence component. The software tracks students' work, tailoring feedback and hints along the way. By collecting information on a particular student's performance, the software can make inferences about strengths and weaknesses, and can suggest additional work.'
- 'In particular, ITSs are computer-based learning systems which attempt to adapt to the needs of learners and are therefore the only such systems which attempt to 'care' about learners in that sense. Also, ITS research is the only part of the general IT and education field which has as its scientific goal to make computationally precise and explicit forms of educational, psychological and social knowledge which are often left implicit.' (Self, 1999)

We may distil from these definitions, that they stress the expert systems' point of view and they consider ITS as a monolithic system.

Theoretical Foundations for Intelligent Tutoring Systems

It is generally accepted (as it is seen also from the above mentioned definitions) to refer to an ITS if the system is able to:

- build a more or less sophisticated model of cognitive processes,
- adapt these processes consecutively and
- control a question-answer-interaction.

Conventionally, ITS provides individualized tutoring or instruction and has the following 4 models or software components (Kearsley, 1987)

- knowledge of the *domain* (i.e. knowledge of the domain expert, refers to the topic or curriculum being taught)
- knowledge of the *learner* (e.g., what he/she knows, what he/she's done, how he/she learns, …)
- knowledge of *teacher strategies* (or pedagogical issues i.e. how to teach, in what order, typical mistakes and remediation, typical questions a student might ask, hints one might offer a student who is stuck)
- *User interface* (i.e. interactive environment interface)

We observe in general the following two approaches in building components of the ITS:

Deductive inference: In this case we think, whether particular statement(s) coincide with a general theory. Deductive systems provide inference engines to conduct the deduction. The task is to prove that the input predicates fulfill the general theory. E.g. applications based on Prolog programming language represent such systems.

Inductive inference: In this case software engineers are building, or inferring, a general rule from the special input examples. In other words, we are seeking a rule, which covers the particular set of examples. There may exist always one more example, which could modify the recently obtained rule. Inductive inference methods are used for inferring and maintaining the learner model. Application areas are as follows:

- Programming by examples—PBE (Leiberman, 2001) (e.g. programming of robots)
- Inference of grammars (Fu, 1985)
- Pattern recognition (Bhagat, 2005)

Although CAI systems may be somewhat effective in helping learners, they do not provide the same kind of individualized attention that a student would receive from a human tutor. For a computer-based educational system to provide such attention, it must reason about the domain and the learner. This has prompted research in the field of intelligent tutoring systems (ITS). ITS offer considerable flexibility in presentation of material and a greater ability to respond to distinctive, idiosyncratic and characteristic student needs. These systems achieve their "intelligence" by representing pedagogical decisions about how to teach as well as information about the learner. This allows for greater flexibility and versatility by altering the system's interactions with the pupil or student. We could say that "ITS are computer-based instructional systems that have separate data bases or knowledge bases, for instructional content (specifying what to teach) and for teaching strategies (specifying how to teach) and they attempt to use inferences about a student's mastery of topics to dynamically adapt instruction. ITS design is founded on two fundamental assumptions about learning. First, that individualized instruction by a component tutor is far superior to classroom-style learning because both the content and style of the instruction can be continuously adapted to best meet the needs of the situation. Second, that students learn better in situations which more closely approximate the situations in which they will use their knowledge, i.e., they "learn by doing", learn via their mistakes and learn by constructing knowledge in a very individualized way. ITS use techniques that allow automated instruction to come closer to the ideal by more closely simulating realistic situations and by incorporating computational models (knowledge bases) of the content, the teaching process and the student's learning state.

Comparison between ITS and Traditional CBI Systems

The comparison between the two instructional systems is presented in the Table 6.1.

Table 6.1

Issues	*Computer-Based Instruction (CBI)*	*Intelligent Tutoring System (ITS)*
1. Development Goal	Practical for instructional improvement	Exploration of new technology (AI) in instruction
2. Theoretical Base	Existing theories and principles of learning and instruction	Information processing theories and cognitive science (SC)
3. System Structure and Process	Frame-oriented static and single structure; pre-specified algorithmic system-initiative process	Process-oriented dynamic modular structure; generative, mixed initiative process
4.Instructional Principles	Various but mostly program-initiated expository approach	Mostly student-centered discovery approach
5.Knowledge Structuring Methods	Mainly task analysis for identifying sub-tasks and content elements	Knowledge representing techniques for structuring knowledge into the system
6. Student Modelling Method	Binary judgement or qualitative assessment	Reasoning and qualitative evaluation
7.Instructional Formats	Mostly expository tutorials, drill-and-practice, games and simulations	Mostly inquiry tutorials, games and simulations
8. Subject Matter Areas	Virtually every area	Limited to well-structured areas
9. Development Process and Team	Systems approaches, instructional designers, subject matter experts and programmer	Prototyping approach, mostly AI expert (or knowledge engineer only)
10. Evaluation	Formative and summative evaluation, instructional effectiveness	Validation of functional running; mainly technical debugging
11. Hardware and Software	Mostly general-purpose hardware and software or authoring tools	AI-purpose hardware and software (LISP and PROLOG)

Intelligent Tutoring Systems (ITS) are computer programmes that instruct the student in an intelligent way. They are designed to incorporate techniques from the artificial intelligence (AI) community to provide tutors, which know what they teach, who they teach and how to teach. The goal of an Intelligent

Tutoring Systems (ITS) is to apply artificial intelligence methods and techniques to develop highly individualized computer-based instructional environment in which the student and computer tutor can have a flexibility that closely resembles what actually occurs when student and human tutor sit down one-on-one and attempt to teach and learn together. Such flexibility is important because without it, the system cannot be fully adaptive to the individual student's on-going learning needs during instruction.

What Makes a Computer-Aided Learning System Intelligent?

Intelligence is attributed to computer-aided learning system if they do not require every decision to be made for them in advance; instead they have the capability to make reasonable decisions themselves. A significant difference between intelligent CAI and conventional CAI lies predominantly in the location of decision-making expertise. With computer-aided learning system (CAL) the system designer has knowledge of the domain and a view on how it should be taught. The designer makes decisions about how the domain knowledge should be taught, such as the sequence, difficulty level and presentation (graphics, text, multimedia, etc.). The result of this decision-making process is a set of decisions, which are then encoded in the system. During the presentation, the computer merely follows the decisions given to it by the designer. It has little occasion to deviate from the prescribed presentation and consequently is incapable of dealing with unexpected situations. Situations the designer did not anticipate and correspondingly did not provide a solution for them.

In contrast, when designing an intelligent computer assisted/aided learning (ICAL) system, the designer does not make the decisions about interaction and how domain knowledge content is taught. Various knowledge elicitation methods will allow the designer to specify the domain knowledge in a usable model (often as rules, e.g. Clancey, 1987) and similar analysis might offer pedagogic knowledge in a complementary format.

Pedagogic knowledge embodies the principles used by experienced teachers in making decisions about presentation rather than the results of decision-making. Thus, by providing the system with access to this body of knowledge, it has the capability of performing the same decision-making process to obtain decisions about presentation, as the designer would perform in the design of CAL. Since the computer makes its own decisions, in principle it has the flexibility of reasoning about any situation that might arise. The utility of its reasoning, however, depends on the accuracy, reliability and completeness of the knowledge model it accesses (Khan, T. and Yip, Y.J.; 1996).

The central point is made that the computer in CAL is still acting as a presentation device for predefined material. This includes hypermedia-browsing systems that allow free navigation within the network (e.g. World Wide Web or Internet) where nodes contain predefined information pages. The most noticeable problem with traditional CAL is that the student has little control over what is taught.

The Mean of "I" in ITS

Now many questions arise here, e.g., What is meant by intelligent tutoring system?, When a computer assisted instructional programme works intelligently? The answers of these questions is given below in the words of AI experts:

Sharon Derry (1993)—"An intelligent instructional system can observe what the student is doing during problem solving and/or has done over a series of problem-solving session and from this information draw inferences about the student's knowledge, beliefs and attitudes in terms of some theory of cognition. A system can be intelligent whether or not it makes instructional decisions based on this information but if it doesn't use such information in instructional decision-making, then I don't think of it as a tutoring system but rather a tool that has some diagnostic capabilities".

Lee Gugerty (1993)—"Intelligent tutoring involves: (a) explicit modelling of expert representations and cognitive processes; (b) detection of student errors; (c) diagnosis of student's knowledge (correct, incorrect and missing); (d) instruction adapted to student's knowledge state (via problem selection, hints, feedback and explicit didactic instruction) and (e) doing all of the above in a timely fashion as the student solves problems (not post hoc)".

Susanne Lajoie (1993)—"The 'I' in Its means that the computer can provide adaptive forms of feedback to the learner based on a dynamic assessment of the student's 'model' of performance. Intelligent feedback means that the assessment of the learner is ongoing, the feedback is appropriate to that particular learner in the context of where an impasse has been encountered and it is not canned but generated on the spot, based on student needs".

Matt Lewis (1993)—"An 'intelligent' tutoring system contains, at a minimum, a reasonably general simulation of human problem solving in direct service of communicating knowledge and like a good human tutor, separates domain knowledge from pedagogical knowledge. The simulation might solve domain-specific problems in the target instructional domain (e.g., a human like approach and solution to the problem of writing a fugue) or solve pedagogical problems (e.g., error diagnosis and attribution or solution of appropriate response)".

Sig Tobias (1993)—"Intelligent, in an ITS context, means that the programme is flexible in the method and sequence with which instructional materials are presented to the student. Furthermore, the system is capable of adapting instructional parameters to student characteristics by using data collected prior to or during, instruction for such decisions. Finally, it suggests that the instructional system can advise the student regarding options most likely to be successful for the student."

From the above definitions, it is clear that everyone agrees that the most critical element is real-time cognitive diagnosis (or student modelling). The next most frequently cited feature is adaptive remediation.

7

Learning Theories and Intelligent Tutoring System

There is a wide range of educational schools of thought and learning theories, as modern educational thinkers testify (Greeno *et al.*, 1996). Many of these theories can be mapped to three broad pedagogical approaches: behaviourism, cognitivism and constructivism. Thus, the educational principles behind conventional learning are not fundamentally different from the principles underpinning computer based learning (Alexander, S., 2001) therefore, any of these theories may be applied in computer based learning.

Behaviourism

The first of the psychocognitive theories is behaviourism which embodies a model of the learner as a solitary driver for understanding (Jones, A. and Mercer, N., 1993) and the acquisition of knowledge as an abstract platonic form. Behaviourism requires subject matter to be analysed as specific associations, expressed as behavioural objectives. This kind of analysis was developed by Gagné (1985) into an instructional task analysis system of discriminations, classifications and response sequences. Instructional Systems Design (ISD) may be seen as one of the pedagogies derived from behaviourism by offering guidelines and procedures for the decomposition of complex tasks into learning hierarchies and detailed prescriptions for the design of instructional programmes based on such hierarchies. Also Saettler (1990) identified the impact of behaviourism on educational technology with areas such as computer-assisted learning and the programmed instruction movement.

Cognitivism

In response, the cognitive theory emerged. Although it accepts behaviouristic concepts, cognitivism views learning as involving the acquisition or reorganisation of the cognitive structures through which, students process and store information (Ravenscroft, A., 2001). Therefore this approach provided a basis for analysing concepts and procedures of subject matter curricula in terms of information structures, and gave rise to new approaches to pedagogy. However, as in behaviourism knowledge is assumed to be provided by the teaching and learning context and the student's role is to acquire it. Within this broad perspective, particular sub-areas of cognitive research can be highlighted as particularly influential (e.g. metacognitive processes, mental models, schema theory, and information processing theories of problem solving and reasoning). The influence of cognitive science on instructional design is evidenced by the computer tutors developed by Anderson *et al.* (1995) which are based on the 'expertise' view of learning.

Constructivism

Constructivism is a perspective which is becoming influential in shaping emerging practice in the use of ICTs (Levy, P. and Fowell, S., 1999). According to the constructivist theory, knowledge is being actively constructed by the individual and knowing is an adaptive process, which organises the individual's experiential world:

> "*Learning is a constructive process in which the learner is building an internal representation of knowledge, a personal interpretation of experience. This representation is constantly open to change, its structure and linkages forming the foundation to which other knowledge structures are appended. Learning is an active process in which meaning is developed on the basis of experience.*"(Bednar, 1992)

The above definition does not consider the learner as a controlled respondent to stimuli as in the behaviourist approach but as "already a scientist" [28] who actively constructs knowing while trying to make sense of the world through personal experiences, goals, curiosities and beliefs. Constructivists therefore, emphasise the need to engage with the connections between concepts and contexts, through participation in authentic activities in contexts which retain complexity (Levy, P. and Fowell, S., 1999). Authentic learning occurs from engaging in real life complexities and occurrences where the individual is an active processor of information through interaction with rich learning environments allowing students to develop, compare, and understand multiple perspectives on an issue.

This need for encouraging multiple representations of knowledge from different conceptual and case perspectives suggests that different teaching strategies may be adopted to provide support for learners to develop their capacity for self-management and other skills needed to become 'intentional' lifelong learners. The adoption of these different teaching strategies creates learning environments that Granbinger and Dunlap (1995) term Rich Environments for Active Learning (REALs). REALS promote the need for learners to: identify personal learning strengths and weaknesses; set goals; make and implement plans; manage time effectively; develop metacognitive (reflexive) awareness; and revise plans and actions based on that awareness. More broadly, Grabinger and Dunlap suggest that learners need opportunities to evaluate their own learning and learning strategies by focusing to a wide range of issues related to "content, process, and tools and resources" (Granbinger, S. and Dunlap, J., 1995).

Constructivist perspectives on learning exist across a wide spectrum, embracing more individual-cognitivist and more social constructivist epistemologies (Levy, P., 2006). Cobb (1994), Duffy and Cunningham (1996) distinguish between cognitive constructivism and social constructivism. The former tend to draw insight from Piaget and focus on individual constructions of knowledge discovered in interaction with the environment and the latter strand of constructivism is derived from the Vygotskian approach and views learning as connection with, and appropriation from, the sociocultural context within which individuals are immersed (Cobb, P., 1994). The importance of social constructivism for e-learning is that it offers the potential for collaboration and provides the learner to obtain alternative perspectives on issues and offer personal insights; in effect, to engage in meaning making and knowledge negotiation (Duffy, T. and Cunningham, D., 1996). In a setting of collaborative learning, students may criticise their own and other students' contributions, may ask for explanations and may give counter arguments and, in this way, students will stimulate themselves and other students. (McConnell, D., 2000) presents a detailed exploration of collaborative learning). On the other hand cognitive constructivists focus on making learning more relevant, building on student prior knowledge, posing contradictions, and addressing misconceptions. Across both viewpoints, constructivist educational practices and orientations emphasise active, generative learning, with curricula where teachers continue to perform a critical learning function as learning consultants and guides.

Constructionism, Instructionism and AI in Education

It is known that most computer Based Learning systems, such as tutorial systems, drill-and-practice programmes, simulations and mind tool, basically follow two pedagogical methods for teaching and learning:

Instructionism: The learner is seen as a passive human being, who can absorb much information given by the instructor or instructional media and translate it into his/her knowledge. A learning system responds acceptably with respect to some performance criteria within a time interval following a change in its environment.

Constructionism: The learner actively constructs his/her knowledge by gathering information from his/her surroundings and combining it with his/her previous knowledge. Learning is a piecewise refinement of schema due to encoding and discovering new chunks of knowledge.

One of the weaknesses of the instructionism method is that there are discrepancies between the concepts that the learners absorb and the contexts or situations where those concepts may be applied. In general, instructionism based systems can only cover a limited level of information processing. On the other hand, constructionism based systems may provide learning environments where the learners interact not only with the tutorial system but also with many other tools and facilities to do their tasks or to solve their problems. At their own wish, learners may also get some guidance or advice from a tutor, who can a human or from other components of the system. In general, constructionism based systems allow learners to apply a learning style that is directed by their particular goals.

Even though constructionism based systems promise a better understanding of learning materials to learners, they must acquire certain learning skills before this promise can be fulfilled. Learners must be able to define their own goals. Furthermore, they have to be able to direct, plan and monitor their learning activities. In short, learners must have a "self directed" capability. Such a capability needs to be developed and a Computer Based Learning Environment may be designed, in addition, to help them to understand the learning materials. Constructivism and Constructionism are relatively new ideas in the field of learning. These ideas were presented by Papert (1980) as alternatives to Instructionism, the dominant learning method. Papert described constructivism and constructionism and the difference between them as follows:

> "The word with the **v** express the theory that knowledge is built by the learner, not supplied by the teacher. The word with the **n** express the further idea that this happens felicitously when the learner is engaged in the construction of something external or at least sharable...a sand castle, a machine, a computer programme, a book."

Constructivism is therefore the theory where the new knowledge is reached by the understanding and appreciation in a context that one builds oneself. One makes ideas about the world, as opposed to getting ideas about it. When one encounters a new idea, one tries to relate a knowledge already acquired. Traditional teaching methods provide large amounts of knowledge for students to memorize, hoping that learning will come about, as opposed to actually encouraging students to think for themselves as they learn. Constructionism is the practical manifestation of constructivism. Constructionism actually involves two instances of construction in a student, the construction of ideas in the student's mind and the actual real world construction of personally meaningful objects. A constructionist environment could therefore be imagined as:

> "A place where learners work together and support each other's work as they use a variety of tools and information resources in their guided pursuit of learning goals and problem-solving activities."

In the heated debate between learning by construction versus instruction, it is easy to overlook that the disagreement has an empirical base. The central disagreement concerns the person in the best position to make key decisions needed to promote learning. A knowledgeable teacher (automated or otherwise) would be essential to choose appropriate tasks, to provide rich and individualized feedback and to situate learning in automatic tasks. Students working with tools that act as intelligent cognitive amplifiers and in a supportive context that includes peers and mentors-make these decisions themselves. The concern centers on the students' possibilities to generate better feedback for learning than that of a tutor in rich but passive environments or if the students are in a better position to know what information they need for learning than the teacher is.

To clarify the above concerns, several research strategies are feasible. One pragmatic approach is to push the extreme alternatives as far as they would go. For Intelligent Tutoring System (ITS), thios means watching the functions of human tutors that can be usefully automated and assessing the quality of student learning they engender. The central question is about the possibility of developing computer-based agents that are able to suggest interesting tasks at the edge of students' skills or agents that are able to coach students and provide adequate feedback. If this were possible, the question turns into the development of agents for specific subjects and topics of learning and also into the quality of learning, that is, the skills and depth of understanding.

By the same token, pushing the Individualized Learning Environment (ILE) alternative as far as it will go means developing increasingly effective empowering tools and technologies for learning, embedding them in congenial learning environments and demonstrating the efficiency of largely self-guided or inquiry-based learning. At this point, the doubts turn to:

- How dramatically can such ILE magnify self-directed learning skills?
- How crucial for learning is the support of peers, mentors and the broader culture of learning?
- What quality of learning do such highly student-controlled environments yield?
- Do students acquire ideas inefficiently because their searches too often just wander?
- Do they develop a deeper conceptual understanding of ideas and of inquiry itself?

Research in human tutoring and the increasing popularity of mixed-initiative tutoring systems suggests that the best learning environments will be completely controlled neither by students not by tutors. The most effective learning environments include a mix of direct teaching, more passive support for learning, together with substantial student choice. For example, in studies of inquiry-based tutoring by humans noticed that even teachers experienced in orchestrating student-centered inquiries, often interpolated bouts of lecture and tutor-directed coaching. However, active roles in learning are typically associated with mentors, co-workers and peers, who engage learners in rich dialogues. In those environments, the role of technology is largely to provide a useful collection of tools that can amplify, enhance or even transform the nature of those dialogues where learning takes place.

The constructionist approach imposes an external reality onto the learner where the teacher presents the knowledge-determined by specified objectives. The constructivist approach views learning as being constructed by a learner from his/her own perceptions and interpretations and of the external world. The learner is actively involved in the process by reflection on information and creating his/her own learning environment and knowledge base. Teachers should change their role from instructor to facilitator. From a methodological point of view, the relationship between constructivism and instructionism should not be based upon the format "either-or" but rather upon the "and-and" format. This means that a balance between those two approaches should be found. A multimedia programme should ensure opportunities for both constructivistic and instructionistic activities. The focus of control should be imposed both on the system (instructionism) and on the learner (constructivism).

Need to Facilitate Active Learning: A Solution

In the conventional teaching format, instruction is viewed as a process of transmission (Wheatley, 1991). In this viewpoint, ideas and thoughts are communicated in the sense that meaning is packaged into words and "sent" to another who unpacks the meaning from the sentences. Here the learner is like a sponge. This passive view of learning is one of the major causes of turning students into memorizers and poor problem-solvers. According to Wheatley (1991)

> The workplace metaphor seems to describe activities in many classrooms. Students are engaged in exchanging performances for grades, much as a worker's reward depends on their productivity. Students are "paid" for their products (assignments, tests) with praise and grades.... Learning is not a goal of such a work oriented environment, learning is a by-product of the "work" if it happens at all.

Current research in cognitive science is changing our view of how people learn. As Resnick (1983) noted, in the last few years a new consensus on the nature of learning has begun to emerge. She further noted that "This emerging conception of learning has a direct bearing on how ... science ... can be taught most effectively".

Resnick (1983) described the evolving model of the learner in terms of a series of propositions. (1) Learners do not passively receive knowledge but rather actively build (construct) it. That is, as much as we would like to, we cannot put ideas in student's heads, they will and must construct their own meaning. (2) To understand something is to know relationships. Human knowledge is stored in clusters and organized into schemata that people use both to interpret familiar situations and to reason about new ones. Bits of information isolated from these structures are forgotten or become inaccessible to memory. (3) All learning depends on prior knowledge. Learners try to link new information to what they already know in order to interpret the new material in terms of established schemata. (4) Successful problem-solving requires a substantial amount of qualitative reasoning. Good problem-solvers do not rush into applying a formula or an equation. Instead, they try to understand the problem situation; they consider alternative representations and relations among the variables. Only when they are satisfied that they understand the situation and all the variables in it in a qualitative way do they start to quantify it.

From these findings it can be argued that active forms of learning can provide a solution to learning a non-integrated knowledge base. Active learning can also promote the acquisition of problem-solving skills. But active learning requires the role of the teacher to be radically changed. Here the teacher should create an environment that encourages students to take responsibility for their own learning (Michael & Modell, 1993). This environment should be cooperative rather than competitive and here the teacher should be a *facilitator* rather than a transmitter of knowledge (Wheatley, 1991). Teachers also need to focus on the qualitative aspects of the problem situation (Resnick, 1983).

Tutoring: A Method of Facilitating Active Learning

One-on-one tutoring is a method that facilitates active learning in the student. In this method the student and the tutor collaborate in the process of instruction (Goodyear, 1991). Here the tutor provides individualized instruction and attention to the student (Wenger, 1987). Studies have shown that one-on-one tutoring is one of the most effective educational delivery methods (Bloom, 1984; Anderson *et al.*, 1985; Woolf, 1986; Cohen *et al.*, 1982). A study by Bloom (1984) shows that students involved in one-on-one tutoring seem to perform at about the 98th percentile as compared with students who are traditionally trained (via the group instruction method). Hence, if our educational system adopts tutoring as the educational delivery method then students will be active while learning. This would probably help them to build coherent models of domain from the subject matter content, which would not only help to enhance their understanding but also help to develop their problem-solving skills. So if tutoring is so advantageous why are students still learning in groups via the traditional classroom teaching method? As Galdes (1990) noted that "The answer is simple—there just aren't enough skilled human tutors to do all of the necessary tutoring".

Why Tutoring is Effective?

One vision of artificial intelligence and education is to produce a "teacher for every student" or a "community of teachers for every student." This vision includes making learning a social activity, accepting multimodal input from students (handwriting, speech, facial expression, body language) and supporting multiple teaching strategies (collaboration, inquiry, and dialogue).

We present several vignettes of successful intelligent tutors in use. The first is a child reading text from a screen who comes across an unfamiliar word. She speaks it into a microphone and doesn't have to worry about a teacher's disapproval if he/she says it wrong. The tutor might not interrupt the student, yet at the end of the sentence it provides her the correct pronunciation (Mostow and Beck, 2003). Now we shift to a classroom at a medical school. First-year students are learning how the barometric (blood pressure) response works. Their conversation with a computer tutor does not involve a microphone or avatar, yet they discuss the qualitative analysis of a cardio physiological feedback system and the tutor understands their short answers (Freedman and Evens, 1997). Consider the likely scenarios when such intelligent tutors are available any time, from any place, and on any topic. Student privacy will be critical and a heavily protected portfolio for each student, including grades, learning level, past activities, and special needs will be maintained.

Intelligent Tutors Know Individual Student Differences

Tutors have knowledge of each student's background, learning style, and current needs and choose multimedia material at the proper teaching level and style. For example, some students solve fraction problems while learning about endangered species; premed students practice fundamental procedures for cardiac arrest; and legal students argue points against a tutor that role-plays as a prosecutor.

Such systems infer student emotion and leverage knowledge to increase performance. They might determine each student's affective state and then respond appropriately to student emotion. Systems recognize a frustrated student (based on facial images, posture detectors, and conductance sensors) and respond in a supportive way with an animated agent that uses appropriate head and body gestures to express caring behaviour. Such systems can also recognize bored students (based on slow response and lack of engagement) and suggest more challenging problems.

Intelligent tutors work with students who have various abilities. If a student has dyslexia, the tutor might note that he is disorganized, unable to plan, poorly motivated, and not confident. For students who react well to spoken text messages, natural language techniques simplify the tutor's responses until the student exhibits confidence and sufficient background knowledge. During each interaction, the tutor updates its model of presumed student knowledge and current misconceptions.

Students Work Independently or in Teams

Groups of learners, separated in space and time, collaborate on open-ended problems, generate writing or musical compositions, and are generally in control of their own learning. In team activities, they work with remote partners, explaining their reasoning and offering suggestions. They continue learning as long as they are engaged in productive activities. Teachers easily modify topics, reproduce tutors, at an infinitesimal cost to students and schools and have detailed records of student performance.

Intelligent Tutors Know How to Teach

Academic material stored in intelligent systems is not just data about a topic (i.e., questions and answers about facts and procedures). Rather, such software contains qualitative models of each domain to be taught, including objects and processes that characterize trends and causal relations among topics. Each model also reasons about knowledge in the domain, follows a student's reasoning about that knowledge, engages in discussions, and answers questions on various topics. New tutors are easily built and added onto existing tutors, thus augmenting a system's teaching ability. Tutors store teaching methods and processes (e.g., strategies for presenting topics, feedback, and assessment). This knowledge contains rules about how outstanding teachers behave and teaching strategies suggested by learning theories.

These scenarios describe visions of fully developed, intelligent instructional software. Every feature described above exists in existing intelligent tutors. Some tutors are used in classrooms in several instructional forms (simulations, games, open-learning environments), teaching concepts and procedures from several disciplines (physics, cardiac disease, art history).

Necessary Hardware and Software

Students work on personal computers or with sophisticated servers managed within a school district. Using high-speed Internet connections, they explore topics in any order and are supported in their different learning styles (e.g., as holists and serialists) (Pask, 1976; Self, 1985). They ask questions (perhaps in spoken language), practice fundamental skills, and move to new topics based on their interests and abilities. Tutors generate natural language responses. Metacognitive strategies identify each student's learning strengths (e.g., the student requests hints and knows how to self-explain new topics).

These educational scenarios are not just fixes or add-ons to education. They may challenge and possibly threaten existing teaching and learning practices by suggesting new ways to learn and offering new support for students to acquire knowledge (McArthur *et al.*, 1994). Technology provides individualized attention and augments a teacher's ability to respond. It helps lifelong learners who are daily called on to integrate and absorb vast amounts of knowledge and to communicate with multitudes of people. The educational community needs to think hard about its mission and its organization:

School Structure: What happens to school structures (temporal and physical) once students choose what and when to study and work on projects by themselves or with remote teammates independent of time and physical structure?

Teachers and Administrators: How do teachers and administrators react when their role changes from that of lecturer/source to coach/guide?

Classrooms: What happens to lectures and structured classrooms when teachers and students freely select online modules? What is the impact once teachers reproduce tutors at will and at infinitesimal cost?

Student Privacy: How can students' privacy be protected once records (academic and emotional) are maintained and available over the Internet?

> We are not going to succeed [in education] unless we really turn the problem... around and first specify the kinds of things students ought to be doing: what are the cost-effective and time-effective ways by which students can proceed to learn. We need to carry out the analysis that is required to understand what they have to do—what activities will produce the learning—and then ask ourselves how the technology can help us do that. Herbert A. Simon (1997)

Effective Teaching Methods

For hundreds of years, the predominant forms of teaching have included books, classrooms, and lectures. Scholars and teachers present information carefully organized into digestible packages; passive students receive this information and work in isolation to learn from fixed assignments stored in old curricula. These passive methods suggest that a student's task is to absorb explicit concepts and exhibit this understanding in largely factual and definition-based multiple-choice examinations. In this approach, teachers in the classroom typically ask 95 per cent of the questions, requiring short answers or problem-solving activities (Graesser and Person, 1994; Hmlo-Silver, 2002).

These teaching approaches are not very effective (Waterman *et al.*, 1993); they have succeeded only with the top fourth of each class, often motivated and gifted students. Student achievement in classroom instruction (1:30 teacher/student ratio) was found to differ from achievement based on individual tutoring (1:1 teacher/student ratio) by about two standard deviations (Bloom, 1984). That is, the typical bell curve of achievement was centered on the 50th percentile for traditional lecture-based teaching and was raised to the 98th percentile by one-to-one human teachers (see Figure 7.1).

Other effective teaching methods (e.g., *collaboration, inquiry*, and *teaching meta-cognition*) actively engage students (including the disadvantaged, financially insecure, and unmotivated) to create their own learning. However, these methods are nearly impossible to implement in classrooms without technology, as they are so time and resource intensive. For example, one-to-one tutoring (adapting teaching to each learner's needs) requires one teacher for each student (Bloom, 1984). Collaboration (facilitating

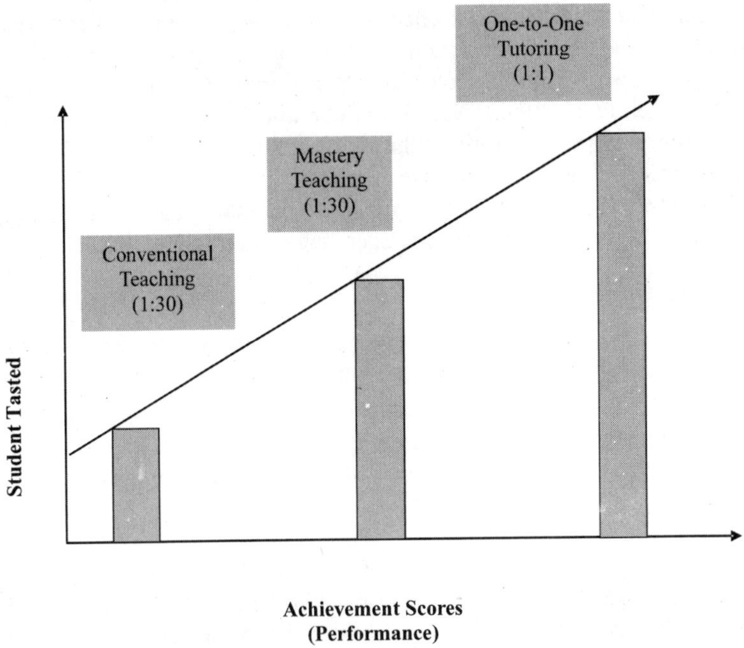

Figure 7.1: Advantages of one-to-one tutoring (Adapted from Bloom, 1984)

students to work in groups and explain their work to each other) often results in students learning more than the best student in the group but requires individual attention for each group of one to three students. Inquiry learning (supporting students to ask their own questions, generate research hypotheses, and collect data) is powerful because students are engaged in authentic and active work and use information in a variety of ways. However, inquiry learning requires teachers to guide students in asking their own questions and gathering and analyzing evidence. Teaching about *metacognitive skills* (students focus on their own learning approaches, e.g., asking for hints, self-explanation) sometimes results in more effective learning, yet requires teachers to individually guide each student. Most schools in most disciplines cannot provide this individual attention, although many nations support one teacher for every student in high-risk professions (airplane pilots or controlling nuclear reactors) or in the arts (music or painting).

One example of ineffective teaching methods is the tradition of only transmitting facts to students. Understanding the components and data of a discipline is not as effective as understanding its structure. This distinction is particularly true in fields such as science, mathematics, and engineering, where students need to know the processes by which the discipline's claims are generated, evaluated, and revised.

Information technology is effective in teaching and improves productivity in industry and the military. Intelligent tutors produce the same improvements as one-to-one tutoring and effectively reduce learning time by one-third to one-half (Regian *et al.*, 1996). Recall that one-to-one human tutoring increases classroom performance to around the 98th percentile (Bloom, 1984). Intelligent tutors are 30 per cent more effective than traditional instruction (Fletcher, 1995; Regian *et al.*, 1996), and networked versions reduce the need for training support personnel by about 70 per cent and operating costs by about 92 per cent.

Computers in Education

Computers have been used in education since 1959 when PLATO was created at the University of Illinois (Molnar, 1990; Office of Technology Assessment [OTA], 1982). This several thousand-terminal system served elementary school, undergraduate, and community college students. In 1963, another system used a drill-and-practice, self-paced programme in mathematics and reading, thus allowing students to take a more active role in the learning process (Suppes, 1981).

The programming language LOGO was developed in the early 1970s to encourage students to think rigorously about mathematics, not by teaching facts and rules but by supporting the use of mathematics to build meaningful products, such as drawings and processes (Papert, 1980). Because LOGO was user-friendly, students could easily express procedures for simple tasks. It was used in various "micro-world" environments, including robotic building sets (Lego Mindstorms) that could be used to invent robotics solutions, trucks, spaceships, and mobile artifacts. In building computer-driven LOGO inventions, students defined a problem and developed the skills needed to solve it.

Other engaging uses of computers in education involved project-oriented, case-based, and inquiry-oriented education. For example, the National Geographic Kids Network invited students to measure the quality of their regional water and its relationship to acid rain (Tinker, 1997). Students in more than 10,000 elementary schools at 80 sites in 30 countries gathered data, analyzed trends, and communicated by e-mail with each other and with practicing scientists. Student results were combined with national and international results, leading to the discovery that school drinking water and air pollution standards were not being met. The network provided low-cost devices for measuring ozone, soil moisture, and ultraviolet radiation to calibrate the effects of global warming. In 1991, students measured air and soil temperatures, precipitation, bird and insect presence, and stages of plant growth, thus linking meteorological, physical, and biological observations to a major seasonal event and creating a "snapshot" of the planet. Most teachers using KidsNet (> 90%) reported that it significantly increased students ' interest in science and that their classes spent almost twice as much time on science than before.

In another example, the Learning Network was used by 35,000 kids from

23 nations to explore social studies and literature issues. It was run by AT & T and managed by state and grassroots organizations.

These projects have powerful significance. Networks permit all students to participate in experiments on socially significant scientific problems and to work with real scientists (Molnar, 1990). Students create maps of a holistic phenomenon drawn from a mosaic of local measurements. Teachers' roles change, and they act as consultants rather than as leaders.

Computer-based education has been well documented to improve learning at the elementary, secondary, higher-, and adult-education levels. A meta-analysis of several hundred well-controlled studies showed that student scores increased by 10 per cent to 20 per cent, the time to achieve goals decreased by one-third, and class performance improved by about one-half standard deviation (Kulik and Kulik, 1991).

However, these early computer-based instructional systems had several drawbacks.

Many systems used *frame-based* methods, in which every page, computer response, and sequence of topics was predefined by the author and presented to students in lockstep fashion. Directed learning environments, including tutorials, hypermedia, and tests, typically presented material in careful sequences to elicit correct learner action (Alessi and Trollip, 2000).

In some systems, computer responses were similar for every student, no matter the student's performance, and help was provided as a pre-worded, non-customized response. For each student and every situation, "optimal" learning sequences were built in. This approach is similar to playing cops and robbers with predefined paths for chasing robbers. No matter what the robber does, the law enforcer runs down a preset list of streets and crosses specified corners. This model has limited impact; it clearly fails to capture the one-on-one approach of master human teachers who remain opportunistic, dynamically changing topics and teaching methods based on student progress and performance.

Nonetheless, many educational simulations were clearly effective. They allowed students to enter new parameters, watch changing features, start or stop simulations, or change the levels of difficulty, as exemplified by SimCity and SimArt (released by Electronic Arts in 1998) and BioLab Frog (released by Pierian Spring Software in 2000). However, if a student's concept of the modeled interaction differed from that of the author, the student could not ask questions, unless those questions were already programmed into the environment. Students received preformatted responses independent of their current situation or knowledge. They watched the simulation, but typically could not change its nature or learn why the simulation worked as it did.

Other early systems used open-ended learning environments (OLE) that allowed students to experiment, interpret, and learn from errors and to revise their knowledge; these included Jasper Woodbury (Vanderbuilt, Cognition and Technology Group, 1997), EarthTrails (Iowa Public Television, 1997), and Geometer's Sketchpad (Key Curriculum Press, 1995). These systems often provided excellent tools (drawing, measuring, calculating), but many OLEs were very directed and not adaptable. The system pursued a list of problems or cases in a fixed order, and students could not ask questions or alter the programme's order. Using these systems required classroom teachers to be trained and remain as central guides during the classroom experience. Teachers divided tasks among collaborative learners and decided which steps each group would tackle and which parameters to enter. OLEs such as Rainforest Researchers or Geography Search (Tom Snyder Productions, 1998, 1995) supported team activities, but did not interact individually with students to help them manage the environment. Neither did they support group creation, group dynamics, role-playing, or planning the next strategy.

Intelligent Tutors: The Formative Years

The field of artificial intelligence and education was established in the 1970s by a dozen leaders, including John Self (1974, 1977, 1985), Jaime Carbonell (1970a, 1970b), and William Clancey (1979). The earliest intelligent tutor was implemented in the 1970 Ph.D. thesis of Jaime Carbonell, who developed Scholar, a system that invited students to explore geographical features of South America. This system differed from traditional computer-based instruction in that it generated individual responses to students' statements by traversing a semantic network of geography knowledge.

The first intelligent tutor based on an expert system was GUIDON developed by William Clancey (Clancey, 1979, 1987). This system was named GUIDON, was also the first to teach medical knowledge. Another knowledge representation, NEOMYCIN, was later designed for use in GUIDON 2 (Clancey and Letsinger, 1981). The GUIDON project became relevant in developing future medical tutors (Crowley *et al.*, 2003) because of key insights: the need to represent implicit knowledge, and the challenges of creating a knowledge representation sufficiently large, complex, and valid to help students learn real medical tasks.

In 1988, Claude Frasson at the University of Montreal, Canada, organized the first conference of the field. The International Conference of Intelligent Tutoring Systems (ITS) provided a forum for researchers and practitioners to exchange ideas, experiments, and techniques in all areas of computer science and human learning. These ITS conferences continued every few years for 20 years under the leadership of Claude Frasson. The first conference of the fledgling field of artificial intelligence and education (AIED), AIED93, was held in Edinburgh, United Kingdom, with Helen Pain as the organizing committee chair. AIED95 was held in Washington, with Jim Greer as the programme committee chair, and AIED, in Osaka directed by Riichiro Mizoguchi. The conference goals are to advance research and development; to support a community from computer science, education, and psychology; and to promote the rigorous research and development of interactive and adaptive learning environments.

Learning Theories as the Basis of Tutor Development

Philosophers, psychologists, and researchers have postulated theories about human learning, indicating a variety of components and processes (Bruner, 1986, 1990; Lave and Wenger, 1991; Piaget and Inhelder, 1969). However, no single teaching environment has been shown to be appropriate for a majority of people or even a majority of domains, in part because human learning is imperfectly understood.

Several principles of human learning have remained fairly consistent. First, students need to be involved, engaged, and active in authentic and challenging learning. Learning is most effective when students are motivated to learn. Page turning, flashy graphics, and simulations are not enough; the experience must be authentic and relevant (Schank, 1994; Woolf and Hall, 1995). Systems that simply present text, graphics, or multimedia often encourage passive learning and provide little learning advantage. Students do not learn by simply pressing buttons, even if the new pages contain animations, images, sounds, or video. Exercises should preferably involve students in the material and be adaptable to different learning needs. A second consistent learning principle is that people learn at different rates and in different ways (Vygotsky, 1978). No one method works for all people. Students seem to learn more effectively and efficiently when material is customized and individualized. Learning approaches should be adapted to learners and their situations, yet it is still not known exactly which materials should be provided to which students.

These learning principles have not always been followed in the three main types of learning theories used in teaching environments: behaviourism, cognitive science, and constructivism. Affiliations to these learning principles among psychologists, educators, and philosophers have changed several times during the 20th century (Alessi and Trollip, 2000):

Behaviourism maintains that learning is a set of changes created in an individual as a function of events in the environment. Thus, learning is a process of memorizing, demonstrating, and imitating. The teaching implication is that learners should be provided with explicit and planned stimuli. Computer instruction based on this principle typically presents pages of text and graphics, carefully arranged, planned, and controlled by the computer, not the learner. Such learning strategies target primarily memory tasks and recall. The teacher or computer is the source of knowledge and often the lecturer.

Cognitive Science holds that learning is influenced by unobservable and internal constructs; e.g., memory, motivation, perception, attention, and metacognitive skills. Computer instruction based on this principle considers the effects of attention and perception and is based on individual learning needs and differences. Here the computational focus is on screen design and interactions in which learners share control with computers. The primary results are active learning, transfer of learning, comprehension, and metacognitive skills, with the teacher as coach, facilitator, and partner.

Constructivism claims that individuals interpret and construct the world in their own way. Thus, learning is an individual process manipulating and interpreting the surrounding world. In the extreme, this view implies that reality is constructed by each individual. The implication for teaching is to focus on student learning, not on teaching, and on the actions of learners rather than those of teachers. The primary target of this strategy is supporting a process of construction for individual students.

These paradigms are typically embraced simultaneously by developers of online learning, because authors recognize that each principle contains a bit of truth about learning. Thus, rather than build a pure discovery environment in which students freely explore activities with no outside influence (radical constructivism), developers build modified constructivist environments that guide and structure discovery environments.

A behaviourist philosophy has been built into many CAI systems. A window of material (text, graph, animation) is presented to students who are then asked questions, followed by new windows of material. Such systems have been used for more than 30 years in schools, industry, and the military and are fully described in other books. We do not discuss these systems in this book. *Cognitive learning* theory is the foundation of several intelligent instructional systems (cognitive tutors, model tracing tutors) described in this book. This theory has been used as the basis of some of the most successful intelligent tutors, in which mental processes are first identified and knowledge transferred to learners in the most efficient, effective manner possible. A constructivist philosophy has been applied in classrooms to teaching practice and curriculum design, but few intelligent tutors fully implement the constructivist perspective.

Constructivist Teaching Methods

The last learning theory, *constructivist teaching*, is the most difficult to implement in a classroom or computer, but it may have the greatest potential to enhance human learning, particularly through methods based on one-to-one, inquiry, apprenticeship, and collaboration. Inquiry learning is seen as central to developing critical thinking, problem solving, and reasoning (Goldman, 1992; Scardamalia *et al.*, 1989; Slavin, 1990b; Kuhn 1970; Newman *et al.*, 1989). Apprenticeship and collaboration have been adjuncts to learning for centuries. These methods challenge existing educational practice (class and lecture based), which is organized by time and place and does not permit students to freely query processes, make mistakes, or monitor their own processes (Cummins, 1994; O'Neil and Gomex, 1994; Slavin, 1990b). In constructivist methods, teams of students might work with remote colleagues to pursue independent goals and answer questions that only they may be asking. This approach is difficult to support in classrooms where learning is regimented to physical and temporal blocks, and teachers are responsible for up to 300 students.

Constructivist activities are also expensive in terms of teacher time, resources, and labour, and might require hiring more instructors. Teachers want to use inquiry methods, team learning, or metacognitive skills, but administrators typically cannot provide extra resources, e.g., one teacher for each group of three students. Because student centered methods often require extra class time and attention, they also limit the coverage of content in lectures, further biasing classroom teachers against such methods. Constructivist activities can rarely be employed by teachers without technology mediated environments. Electronic media, on the other hand, is well suited to support and strongly promote constructivist teaching (Table 7.1). Such media supports learning as a unique process for each individual. Students become the focus, reducing the centrality of the teacher. Tutors respond to students and dynamically modify their own reasoning about students' knowledge. One goal of AI and education is to extend constructivist activities to large classrooms and to engage students in critical thinking, collaboration, and their own research.

Table 7.1: Constructivist-Teaching Methods with Classroom and Online Examples

Constructivist Learning Method	*Description and Classroom Example*	*Computational Example*
One-to-one tutoring	Students and teachers enter into a dialogue in which teachers repair student errors; Students discuss their understanding with teachers or older students.	Intelligent tutors generate appropriate problems and hints (e.g., PAT, AnimalWatch).
Case-based inquiry	Students are presented with real-life cases, e.g., a patient's medical symptoms. Learning begins when students hypothesize probable diseases and provide supporting evidence.	Computer-rich interfaces (e.g., Rashi) transparently support the exchange and sharing of information/documents, and encourage students to question processes, make mistakes, and monitor their processes.
Apprenticeship learning	Students practice by studying with an expert. Students are engaged in authentic environments such as a complex piece of machinery.	Computer environments replicate a complex environment (e.g., Sherlock, Steve).
Collaboration	Students work in teams to explain their reasoning about a topic, e.g., why dinosaurs became extinct. They learn how knowledge is generated, evaluated, and revised.	Multiuser environments and computer support for collaborative learning methods (Belvedere) encourage students to work together.

Effective Classroom and Online Environment

The very nature of teaching, learning, and schooling is being reconsidered by educators from preschool to graduate school, based on the demands of a global information society and opportunities provided by electronic media. To fully realize the educational potential of these media, new theoretical frameworks are needed that begin with the premise that proposed computer-mediated learning should keep students engaged, motivated, and active in authentic and challenging work (i.e., moving beyond the "tyranny of the button") (Woolf and Hall, 1995).

This section proposes a brief theoretical framework for building classrooms and online learning environments and uses that framework to evaluate existing environments. Modeled after Bransford (2004), this framework is based on ideas expressed in the National Academy of Sciences report, *How People Learn* (see Bransford *et al.*, 2000b), which suggests that learning environments should be knowledge, student, assessment, and community centered (Table 7.2).

Effective learning environments should be *knowledge-centered* or able to reason about the knowledge of the domain, know what students need to know, and know what they will do when they finish learning. Environments should prioritize important content (rather than present pages of unstructured material) and design learning opportunities based on understanding what students will do at the end of their learning. Many academic departments are renewing their curricula to reflect the fact that many disciplines have become integrated (e.g., biomechanical engineering), many topics cut across disciplines (e.g., renewable energy, computational science, environmental studies), and many students want classes related to current issues (e.g., a course about My DNA and modern applications of genetics).

An obvious example of a knowledge-centered environment is one-to-one human tutoring in which the teacher knows the domain and provides just the knowledge needed by the students. However, traditional lecture-style classrooms often fall short in providing this feature, especially when material is unstructured and unchanged from year to year. Similarly, standard electronic resources (static pages of information, web portals, virtual libraries) fall short as they provide unstructured and non-prioritized information. Students might spend days searching for a single topic on the Internet, which contains all the information potentially available, yet they cannot reliably find what they seek. Efforts to order and structure static material for instruction have great potential.

An effective learning environment should be *student-centered*, or recognize prior and evolving student knowledge. It should understand students' version of the discipline, their evolving knowledge, and should consider their preconceptions, needs strengths, and interests (Bransford, 2004). The basic assumption is that people are not blank slates with respect to goals, opinions, knowledge, and time. The learning environment should Honour student preconceptions and cultural values. This feature is definitely provided by one-to-one human tutoring, because human tutors often organize material and adopt teaching strategies for individual students. The criterion of delivering a student-centered environment is also satisfied by computer tutors that model student knowledge and reason about students ' learning needs before selecting problems or hints, adjusting the dialogue.

Table 7.2: Four Features of Effective Learning Environments and the Lack of Availability of Each Feature

Features of Effective Learning Environments	Knowledge-Centered	Student-Centered	Assessment-Centered	Community-Centered
Books		x	X	X
Lecture-based classrooms		x	X	X
One-to-one human tutoring				Available
Online environments				
Static information (web)	X	x	X	X
Courses/homework		x		Available
Hypermedia		x	X	Available
Virtual/linked laboratories		x	Possible	
Simulations		x	Possible	Available
Intelligent tutors				Available

However, this feature is not provided by most frame-based or directed resources, especially static information on the Internet, which provides the same material to all students. Similarly, other instructional approaches, such as traditional lectures and simulations are typically not student-centered and do not recognize the student's actions, goals, or knowledge.

An effective learning environment should be *assessment-centered*, or make students' thinking visible and allow them to revise their own learning. This feature goes beyond providing tests organized for assessments. Teachers are often forced to choose between assisting students ' development (teaching) and assessing students ' abilities (testing) because of limited classroom time. Formative assessment in an electronic learning environment provides not only feedback for students but also empirical data to teachers, allowing them to assess the effectiveness of the materials and possibly modify their teaching strategy. For example, to help teachers better use their time, a web-based system called ASSISTment integrates assistance and assessment (Feng and Heffernan, 2007; Razzaq *et al.*, 2007). It offeres instruction in 8th and 10th grade mathematics while providing teachers a more detailed evaluation of student abilities than was possible in classrooms. Web-based homework systems assess student activities, broken down by problem, section, topic, or student. Several of these systems have shown powerful learning results, including significant increase in classes ' grades; these include Online web-based learning (OWL) (Mestre *et al.*, 1997), Interactive MultiMedia Exercises (IMMEX) (Stevens and Nadjafi, 1997), and Diagnoser (Hunt and Ministrell, 1994). OWL, which teaches several college level chemistry classes, provides feedback and opportunities for students to receive similar problems with different values or parameters, thus enabling students to improve their skills. Many web-based intelligent tutors provide individual assessment based on student modeling. Laboratory and simulation materials can make a student's thinking visible by indicating correctly accomplished procedures and providing helpful feedback. Such systems might also indicate how learners' knowledge or strategies are inconsistent with that of an expert.

Most classroom learning environments do not provide an assessment-centered environment, primarily because such opportunities require a great deal of teacher effort and time. Some static web-based pages clearly do not satisfy this criterion, nor do typical distance-education courses that simply provide teacher slides or pages of text.

An effective learning environment should also be *community-centered* or help students feel supported to collaborate with peers, ask questions, and receive help (Bransford, 2004). Such communities are provided in only the best classrooms. Many classrooms create an environment in which students are embarrassed to make a mistake. They refuse to "get caught not knowing something."

Some online systems support student, teacher, and researcher communities. The nature of the community, whether or not students feel supported, depends in part on the nature and policy of the community facility. Some communities provide homework help; for example, "Ask Dr. Math" provides answers to mathematics problems (Math Forum, 2008), and "Buzz a tutor" (Renseelear) allows students to contact a human tutor. The quality of a community is very important to its participants, especially if students are contributing (publishing) their own input to a site. People prefer to get to know the participants in an online community before deciding how to frame their own contribution—can they suggest off-the-wall ideas or does this audience require detailed references? As in any physical community, "people-knowledge" and trust are important in defining an online community.

Many distance-education courses and web-based sites require students not only to complete assigned work but also to participate in chat sessions and community-building efforts. Class members may access a chat facility while pursuing static pages, though the static information itself does not provide a community.

The potential for a learning environment to be knowledge-student, assessment, and community centered is greater for computer-and web-based learning environments than for most classrooms. Educational material on the web can be made knowledge-ecentered, possibly the web's greatest advantage. The remainder of this book describes how web materials can be made knowledge-student, and assessment centered.

Computer Science, Psychology and Education

One hallmark of the field of AI and education is using intelligence to reason about teaching and learning. Representing what, when, and how to teach requires grounding from within several academic disciplines, including computer science, psychology, and education.

Many of the methods and tools of computer science, psychology, and education are complementary and collectively supply nearly complete coverage of the field of AI and education (Figure 7.2). *Artificial intelligence* addresses how to reason about intelligence and thus learning. *Psychology*, particularly its subfield *cognitive science*, addresses how people think and learn, and *education* focuses on how to best support teaching. Human learning and teaching are so complex that it is impossible to develop a *computational system* for teaching (the goal of artificial intelligence) that is not also supported by an underlying theory of learning (the goals of education and cognitive science). Thus, fulfilling the goal of developing a computational teaching system seems to require an underlying theory of learning. However, current models of learning are incomplete, and it is unreasonable to put off building these systems until a complete model is available.

Thus, researchers in the field simultaneously pursue major advances in all three areas: learning models, human information processing, and computational systems for teaching. Because computational models must first explore and evaluate alternative theories about learning, a computational model of teaching could provide a first step for a cognitively correct theory of learning. Such a model could also serve as a starting point for empirical studies of teaching and for modifying existing theories of learning. The technological goal of building better intelligent tutors would accept a computational model that produces results, and the cognitive goal would accept any model of human information processing verified by empirical results.

Cognitive science is concerned with understanding human activity during the performance of tasks such as learning. Cognitive modeling in the area of learning has contributed pedagogical and subject-matter theories, theories of learning, instructional design, and enhanced instructional delivery (Anderson *et al.*, 1995). Cognitive science results, including empirical methods, provide a deeper understanding of human cognition, thus tracking human learning and supporting flexible learning. Cognitive scientists often view human reasoning as reflecting an information processing system, and they identify

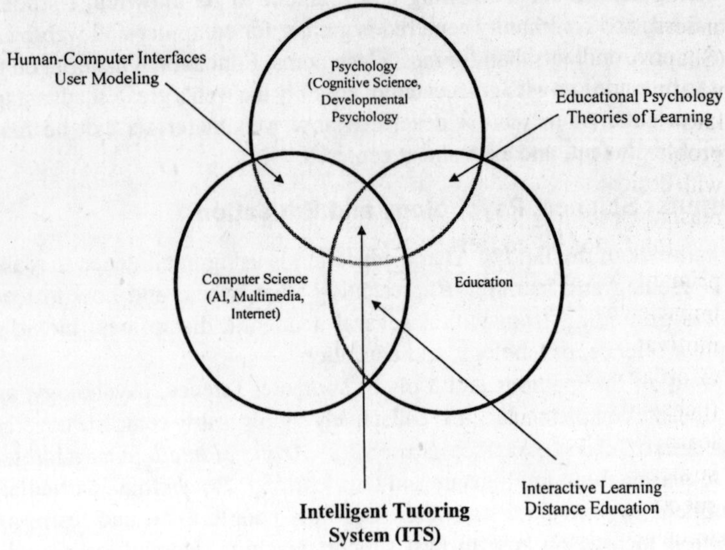

Figure 7.2: The Field of Artificial Intelligence and Education is Grounded in Three Disciplines: Computer Science, Psychology, and Education

initial and final states of learners and the *rules* required to go from one state to another. A typical cognitive science study might assess the depth of learning for alternative teaching methods under controlled conditions (Corbett and Anderson, 1995), study eye movements (Salvucci and Anderson, 2001), or measure the time to learn and error rate (accuracy) of responses made by people with differing abilities and skills (Koedinger and MacLaren, 1997).

Artificial intelligence (AI) is a subfield of computer science concerned with acquiring and manipulating data and knowledge to reproduce intelligent behaviour (Shapiro, 1992). AI is concerned with creating computational models of cognitive activities (speaking, learning, walking, and playing) and replicating commonsense tasks (understanding language, recognizing visual scenes, and summarizing text). AI techniques have been used to perform expert tasks (diagnose diseases), predict events based on past events, plan complex actions, and reason about uncertain events. Teaching systems use inference rules to provide sophisticated feedback, customize a curriculum, or refine remediation. These responses are possible because the inference rules explicitly represent tutoring, student knowledge, and pedagogy, allowing a system to reason about a domain and student knowledge before providing a response. Nonetheless, deep issues remain about AI design and implementation, beginning with the lack of authoring tools (shells and frameworks) similar to those used to build expert system.

Cognitive science and AI are two sides of the same coin; each strives to understand the nature of intelligent action in whatever form it may take (Shapiro, 1992). Cognitive science investigates how intelligent entities, whether human or computer, interact with their environment, acquire knowledge, remember, and use knowledge to make decisions and solve problems. This definition is closely related to that for AI, which is concerned with designing systems that exhibit intelligent characteristics, such as learning, reasoning, solving problems, and understanding language.

Education is concerned with understanding and supporting teaching primarily in schools. It focuses on how people teach and how learning is impacted by communication, course and curriculum design, assessment, and motivation. One long-term goal of education is to produce accessible, affordable, efficient, and effective teaching. Numerous learning theories (behaviourism, constructivism, multiple intelligence) suggest ways that people learn. Within each learning theory, concepts such as memory and learning strategies are addressed differently. Specific theories are often developed for specific domains, such as science education. Education methods include ways to enhance the acquisition, manipulation, and utilization of knowledge and the conditions under which learning occurs. Educators might evaluate characteristics of knowledge retention using cycles of design and testing. They often generate an intervention—a circumstance or environment to support teaching—and then test whether it has a lasting learning effect.

8

History of Intelligent Tutoring System

Computer Assisted Instruction systems have existed as early as 1961 (Bitzer, D.L. and Easley, J.A., 1965). In the decades since, many excellent implementations of CAI systems have been developed (Brusilovsky, P., 2004; Burns, H. & Capps, C., 1998; Alexandra C. & Toshio O., 2000; Graesser, A. *et al.*, 2001; Libbrecht, P. *et al.*, 2001; Prentzas, J. *et al.*, 2001; Sleeman, D. and Brown, J.S., 1982 and Hai Zhuge and Yanyan Li., 2004). These systems have gone under the names Computer Assisted Instruction, Computer Aided Learning, Intelligent Tutoring Systems, eLearning Systems, Web-Based Education, Educational Hypermedia and others. Soon after the earliest use of computers in education, the practice was referred to as Computer Assisted Instruction in the US and Computer Aided Learning in Europe. As developments in AI, multimedia, hypermedia and communications technologies improved, projects were started in order to take advantage of these advancements in the context of CAI and CAL.

A noteworthy improvement in these systems was the addition of a Student Model which represents the knowledge and learning process of the student based on an analysis of the student's behaviour, especially in terms of the correctness of answers given by students during quiz sessions. The system can use this model to adapt the instruction to the student's needs. Systems that make use of a student model to determine which questions should be asked, are called Intelligent Tutoring Systems (ITS), or generally, Intelligent Computer Assisted Instruction.

Another improvement distinctive of Intelligent Computer Assisted Instruction is the inclusion of an expert system containing facts and rules regarding the domain being learned. This expert system allows for a much larger set of questions that may be asked of the student, as these questions can be formulated rather than directly authored. There is still a moderate amount of work involved in tracing "paths" through the knowledge content of the expert system, but many toolkits have been developed to assist this process (Aleven, 2006). Some of these ICAI systems also store facts and rules about various learning strategies of students so that the system can adapt its presentation of the material and questions to better suit the learner. An architecture for such a system, taken from (Lelouche, R., 1998), can be found in Figure 8.1.

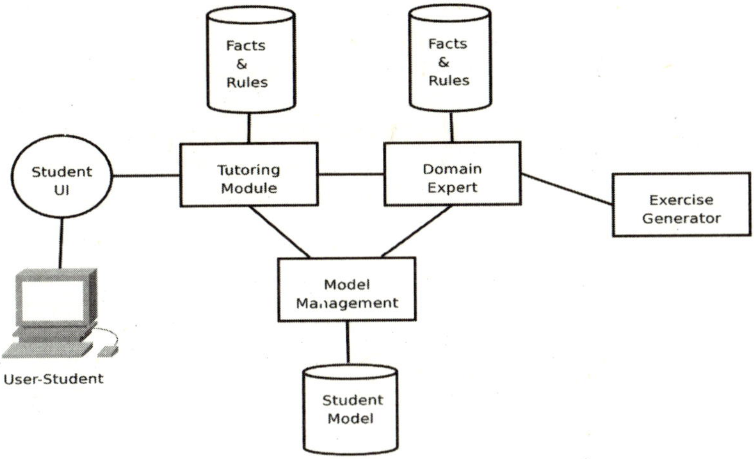

Figure 8.1: An Example Architecture for an Intelligent Computer Assisted Instruction System

Advances in hypermedia and network communications have led to another improvement in Computer Assisted Instruction that of providing instructional resources through the World Wide Web (Prentzas, J. *et al.*, 2001 and Brusilovsky, P. *et al.*, 1998). These systems, called eLearning systems or Web-Based Education systems, take advantage of the increasing availability of the WWW to make course-related resources available to students from any internet-connected computer at any time of the day. This has had far-reaching impact on Distance Education and has in some ways decreased the burden on instructors and teaching assistants.

The sophistication of these systems ranges from simply storing course material to presenting an interface tailored especially to the student using it. Many of the less sophisticated of these systems are based on the Content Management Systems popular in business environments and have been termed Learning Management Systems (LMS). Although they offer a convenient interface for storing and retrieving class materials, they do not inherently have any learning-related functionality. An aspect of the World Wide Web, and more specially hypertext, the predominant format for documents, is the nature of linking the contents of one document to the location of another WWW document. This simple concept has created an entire area of research in Hypermedia. Combining this idea with that of a user model gives rise to Adaptive.

Hypermedia, wherein hypertext links are shown or hidden (adaptive navigation) or their colour/size changed (adaptive presentation) based on user preferences determined from the user's previous navigation behaviour. When the user model is replaced or supplemented with a student model, as in Adaptive Educational Hypermedia (Brusilovsky, P., 1996), the student is presented with course material appropriate to their level of knowledge and they avoid potentially getting lost or confused in the face of too much learning material (Brusilovsky, P. and Pesin, L., 1998). This is especially valuable in student-directed learning, as well as in the context of University courses.

Research in this area has also explored the use of dialogue in Intelligent Computer Assisted Instruction systems (VanLehn, K., 1998 and Graesser, A. *et al.*, 2001). This may allow for more direct observation of the student's knowledge, especially if semantic and pragmatic aspects of the student's writings are interpreted. While all of these systems certainly have their benefits, they are typically used outside of the traditional lecture context of University courses. Furthermore, there are activities in the normal workflow of this lecture environment, namely student note-taking, that produce artifacts which such Intelligent Computer Assisted Instruction systems could use to further assess knowledge and learning of the student.

Before understanding the architecture and functioning of the ITS, it is important to understand the important issues related to ITS development.

Important Issues Related to ITS Development

1970s	*1980s*	*1990s*
Problem Generation	**Model Tracing**	**Learner Control**
Simple student modeling	More buggy-based systems	Individual vs. collaborative learning
Knowledge representation	Case-based reasoning	Situated learning vs. information processing
Socratic tutoring	Discovery worlds	Virtual reality
Skills and strategic knowledge	Progression of mental models	
Reactive learning environments	Simulation	
Buggy library	Natural language processing	
Expert systems and tutors	Authoring systems	
Overlay models/Genetic graph		

Up through the 1970s: Defining the Issues

Computer assisted instruction developed before the 1970s was inflexible and didactic because the systems had very limited capabilities (i.e., memory capacity and computational speed) for adaptive diagnosis and feedback. Furthermore, the only theory available to guide instructional development was behaviour theory, which poorly matched the cognitive goals of education. Over time, researchers in AI and cognitive psychology joined forces and together provided a basis for a new generation of computer based teaching programmes. Some of the research issues that dominated the 70's are discussed below:

Real Time Problem Generation

The earliest systems to incorporate some now "classic" ITS elements were programmes that generated problems and learning tasks, representing a big departure from the canned problems stored in CAI databases. The next major advance in this area came in the form of computer programmes that generated problems that had been tailored to the knowledge and skill level of a particular student, thus providing the foundation for student modeling.

Simple Student Modeling

The Basic Instructional Programme (BIP) develops procedural skills required in learning the programming language BASIC (Barr, Beard and Atkinson, 1976). It did so by selecting problems based on what the student already knew (past performance), which skills should be taught next and its analysis of the skills required (problems in the curriculum). Exercises were dynamically and individually selected per person (from a pool of 100 sample problems); then teaching heuristics were applied to the student model to identify skills to be taught and exercises were selected that best involved those skills. Selection of appropriate exercises was based on information contained in a network called the Curriculum Information Network (CIN), relating tasks in the curriculum to issues in the domain knowledge. Thus, a programming task in the tutor was represented in terms of its component skill requirements.

Knowledge Representation

Classic CAI used pages of text to represent knowledge but with little psychological validity. In contrast, Carbonell's (1970) SCHOLAR programme (often credited with being the first true ITS) used a semantic net to represent domino knowledge as well as the student model nodes in the network had tags to indicate whether the student knew the concept. This novel application of semantic network as a general structure of knowledge representation supported mixed initiative dialogues with students. Not only could the computer ask questions of the student but also the student could, theoretically, ask questions of the computer. One major limitation of this semantic knowledge representation was the difficulty of representing procedural knowledge.

Socratic Tutoring

Carbonell's research spawned another line of work concerned with enabling systems to engage in Socratic dialogues, believed to involve the learner more actively in the learning process. Collins (1977) outlined a set of tutorial rules for Socratic tutoring that was incorporated into a system called WHY (Stevens and Collins, 1977). For example, consider the following IF/THEN string: If the student gives an explanation of one or more factors that are not sufficient, THEN formulate a general rule for asserting that the given factors are sufficient and ask the student if the rule is true. Instead of semantic nets, the domain knowledge was stored in a "script hierarchy" containing information about stereotypical sequences of events.

Skills and Strategic Knowledge

Another attempt to stimulate thought among students was the focus of a group of researchers at Xerox PARC in the mid-to-late-1970s. For instance, WEST (Burton and Brown, 1976) was developed to help students learn/practice skills involved in the manipulation of arithmetic expressions. In this system, not only the basic arithmetic skill was involved but also strategic knowledge was required. The system was attentive to all levels of knowledge and skills, but the "coach" was somewhat unobtrusive, sitting in the background monitoring the student's moves, intervening only when it was clear that the student was floundering. Then the coach would make a few suggestions to enhance student skills. WEST's coaching goals were accomplished by focusing on the strategy used to construct a move.

Reactive Learning Environments

In reactive learning environments, the system responds to learners' actions in a variety of ways that extend understanding and help change entrenched belief structures using examples that challenge the learner's current hypotheses. An early, excellent example of this kind of environment was SOPHIE (Sophisticated Instructional Environment), designed to assist learners in developing electronic troubleshooting skills. For instance, in SOPHIE I, learners located faults in a broken piece of equipment. They could ask SOPHIE questions in English (e.g., to obtain values of various measurements taken on the device). SOPHIE I included three main components: a mathematical simulation, a programme to understand a subset of natural language and routines to set up contexts, keep history lists and so on. A student, troubleshooting a simulated piece of equipment, could offer a hypothesis about what was wrong. SOPHIE I reacted to the request by comparing the hypothesis to the measurements entered by the student. SOPHIE II extended the environment of its predecessor by adding an articulate expert bases on the pre-stored decision tree for troubleshooting the power supply that was annoted with schema for producing explanations. SOPHIE III contained an underlying expert based on a causal model rather than on a mathematical simulation. In SOPHIE I, the simulator worked out a set of equations not using human-like, causal reasoning, so it wasn't possible for the system to explain its decision in any detail. But SOPHIE III did employ a causal model of circuits to deal with the student feedback deficiency. Research with SOPHIE spawned a lot of later research in troubleshooting, reactive learning environments and articulate experts.

Buggy Library

Brown and Burton (1978) developed BUGGY to the diagnosis of student errors and it was based on the "buggy" library approach system. BUGGY was a framework for modeling misconceptions underlying procedural errors in addition and subtraction where students' errors were represented as the results of "bugs" (errors) in an otherwise correct set of procedures. DEBUGGY (Burton, 1982) was developed as an off-line version of the system based on the BUGGY framework using the pattern of errors from a set of problems to construct a hypothesis concerning a bug or combination of bugs, from the library that generated the errors. IDEBUGGY (Burton, 1982) was an on-line version of BUGGY, diagnosing the student's procedure bit-by-bit while giving the learner new problems to solve. The major limitation of these kinds of systems was the inability to anticipate all possible misconceptions.

Expert Systems and Tutors

MYCIN (Shortliffe, 1976) was a rule-based expert system for diagnosing certain infectious diseases such as meningitis. GUIDON (Clancey, 1979) was constructed to interface with MYCIN for tutoring interactively presenting the rules in the knowledge base to a student. This tutoring operated as follows. GUIDON described case dialogues of a sick patient to the student in general terms. The student had to adopt the role of a physician and ask for information that might be relevant to the case. GUIDON compared the student's questions to those which MYCIN would have asked and then responded accordingly.

Overlay Models/Genetic Graph

The definition of an overlay model is one of a novice-expert difference model representing missing conceptions. It's typically implemented as either an expert model annotated for missing items or an expert model with weights assigned to each element in the expert knowledge base. To illustrate how it works, consider the on-line coach for the game WUSOR (Stansfield, Carr & Goldstein, 1976). The WUMPUS player had to traverse through successive caves to locate the hiding wumpus. Many dangers faced the player but applying logical and probabilistic reasoning to information obtained along the way could solve the problem. The goal of the game was to shoot an arrow into the wumpus' hiding spot before you were killed. WUSOR had three generations, each with a progressive more sophisticated student model. The first version (I) had only an expert and advisor and did not try to diagnose the learner's state of knowledge. The next version (II) incorporated and overlay model (Carr & Goldstein, 1977) where the expertise was represented as rules and the student's knowledge state was a subset of the expert's knowledge. Goldstein (1979) made the WUSOR (III) by including the genetic graph combining overlay modeling (rule-based representation) with a learner-oriented set of links between curricular elements. "Genetic related to the notion of knowledge being evolutionary and graph denoted the relationships between parts of knowledge expressed as links in a network. A genetic graph could represent type of links (e.g., generalization, analogy, refinement) as well as deviation links.

1980s: Standardized Approaches and Environments

The 1980s were characterized by enormous growth and momentum in the ITS field. Sleeman (1984) attempted to focus research efforts by outlining four main problems with ITS at that time:

1. *Feedback Specifically*: Instructional feedback was often not sufficiently detailed for a particular learner.
2. *Non-adaptability*: Systems forced students into their own conceptual framework rather than adapting to a particular student's conceptualization.
3. *Theoretical Foundation*: Tutoring strategies used by the systems lacked a theoretical cognitive foundation.
4. *Restrictive Environment*: User interaction and exploration was too restricted.

The above main criticisms were addressed to varying degrees during the 1980s.

Model Tracing

Anderson and his colleagues at Carnegie Mellon University developed a model tracing approach to tutoring based on production systems as a way of modeling student behaviour. The model tracing approach has been employed in a variety of tutoring systems, such as the LISP tutor (Anderson, Boyle & Reiser, 1985) and the Geometry Tutor (Anderson, Boyle & Reiser, 1985). Model tracing provides a powerful way to both validate cognitive theories and to deliver low-level personalized remediation. This approach works by delineating many hundreds of production rules that model curricular "chunks" of cognitive skill. The drawback of this approach is that, while it works very well in modeling procedural skill acquisition, it does not work well for domains that are ill structured or that are not rule-based.

More Buggy-Based Systems

During this time period, a plethora of tutors were developed based on the "Buggy" library approach. While these systems do provide very specific feedback about the nature of the learner's error, the system response is dependent on the programme's ability to match the student's error with that of a stored "bug". As with model tracing, novel bugs are ignored; thus there is no way to update the buggy library or adapt to the learner's current conceptualization. This approach is theoretically based on the notion of cognitive errors in specific procedures, impasse learning and repair theory (Van Lehn, 1990).

Case-Based Reasoning (CBR)

Another category of systems emerging at this time came from case-based reasoning research (Schank, 1982; Kolodner, 1988). Proponents of this approach suggest that the goal of ITS should be to teach cases and how to index them. This system affords the learner greater freedom and promotes a more adaptive learning environment. Furthermore, whereas the model-tracing tutors work poorly in ill structured domains, CBR works well in those areas (e.g., politics, philosophy). CBR systems also perform well in domains where there are too many rules or too many ways in which rules can be applied (e.g., programming, game playing). CBR suggests approximate answers to complex problems thereby limiting how many rule combinations should be explored. There are two main processes involved with CBR: indexing (labeling new experiences for future retrieval) and adaptation (changing a retrieved case to fit a current situation). Further, two kinds of indices are required: concrete and abstract. Concrete indices refer to objects and actions usually directly mentioned in the case while abstract indices refer to more general characterization. According to Reisbeck and Schank (1990)-" *case-based reasoning serves as a model of cognition and learning.* But, while these systems present a provocative and well-conceived approach that has many practical and obvious merits, they cannot be said to possess a solid theoretical foundation. A major limitation of this approach includes the problem of anticipating and representing a sufficient number of cases to be cataloged.

Discovery Worlds

Learning from computers in the 1960s and 1970s was characterized by inflexible presentations of didactic material. But an opposition movement arose in the 1970s that gained steam in the 1980s. Development of discovery learning environments were the result of this movement. The typical example of this type of discovery worlds as—a computer simulation environment with simple interface and tools. These computerized systems were designed to make it possible for students to acquire various knowledge and skills on their own. For example, students could learn LOGO or Newton's laws of motion within discovery (or micro) worlds. One of the main strengths of these systems was their great adaptability to a range of different learners. Students were free to explore and act within the micro world as they chose with the ramifications of their actions immediately revealed. This movement was based on the theoretical premise that in discovery learning one can radically alter the perceptual relationship between the learner and the knowledge or skills to be acquired. This position was epitomized by Piget (1954), who stated that-" *an education which is an active discovery of reality is superior to one that consists merely in providing the young with ready-made wills to will with and ready-made truths to know with.* " A major drawback of these systems is that all persons are not skilled in the requisite inquiry behaviours necessary to achieve success in those environments. For a successful learning, an individual should be able to: formulate efficient experiments, state, confirm and negate hypotheses, approximately relate hypotheses and experiments, plan future experiments and tests, engage in self-monitoring and so on.

Progression of Mental Models

White, Frederiksen and their colleagues (Frederiksen, White, Collins & Eggan, 1988; White & Frederiksen, 1987; White & Horowitz, 1987) incorporated ideas from (a) AI research on mental models and (b) qualitative reasoning to develop QUEST (Qualitative Understanding of Electrical System Troubleshooting) as well as 'Thinker Tools'. These systems work by motivating students to want to learn by pointing out errors and inconsistencies in their current beliefs. Then students are guided through a series of micro worlds, each more complex than the one preceding, toward the objective of more precise mental models of the evolving subject matter. Finally, students formalize their developing mental models by evaluating a set of laws describing phenomena in the micro world then they apply the selected law to see how well it predicts real-world events.

Simulations

Graphical simulations have become more central to the ITS enterprise as the power of computers has grown. Simulations are useful wherever real objects are involved in a learning task and they provide many benefits over real devices. Simulations not only display aggregate behaviour but they are decomposable into constituents that mimic novice or expert mental models. This decomposability of graphic displays and simulations mimic the power of productions in expert systems for creating natural chunks that promote learning.

Natural Language Processing (NLP)

This technique was an important part of ITS right from the beginning. SOPHIE was built on a powerful and original NLP technique called Semantic Grammar (SG). NLP is used to communicate information to the learner or accept input from the learner.

Authoring Systems

The creation of computer-based environments to facilitate the design and development of ITS has been an important and continuing thread of research. The goal of authoring systems is to give relative computer novices, a software tool kit to take advantage of the power of computers for designing instruction. An example of one powerful graphic authoring system developed over the last decade is that by Towne and Munro (1992). Quite powerful CBT systems have been made available over the years. Research, beginning in the 1980s, attempted to adapt such systems as authoring shells for developing ITS. Miller and Lucado (1992) were among the first to integrate the power of CBT authoring environments with the technology of ITS.

1990s: Great Debates

The four hot ITS topics right now may be broadly characterized as:

(a) How much learner control should be allowed in systems?
(b) Should learners interact with ITS individually or collaboratively?
(c) Is learning situated, unique and ongoing or symbolic and does it follow an information-processing model?
(d) Does virtual reality uniquely contribute to learning beyond CAI, ITS or even multimedia?

Degree of Learner Control

The debate over the amount of learner control that should be a part of the learning process has raged for many years. On the one hand, some have argued that discovering information on one's own is the best way to learn (e.g., Bruner, 1961). On the other hand, structure and direction have been stressed as the important ingredients in the promotion of student learning (e.g., Ausubel, 1963). The same debate has appeared in the ITS arena. Two differing perspective, representing the ends of this continuum, have arisen in response to the issue of the optimal ITS learning environment. One approach is to develop a computerized environment containing assorted tools and allow learners freedom to explore and learn independently (e.g., Collins & Brown, 1988; Shute, Glaser & Raghavan, 1991; White & Horowitz, 1987). Advocates of the opposing position argue that it is more effective to develop straight forward learning environment with no digressions permitted (e.g., Anderson, Boyle & Reiser, 1985; Corbett and Anderson, 1989; Sleeman, Kelly, Martinak, Ward & Moore, 1989). Merrill, Reiser, Ranney and Trafton (1992) investigated how human tutors dealt with the issue of learner control. They compared human-to-computer-tutoring techniques and found that while expert human tutors did sometimes act like model tracers, they actually maintained a 'delicate balance' between (a) allowing students freedom and control and (b) giving students sufficient guidance. In general, pedagogical research findings differ with regard to the amount of learner control to allow in automated systems.

Individual vs. Collaborative Learning

Traditionally, ITS have been designed as single-learner enterprises. Bloom (1984) and others have presented compelling evidence that individualized tutoring (using human tutors) engenders the most effective and efficient learning across an array of domains. Furthermore, intelligent tutoring systems epitomize this principle of individualized instruction. In his often-cited 1984 paper, Bloom presented a challenge to instructional researchers that has been called the "two sigma problem. The goal is to achieve two standard deviation improvements with tutoring over traditional instruction methods. So far, this goal has yet to be attained using individualized ITS.

An alternative approach to individualized instruction is collaborative learning. Students can learn more than by themselves, especially when they bring complementary, rather than identical. Collaboration is denied as a process by which *"individuals negotiate and share meanings relevant to the problem-solving task at hand."* (Teasley & Roschelle, 1993) and is distinct from co-operation, which relates to the division of labour required to achieve task. Some basic questions related to collaborative learning are: (a) Are two heads better than one? and (b) Can intelligent computer systems support collaborative learning endeavors? Recently, research is beginning to shed light on both of these questions. For example, many researchers have shown impressive student gains in knowledge and skill acquisition from collaborative learning environment (e.g., Brown, & Palincsar, 1989; Lampert, 1986; Palincsar & Brown, 1984; Scardamalia, Bareiter, Mc Lean, Swallow & Woodruff, 1989; Schoenfeld, 1985). Furthermore, the few studies of the effectiveness of collaborative learning in computer-based learning environments have also been positive (eg., Justen, Waldrop & Adams, 1990; Katz & Lesgold, 1993; Papert, 1980).

There are basically two ways of implementing collaborative learning environments using computers: (a) a small group of learners interact with a single intelligent computer system or (b) the computer system itself serves as the "partner" in the collaboration. The first way (i.e., a small group using one computer) represents an extension of the research on collaborative learning in classrooms. In this case, some of the issues that need to be addressed have been out lined by Teasley and Roschelle (1993). The system must be able to: (a) introduce and accept knowledge into a joint problem-solving space, (b) monitor on-going activities for evidence of divergences in meaning and (c) repair divergences that impede the progress of collaboration. The difference between this list and general modeling issues in ITS is that it deals with a student model that's built upon a joint, rather than single problem solving space. The second way of implementing collaboration (i.e., assigning the computer as the learner's partner). Cummings and Self (1989) proposed a collaborative Intelligent Education System (IES) that engages the learner in a partnership. Here, the computer serves as a collaborator not as an authoritarian instructor. In both cases, a student model still must be derived either that of an individual or a group.

For a variety of reasons (eg., greater range of shared knowledge, resource limitations, etc.), the notion of collaborative learning environments is appealing. However, there are a lot of unanswered research questions that need to be addressed. Some of these (listed in Katz & Lesgold, 1993) include: (1) What parts of the curriculum should be learned collaboratively and what parts learned individually? (2) What teaching methods should be used to achieve the instructional goals and how should they be sequenced to optimize learning? (3) What should the computer tutor do while students work on problems? (4) What additional roles could the computer coach perform?

Situated Learning vs. Information Processing

Situated learning is not just a trend but a radically new perspective or philosophy that supports the integration of psychological theories of physical and cognitive skills, uniting emotions, reasoning and development in a neuro-biologically grounded way. It has also been referred to in the literature as "situated action" and "situated cognition". Knowledge would be understood as a relation between an individual and a social or physical situation rather than as a property of an individual. Next consider the nature of knowledge from the information-processing perspective. Anderson's (1983) ACT theory proposed two fundamental forms of knowledge: procedural, represented in the form of a production system and declarative, represented in the form of a node-link network of propositions. Both representations are believed to operate within long-term and short-term memory structures.

These two positions present quite different views on how learning or knowledge acquisition occurs. In the first case (situated cognition), learning is a process of creating representations, inventing languages and formulating models for the first time. Learning is ongoing, occurring with every thought, perception and action and is situated in each unique circumstance. Situated cognition argues for an instructional system rich with explicit tools and varied exemplars than can support and extend learner's discovery processes. The second position (information processing) sees learning as progressing from declarative knowledge to procedural skills, to automatic skills dependent upon enablers (i.e., what one already knows and can transfer to new situation and mediators i.e., cognitive processes determining what one can acquire such as working-memory capacity and information processing speed).

Virtual Reality

A collection of techniques known as Virtual Reality (VR) has recently been exciting the instructional technology community. This new technology refers collectively to the hardware, software and interface technologies available to the user interested in experiencing certain aspects of a simulated 3-dimensional environment. VR changes the relationships between learning and experiencing, highlighting the role of perception in learning. The current question is: Does VR represents the next logical, developmental step in the design of instructional systems? Virtual Reality shows promise in the construction of micro worlds for physics and other science instruction. For instance, Loftin and Dede (1993) are creating a virtual physic laboratory from the base facilities of a VR world created for NASA astronaut training. In their virtual laboratory students can conduct experiments in a virtual world.

9

Intelligent Tutoring System

Early systems that were developed for teaching purpose were known variously as Computer Aided Instruction or Computer Aided Learning systems. These traditional systems were developed to provide users with knowledge in a particular area and then assess the user retained knowledge by posing questions, usually multiple choice, to direct the course of study. The structure of such a system is shown in Figure 9.1.

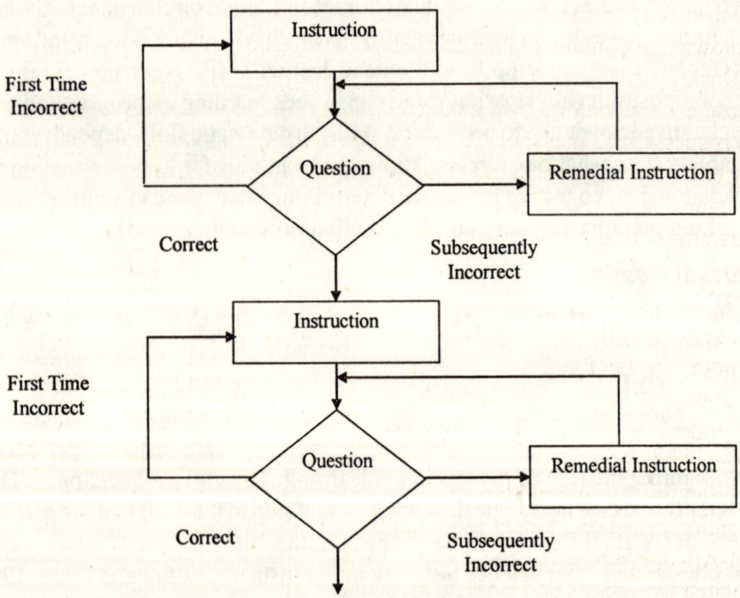

Figure 9.1: Routing within a Computer Aided Instruction System

Examinees are presented with information after which a series of question are asked. If the user answers correctly the next phase of instruction is entered. There may be a summary set of questions at the end of the instruction to gauge how well the student has performed.

If an examinee answers the questions incorrectly the instructional material is presented again, perhaps in a slightly different format. If, after the material has been repeated, the examinee again answers incorrectly then remedial instruction may be presented. In this kind of systems, the instruction was not individualized to the learner's needs. In general the decisions about how to move a student through the material were script-like, such as "if question 21 is answered correctly, proceed to material 54; otherwise go to material 33".

Such systems can appear to imitate intelligence by being able to adapt to student misconceptions. However, this appearance is a result of the system designer anticipating all possible errors that the student may make. These are built into the system at design time and encoded within the branching structure. If the designer of the system has not anticipated an incorrect interpretation of the instructional material then the system will not be able to provide feedback to help the examinee resolve the misunderstanding. These systems are incapable of dynamically generating a response to a particular situation as a human tutor would be able to do.

So, while CAI may be somewhat effective in helping learners, they do not provide the same kind of individualized attention that a student would receive from a human tutor. For a computer based educational system to provide such attention, it must implement more advanced algorithms to parse the knowledge domain and related learner feedback.

During last few years there have been many systems developed for this purpose each having its own characteristics. Until now the majority of such ITSs is specialized in a specific knowledge domain. In literature we can find many examples of specialized ITS operating in various knowledge domain.

Over the years, various tutoring systems have been built to teach programming (e.g., Proust [Johnson, W.l., and Soloway, E. Proust (1985)], Meno-II [Soloway, E., Rubin, E., Woolf, B., Johnson, W.L., and Bonar, J. (1983)], and ELM-PE [Weber, G., and Mllenberg, A. (1995)]). They analyze the user's solutions to exercises and provide feedback to identified misconceptions or missing skills based on the analysis. Other approaches have also appeared in intelligent tutoring paradigm. Kumar's model-based tutor asks students to predict C++ programmes' output and identify semantic and run-time errors [A.N., K. (2002)]. It provides explanations of programme execution line by line to help students understand code behaviour. Adaptive navigation based on student modeling is used in a web-based system called ELM-Art II [Weber, G., and Specht, M. (1997)] to provide individualized annotated hyperlinks and curriculum sequencing.

Expert critiquing systems provide useful feedback to users' work in many domains. Such feedback includes alerts to problematic situations, relevant information to the task at hand, directions for improvement, and prompts for reflection [Silverman, B.G. (1992)]. One of these systems is "Java Critiquer" that uses an incremental authoring approach to amortize the high development cost [Qiu, L., and Riesbeck, C. (2004)].

Other systems like "CTutor" [Song, J.S., Hahn, S.H., Tak, K.Y., and Kim, J.H. (1997)], "Prolog Tutor" [Hong, J. (2004)] and "Java Intelligent Tutoring System" [Sykes, E.R., and Franek, F. (2003)] adopts advanced code analysis to see what is the intention of student and give feedback based on this analysis.

There are also tutoring system based on natural language like CIRCSIM-Tutor that is a language-based intelligent tutoring system for first-year medical students to learn about the reflex control of blood pressure. Students solve small problems and are tutored by dialog with the computer.

Despite of the great variety of ITS in the literature we chose to focus our attention on tutoring system that define a generic architecture. It is possible, in principle, to inject knowledge base of every kind in this type of system so that the process of learning can start in whatever domain of knowledge. This choice will enable us to develop a system for knowledge acquisition that tries to be independent from the specific domain in which an ITS can be developed.

Intelligent tutoring systems (ITSs) are computer programmes that are designed to incorporate techniques from the AI community in order to provide tutors which know *what* they teach, *who* they teach and *how* to teach it. AI attempts to produce in a computer behaviour which, if performed by a human, would be described as 'intelligent': ITSs may similarly be thought of as attempts to produce in a computer behaviour which, if performed by a human, would be described as 'goad teaching' (Elsom-Cook, 1987). The design and development of such tutors lie at the intersection of computer science, cognitive psychology and educational research; this intersecting area is normally referred to as cognitive science. For historical reasons, much of the research in the domain of educational software involving AI has been conducted in the name of 'ICAI', an acronym for 'Intelligent Computer-Aided Instruction'. This phrase, in turn, evolved out of the name 'Computer-Aided Instruction' (CAI) often referring to the use of computers in education. Nevertheless, to all intents and purposes, ITSs and ICAI are synonymous. However, though some researchers still prefer 'ICAI' (e.g. Self, 1988a, uses it in the title of his recent book), it is now often replaced by the acronym 'ITS' (Sleeman & Brown, 1982b). However, some researchers are understandably hesitant to use the term 'intelligent', instead opting for labels such as 'Knowledge-Based Tutoring System' (KBTS) or 'Adaptive Tutoring System' (ATS) (e.g. Streitz, 1988): Wenger (1987) prefers the label Knowledge Communication Systems. Nevertheless, most researchers appear to be reasonably content with the acronym ITS. This is fine as long as everyone involved with the area understands that the usage of the word 'intelligent' is, strictly speaking, a misnomer. This does not appear to be the case, resulting in some very ambitious goals/claims, particularly in the more theoretical parts of the literature: this also appears to be a valid criticism of the entire AI literature.

The fact that ITS research spans three different disciplines has important implications. It means that there are major differences in research goals, terminology, theoretical frameworks, and emphases amongst ITS researchers.

ITS research also requires a mutual understanding of the three disciplines involved, a very stressful demand given the problems of keeping abreast with even a single discipline today. However, some researchers have stood up to the challenge. As a result, a great deal has been learnt about how to design and implement ITSs.

Tutoring programmes have evolved dramatically from the simple prompt for remediation based on a wrong answer to the complex, adaptive systems of today that truly qualify as intelligent. Modern intelligent tutoring systems (ITSes) incorporate 5 different models that interact to effectively lend pedagogical assistance to a learner (Beck, Stern, Haugsjaa 1996). These researchers have identified the following models (or modules) that constitute an ITS. The Student Model stores information that is specific to each learner. The Pedagogical Model defines the teaching process that the ITS will employ. The Domain Model contains the information about the subject being taught and as such usually constitutes the most area. The Communications Model includes the screen layout and dialogues with the learner. The Expert Model is a model of how someone who is an expert in that domain would represent this information.

ITSes like "Cognitive Tutor" from Carnagie Learning are proving themselves in classrooms today by helping students improve their abilities in math. As students solve problems, the software adapts to provide feedback that is appropriate to their problem solving and learning style.

Overview of the Evolution of Intelligent Tutoring Systems

A Short Historical Perspective

As illustrated in the following Figure 9.2, the advent of ITSs is around the late sixties.

The differentiation of the two main streams is based on the one hand side by modeling the human cognition by the application of the deduction and the induction concepts. Deduction based applications evolved later, around the late eighties, into the application of the PROLOG (Ivan, 2000) and similar programming languages in building expert systems. It was also the era of the fifth generation computers initiative (Edward, 1983) launched by the Japans. On the other hand-side were the dedicated applications, based on procedural languages, for supporting pedagogical purposes, like tracking the assignments and their evaluation. There are many monolithic tutoring (or e-learning) systems, which aim is to conduct and track the students' progress in special areas.

We observe in Figure 9.2 that computers have been used in education for over 30 years. Computer Based Instruction (CBI) and Computer Based Training (CBT) are the predecessors of ITSs. The field of *automating tutoring* (e.g. Computer Aided Instruction—CAI or Intelligent Computer Aided

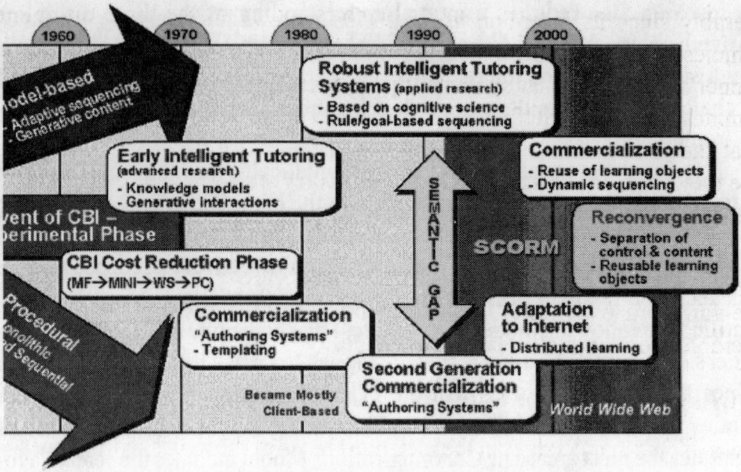

Figure 9.2: The Evolution of E-learning

Instruction—ICAI) was one of the first most fruitful fields, which served aims of AI researchers. Application of machine learning algorithms in tutoring has a long history. The field of automating tutoring was one of the first most fruitful fields, which served aims of *artificial intelligence* (AI) researchers. These were more or less monolithic systems with low level of flexibility.

Splitting of the practice into two streams has begun since the beginning of the late sixties mainly due to the different research orientation. In further decades we observe a gradual convergence and synthesis mainly due to the penetration of the Internet.

The upper stream is characterized by the application of the artificial intelligence algorithms and computational architectures, such as production rules systems, generative grammars, Bayesian networks, Markov models, neural networks, higher-order semantic spaces, fuzzy control systems, and non-linear dynamical systems. With these methods ITSs use tutorial dialogue to adaptively respond to the learner's motivational states, and efficiently bridge the man-machine interface, adapting to a learner's profile. One of the aspects of the profile of the learner or elearning user is a user model. The user model can be used for solving the problem of e-learning users' cognitive load.

The bottom stream is characterized by the application of actual software technologies to support functionalities which a human teacher might do: select (or generate) appropriate material, set up the exercise, monitor student activity, give hints during exercises and feedback afterwards, understand why students make mistakes, customize presentation style to the student's style, ask and answer questions.

Computer-assisted instruction/learning (CAI/CAL) has evolved considerably since its inception in the 1950s with Skinnerian type 'linear programmes'. This has happened despite being set off in the wrong direction by Skinner's insistence that students' responses could be ignored in linear programmes (O'Shea & Self, 1983). The central problem with early systems was that they were unable to provide rich feedback or individualization, because they were not designed to know what they were teaching, who they were teaching or how to teach it. In order to solve this problem, CAI/CAL systems have evolved over the past three and a half decades into what are now usually termed 'Intelligent Tutoring Systems' (ITSs). Although we may still be far from truly intelligent tutoring systems, most would agree considerable progress has already been made.

From CAI *to* ITSs: Major Stages

There were some major stages in the metamorphosis of the linear programmes of the 1950s into the ITSs of the 1980s (see Fig. 9.3). The path has spanned a period of almost four decades. It began in the 1950s with simple 'linear programmes' which were based on the principle of operant conditioning. The main proponent of such linear programmes was the psychologist B.F. Skinner (1954, 1958). Material which had been selected and arranged to take the student step by step towards the desired behaviour was presented in a series of 'frames'. Most frames had very simple questions (e.g. involving only the filling in of a missing space or two), and the student was told immediately whether the answer was right or wrong. The system proceeded to present the next frame regardless of the correctness of the student's response. To be fair, Skinner held that students should not be allowed to make mistakes because this gives negative reinforcement. If the designer succeeded in this aim, all the responses would be correct and so could legitimately be ignored. Unfortunately, experience showed that such an ideal situation was usually not attainable. The major limitations of linear programmes then became glaringly apparent: they did not provide individualization, which meant that all students, irrespective of their abilities, background, or previous knowledge of the domain, received exactly the same material in exactly the same sequence; neither did they provide feedback, as the students' responses were ignored. This style of CAI has been dubbed *ad-hoc* frame-orientated (AFO) CAI by Carbonell (1970) to stress its dependence on author-specified units of information. Carbonell concluded that 'in most CAI systems of the AFO type, the computer does little more than what a programmed text book can do, and one may wonder why the machine is used at all when teaching sequences are extremely simple, perhaps trivial, one should consider doing away with the computer, and using other devices or techniques more related to the task' (Carbonell, 1970, pp. 194,201). Overcoming these limitations prompted the chain of events which has culminated in today's ITSs.

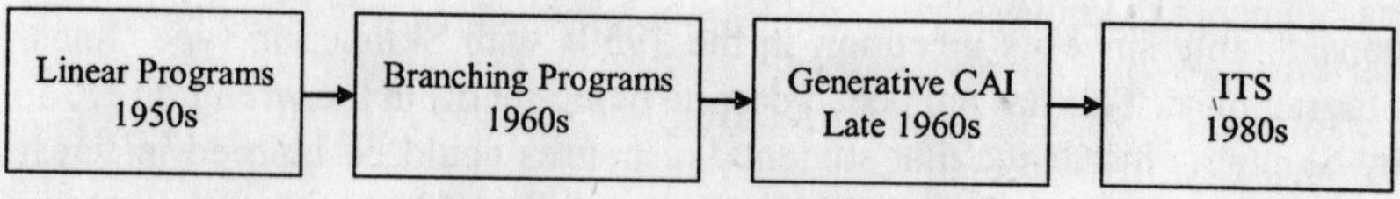

Figure 9.3: From CAI to ITS

Crowder (1959) overcame some of the limitations of Skinnerian systems by ceasing to ignore students' responses. He proposed using them to control the material shown to the student. The 'branching programmes' that resulted still had a fixed number of frames, but were able to comment on a student's response and then use it to choose the next frame, possibly repeating an earlier one. Pattern-matching techniques allowed alternate answers to be treated as acceptable or partially acceptable rather than as totally correct or incorrect as demanded by Skinnerian systems. However, the teaching material became too large to be manageable through straightforward programming and so a special breed of programming languages, called 'author languages', were developed for creating CAI material.

In the late 1960s and early 1970s, 'generative systems' came into being (also called 'adaptive systems'). These emerged from the recognition of the fact that the teaching material could itself be generated by the computer. A generative system has the ability both to generate and solve meaningful problems. In some domains like arithmetic, researchers realized they could do away with all the pre-stored teaching material, problems, solutions and associated diagnostics, and actually generate them. The potential advantages, if exploited, were enormous. They included drastically reduced memory usage and the generation and provision of as many problems (to some desired level of difficulty) as the student needed. Most notably, Uhr and his team implemented a series of systems which generated problems in arithmetic that were 'tailor-made' to a student's performance (Uhr, 1969). Suppes (1967) and Woods & Hartley (1971) produced systems with similar abilities. Wexler (1970) describes a system which combines generative CAI with frame-orientated CAI in which the course-author must specify certain question formats. The system generates parameters for these formats and searches the database to determine the correct answer. Nevertheless, a major shortcoming was the restriction to drill-type exercises in domains as well-structured as mathematics.

Only parametric summaries of behaviour were used to guide problem generation, rather than an explicit representation of the student's knowledge (Sleeman & Brown, 1982b). Sleeman (1983) notes that in the initial version of the Leeds Adaptive Arithmetic System (which later evolved to the Leeds Modelling System, LMS, Sleeman & Smith (1981) and from there to the PIXIE system (Sleeman, 1987)), the model of the student consisted merely of an integer to indicate the level of the student's competence.

Generative CAI was the main precursor of ITSs. Although individualization and feedback had been improved, there was a rather shallow knowledge representation. Yazdani (1986) notes that 'none of these systems has human-like knowledge of the domain it is teaching, nor can it answer the serious questions from the students as to "why" and "how" the task is performed.' Such sentiments have also been echoed by other researchers (e.g. O'Shea & Self, 1983). Hence, many problems remained unsolved. Sleeman & Brown (1982b) and Hawkes *et al.* (1986) point out that these systems were found to be lacking for a number of reasons:

(1) They attempted to produce total courses rather than concentrating on building systems for more limited topics.
(2) They had severe natural language barriers which restricted users' interaction with them.
(3) They had no 'knowledge' or 'understanding' of the subject they tutored or of the students themselves; this is sometimes referred to in the literature as the 'Eliza' syndrome. Consequently, they tended to assume too much or too little student knowledge, and they could not conceptualize so as to diagnose a student's misconception within his/her own framework.
(4) They were extremely ad *hoc.* Building tutoring systems was not recognized to be a non-trivial task—a task requiring detailed psychological theories of learning and mislearning. Anyone with a knowledge of computing attempted to build a tutor. Consequently, there was little or no co-operation among educators, psychologists and computer scientists ill the development phase of the tutors.
(5) They tended to be static rather than dynamic. There was little experimentation with systems in order to improve them. Human tutors learn about their students and about the subjects they teach every day, and so should machine tutors.

A model of computer-assisted instructions (CAI) is given in Figure 9.4. In response to the problems CAI faced, Self, in his interesting and classic paper, argued that a computer tutorial programme should have a representation of *what* is being taught, *who* is being taught and *how* to teach him/her (Self, 1974). Carbonell (1970) argued that a solution to this problem could not be achieved without the use of AI techniques. Jaime Carbonell's important contribution to cognitive science is best summarized in the title of his first-rate 1970 publication *AI in CAI.* He wanted to put AI into CAI systems. He dreamed of a system which had a database of knowledge about a subject matter and general information about language and principles of tutorial instruction. The system could then pursue a natural language dialogue with a student, sometimes following the student's initiative, sometimes taking its own initiative, but always generating its statements and responses in a natural way from its general knowledge. Such a system sharpedly contrasted with existing CAI systems at the time in which a relatively fixed sequence of questions and possible responses had to be pre-determined for each topic. He

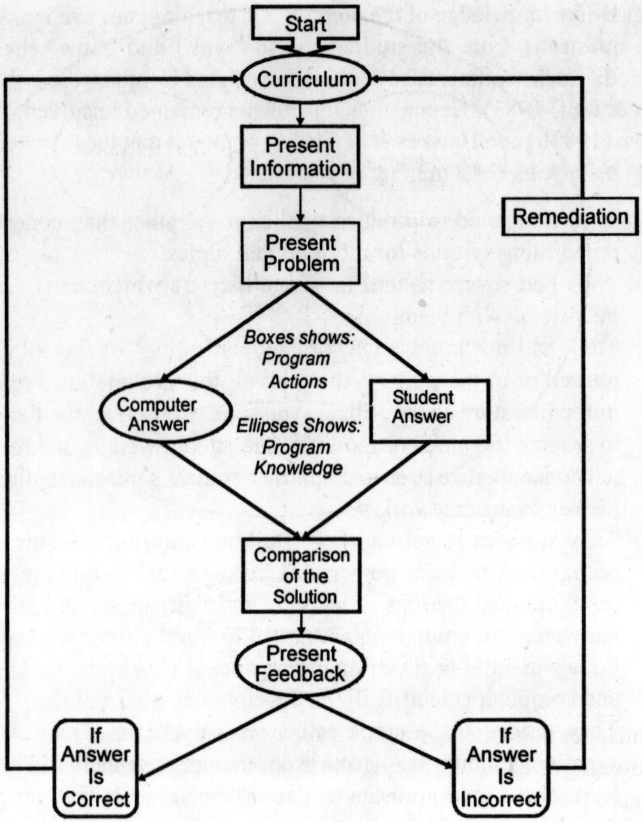

Figure 9.4: A Model of CAI

constructed an early version of his dream, a classic system he called *SCHOLAR* (Carbonell, 1970, 1971), but he died before it was fully realized. Carbonell's introduction of AI into CAI marked the beginning of the era of ITSs which therefore emerged to provide answers to the limitations of generative CAI.

It is claimed that ITSs combine AI, psychological models of the student and the expert, and educational theory. The psychological models allow for simulations of student performance and can be experimented upon until they closely represent the behaviour exhibited by the student. Summarizing, providing a truly 'intelligent' system was recognized to be a nontrivial task which needed experts from several other disciplines; a need which could be provided by the AI research community, which contains computer scientists, psychologists and educationists.

Most of the present-day work in ITSs is being carried out by AI researchers or enthusiasts, and AIs influence has been so great that Yazdani (1983)

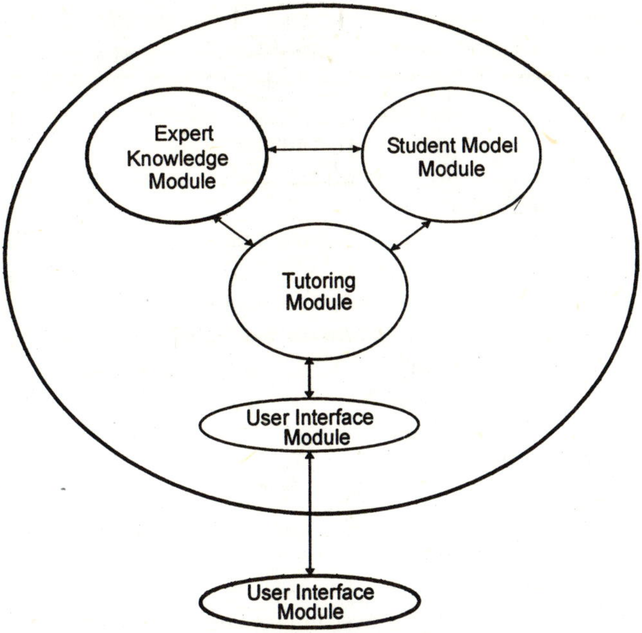

Figure 9.5: General ITS Architecture

concludes that 'intelligent tutoring systems are AI's answer to CAL packages.' However, it is worth making the point that most so-called ITSs still do not escape the bulk of the criticisms discussed above, so that there is considerable scope for further work. Some of the major differences between ITSs and CAI programmes are (or should be):

(1) ITSs provide a clear articulation of knowledge for a limited domain;
(2) ITSs have a model of student performance which is dynamically maintained and is used to drive instruction;
(3) the ITS designer defines the knowledge and the inference rules, but not the teaching sequence, which is derived by the programme;
(4) ITSs provide detailed diagnostics of errors rather than simply drill and practice;
(5) students can pose questions to an ITS (this is the main characteristic of 'mixed initiative tutors').

Intelligent Tutoring System (ITS)

Discussions concerning computer use in education have rapidly passed through different phases. The first phase is centered on the need for "computer literacy", generally defined as computer awareness and computer programming. In the second phase of the computer literacy debate, the emphasis shifted to the role of the computer as a tool and as a method for solving problems. The third phase addresses issues related to computer application in support of the curriculum.

Computers have been used in education for over 20 years. Computer-Based Training (CBT) and Computer Aided Instruction (CAI) were the first such systems developed to teach using computers. In these kinds of systems, the instruction was not individualized to the learner needs. The learner abilities were not taken into account.

While both CBT and CAI may be somewhat effective in helping learners, they do not provide the same kind of individualized attention that the student would receive from a human tutor (Bloom, 1984). A computer-based educational system, designed to provide such attention, must include tasks about the domain and the learner. This has prompted research in the field of Intelligent Tutoring Systems (ITS) and it has supposed a great challenge for researchers in educational technology and a support to testing cognitive theories (Nwana, 1990).

An Intelligent Tutoring Systems (ITS) has its roots in the generative Computer-assisted instruction (CAI) and is often known as Intelligent Computer-Assisted Instruction (ICAI) (Sleeman & Brown, 1982). Computer-aided instruction were the forbears to ITS, which started in the late 1950s. The more sophisticated tutoring systems were developed due to the common use of artificial intelligence, which basically started in the 1970s. The intelligent CAI system has the potential to provide the necessary interaction to suit various learners, and differentiates clearly between Computer-Assisted Instruction (CAI) and Intelligent Computerassisted instruction (ICAI) (Boulay, 1998). Table 9.1 briefly lists the main differences between CAI and Intelligent CAI.

Table 9.1: Guide to Differentiating Intelligent CAI Systems from CAI Systems

Computer-assisted instructional systems (CAI)	*Intelligent computer-assisted instructional systems (ICAI)*
Knowledgeable	Highly knowledgeable
Can be intelligent	Maximum intelligence
Slow learning	Fast learning
Tutor controlled	Student controlled
Active feedback	Interactive feedback

The Intelligent Tutoring System is one of the fast developing and most popular areas of Computer-Assisted Learning (CAL). According to Ong and Ramachandran (2000), the beauty of ITS technology is that it provides learners with highly interactive learning environments that enable students to practice their skills by carrying out learning tasks. The use of intelligent machines for teaching in education has been around since 1926, when Sidney L. Pressey built a machine with multiple choice questions and answers, which also provided immediate feedback to the user (Thomas, 2003). The three essential components or models of ITS are as follows:

- Knowledge of the domain or expert model;
- Knowledge of the learner or student model;
- Knowledge of teacher strategies or instructor model (Thomas, 2003, Ong & Ramachandran, 2000).

The important contribution of AI in computer-based education is to provide knowledge-based access to resources. Wilson and Welsh (1991) divided AI into three broad areas where knowledge-based systems or expert systems can have important implications for education and training. The history of computerised educational measurement system shows that each generation of educational measurement has shown an increased use of AI and expert systems approaches in order to improve educational measurement activities (Olsen, 1991). The four important generations highlighted by Olsen (1991) are:

- Computerised testing;
- Computerised adaptive testing;
- Continuous measurement;
- Intelligent measurement.

ITS Performance

The concept known as Intelligent Tutoring System (ITS) or Intelligent Computer-Aided Instruction (ICAI) has been pursued for more than three decades by researchers in education, psychology and Artificial Intelligence (see Figure 9.6). Nowadays, prototype and operational ITS provide practice-based instruction to support corporate training, college education and military training. Additionally, the technology is now ready to support computer learning for the first time.

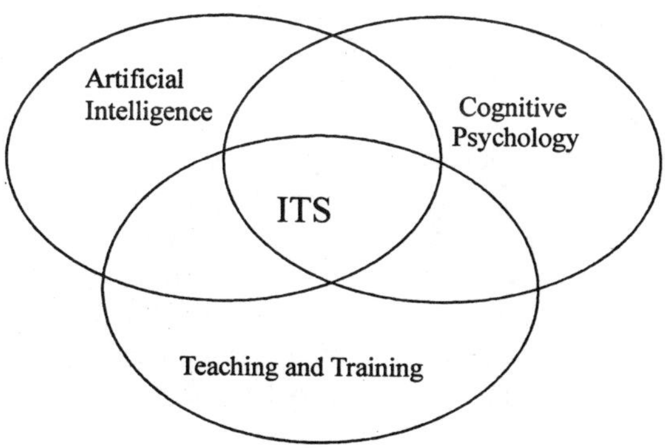

Figure 9.6: ITS Domain

The goal of an ITS is to provide the benefits of one-to-one instruction automatically and cost effectively. Like training simulations, ITS enable participants to practice their skills by carrying out tasks within highly interactive learning environments. However, ITS go beyond training simulations by answering user questions and providing individualized guidance. Unlike other computer-based training technologies, ITS systems assess each learner's actions within these interactive environments and develop a model of learner's knowledge, skills and expertise. Based on the learner model, ITS can tailor instructional strategies, in terms of both the content and style and provide explanations, hints, examples, demonstrations and practice problems as needed.

ITS apply Artificial Intelligence (AI) techniques to the development of educational systems based on computers with the purpose of building systems able to adapt dynamically to the learning evolution. ITS also offer considerably flexibility in presentation of material and a greater ability to respond to idiosyncratic student needs. These systems achieve their "intelligence" by representing pedagogical decisions about how to teach as well as information about the learner. Major (1995) states that an ITS should adapt to a particular student by varying "difficulty of material", presentation style, help offered, path taken and generality of the material". He further states that the path through the courseware is calculated whilst the student is using the system (i.e., it is not pre-programmed).

However, an ITS will typically constrain the student to learning by a predetermined method or strategy [Ridgeway (1989) and Kinshuk (1997)]. ITS use a model of the student's knowledge (student model) so that the student is presented with new information only when he/she requires it. This is carried out in order to reinforce a point, to progress in the learning and/or to identify misconceptions and wrong-rules (Sleeman, 1982). Such systems have been criticized for constraining the student to solving a problem in a particular way (Ridgeway, 1989). In most complex problem domains, there can be many methods to achieve a correct solution. Some people may find one particular method that suits their way of thinking better than others. It has been argued that students should be able to experiment with their own ideas and find methods that naturally suit them.

Elsom-Cook (1989) reviewed some Computer-Based Learning (CBL) and ITS packages and graded them between two extremes: totally constrained and totally unconstrained. He argued that ITS lie at the constraint end of this spectrum, whereas an electronic textbook type system would be unconstrained. He also argued that the perfect tutoring system should be able to "slide" between these two extremes according to the student's needs and the state of knowledge.

Therefore, a system could appear as a traditional ITS to a novice student or as a discovery learning hypermedia system to an advanced student. Hartley

(1993) reinforces this point by stating that when there is a mismatch between strategies) of the learning system) and learning style (of the student), then performance is degraded. He also states that support for different styles and viewpoints of users is required.

Further research has shown that the learning process is improved when a student is allowed to follow pathways of their own choice, at their own pace and is able to monitor their progress by instant feedback to questions (Kibby 1990). These ideas are similar to the idea of cognitive scaffolding" [Henze (1999) and Robotham (1995)], whereby a learner is supported in their learning activity when he/she needs support. Nevertheless, the support is reduced as he/she becomes more capable and hence is empowered to go through learning in his/her style.

Working of an ITS

The three major components of any ITS coordinate and work together in order to produce better learning outcomes. These components are listed as below:

- Teacher strategies;
- Learner knowledge; and
- Domain knowledge.

Although each component has its specific identity and functioning ability, they always interact and coordinate with each other that help in guiding learners and interfacing them to expert in the subject. In a typical formal teaching situation, guidance is provided based on the learner's performance observed and gained during the instruction. However, in ITS-based learning, highly interactive techniques, such as simulations, AI and expert systems are incorporated with the learning in order to perform the action. The information received by the learner is again used as a feedback to provide further instructions and the cycle is repeated. Beck *et al.* (1996) categorized ITSs on two dimensions, namely: abstraction of the learning environment and the knowledge type of the instruction.

ITS Components

Each ITS must have the following four model components (see Figure 9.7):

- Knowledge of domain (domain model)
- Knowledge of teaching strategies (pedagogic model)
- Knowledge of learner (learner model)
- Communication model

This basic outline of requirements has been around since 1973 when it was introduced by Derek H. Sleeman and J.R. Hartley. The goal of every ITS is to effectively communicate to the student its embedded knowledge by using the communication model (Wenger, 1987)

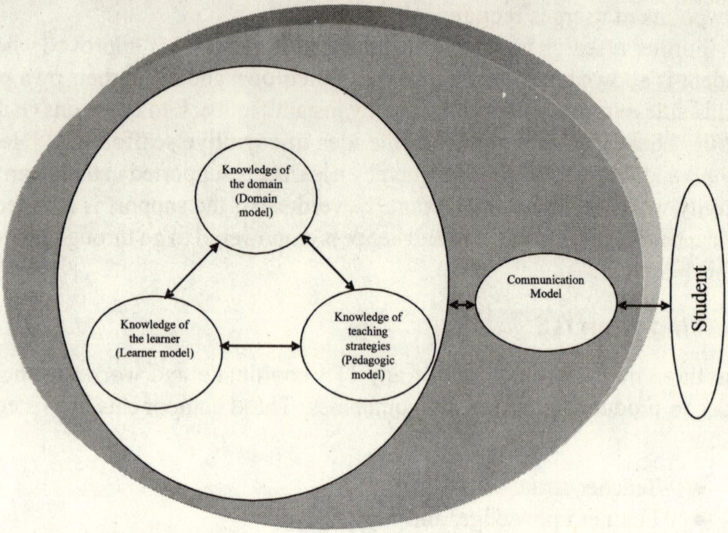

Figure 9.7: The Necessary Base for an Effective Teaching in ITS

Domain Model

The domain model contains the knowledge of the matter to be trained and is usually pedagogically organized to facilitate the task of the pedagogic model. The knowledge presented in this module is used to determine what should be presented to the student and how to evaluate his/her actions and answers.

Pedagogic Model

Through the pedagogic model the different teaching strategies are represented and the methods for controlling the session are implemented by means of the appropriate selection and sequencing of these strategies. This module takes charge of promoting the learning by designing, regulating and organizing the instruction that will be carried out for each student. It also is able to decide, using the information which should be offered at each moment, how to present each concept and when and how to interrupt the student.

Learner Model

The learner model represents the image of the system that has the knowledge which the student has acquired during the instruction process. It also incorporates other aspects of his/her behaviour and knowledge with possible repercussions on his/her performances and learning, the type of student, favourite learning styles, motivation level, etc. The learner model evaluates each learner's performance to determine his/her knowledge, perceptual abilities and reasoning skills. It stores specific information of each individual learner. At least, such a model tracks the way a student is performing on the material being taught. A possible addition can be recording misconceptions. Since the purpose of the learner model is to provide data for the pedagogical module of the system, all of the information gathered should be able to be used by the tutor.

Communication Model

Interactions with the learner, including the dialogue and the screen layouts are controlled by the communication model.

Structure of ITSs

General Architecture

Existing ITSs vary tremendously in architecture. In fact, it is almost a rarity to find two ITSs based on the same architecture. This results from the experimental nature of the work in the area: there is yet no clear-cut general architecture for such systems (Yazdani, 1986, 1987). Previously, there was considerable consensus in the literature that ITSs consist of at least three basic components (Barr & Feigenbaum, 1982; Bonnet, 1985).

1. The expert knowledge module.
2. The student model module.
3. The tutoring module.

The expert knowledge module comprises the facts and rules of the particular domain to be conveyed to the student, i.e. the knowledge of the experts. In the transition from CAI to ITSs, such knowledge has been the first aspect of the teacher's expertise to be explicitly represented in systems. It has already been mentioned that in traditional CAI, the expertise to be communicated is contained in pre-stored presentation material called 'frames', which are designed by the expert teacher and simply displayed to the student under given conditions. Such implicit representation of knowledge has since been recognized to be inadequate: in fact a major lesson learned from all the research on expert systems is that any expert module must have an abundance of specific and detailed knowledge, derived from people who have years of experience in a particular domain. Consequently, in ITSs, much effort is expended in discovering and codifying the domain knowledge, i.e. distilling years of experience into a knowledge representation.

Knowledge elicitation and codification can be a very time-consuming task, especially for a complex domain with an enormous amount of knowledge and interrelationships of that knowledge. Thus, investigating how to encode knowledge and how to represent it in an ITS remains the central issue of creating an expert knowledge module. In effect, this process aims to make the knowledge stored in this module more explicit. So, in current ITSs, expert knowledge is represented in various ways, including semantic networks, frames and production systems. It must not only include surface knowledge (e.g. the descriptions of various concepts that the student has to acquire), but also the representational ability that has been recognized to be a critical part of expertise. Expert knowledge must include the ability to construct implicit representational understanding from explicitly represented information (Mandl & Lesgold, 1988).

Expert knowledge modules can be classified along a spectrum ranging from completely opaque or 'blackbox' representations, whereby only final results are available (e.g. in tutors like *SOPHIE I,* reviewed in the next section), to fully transparent or 'glassbox' ones, where each reasoning step can be inspected and interpreted (e.g. *SOPHIE III,* also reviewed later).

The expert knowledge module or domain expert, as it is alternatively termed, fulfils a double function. First, it serves as the source of knowledge to be presented to the student, which includes generating questions, explanations and responses. Secondly, it provides a standard for evaluating the student's performance. For this latter function, it must be able to generate solutions to problems in the same context as the student, so that respective answers can be compared. The module must also be able to detect common systematic mistakes, and if possible identify any gap in the student's knowledge that may be the cause of this. If the ITS is to monitor students in solving problems, the expert module must also be able to generate sensible, and possibly multiple, solution paths so that intermediate steps can be compared.

Also, in its function as a standard, the expert knowledge module can be used to assess the student's overall progress. To achieve this required the establishment of some criteria to compare knowledge. This type of comparison is possible only if the knowledge has been explicitly represented. Hence, ITSs differ considerably from traditional CAI programmes in that the knowledge in the latter is implicitly represented within its code.

It is also worth recognizing that the expert knowledge module by necessity embodies a specific view of the domain—that of the designer. Thus, tutoring can be compromised if the student does not understand the system's instruction or because the system cannot interpret the student's behaviour in terms of its own view of the knowledge (Wenger, 1987). Of course, human teachers also have their own views, but they do also have the incredible ability to adapt them accordingly in order to perceive that of the student. This issue touches on the central problem of knowledge representation in AI; a problem which is often said to be the main bottle-neck to AI's success. The solution to this bottle-neck is particularly relevant to ITSs because of its deep pedagogical implications.

The student model module refers to the dynamic representation of the emerging knowledge and skill of the student. No intelligent tutoring can take place without an understanding of the student. Thus, along with the idea of explicitly representing the knowledge to be communicated came the idea of doing likewise with the student, in the form of a student model. Most researchers agree that an ITS should have a student model (Hartley & Sleeman, 1973; Self, 1974, 1987a, 1987b, 1988b; Rich, 1979; Sleeman, 1985: Tobias, 1985; Zissos & Witten, 1985; Ross *et al.,* 1987; Gilmore & Self, 1988: Wachsmuth, 1988). Ideally, this model should include all those aspects of the student's behaviour and knowledge that have possible repercussions on his/her performance and learning. However, the task of constructing such a complete model is not only non-trivial but, probably, impossible, especially considering that the communication channel, which is usually the keyboard, is so restrictive. Human tutors would normally combine data from a variety of other sources, like voice effects or facial gestures. They may also be able to detect other phenomenological factors such as boredom or motivation which are also crucial in learning.

In a recent review, Self (1988b) identified twenty different uses that had been found for student models in existing ITSs. *From* analysing this list, he notes that the functions of student models could be generally classified into six types.

1. *Corrective*: to help eradicate bugs in the student's knowledge.
2. *Elaborative:* to help correct 'incomplete' student knowledge.
3. *Strategic:* to help initiate significant changes in the tutorial strategy other than the tactical decisions of 1 and 2 above.
4. *Diagnostic:* to help diagnose bugs in the student's knowledge.
5. *Predictive:* to help determine the student's likely response to tutorial actions.
6. *Evaluative:* to help assess the student or the ITS.

Self's *preceding* list is still far from *comprehensive;* it could be narrowed down much further, and the student model could be seen to fulfil a double function. On the one hand, it acts as a source of information about the student. On the other hand, it serves as a representation of the student's knowledge. Wenger (1987) also supports this view. The next few paragraphs will attempt to justify this aforementioned viewpoint.

In its function as a source of information, it infers unobservable aspects of the student's behaviour from the model. Such an inference could produce an interpretation of his/her actions and also lead to a reconstruction of the knowledge that gave rise to these actions. Such knowledge is vital for the pedagogic component of the ITS as it could be used in either of the six ways noted by Self.

The student model is also likely to be formed out of the system's representation of the target knowledge in the expert knowledge module. Accordingly, the student model can include a clear evaluation of the mastery of each unit of knowledge in the expert module (the function of the student model here is evaluative). This allows the student's state of knowledge to be compared with the expert knowledge module, and instruction would then be biased towards portions of the model shown to be weak (thus, the student model's function here is elaborative). This form of student modelling is referred to as 'overlay' modelling (Goldstein, 1982), because the student's state of knowledge is viewed as a subset of the expert's. Again, this shows how the student model acts as a source of information.

However, incorrect or suboptimal behaviour does not always result from incomplete knowledge. It could also be due to incorrect versions of the target knowledge. Therefore a more formative student model should also provide explicit representations of the student's incorrect versions of the target knowledge for remediation purposes (clearly, the function of the student model here is diagnostic and corrective). In such a capacity, it serves as a representation of the student's knowledge. This approach to modelling is called the 'buggy' approach (Brown & Burton, 1978a).

Student models are also expected to be executable or runnable. This allows for exact prediction about a particular student in a particular context (thus, the function of the student model here is predictive). The tutoring module would also be making use of such executable representations for pedagogic purposes (i.e., the knowledge represented in the student model is being used in a strategic way). The student model is also serving here as a representation of the student's knowledge.

In conclusion, student models could be seen to perform two 'super' functions: acting as a source of information about the student, and serving as a representation of the student. In achieving these functions, they act in roles including corrective, elaborative, strategic, diagnostic, predictive and evaluative.

The tutoring module is the part of the ITS that designs and regulates instructional interactions with the student. In other architectures, this module is referred to as the teaching strategy or the pedagogic module. It is closely linked to the student model, using knowledge about the student and its own tutorial goal structure to decide which pedagogic activities will be presented: hints to overcome impasses in performance, advice, support, explanations, different practice tasks, tests to confirm hypotheses in the student's model, etc. (Self, 1988b). The tutorial component is thus the source and the orchestrator of all pedagogic interventions. The decisions involved are subtle. The order and manner in which topics are treated can produce very different learning experiences. In tutorial, it is sometimes more effective to let the student flounder for a while before interrupting; sometimes, the student will get stuck or lost if left completely to himself/herself (however, no good human tutor will destroy a student's personal motivation or sense of discovery). Consequently, the tutoring in existing ITSs can be classified along a spectrum ranging from systems that *monitor* the student's every activity very closely, adapting their actions to the student's responses but never relinquishing control, to *guided discovery learning* systems where the student has almost full control of the activity, and the only way the system can direct the course of action is by modifying the environment. In the middle are *mixed-initiative* systems where the control is shared by the student and the system as they exchange questions and answers. The existence of this spectrum clearly highlights the fact that tutoring is an art that requires great versatility which is still extremely difficult to articulate and represent in an ITS. Nevertheless, some progress is being made, albeit limited.

ITSs also aim at explicitly representing the knowledge found in the tutoring module. This creates the potential to adapt and improve strategies over time (as in the case of self-improving tutors), and for the same strategies to be used for other domains. Once more this is contrasted with traditional CAI systems where such pedagogical knowledge is deeply buried in the various pieces of code that control the tutorial interaction.

The* user *interface module is the communicating component of the ITS which controls interaction between the student and the system. In both directions, it translates between the system's internal representation and an interface language that is understandable to the student. Because the user interface can make or break the ITS, no matter how 'intelligent' the internal system is, it has become customary to identify it as a distinct component of its own. In fact, it would be a mistake to consider it a secondary component of the ITS for two main reasons. First, when the ITS presents a topic, the interface can enhance or diminish the presentation. Since the interface is the final form in which the ITS presents itself, qualities such as ease of use and attractiveness could be crucial to the student's acceptance of the system. Secondly, progress in media technology is increasingly providing more and more sophisticated tools whose communicative power heavily influences ITS design.

Current ITSs provide user interfaces which, for the input, range from the use of fixed menus with multiple-choice answers to a fairly free treatment of a pseudonatural language. For the output, they range from the mere display of pre-stored texts typical of CAI, to the use of fairly complicated generic frames. Within these two ends of the spectrum there is also a varying flexibility (Wenger, 1987).

Some ITSs are making their interaction with the student more 'user friendly' by substituting pictures and pointing for text and typing. In some, the treatment of text is only supplemented by pictures and graphics; much more cognitive research into the use of such interfaces is still required. However, the most one expects to see, in the near future, is ITSs communicating with the student primarily via graphics, as research in natural language understanding and computer speech recognition/generation are still at such early and primitive stages. In fact, research into user interfaces is just commencing, as they have only recently been acknowledged as distinct parts of ITSs.

Other Architectures of ITS

Other architectures have been suggested, some largely similar but others radically different. For example, there are four components to Anderson's Advanced Computer Tutoring (ACT) ITS architecture (Anderson *et al.*, 1985a, b) (see Fig. 9.8).

1. The domain expert (ideal student model): this module contains all the correct rules used for solving problems in the domain.
2. The bug catalogue: this is an extensive library of common misconceptions and errors for the domain.
3. The teaching knowledge (tutoring module).
4. The user interface.

This architecture is not only a proposal; at least two tutors are based on it including the Geometry tutor and the Lisp tutor (Anderson *et al.,* 1985a).

Hartley & Sleeman, whose 1973 architecture is probably the closest proposal to the general architecture depicted in Fig. 9.8, suggest that an ITS ought to have four distinct knowledge bases:

1. knowledge of the domain (expert knowledge),
2. knowledge of the person being taught (student model),
3. knowledge of the teaching strategies (tutoring knowledge),
4. knowledge of how to apply the tutoring knowledge to the needs of an individual,

Hartley & Sleeman's proposals differ from Anderson's inasmuch as they do not give the misconceptions in the domain (the bug catalogue) primary importance but instead introduce the student model as a primary component (Yazdani, 1987). Furthermore, this proposal subsumes the user interface in a more tutoringorientated module which includes meta-rules that guide the tutoring rules. These differences also reflect the different tutoring philosophies involved in both architectures; Anderson plays down the importance of the student model and, in its place, substitutes two knowledge bases of ideal and

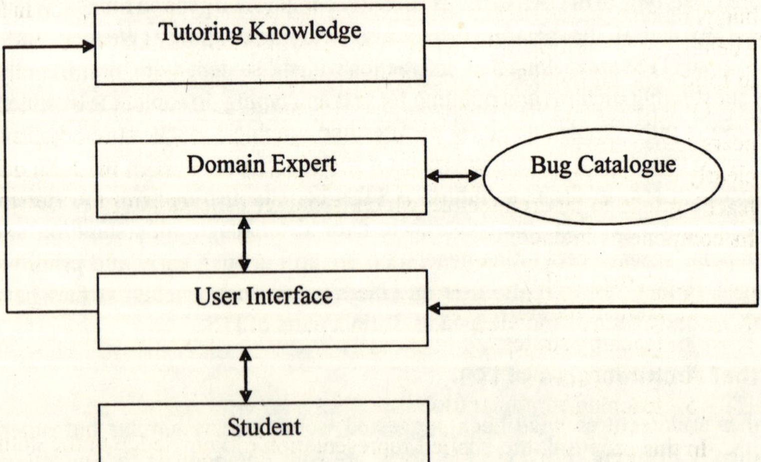

Figure 9.8: Anderson ITS Architecture

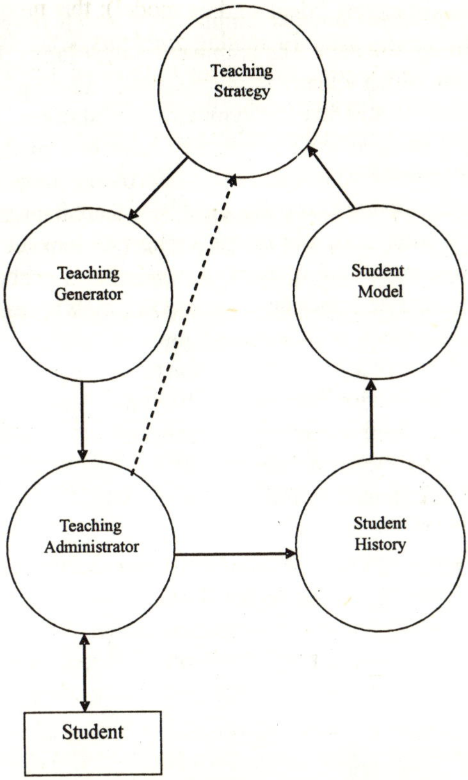

Figure 9.9: O'Shea *et al.* ITS Architecture

buggy representations of knowledge of the domain (see Fig. 9.8). Immediately a behaviour is exhibited which indicates an error or bug, the student is nudged to follow the correct path by being presented with the ideal solution.

O'Shea *et al.* (1984) present a five-ring model as shown in Fig. 9.9, This bears some similarity to the Hartley & Sleeman architecture. However, it also clearly demonstrates how differences in emphasis on student modelling and teaching lead to an architecture which is starkly different from Anderson's. Its components include:

1. student history,
2. student model,
3. teaching strategy,
4. teaching generation,
5. teaching administration.

In this proposal, the explicit representation of knowledge in the domain (expert knowledge), and the common misconceptions in the domain (the bug catalogue), are undermined in favour of teaching skills: hence the introduction of the teaching generation and teaching administration components.

Figure 9.10 presents another architecture which introduces the self-improving {learning) concept. The architecture thus forms the basis of self-improving systems which attempt to improve their tutoring capabilities over time. Such systems are still rare and typically consist of two components: an adaptive teaching programme (which may have any of the architectures discussed earlier or some other), and a self-improving component that makes experimental changes using data collected during teaching sessions. O'Shea's (1982) Quadratic tutor was one of the earliest to exploit this idea. This ambitious architecture, which attempts to automate a process that is even difficult for humans, is an important contribution; most researchers agree but pay lip service to the fact that ITSs should improve or learn over time as good human tutors do. Kimball's (1982) Integration tutor is generally acknowledged to be the first self-improving tutor to have been developed. In addition to the above architectures, more recent systems concentrate on other features such as planning (e.g. see Peachey & McCalla, 1986). The SCENT-3 architecture evolved by McCalla's team (McCalla & Greet, 1988) is much more complex and interested readers are referred to this paper. Suffice to say that it is based on a blackboard philosophy; the blackboard mediates communication among the numerous components of the architecture.

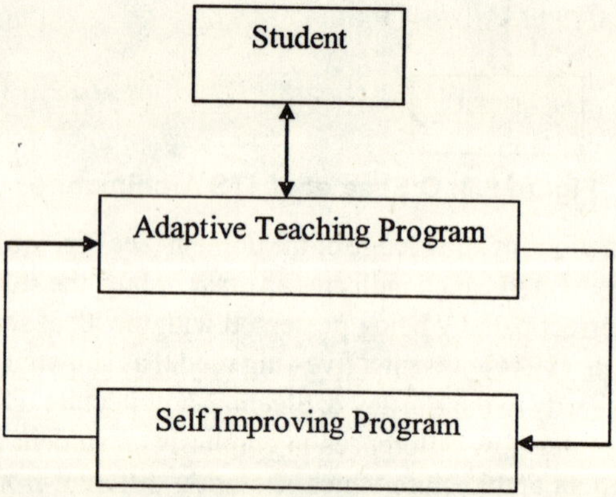

Figure 9.10: Self Improving ITS Architecture

Artificial Intelligence, Expert Systems and Simulations

The principle of AI made computers more useful, as well as intelligent, in order to utilize them in all the fields of human life. The application of AI principles is the next advanced step to a Web-based ITS, which began in the 1970s and 1980s. Since then, the influence of AI on software technology has considerably increased. As a result, the use of AI techniques in teaching/learning, such as expert systems, simulations and robotics, etc., has become a major factor in the development of Web-based intelligent authoring systems. AI is an advanced scientific technology that is used for efficient computer-based problem-solving techniques in various disciplines. The literature survey shows that the advancement in hardware and software systems has resulted in the development of numerous AI-based authoring tools with the help of sophisticated programming languages, such as LISP or Prolog. There are numerous interactive simulation tools developed in basic engineering disciplines, for example: a prototype of an intelligent case-based process planning system (Yang & Lu, 1993) and three-dimensional mechanical assemblies (Fang & Liou, 1993). However, most of these simulation systems are standalone in nature.

ITS and World Wide Web

Most of the traditionally developed ITSs use static media, such as CD-ROMs. However, it is very difficult to deploy the advancement and changes in the courseware in such systems; hence it is generally not suitable for basic learning strategies. The way to minimise the disadvantages inherent in traditional Intelligent Tutoring Systems is to utilise World Wide Web (WWW). Since its inception in 1990, the Internet (WWW or Web) has quickly emerged as a powerful new tool for connecting people and information on a global scale (Reed & Afjeh, 1998). The Web technology can also be utilised for various learning programmes based on multimedia/hypermedia techniques. ITS developers mostly concentrate on designing a programme that can provide effective instructions for the desired learning task. The developer's task has become more advanced and useful but challenging due to the common use of Internet technology in educational instructional systems. Recently, several advanced ITSs have been used for open and distance learning in many universities that provide learners with adequate sources of learning material for unlimited, unconditional use via the Internet.

10

Development of Intelligent Tutoring System

In the initial phase of ITS developments, several efforts have been undertaken to develop tutoring systems, mostly for teaching computer programming to students at the university level (Larkin and Chabay, 1992). However, recent research on ITS developments indicates that there are few dedicated ITSs developed in the engineering domain. Dear (1991) identified the trend in developing computerassisted instruction regarding the relationship of the content and the code. According to him, in traditional authoring systems developed with general purpose programming languages (e.g BASIC, COBOL, PASCAL, etc), the code and the contents were one and the same, yet this trend is changing with regard to AI-based authoring systems in which content is being separated from the code.

Curilem *et al.* (2006) propose a mathematical model of Intelligent Tutoring Systems (ITS), based on observations of the behaviour of these systems. One of the most important problems of pedagogical software is to establish a common language between the knowledge areas involved in their development, basically pedagogical, computing and domain areas. Authors presented an example demonstrating how the formalization was used to design the adaptive mechanism of and to adapt its Interface Module to some student characteristics.

Crowley and Medvedeva (2006) described the development of a general intelligent tutoring system for teaching visual classification problem solving. The architecture incorporates aspects of cognitive tutoring system and knowledge-based system design within the framework of the unified problem-solving method description language component model. Based on the domain ontology, domain task ontology and case data, the abstract problem-solving methods of the expert model create a dynamic solution graph. Student interaction with the solution graph is filtered through an instructional layer, which is created by a second set of abstract problem-solving methods and pedagogic ontologies, in response to the current state of the student model.

Huang *et al.* (2006) proposed three kinds of learning parameter improvement mechanisms to establish effective parameters that are frequently used in the learning platforms. The proposed learning parameter improvement mechanisms can calculate the students' effective online learning time, extract the portion of a message in discussion section which is strongly related to the learning topics, and detect plagiarism in students' homework, respectively. The derived numeric parameters are then fed into a Support Vector Machine (SVM) classifier to predict each learner's performance in order to verify whether they mirror the student's studying behaviours. The experimental results show that the prediction rate for the SVM classifier can be increased up to 35.7 per cent in average after the inputs to the classifier are "purified" by the learning parameter improvement mechanisms.

Woo *et al.* (2006) main research objective was to build an intelligent tutoring system capable of carrying on a natural language dialogue with a student who is solving a problem in physiology. Analysis of a corpus of 75 hour-long tutoring sessions carried on in keyboard-to-keyboard style by two professors of physiology tutoring first-year medical students provided the rules used in tutoring strategies and tactics, parsing, and text generation. The system presents the student with a perturbation to the blood pressure, asks for qualitative predictions of the changes produced in seven important cardiovascular variables, and then launches a dialogue to correct any errors and to probe for possible misconceptions. The natural language understanding component uses a cascade of finite-state machines. Results of experiments with pretests and posttests have shown that using the system for an hour produces significant learning gains and also that even this brief use improves the student's ability to solve problems more then reading textual material on the topic. Han *et al.* (2005) described an intelligent tutoring in a collaborative medical tutor for Problem Based Learning (PBL). Authors used Bayesian networks to model individual student clinical reasoning, as well as that of the group. The prototype system incorporates substantial domain knowledge in the areas of head injury, stroke and heart attack. Tutoring in PBL is particularly challenging since the tutor should provide as little guidance as possible while at the same time not allowing the students to get lost. From studies of PBL sessions at a local medical school, the authors identified and implemented eight commonly used hinting strategies.

Stathacopoulou *et al.* (2005) proposed a neural network implementation for a fuzzy logic-based model of the diagnostic process is proposed as a means to achieve accurate student diagnosis and updates of the student model in Intelligent Learning Environments. The neuro-fuzzy synergy allows the diagnostic model to some extent "imitate" teachers in diagnosing students' characteristics, and equips the intelligent learning environment with reasoning capabilities that can be further used to drive pedagogical decisions depending on the student learning style. The neuro-fuzzy implementation helps to encode both structured and non-structured teachers' knowledge: when teachers' reasoning is available and well defined, it can be encoded in the form of fuzzy rules; when teachers' reasoning is not well defined but is available through practical examples illustrating their experience, then the networks can be trained to represent this experience. Jaques and Vicari (2006) described the use of mental states approach, more specifically the belief-desireintention (BDI) model, to implement the process of affective diagnosis in an educational environment. Authors used the psychological OCC model, which is based on the cognitive theory of emotions and is possible to be implemented computationally, in order to infer the learner's emotions from his actions in the system interface. The proposed architecture profit from the reasoning capacity of the BDI model in order to infer the student's appraisal (a cognitive evaluation of a person that elicits an emotion) which allows to deduce student's emotions. The system reasons about an emotion-generating situation and tries to infer the user's emotion by using the OCC model. Besides, the BDI model is very adequate to infer and also model student's affective states since the emotions have a dynamic nature.

Aberek and Popov (2004) presented an intelligent tutoring system STATFAG for education on design, optimisation and the manufacturing of gears and gearing. STATFAG serves several purposes. It helps lecturers to plan and execute optimal lessons for various subjects; it makes self-studies of students of higher level of education at the Faculty of Mechanical Engineering much more efficient; and also assists less experienced graduates who must independently design gear assemblies in companies. Hwang (2003) proposed a conceptual map model, which provides learning suggestions by analyzing the subject materials and test results. A testing and diagnostic system is also implemented on computer networks based on the novel approach. Experimental results have demonstrated that the novel approach benefits students and deserves further investigation.

Architecture of Intelligent Tutoring System

Various architectures are proposed in literature for ITS systems and it is almost impossible to find two ITSs based on same architecture. There are currently no clear-cut guidelines available regarding the general structure of the ITS architecture. Previously, there was some consensus that the architecture of an ITS consists of at least three basic components:

- The Expert Knowledge Module
- The Student Model Module
- The Tutoring Module

Afterwards one more component has been identified and has been added as fourth one in the list.

- The User Interface Module

As stated above that there is no single method to design an ITS system. Nowadays some more components have been identified. Here we are giving there different models of ITS architecture.

First ITS Architecture Model

This model has mainly 5 major components for ITS development. The figure 10.1 shows the architecture model.

- Domain Expertise Component
- Student Expertise Component
- Teaching Expertise Component
- Communication Component
- System Learning Component
- Control Component

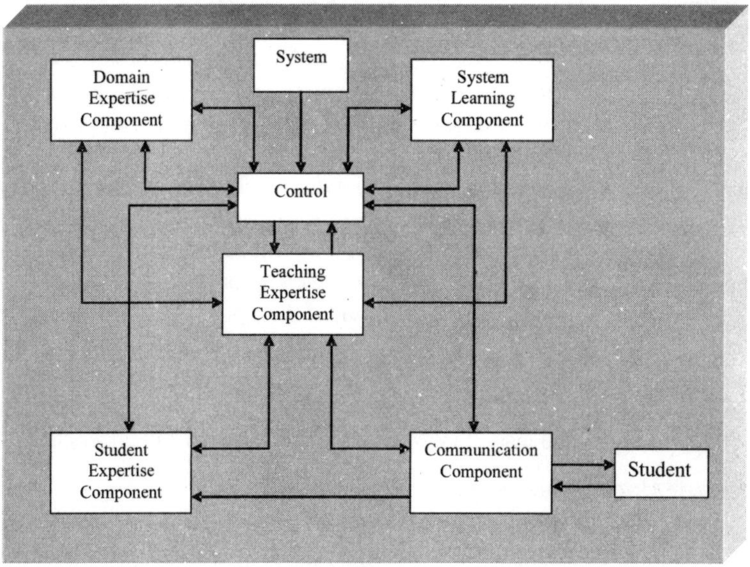

Figure 10.1: Architecture of ITS Model

Domain Expertise Module

This component is also known as expert knowledge module. In order to generate the information required by the student, the ITS (like a teacher) must possess the knowledge of the subject area or domain. The domain expertise module contains all the knowledge or subject matter in a knowledge base. This knowledge has to be represented in structures, which understandable and can be manipulated by the computer system. Traditional CAL does not have expert modules of this sort because it is not required to actually solve the problems presented to students other than those solvable through algorithmic methods, i.e., mathematical problems. The difference becomes apparent in domains where heuristic reasoning on domain concepts is needed rather than execution of algorithms. In this type of domain solutions cannot be generated by running algorithms because the procedure for solving a problem is not fully defined and therefore, some uncertainty always exists.

Currently expert knowledge in ITS is represented in various ways, including semantic networks, frames and production systems and includes both surface knowledge (e.g., the description of various concepts that the student has to acquire) and the representational ability, which is a critical part of expertise. Expert knowledge modules range from completely opaque or 'black-box' representations whereby only final results are available (a classical example is tutor SOPHIE I), to fully transparent or 'glass-box' ones, where each reasoning step can be inspected and interpreted (e.g., SOPHIE III). These modules, on one hand, serve as the source of knowledge to be presented to the student, which includes generating questions, explanations and responses and on other hand, they provide a standard for evaluating the student's performance by generating comparable solutions to problems in the same context as the student. The modules must also be able to detect common systematic mistakes and any resulting gap in the student's knowledge. The expert module must also be able to generate sensible and possibly multiple solution paths to compare intermediate steps to provide student monitoring.

The domain expertise module by necessity embodies a specific view of the domain of the designer. Thus, tutoring can be compromised if the student does not understand the system's instruction or if the system cannot interpret the student's behaviour in terms of its own view of the knowledge. Of course, human teachers also have their own views and styles of teaching which students may find difficult to understand but these human teachers have the incredible ability to adopt the styles and way of expressions which students can understand.

Student Model Module

The student model is the component of an ITS that represents the student's current state of knowledge. The role of the student model module is to build up a picture of the student in terms of what the student does and does not know in order to provide him individualized instructions. It should infer what the student already knows about the subject matter and how well the student is progressing. This information is used to decide what next is to present to the student.

The student model module evaluates each learner's performance to determine his/her knowledge, perceptual abilities and reasoning skills. To understand this imagine that three learners are presented with addition problems that they answer as follows:

Though all three participants answered incorrectly, different underlying misconceptions caused each person's errors. Student A fails to carry, student B always carries (sometimes unnecessarily) and student C has trouble with single-digit addition. In this example, the student supplies an answer to the problem and the tutoring system infers the student's misconceptions from this answer. By maintaining and referring to a detailed model of each user's strengths and weaknesses, the ITS can provide highly specific and relevant instruction.

ITS attempts to capture the student's profile while the student is interacting with the computer through a variety of parameters, such as type of information requested, speed of acquisition of information, response time, etc. The system than builds up a cognitive model of the student and/or a model(s) of the student's view of the subject also called domain model. The cognitive model represents the general intellectual abilities of the student while the domain model represents the perception of the student of the discipline under study. It is not uncommon to have more than one domain model for the same domain. These are dynamic models, which go on changing with every interaction. The ITS or ICAI uses these models to analyze the thought process of the student or the domain knowledge of the student in the overall context to decide how much the student understood and to identify the weak areas. Since the purpose of the student model is to provide data for the pedagogical module of the system, all of the information gathered should be able to be used by the tutor module.

The Relationship of the Student Model Module to the Domain Expertise Module

The construction of the student model is generally based on the model of the subject matter or the expert's knowledge model. According to the relation between this model and the student model, student models are usually classified into three types in the literature. These three types of models are—overlay, differential and perturbation.

Overlay Model: The overlay model assumes that all differences between the student's behaviour and the behaviour of the expert model can be explained by the lack of skills on the part of the student.

Differential Model: Differential modeling divides the class of things of which the system believes the student does not know into those which the student should know (if they are to behave like the expert) and those things which the student could not be expected to know. Both overlay and differential models assume that knowledge of the student is only a subset of the knowledge of the expert and therefore do not represent any belief of the user which is outside the domain knowledge of the expert.

Perturbation Model: In perturbation models the student model can differ on the basis of small perturbations, from some of the knowledge in the expert model. A lack of knowledge is just another form of perturbation—for instance, common bugs or misconceptions.

Teaching Expertise Module

The teaching expertise module or instructional module is the part of the ITS that designs and regulates instructional interactions with the student. In other architectures, this module is referred to as the tutoring strategy or the pedagogic module. This module decides the teaching strategies to be used for imparting the instruction to a particular student and so incorporates the knowledge regarding the pedagogical principles and practices. As teaching is not merely an orderly presentation of the instructional material, it must use the knowledge about the learner capabilities from the student model and his/her own goal structure to decide what instructional activities will have to be presented. It is closely linked to the student model, using knowledge about the student and its own tutorial goal structure to decide which pedagogic activities will be presented: hints to overcome impasses in performance, advice, support, explanations, different practices tasks, tests to confirm hypotheses in the student's model, etc. It may decide to present new material or revise previously taught material. It will decide when the student needs help and give the appropriate help. Questions will be asked when this module decides the student should be tested. Explanations will be given when it decides the student is confused. Thus, this module designs and regulates the instructional interactions of the student with the computer.

Communication Module

The communication or user interface module is the communicating component of the ITS, which controls interaction between the student and the system. In both directions, it translates between the system's internal representation and an interface language that is understandable to the student. This module is responsible for all the interaction of computer with the student. Ideally, this interaction should be bi-directional and in the natural language (NL) of the student. The conventional CAI system permit only limited communication from computer to student but the communication from student to computer is highly restricted and non-existent. But in ICAI there is an effort to give the opportunity to student to improve his/her computer communication.

The communication module analyses the student's questions or responses and presents the interpreted information to the ICAL system. The teaching expertise module looks at this information and then on the basis of this information and information provided by the domain expertise module, it prepares the information to be provided to the student. This information is given to communication module, which packages it in natural language and presents it to the student.

System Learning Module

This module helps the system to acquire domain knowledge or teaching expertise during its interactions with students. Thus, this module permits the system to simulate human teacher who is characterized by his ability to learn during his interactions with others. This component is responsible for improving the overall abilities of the system.

Control Module

This module provides overall control, co-ordination and communication between various modules.

Second ITS Architecture Model: The GET-BITS Model

Intelligent tutoring systems are becoming more common and are proving to be increasingly effective in their basic goal of individualizing the learning process. But, the fact is that the definition and implementation of a typical ITS needs a quite large development environment and this process is very time consuming, i.e. the accomplishments of an average ITS require huge computing resources, lot of money and time. Traditional ITSs are concentrated on the domain knowledge they are supposed to present and teach; hence their control mechanisms are often domain-dependent. More recent ITS's pay more attention to generic problems and concepts of the tutoring process, trying to separate architectural, methodological and control issues from domain knowledge as much as possible. In other words, there are interactive and integrated development tools for building ITS. Such integrated tools are often referred to as shells (eg., ITS Shells or ILE Shells or IES Shells etc.), which usually require a knowledge engineer in order to be fully used or authoring tools, which can be also used by human instructors who do not necessarily have knowledge engineering experience.

Authoring tools or shells can speed ITSs development and reduce costs by providing essential infrastructure along with a conceptual framework within which to approach an educational problem. Some of the ITS tools are:

ITS Tools	Developers
PIXIE	Sleeman, 1988
Byte-sized Tutor	*Bonar, 1988*
IDE	Russell et. al., 1988
ID Expert	Merrill, 1989
KAFITS	Murray and Woolf, 1990
COCA	Major and Reichgelt, 1992
GTE	Van Marcke, 1992
RIDES	Munroe et. al., 1994
EON	Murray, 1997

Some major limitations with these ITS tools are as follows:

- They are too complicated and complex because they are based primarily on theoretical concerns or AI techniques;
- Using them still needs a big development team and huge computer resources so the product is still expensive;
- These shells and tools are very inappropriate for changing their elements (they simply copy the philosophy of expert systems shells), i.e. the definition of the elements are buried in the source code, so some changes could require the complete re-design of the shell;
- Most of them are based on a specific instructional approach;
- The domains of application are limited because the system was

modeled from an existing task—specific intelligent tutor and generalized to similar domains; and

- They provide tools for structuring and using knowledge but not for creating appealing student interfaces or learning environments.

The GET-BITS (Generic Tools for Building ITS) Approach

Instead a traditional expert systems shells approach (like most of the above shells and tools) we can solve these problems with ITSs, authoring tools and ITSs shells using the object-oriented approach combined with component based-architecture. Figure 10.2 shows the ITS Architecture of GET-BITS Approach.

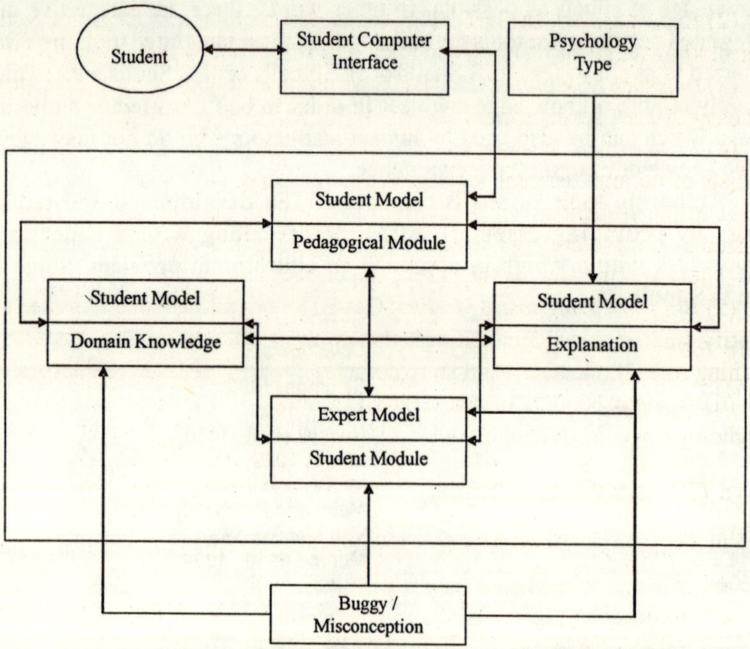

Figure 10.2: The ITS Architecture (GET-BITS Approach)

(1) *Knowledge Base*: In GET-BITS, the knowledge base has three parts—domain knowledge (i.e. a model of experts' knowledge), control knowledge (i.e. a model of the teaching process) and the third part is explanatory knowledge.

(i) *Domain Knowledge*: In GET-BITS, the domain knowledge expert module is represented with a knowledge network of semantically connected frames. That knowledge network represents the content to be taught in terms of lessons, concepts, rules, tasks, questions, actions, examples and their inter relationships. It can be thought of as more than just a network of facts. The knowledge network could be coupled to a domain expert or it could be a collection of text, pictures, simulation procedures and/or voice.

(ii) *Control Knowledge*: The content of the ITS's control knowledge are abstract, explicit and more or less domain independent descriptions of the way to learn some facts during the ITS's operation.

(iii) *Explanatory Knowledge*: The primary purpose of the part of the knowledge base that we refer to as the explanatory knowledge is to define the contents of explanations and justifications of the ITS's learning processes, as well as the way they are generated. Explanatory knowledge is related to both domain and control knowledge and often that knowledge are treated as a part of the other two components of knowledge bases.

(2) *Expert Model*: In GET-BITS, the expert module is represented with control knowledge and with the concept of transactions.

(3) *Interface Module*: In GET-BITS we use a menu-driven, icon-managed and easy-to-use user interface.

(4) *Pedagogical Module*: In GET-BITS the pedagogical or tutor module consists of various teaching strategies, the rules that decide what should be taught to the student given the current state of the student model. This is realized by parameterizing a semantic network of frames with the combination of If-Then-Action rules, as the part of the control knowledge.

(5) *Buggy or Diagnostic Module*: Get-BITS consists of the rules used to identify student misunderstandings, update the student model, manage the teaching rules if necessary and store common student mistakes and errors.

(6) Student Model: In the GET-BITS model there is an addition of psychology type in student model.

Third ITS Architecture Model

This model consists of seven major modules or components, such as:

- Domain Knowledge Base
- Problem Solver
- Student Modular
- Instructional Planner
- Input Under stander
- Text Generator
- Screen Manager

The three modules, namely "Domain Knowledge Base", "Student Modular" and "Instructional Planner" are discussed above. Now we discuss the next components one by one:

(1) *Problem Solver*: The intelligence of an ITS comes from its ability to solve the problems. The problem solver solves the problems presented to the student or asked by the student. If the problem solver solves the problems but

cannot explain how it solves them, it may just as well retrieve stored answers. The ability to solve the problem, using the expert's problem solving behaviour, can be used to identify the student's misconceptions, to give an explanation and to provide a basis for tutoring strategies.

(2) *Input Under stander*: The input under stander is responsible for understanding, the student's natural language input. It handles not only well formed but also ill-formed student inputs. The student input may be either an answer to the tutor's question or a question from the student.

(3) *Text Generator*: The text generator is responsible for turning the tutor's output into a natural language sentence. It receives necessary information as a logical form from the planner and generates a natural language sentence or sequence of sentences. This information includes the current topic and text styles, question hint, answer etc.

(4) *Screen Manager*: The screen manager takes care of the interaction between the student and the system. The planner closely controls the interaction, the planner tells the screen manager what to display and the screen manager sends back the student's input to the planner. Thus, every interaction passes through the planner. The screen manager may display its own messages such as help messages or warning messages.

Intelligent Tutoring System Architectures

This section examines selected intelligent tutoring systems spanning the period 1988-1999, and classifies them into three categories, namely three-model, four-model and new generation architectures. The ITS architectures have in the main been named after their respective designers for easy referencing.

Three-Model Architectures for ITSs

A three model architecture typically comprises three major building blocks or components, namely the systems domain expertise, student knowledge and skill, and tutoring expertise. Two examples representing the three-model architecture are discussed below.

(1) *Derry* et al. *Architecture*

Derry, Hawkes & Ziegler [1988] proposed an ITS architecture comprising three major components, namely a tutoring model, expert domain model, and student knowledge model. Each of these components will be discussed below.

Tutoring Model: This model makes use of heuristically guided routines to perform three levels of instructional activity, namely planning an individual's route through a curriculum (the agenda); planning lessons (using action schemata); and online tutorial intervention. At each of these instructional levels, student performance data can be compiled and made available to other levels. This model uses three sub-components, namely a curriculum planner, lesson planner and intervening monitor for performing the three levels of instructional activity.

Expert Domain Model: This model provides information to guide routines in the tutoring model.

Student Knowledge Model: This model also informs the routines of the tutoring model.

Derry *et al.* [1988] combines the planning and opportunistic architectures for intelligent tutoring, by using global models of domain knowledge to structure the student's learning experience, and bases didactic decisions on the learner's operational model of performance. This architecture has a well-defined tutorial component embodying curriculum planning, lesson planning, and tutorial monitoring and intervention with the ultimate goal of moving the student toward the expert model of knowledge. The functionality of the expert domain and student knowledge models appears to be limited to providing information to routines in the tutoring model. A shortcoming of this architecture is the omission of the user interface component and allied usability issues. A major strength of this architecture is the use of heuristically guided routines in the tutoring model, which provides dynamic student-centred tutoring. This architecture is recommended for problem-solving or procedural task application domains.

(2) *Siemer and Angelides Architecture*

The next architecture described by Siemer and Angelides [1998] also supports a basic three-model structure, comprising domain expertise, student knowledge and skill, and tutoring expertise. The point of departure between this architecture and the previous one is that it explicitly identifies the processes manipulating the three knowledge bases in each of the models, and incorporates an additional process to co-ordinate the three models. The three major architectural components and the overall system control are described below.

The Domain Model: The domain model contains knowledge relating to the subject matter. The intelligent tutoring system utilises its domain knowledge to reason with and solve problems, or to answer questions posed by students. Different knowledge representations of the same domain knowledge may be incorporated to support alternative teaching strategies. Domain knowledge processes, referred to as the *expertise* provide for the content of tutorial interactions.

The Tutoring Model: The tutoring model provides the knowledge needed to attain teaching goals. It should have: control over the sequence and selection of subject material to be presented to the student; response mechanisms to answer learners' questions with appropriate answers; and knowledge of when learners need help, in the course of solving a problem or practising a skill, and what type of help to offer. To achieve this, the tutoring model needs to embrace different teaching strategies (styles of delivery).

The tutoring knowledge processes referred, to as the *didactic aspect* is responsible for selecting teaching goals, and for determining appropriate teaching strategies for learners on the basis of their student models, learner's needs and/or preferences, learning experiences, the domain of discourse and the instructional objectives of the intelligent tutoring system.

The Student Model: The student model represents the learner's emerging knowledge and skills. Information such as learning preferences, past learning experiences and advancement may also be relevant in adapting the teaching process. It may also record the learner's errors and misconceptions. The student knowledge processes, known as *diagnostics*, analyse the behaviour of the student.

Overall System Control: The overall system control process is needed to co-ordinates the three-knowledge models to provide student-centred tutoring. For example, an intelligent tutoring system has to select teaching strategies and presentations for each subject area, in accordance with an individual learner's needs and preferences stored in the student model.

Additional flexibility may also be provided with a student or system initiated help system.

This architecture provides a comprehensive description of the knowledge and functional requirements related to the various architectural components comprising an ITS. It does not delve into implementation issues or operability mechanics. This architecture extends the concept of lesson planning and dynamic adaptation thereof in the previous architecture, to embrace multiple knowledge representations and teaching strategies. Each of the models are welldefined in terms of the knowledge bases and processes supported. Furthermore, an additional process is identified for managing and co-ordinating the activities of the three models, which is not evident in the previous architecture. Since this is a general Intelligent Tutoring System architecture, it can be adopted and/or adapted for use in any application domain.

In summary, the three-model architecture represents the traditional architecture of ITSs comprising three main components that are commonly referred to as domain model, student model, and tutoring model. The three-tier architecture of ITSs made way for the four-model ITS architecture, which is discussed next.

Fourth-Model Architecture for ITSs

The four-model architecture retained the three major components of the traditional three model architecture, and added the *user interface* as a fourth component. This architecture became the classical standard architecture for ITSs.

Dede's Architecture: A typical example of a four-model architecture comprising the *knowledge base, student model, pedagogical module,* and *user interface* is described below [Dede, 1986]. A brief discussion on each of these components follows:

Knowledge Base: A tutor or coach incorporates declarative (what), procedural (how), and metacognitive (thinking about what and how) knowledge. This component is synonymous with the domain model of other architectures.

Student Model: An internal model representing cognitive processes (such as information retrieval, calculation and problem solving), meta-cognitive strategies (for example, learning from errors) and psychological attributes (developmental level, learning style, and interests) are maintained for each learner.

Pedagogical Module: This module is similar to its counterpart the tutoring model in other architectures. It uses a model of the learner's present comprehension to select an efficient path through its knowledge representation to generate expert behaviour by the learner. It employs different teaching strategies on the basis of an evolving student model, and an underlying instructional theory that determines which pedagogical means is most efficient to accomplish a given end, alternative approaches to dialogue management (adjusting to different learning styles), and domain-dependent teaching heuristics. A teaching module is recommended to facilitate integration and co-ordination of the functions of the other components.

User Interface: This component integrates three types of information that are needed in carrying out a dialogue: knowledge about patterns of interpretation (to understand a speaker) and action (to generate utterances) within dialogues; domain knowledge needed for communicating content; and knowledge needed for communicating intent. The four-model architecture makes a number of important contributions in that it: incorporates a separate user interface component; embodies cognitive processes, meta-cognitive strategies and learning styles in the student model; and includes domain dependent teaching heuristics in the pedagogical model, all of which are hitherto unmentioned. The user interface is regarded as an internal and integral component of the ITS architecture whereas other architectures viewed this component as external to an ITS. This inclusion has positive consequences in that user-interface design and usability issues have become part of ITS development concerns. Another important contribution is the use of a pedagogical component, which combines instructional theory with pedagogical strategies and dialogue management for providing instruction to learners. This architecture was coined as classical in that it became the industry standard for ITS construction.

New-Generation Architectures for ITSs

New-generation architectures represent a departure from the traditional three-model and classical four-model architectures in that they integrated software development advances, as well as new learning and instructional theories into the design of ITSs. Two of these architectures are described below.

(1) Multi-agent Architecture: A multi-agent architecture called MATHEMA [Costa & Perkusich, 1996] is used as a basis for the design of a computer-based intelligent learning environment, which comprises the following six components:

1. An external motivator (representing human external entities that motivate the learner to work in MATHEMA, for example, a teacher);
2. A human learner;

3. A micro-society of artificial tutoring agents (MARTA), that may co-operate among themselves to achieve problem solving activities in a formal and well-structured knowledge domain, divided into different microdomains, each one covering micro-specialities.
4. A human experts society (HES), working as sources of knowledge to MARTA;
5. An interface agent between a human learner and MARTA, responsible for communication and which includes a mechanism of selection for tutor agent (supervisor); and
6. A communication agent providing interaction between MARTA and HES, and responsible for the communication and maintenance of MARTA.

The main idea underlying this architecture is to integrate human learners in a micro-society of artificial agents with the objective of promoting their learning. Grandbastien [1999] is of the opinion that agent-based architectures are more flexible in that new artificial tutoring agents may be added, existing artificial tutoring agents may be modified and/or deleted without negatively impacting on the operation of the other components within the architecture. Hence modular development would be enhanced, and module reusability would be promoted. This architecture promotes the notion of a computer-based intelligent learning environment, which includes external human motivators and a human expert society. Due recognition is thus given to the environmental context in which learning takes place. This architecture encompasses components of the traditional and classical architectures, albeit in a unique structure and representation. The domain model is embedded in MARTA and HES, the role and functions of the tutoring model is distributed among a micro-society of artificial tutoring agents, the user interface component is represented as interface agent and the human learner is represented as a component of the learning environment, and not as a student model as with other architectures. This architecture is recommended for specific, formal and well-structured knowledge domains such as the classical logic domain.

(2) Self's Architecture: Self [1999] revisits the conventional tripartite division of ITSs into the domain, student and tutoring model from a *constructivist learning perspective*. The new tripartite model of the architecture of computer-based learning environments includes the standard ITS architecture as a subset. The proposed new generation three-model architecture for intelligent tutoring systems comprises the situation, interaction and affordance models. Each of these components is discussed below:

Situation Model: The contexts and the dynamics of the learning process are embodied within a *situation model*, which contains descriptions of resources (although it may also contain representations of aspects of the domain of knowledge), which are available in a learning situation as opposed to a pure domain model, which contain descriptions of target knowledge. A model of domain knowledge may thus be perceived as a subset of the broader notion of a situation model.

Interaction Model: An 'interaction process model' focuses on interaction sequences by considering the learner's actions, the contexts in which they occurred, and the learner's cognitive structures at the time. Here again, the notion of an interaction process model is perceived as a superset of an ITS-style student model.

Affordance Model: An affordance model is developed in terms of 'items of knowledge', which may be learned through particular events (for example, an event such as the presentation of remediational feedback affords the learning of the item of knowledge being remediated). The affordance model is thus broader than the model of teaching as curriculumbased planning.

Self extends the scope of the traditional three-model architecture as a result of new insights gained into the complex nature of the learning process, and strongly recommends that learning resources, interaction sequences, and items of knowledge be modelled into the respective architectural components. Self pays due diligence to, and explicitly incorporates the context of learning into the architecture of ITSs which has not been alluded to in other architectures. The issue of context in learning has become an important research area since an understanding of contexts is needed in order to design better and more usable ITSs [Patel & Russell, 1998]. Self's architecture challenges traditional learning theories and may be regarded as a watershed for the development of future intelligent tutoring systems based on constructivistic processes involved in learning.

New-generation architectures for ITSs have emerged from the need to build specific functionality for specialized application domains, embrace important trends in software development, namely modular and incremental development, global sharing of knowledge, as well as incorporate current trends in learning and instruction.

Genetic Characteristics of Intelligent Tutoring Systems

From the architectures examined, it is evident that intelligent tutoring systems possess a number of generic characteristics and behaviour, which are related to specific architectural components. Table 10.1 outlines five architectural components and their associated characteristics. It is envisaged that these characteristics would be useful for the comparison and evaluation of existing ITSs, as well as guide the design of new ITSs, It should, however, be noted that the architecture and behaviour of ITSs are to some degree influenced/constrained by specific application domains (e.g. geography, programming, mathematics, etc.) and design paradigms (e.g. problemsolving monitors, coaches, diagnostic tutors, microworld etc.). Hence, some of the characteristics may with justification, not be incorporated in certain architectures.

Table 10.1: Generic Characteristics/Behaviour of an ITS

ITS Architecture	Characteristics/Behaviour
Domain Model	*Intelligent tutoring systems should:* Possess system domain knowledge to ma ke inferences or solve problems; Provide explanations of problem solutions; Give alternative explanations of the same concept; Answer arbitrary questions from the student; Incorporate knowledge about common misconceptions and missing concepts.
Tutoring Model	Possess system teaching goals & plans; Provide alternative teaching strategies; Be guided by an underlying instructional theory; Tailor system's teaching strategies with student's needs; Allow student to initiate instructional activities; Provide contextualised, doma in-relevant and engaging learning activities; Diagnose misconceptions and learning needs; Intervene if the student appears to be having difficulty; Relate a diagnosed error to a misconception or a missing concept; Incorporate remedial strategies in order to provide alternative remedial teaching styles.
Student Model	Maintain information about the student's knowledge, and skills (current and advancing) in the student model; Store information on the student's cognitive processes; Store information on student's learning preferences and/or past learning experiences in the student model, if the need arises; Monitor and assess student performance and update student model.
System Control	Provide helpful feedback on student input; Treat all detected errors; Respond if it cannot diagnose an error; Intervene to remediate a misconception or a missing concept; Adapt to student's level of advancement; Adapt to the needs and preferences of the student.
User interface	Promote ease of use; Incorporate natural interaction dialogues; Ensure that the dialogue is task-oriented and adaptive; Possess an effective screen design; Embrace a variety of interaction styles.

Sources: Beverly Park Woolf, University of Massachusetts [1998], Costa & Perkusich, 1996]; [Dede, 1986]; Derry *et al.* [1988]; Dix *et al.* [1993]; Gold [1998]; Self [1999]; and Siemer & Angelides [1998].

An Enhanced Architecture for Teaching

Many intelligent tutoring systems have been proposed, some of which have been developed and experimented (also on a wide scale like PAT tutor), on many types of knowledge domains mainly in scientific ones. In many of the experiences with these systems has been found a benefit for customers that have used them. It is therefore well proved that the use of this kind of systems is, in principle, effective and improves the process of learning in numerous varieties of domains.

The research conducted in the field of ITS is relatively young and there are several problems inherent to the development of this kind of software. In the following we will make some basic hypotheses to reason about and we try to define a system architecture that can solve some of the issues:

- There exist a certain amount of documents that can be retrieved in an easy and fast way and they come from trusted sources. These documents contain non structured information, which is data that cannot be used directly from the system for tutoring purpose (Learning Object, HTML documents, pdf documents, etc...). These documents deal with a specific domain of knowledge;
- There is an expert that is the depositary of the structured domain knowledge of interest and another expert that is the depositary of the instruction strategies to be used for teaching the domain;
- There is a system capable of transferring the structured knowledge from the expert to the computer and it can deduce the same knowledge, or part of it, from the documents that contain non structured information;
- The system delivers the acquired knowledge following a predefined pedagogical plan and improve its performances by means of users feedbacks and interactions.

Having in mind these considerations the main problems for the creation of an ITS are:

- Defining the representation of the semantic and/or syntactic content of documents that contain the non structured knowledge. This kind of representation should be used from the system in order to guide the learning process during the didactic material delivering. The extraction of this information must be carried out in automatic or semi-automatic way;
- Defining and realizing authoring tools that through the interaction with the depositary of the structured knowledge (the domain expert) can generate, in an easy and fast way, the necessary information needed to the system in order to both deliver the contents and guide the problem solving learning for the subject domain;
- Defining the system structure in such way to be highly modular and in such way that it can improve its performance through the several interactions with the users, that is it should learn from experience.

Architecture Proposal: An Overview

The proposed architecture is shown in Figure 10.3. We suppose a scenario where the domain expert is a teacher that has access to this hypothetical system and to a number of electronic documents that she wants to use for creation of didactic material. The final objective will be to enable the teacher to easily author the system without any specific skills on knowledge engineering. The fundamental idea behind this architecture is to automate as much as possible the phase of domain knowledge acquisition and subsequently refinements to both the teaching strategies and domain knowledge. The human intervention is required in the case the system is not able to accomplish one of the task involved in knowledge acquisition. We chose the constraint-based model as the core structure of the system. The domain knowledge is composed by a number of component:

- The set of documents containing unstructured domain information;
- The ontology describing the concepts and relations between them;
- The set of constraints that must be satisfied by a solution state in order to be correct;
- An high level knowledge that groups the constraints in a more coarse-grained fashion.

Ideally the domain expert has to do some tasks that should not require additional competence apart the domain one. These actions are:

- Validate the content of documents, that is the expert has to instruct the system on the validity of the documents in the knowledge base;
- Provide a set of problems along with the related set of solutions. We suppose that solutions are supplied in form of text.

The system has a module that can create an ontology starting from the documents that deal with a determined argument. A number of systems have been proposed for semi-automatic ontology acquisition from text sources such as Asium [Faure, D., Ndellec, C., and Rouveirol, C. (1998)], TextToOnto [Maedche, A., and Staab, S. (2000)], Ontolearn [Navigli, R., Velardi, P., and Gangemi, A. (2003)] and OntoLT [Buitelaar, P., Olejnik, D., and Sintek, M. (2003)] even if there much work to do in order to obtain a system suitable for practical use. A possible integration of these systems should be reasonable.

In a more realistic scenario domain knowledge can be acquired by interacting with human expert that inserts her knowledge by means of an authoring tool capable of both graphic editing and natural language dialog. Both ontology and constraint base of the system can be acquired with this modality.

Once domain knowledge is acquired in the form of constraints, an induction of the structure of knowledge can be done based on ontology and interaction with human expert. In [Martin, B., and Mitrovic, A. (2000)] Martin *et al.* use machine learning to induce the knowledge structure from feedback messages associated with constraints but the mechanisms should be improved considering also the domain ontology. This type of knowledge can be updated, hopefully improving it, by means of learning algorithms that based on student feedback can change or add some kind of relation (like precedence relation between topics).

The expert module of the system uses the set of constraint to check if a partial or total solution, given to certain problem, is in a correct state. An example of this methodology is given in [Martin, B., and Mitrovic, A. (2002a)] where an algorithm for problem solving and generation starting from constraint is presented.

The pedagogical module selects the most suitable action for current student based on student model and domain knowledge. A number of techniques were used to deal with this problem. An overview of student modelling and related issues can be found in [Jameson, A. (1995)] and [Sison, R., and Shimura, M. (1998)]. The pedagogical module can be seen has a black box that takes in input information on student and domain and select the next action based on these information. The policy can be improved applying machine learning algorithms in order to refine teaching strategies.

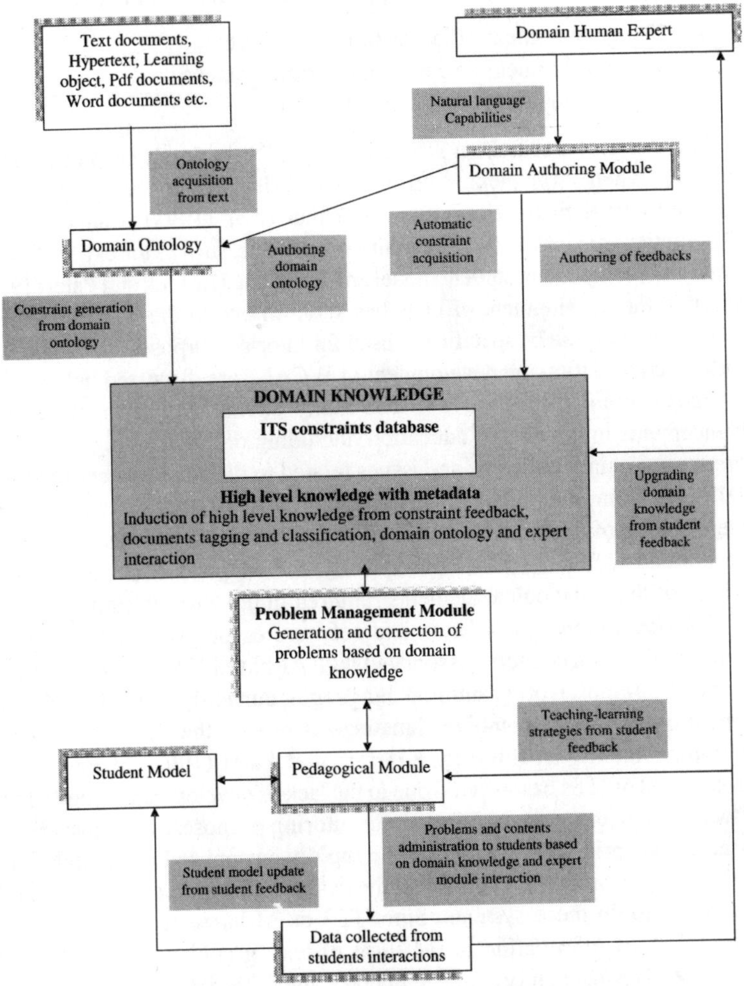

Figure 10.3: Architecture of an Advanced Intelligent Tutoring System

Issues in Developing ITS and Intelligent CAI

Web-based education is being considered as the replacement for traditional classroom-based education at the tertiary level. Barretto *et al.* (2003) claim that user activity and graphic design are two major attributes that influence the development of educational software projects. Although Web-based instructions have distinct advantages over traditional classroom-based learning, the design and development of appropriate Web-based instructional software is a great challenge. CAL or Web-based learning tools offer more dynamic representations of learning materials than traditional blackboard teaching. Although developing any Webbased educational system involves a series of challenges and issues, three major factors of the development that must be considered are namely:

- The development of instructional software;
- The development of the database management;
- The development of assessment tools.

The literature research on ITS shows that ITSs have not been completely successful when implemented on a larger scale, due to various problems associated with their developments. McArthur *et al.* (1993) pointed out that ITS limitations are influenced by certain components, such as the expert system, pedagogical component, student model and interface. Kinshuk and Patel (1997) claim that the development of ITSs has suffered due to the lack of software development that can be specifically used for tutoring purposes. The important issues incurred during the development of WCALP are discussed below:

Pedagogical Concerns: ITS has many advantages given the recent advancements in systems of education, including online learning. However, there are few minor concerns and issues related to the development of ITS or Intelligent Computer-Assisted Instruction. Most of ITS developers lack understanding of the implementation of pedagogical concepts that need to be incorporated within the ITS; consequently, the endproduct design may not fulfil all of the pedagogical elements required in the tutoring strategies.

Software Latency: Hardware and software or programming languages are other important concerns associated with AI-based ITS. There are several advanced computer programming languages currently available, yet the application of proper computer language is one of the essential needs in developing intelligent tutoring. Kinshuk and Patel (1997) claim that the development of ITSs has suffered due to the lack of development of underlying software engineering methodologies for tutoring purposes. This gives rise to a need for generic software that can be rapidly customised as per individual needs. Also, the important concern is the design and maintenance of the large database used in these systems. Since ITS or AI-based tutoring consist of several files of information in the form of text, graphics and audio-visual data, it is somewhat cumbersome to manage all of this data. Also, the research shows that in some of the ITSs, debugging is the main concern in the designed software; it is very difficult to debug problems encountered in authoring programmes due to large file sizes and complicated interfaces.

Courseware Development: Any computer-assisted learning or ITS must have essential courseware design that can easily fulfil the required pedagogical requirements in the learning strategy. In designing the project pedagogy for WCALP, several important factors have been taken into consideration, such as: the content of the course, learner's activities, performance indicators and learning outcomes. The WCALP has been developed using a framework in which three key strategies have been embedded in the model, namely: the tutorial strategy, hint strategy and evaluation strategy. This framework is very much pertinent in the development of Web-based educational software to help teaching/learning.

Authoring Software: The instructional software designed has the following important characteristics that are essential in order to implement the developed system with the appropriate instructional strategies. These characteristics are pertinent in the design of ideal instructional software for Web-based education in the engineering domain. These characteristics are listed as follows:

- The software is user friendly, easy to use and task-oriented.
  The instructional design strategies used in the software are able to provide the most appropriate encouragement for self-motivation.
- The software incorporates simple Web delivery methods with the minimum standards required of the desired content.
- The developed software provides realistic solutions to the problems according to the complex to simple principle.
- The software is learner-centred and not developer-centred, which provides opportunities for learners to test theories and explore their own learning.
- The software also develops active learning and facilitates essential thought processes, which result in a positive impact on the learning outcomes.
- The software utilises appropriate technology and includes educational facilities for self-assessment by learners throughout the learning process (Patil, 2004).

Intelligent Tutoring System Authoring Tools

Intelligent Tutoring Systems (ITSs) are computer-based instructional systems with models of instructional content that specify *what* to teach, and teaching strategies that specify *how* to teach (Wenger 1987, Ohlsson 1987, Shute & Psotka 1996). They make inferences about a student's mastery of topics or tasks in order to dynamically adapt the content or style of instruction. Content models (or knowledge bases, or expert systems, or simulations) give ITSs depth so that students can "learn by doing" in realistic and meaningful contexts. Models allow for content to be generated in real time. ITSs allow "mixed-initiative" tutorial interactions, where students can ask questions and have more control over their learning. Instructional models allow the computer tutor to more closely approach the benefits of individualized instruction by a competent pedagogue. In recent years ITSs have moved out of the lab and into classrooms and workplaces where some have been shown to be highly effective (Shute and Regian 1990; Koedinger *et al.* 1997; Mark & Greer 1991; Person *et al.* 2001; Rosé, *et al.* 2001). While intelligent tutors are becoming more common and proving to be increasingly effective they are difficult and expensive to build. Authoring systems are commercially available for traditional computer aided instruction (CAI) and multimedia-based training, but these authoring systems lack the sophistication required to build intelligent tutors. Commercial multimedia authoring systems excel in giving the instructional designer tools to produce visually appealing and interactive screens, but behind the screens is a shallow representation of content and pedagogy. Researchers have been investigating ITS authoring tools almost since the beginning of ITS research, and over two dozen very diverse authoring systems have been built.

Classification according to Tasks and Tutors

Shells vs. tools. An ITS "shell" is a generalized framework for building ITSs, while an ITS "authoring system" (or authoring tool) is an ITS shell along with a user interface that allows non-programmers to formalize and visualize their knowledge. Inspired by goals of elegance, parsimony, and/or cost effectiveness, software designers seem naturally driven to write software that is general and reusable. Thus there have been many papers published describing ITS "shells" that consist of software architectures, code libraries, or conceptual frameworks that make ITS construction more efficient for programmers. Though some of these systems include form-based data entry to support authoring tasks, most of them are either content acquisition shells or instructional planning shells. For examples, see Goodkovsky *et al.*, 1994 (Pop ITS shell), Ikeda & Mizoguchi, 1994 (FITS), McCalla & Greer, 1988 (SCENT-3), Goodyear & Johnson, 1990 (TOSKA), Anderson & Pelliteir, 1991 (TDK), McMillan *et al.*, 1980 (SIPP), Wasson, 1992 (PEPE), Winne & Kramer, 1989 (DOCENT), Jona & Kass, 1997 (GBS architectures).

A Bags of Tricks vs. A Shelf of Tools. Over two dozen ITS authoring systems have been built. They differ by the types of domains and tasks they are suited for, by the degree to which they make authoring more easy or efficient, and by the depth and fidelity employed to represent the knowledge or skill being taught. Not all of the designers of these systems would describe their systems as being "ITS authoring systems." These systems seem to populate the space of authoring tool features almost uniformly, making it difficult to cluster them into discrete groups in an effort to summarize the field. Since the field is still in a formative stage, this paper is intended to help the reader envision the next generation of authoring tools, more than to select an existing one to use. Therefore its organization is more like the description of a "bag of tricks" that can be mixed and matched to create an authoring tool than a description of a shelf of completed authoring tools.

Early ITS authoring systems fell into two broad categories: those based on a traditional curriculum (or courseware) metaphor and those geared toward device simulation and embodying a "learning environments" instructional metaphor. The majority of current authoring tools fall similarly into two broad categories: pedagogy-oriented and performance-oriented (Murray 1997). Pedagogy-oriented systems focus on how to sequence and teach relatively canned content. Most of them pay special attention to the representation of teaching strategies and tactics. Performance-oriented systems focus on providing rich learning environments in which students can learn skills by practicing them and receiving feedback. Most of them pay special attention to the representation of human problem solving skills or domain-specific processes or systems (either man made ones such as electrical components, or natural ones such as the meteorology). In general, performance-oriented systems focus on feedback and guidance at the level of individual skills and procedural steps, while pedagogy-oriented systems pay more attention to guidance and planning at a more global level, looking at the sequence of topics and the need for prerequisite topics. Some systems have elements of both categories, but those that do tend not to have very complete or deep representational systems for both pedagogy and domain processes. Though it is possible to create a system with full capabilities in both areas, none yet exists. This is probably due to a combination of the fact that supporting each type of authoring is difficult (and each project has limited recourses to spend) and supporting each type of authoring requires a very different kind of expertise.

Proponents of constructivist learning theories (e.g. Jonassen & Reeves 1996) often criticize pedagogy-oriented tutors and the instructional design theories behind them as being too "instructivist." Such critics contend that these systems ignore important aspects of learning such as intrinsic motivation, context realism, common misconceptions, and social learning contexts. Actually these factors are acknowledged by most instructional design theorists (Merrill 1983, Gagne 1985, Reigeluth 1983), but are either seen as not being as important or as being too complex or incompletely understood to incorporate into instructional planning and knowledge representation. Table 10.2 describes the strengths and limitations of each category, along with a summary of how systems within the category differ. The categories are described below in their particular sequence because some build upon concepts developed in previous categories.

Curriculum Sequencing and Planning

Authoring systems in the Curriculum and Course Sequencing category organize

Table 10.2: ITS Authoring Tool Strengths and Limitations by Category

CATEGORY	*STRENGTHS*	*LIMITS*	*VARIATIONS*
Curriculum Sequencing and Planning	Rules, constraints, or strategies for sequencing courses, modules, presentations	Low fidelity from student's perspective; shallow skill representation	Whether sequencing rules are fixed or authorable; scaffolding of the authoring process
Tutoring Strategies	Micro-level tutoring strategies; sophisticated set of instructional primitives; multiple tutoring strategies	(same as above for most systems)	Strategy representation method; source of instructional expertise
Device Simulation and Equipment Training	Authoring and tutoring matched to device component identification, operation, and troubleshooting	Limited instructional strategies; limited student modeling; mostly for procedural skills	Fidelity of the simulation; ease of authoring
Domain Expert System	Runnable (deeper) model of domain expertise; fine grained student diagnosis and modeling; buggy and novice rules included	Building the expert system is difficult; limited to procedural and problem solving expertise; limited instructional strategies	Cognitive vs. performance models of expertise
Multiple Knowledge Types	Differential predefined knowledge representation and instructional methods for facts, concepts, and procedures, etc.	Limited to relatively simple fact, concepts, and procedures; predefined tutoring strategies	Inclusion of intelligent curriculum sequencing; types of knowledge/tasks supported
Special Purpose	Template-based systems provide strong authoring guidance; fixed design or pedagogical principles can be enforced	Each tool limited to a specific type of tutor; inflexibility of representation and pedagogy	Degree of flexibility
Intelligent/ Adaptive Hypermedia	WWW has accessibility & UI uniformity; adaptive selection and annotation of hyperlinks	Limited interactivity; limited student model bandwidth	Macro vs. micro level focus; degree of interactivity

instructional units (IUs, or "curriculum elements") into a hierarchy of courses, modules, lessons, presentations, etc., which are related by prerequisite, part, and other relationships. The instructional units typically have instructional objectives. Some systems include IUs that address misconceptions or remedial material. The content is stored in canned text and graphics. These systems are seen as tools to help instructional designers and teachers design courses and manage computer based learning.

Intelligent sequencing of IUs (or content or topics) is at the core of these systems. To the student, tutoring systems built with these tools may seem identical to traditional computer-based instruction. Screens of canned text and pictures are presented, and interactions tend to be limited to multiple choice, fill-in, etc. Of course, the difference is that the sequencing of the content is being determined dynamically based on the student's performance, the lesson objectives, and the relationships between course modules. Because domain knowledge is not represented in a very "deep" fashion, any arbitrary domain can be tutored (just as a textbook can be about any domain). But the depth of diagnosis and feedback in tutors built with these authoring tools is limited by the shallowness of their domain knowledge representation. This makes them more appropriate for building tutors that teach conceptual, declarative, and episodic types of knowledge, and less pedagogically powerful for building tutors that teach procedural or problem solving skills. Authoring systems in the Curriculum Sequencing category are, generally speaking, the most "basic," or minimally functional (though each system in this category has certain very evolved signature features or capabilities).

Tutoring Strategies

Systems in this category excel at representing diverse teaching strategies. They tend to be similar to the Curriculum Sequencing systems described above, in that content is stored in canned text and graphics and domain knowledge representation is shallow. Systems in this category go beyond Curriculum Sequencing systems to encode fine-grained strategies used by teachers and instructional experts. Systems in the Curriculum Sequencing category tend to focus on the "macro" level of instruction—i.e. the sequencing of topics or modules, while systems in this category also address the "micro" level of instruction. Instructional decisions at the micro level include when and how to give explanations, summaries, examples, and analogies; what type of hinting and feedback to give; and what type of questions and exercises to offer the student. Systems in the Tutoring Strategies category have the most sophisticated set of primitive tutorial actions, compared with systems in other categories. In addition some systems in this category represent multiple tutoring strategies and "meta-strategies" that select the appropriate tutoring strategy for a given situation (e.g. REDEEM and Eon). The availability and intelligent interjection of small grain sized components such as explanations, multiple levels of hints, and analogies can make the tutor appear quite responsive, at times even conversational (as in Socratic strategies).

Simulation-Based Learning

For tutors built by authoring tools in this category, instruction centers around a simulation of a man-made process or phenomena. In RIDES, XAIDA, DIAG, and Instructional Simulator the student is shown a piece of equipment and is asked to identify its components, perform operating steps, perform maintenance steps, or diagnose faulty device behaviour and fix or replace the implicated parts. These authoring tools have been used to build instructional simulations of mechanical, electrical, and hydraulic systems. These types of skills are relatively widespread and generic, so authoring tools that specialize in this area should be widely usable. The expert knowledge for component locations and operational scripts is straightforward to model. Performance monitoring and instructional feedback is also straightforward (e.g. "That is not the Termination Switch," and "You should have checked the safety valve as your next step"). Thus authoring tools can be built which closely match the needs of the author (and student). The most difficult authoring task with these systems is building the simulation. But once the simulation is authored, much of the instructional specification comes "for free." Component location and device behaviour "what if" activities can be generated automatically. However, the device operation procedures must be authored. The four systems mentioned differ in the complexity of the simulation models that they can author. While these systems focus mostly on learning procedural skills, SimQuest focuses more on conceptual knowledge and physical principles. It has features for providing explanations of phenomena, exploratory and hypothesis generation learning activities, and instructional sequences based on a "model evolution" paradigm (White & Frederiksen 1995). SimQuest simulations are based on a set of equations which constitute a model of a physical process. Though they are not covered in this paper, there are other simulation-based and model-based educational software projects that incorporate authoring tools for building models (see a brief summary in Murray, *et al.* 2001).

In contrast to the previous two categories of authoring tools, students using tutors built with tools in this category will be "learning by doing." It is usually assumed that students have a basic familiarity with important concepts and procedures in the domain before using the tutor and students immediately start to practice skills. Specific feedback is given for each skill step, and task difficulty is increased as students progress.

A major differentiating factor among systems in this category is the depth and fidelity of the simulation. Authoring tools range from those supporting static expression-based relationships between device components (XAIDA, which also supports domains other than device simulation, see the Multiple

Knowledge Types category), to those supporting runnable but shallow simulation models (RIDES), to those supporting deeper, more causative or cognitive models of how the device works (SIMQUEST).

Expert Systems and Cognitive Tutors

An important class of intelligent tutors are those that include rule-based cognitive models of problem solving expertise. Such tutors, often called model tracing tutors (Anderson & Pelletier 1991), observe student behaviour and build a fine-grained cognitive model of the student's knowledge that can be compared with the expert model. Authoring tools have been prototyped for such tutors. I also include in this category authoring tools which use traditional expert systems (built to solve problems, not to teach) and produce "value added" instruction for the encoded expertise. These systems are similar to model tracing systems, except the expert system is based on performance competency, rather than cognitive processes. Some systems include buggy or novice-level rules that capture common mistakes, allowing the tutorial to give feedback specific to those errors.

Students using these systems usually solve problems and associated subproblems within a goal space, and receive feedback when their behaviour diverges from that of the expert model. Unlike most other systems described above, these systems have a relatively deep model of expertise, and thus the student, when stuck, can ask the tutor to perform the next step or to complete the solution to the entire problem. Authoring an expert system is a particularly difficult and time-intensive task, and only certain tasks can be modeled in this manner. Demonstr allows authors to build an expert problem solver through demonstration of an example problem solution. D3 trainer and Training Express add a tutorial component onto an existing expert system (authored with an expert system shell). DIAG includes an expert model of fault diagnosis strategies.

Multiple Knowledge Types

Instructional design theories classify knowledge and tasks into discrete categories, and prescribe instructional methods for each category. They tend to be limited to types of knowledge that can be easily defined, such as facts, concepts, and procedures. Though the knowledge types and instructional methods vary for different theories, they typically prescribe instruction similar to the following. Facts are taught with repetitive practice and mnemonic devices; concepts are taught using analogies and positive and negative examples progressing from easy prototypical ones to more difficult borderline cases; procedures are taught one step at a time, with particular attention payed to branching decision steps. Instruction for these knowledge types includes both expository presentations of the knowledge, and inquisitory exercises that allow for practice and feedback. Straight-forward instructional strategies for how to sequence content and exercises, and how to provide feedback, are defined separately for each knowledge type (for example see Merrill 1983). The pre-defined nature of the knowledge and the instructional strategies is both the strength and the weakness of these systems. Domain knowledge for each knowledge type can be easily represented for authors, who fill in templates for examples, steps, definitions, etc. (depending on the knowledge type). The tools support the decomposition of complex skills into elementary knowledge components. Links between knowledge components can be authored and used in instruction (e.g. the concepts or facts that support a procedure or a concept that helps explain another concept). Since instructional strategies are fixed and based on knowledge types they do not have to be authored. Of course, not all instruction fits neatly into this framework, but it has significantly wide applicability (problem solving and other higher order cognitive skills can not be represented in this way).

Authoring systems in the Multiple Knowledge Types category are diverse in many respects, but they all use a knowledge/skill classification scheme and represent and instruct differentially based on knowledge type. Also, they all cite classic instructional design literature as part of the basis for their pedagogical approach.

For the student, tutors built with these systems are similar in character to those in the Multiple Teaching Strategies category. The main difference is for the authors, whose task is more constrained, and thus both easier and less flexible.

Special Purpose Systems

In this category, authoring tools specialize in particular tasks or domains. Systems in the Device Simulation and Multiple Knowledge Types categories are also for particular types of tasks, but systems in the Special Purpose category focus on more specific, less general tasks. There is a rough principle that authoring tools tailored for specific tasks or instructional situations can better support the needs of the student and author for those situations. Systems in this category were designed by starting with a particular intelligent tutor design, and generalizing it to create a framework for authoring similar tutors. Authoring is much more template-like than in other categories of authoring tools. One potential problem with special purpose authoring is that once a task and its instructional approach have been codified enough to become a template, the resulting system reflects a very particular approach to representing and teaching that task; one that may only appeal to a limited authoring audience. On the other hand, preferred design and pedagogical principles can be strictly enforced, since the author has no influence over these aspects. Bell (this volume) calls this approach using a "strong task model" to build "knowledge rich" authoring tools.

Since the only thing that systems in this category have in common is that they support particular types of tasks or domains, we can not say anything in general about the types of tutors built or about students' experience using the tutors. The IDLE-Tool/Imap/Indie systems build tutors for "investigate and decide" GBS (goal based scenario) learning environments. LAT builds tutors to train customer service representatives how to answer product questions. Both of the above mentioned projects involve learning by doing in role playing environments. BioWorld is a learning environment for promoting scientific reasoning in the medical domain. Its authoring tool is a template-based tool allowing teachers to create new medical cases. WEAR builds tutors in algebra-related domains.

Intelligent/Adaptive Hypermedia

As adaptive hypermedia systems and web-based tutors become more sophisticated, they increasingly incorporate methods and models from the field of intelligent tutoring. The functions of these systems overlap with those from the Curriculum Sequencing and Tutoring Strategies categories above (depending on whether the focus is on instruction at the macro or micro level). The level of interactivity and fidelity available to the student is low for tutors built with these authoring tools. They are HTML-based, and do not yet incorporate highly interactive features available through programming languages such as Java and Flash. Unlike systems in the other categories, these systems must manage the hyperlinks between units of content as well as the form and sequencing of the content itself. The links available to the student can be intelligently filtered, sorted, and annotated based on a student model or profile (Brusilovsky 1998).

General Authoring Features

Though the authoring systems described in this paper have a variety of features, a number of features have emerged as being generally important to robust usability, as described below:

1. *WYSIWIG editing and rapid testing.* Authors should be able to easily see and test both the static visual elements of the tutor and the dynamic run-time behaviour of a tutor. Easy movement back and forth from editing to test-run modes facilitates rapid prototyping.
2. *Flexible, opportunistic design.* ITS authoring tools should be designed to work best for those who have had some training. Features that make it easy for a first-time user to get to work should not get in the way of serious longer term use. Tools should allow for a mixture of top down (starting with the abstract curriculum structure) and bottom up (starting with specific screens and content) authoring for different design styles.
3. *Visual reification.* The conceptual and structural elements of a representational formalism should be portrayed graphically with high visual fidelity if ITS Authoring systems are to be used by non-programmers. Such user interfaces relieve working memory load by

reifying the underlying structures, and assist long term memory by providing reminders of this structure. Also, multiple views (visual perspectives) of information are often needed.

4. *Content modularity and re-usability.* Instructional content should be represented and authored modularly so that it can be used for multiple instructional purposes. Include library structures for saving reusable components. Provide productivity tools that capitalize on repetitive or template-like content. Provide tools that make it easy to browse, search for, and reference content objects.
5. *Customization, extensibility, and scriptabilty.* A tool cannot anticipate everything a designer will want. All modern design and authoring software provides for extensibility and scripting. Scripting allows authors with moderate skills to create "generative" ITSs that construct problems, explanation, hint, etc. on the fly.
6. *Undo!* Mundane features such as Undo, Copy/Paste, and Find can be extremely time consuming to build into complex design software such as authoring tools, yet such features are essential components of all robust usable software.
7. *Administrative features*. Only a few of the authoring tools (including RIDES and SimQuest) have administrative facilities for such things as class rostering, grade analysis and statistics, and generating progress reports, such features may be essential to the eventual adoption of ITSs into mainstream education. CREAM Tools is the only system so far to support collaborative authoring with rights management and access security features.
8. *Include customizable representational formalisms.* An authoring system will be based on some underlying representational formalism, and any such formalism will satisfy the needs of authoring some types of tutors yet not be appropriate for authoring other tutors. To achieve greater flexibility, authoring tools should include the ability to customize the representational formalism.
9. *Anchor usability on familiar authoring paradigms, and facilitate evolution to more powerful paradigms.* For those used to building traditional computer-based instruction, building intelligent tutors requires a conceptual shift from "story board" representations of content to more modular knowledge based representations (Murray 1996). It is useful to have some ITS authoring tools have a look and feel similar to common off-the-shelf CAI authoring tools, and to provide features which allow a smooth transition from traditional authoring paradigms to authoring more powerful intelligent tutors.
10. *Facilitate design at a pedagogically relevant level of abstraction.* Provide tools which allow subject matter experts to author using primitives at the "pedagogical level" as well as the media level (Murray

1996). Media level primitive are "graphic," "button," mouse click, etc. Objects at the pedagogical level have instructional meaning, for example "hint," "explanation," "topic," "prerequisite," and "mastered."

Intelligent Tutors and Metacognition

Meta-cognition refers to "*one's knowledge concerning one's own cognitive processes and products or anything related to them*" (Flavell 1976); more informally, meta-cognition has been referred to as "*thinking about thinking*". Metacognitive skills are therefore domain-independent abilities that are an important aspect of knowing how to learn in general. Examples include, among others, the ability to monitor one's learning progress (*self-monitoring*), the tendency to explain instructional material to oneself in terms of the underlying domain knowledge (*self-explanation*), the ability to learn from examples (*analogical reasoning*), the ability to appropriately seek tutoring help. Individuals vary significantly in these abilities, and thus several ITS researchers have been investigating how to devise tutors that can help students acquire the relevant meta-cognitive skills. While some researchers have focused on creating tools that can scaffold meta-cognition by design (e.g., Luckin and Hammerton 2002, Aleven and Koedinger 2002), others have been investigating how to capture a user's need for metacognitive support in real-time during interaction, to enable the ITS to respond accordingly. Roll *et al.*, for instance, have devised a model that enables an ITS to track and scaffold a student's tendency to effectively use the available help facilities [Roll *et al.,* 2007].

11

Intelligent Tutoring System and Active Learning

"Reform"—this word, nowadays, is commonly heard in all educational settings ranging from primary (Anderson, 1992) to professional education (Calderhead, 1988; Jonas, 1978; McGuire *et al.*, 1983; Rothstein, 1987). This reform movement is due to the unsatisfactory state of our current educational system. According to Woolf (1986) "education is in trouble" (p. 1). Anderson (1992) noted that "The situation with respect to low educational achievement has been raised to the status of a national crisis in America" (p. 1). Woolf (1986), citing the literature, further states that ... an NSF study says, "*Most Americans are moving towards virtual scientific and technological illiteracy*" (National Science Foundation, 1983). Naisbitt says, "*The generation graduating from high school today is the first generation in American history to graduate less skilled than its parents* ..." (Naisbitt, 1984). R. Buckminister Fuller says, "*Classrooms are desensitizing, stultifying and boring.*" (Fuller, 1962) ... *Andrew Molnar from NSF says that only 75 per cent of the teachers in America are qualified to teach the courses they are teaching* (Molnar, 1986) ...*America will be short one million teachers within four years ... People graduate without the basic skills necessary to function at the college level.*

The problems are great and there is no single "magical" method available to improve the current state of education. But what we can do is to adopt the "divide and conquer" strategy and solve problems that are linked to this disastrous state of education, as far as possible.

Two Problems

According to Anderson (1984) "Knowledge is not a basket of facts" but rather "the essence of knowledge is structure". A study by Bloom (1984) shows that conventional teaching, which means a teacher presenting material in front of 20-200 people, provides one of the least effective methods for educational delivery. In this conventional form "too often school science and mathematics is studied as a disembodied set of facts and principles" (Wheatley, 1991,

p. 13). Here "the learner is assumed to be, in the John Locke tradition, a *tabula rasa*" (Wheatley, 1991, p. 14). In such a situation, as Anderson (1984) noted, the majority of students "are unlikely to make the inferences required to *weave* the information ... into a coherent overall mental model" (p. 10).

Besides leaving student's knowledge in a *non-integrated (unstructured)* form, the second problem created by the current educational system is that it does not provide opportunities for students to develop higher mental processes such as the ability to solve problems (Bloom, 1984). Michael (1993) says that "American education has, in general, failed to prepare students ... to become problem solvers" (p. 37). According to Bloom (1984):

> ... *Such higher mental processes ... enable the student to relate his or her learning to the many problems he or she encounters in day-to-day living. These abilities ... are retained and used long after the individual has forgotten the detailed specifics of the subject matter taught in the schools. These abilities are regarded as one set of essential characteristics needed to continue learning and to cope with a rapidly changing world ... These higher mental processes are (also) important because they make learning exciting and constantly new and playful.* (p. 13).

Bloom further observes that:

> ... teachers in United States typically make use of text books that rarely pose real problems. These text books emphasize specific content to be remembered and give students little opportunity to discuss underlying concepts and principles and even less opportunity to attack real problems in the environments in which they live. The teacher-made tests (and standardized tests) are largely tests of remembered information ... (p. 13).

These two problems are related to each other. A student having knowledge in a non-integrated form would not be able to *correctly* solve problems, because according to Anderson (1980) problem solving requires a "goal-directed sequence of cognitive operations" (p. 257). A "basket of facts" lacks the needed structure to support the required sequence of operations.

The New Science of Learning

Researchers in the learning sciences seek to uncover fundamental principles of human learning. About 30 year's worth of such findings are summarized in the National Research Council's report *How People Learn* (HPL) (Bransford, Brown, & Cocking, 2000). In this section, we briefly highlight two (of many) consensus points highlighted by this team that have a particular relevance to ITS research. HPL stresses the importance of helping learners develop a *deeper conceptual understanding* when they are learning a new domain. This means going beyond facts and procedures to thinking about applicability conditions and dynamic modification of such knowledge to fit new situations. "When students gain a deeper conceptual understanding, they learn facts and procedures in a much more useful and profound way that transfers to real world settings" (Sawyer, 2006). Allowing learners to actively participate in their own learning is essential to this aim. This guideline is broadly supported by many theories of learning (most prominently those of pioneers such as Piaget and Vygostky). Another finding highlighted in HPL is the *importance of reflection*, or metacognition, in learning. In addition to acquiring factual and procedural knowledge (with deep conceptual understanding, of course), learners should also be improving their ability to learn. Reflective skills, such as planning, questioning, explaining, and criticizing, are generally highly developed in experts but not novices. To accelerate the maturation to expertise, then, it is essential to create learning environments that encourage and support these kinds of activities. Clearly, active learning and reflection go hand-in-hand and should be high priority considerations in the development of computer-based learning environments.

Why is Tutoring Effective?

Although a precise answer to the question of why tutoring is more effective than other forms of instruction has remained elusive, most explanations focus on the fact that the best tutors balance the need for active participation of the student with the provision of guidance. This means the student does as much of the work as possible while the tutor provides just enough feedback to minimize frustration and confusion (e.g., Merrill *et al.*, 1992). Also, effective tutoring has less to do with improved didactic explanations on the part of the tutor and more to do with the interaction between the tutor and student. Chi *et al.* (2001) conclude that "students' substantive construction from interaction is important for learning, suggesting that an ITS ought to implement ways to elicit students' constructive responses" (p. 518). It is a common pattern in ITS research to first identify effective learning events and patterns in human tutoring, then attempt to emulate them in an ITS.

Human and Intelligent Tutoring

There are no known forms of education as effective as a professional human tutor. Students working one-on-one with expert human tutors often score 2.0 standard deviations—roughly two grade levels—higher than students in a conventional classroom (Bloom, 1984). In contrast, the very best intelligent tutoring systems achieve learning gains of about 1.0 standard deviations (Anderson *et al.*, 1995; VanLehn *et al.*, 2005). The best computer-aided instructional systems—computer tutors that do *not* use techniques of artificial intelligence (AI)—produce learning gains of about.4 standard deviations (Niemiec & Walberg, 1987).

Machine Tutors: An Alternative to Skilled Human Tutors

One possible solution to the shortage of human tutors is to build computer-based tutoring systems that are as effective as human tutors. These computer-based tutors are often referred to as Intelligent Tutoring Systems (ITS). It would be incorrect to suggest that intelligent tutoring systems will solve *all* the problems of current educational system (Woolf, 1986) but it is possible that these machines might solve some of the problems that are responsible for the current disastrous state of education.

Research on ITS started in the 1970's (Clancey, 1992; Woolf, 1988a). Since then many systems have been built but only a few are in actual use (Clancey, 1992; Galdes, 1990). Studies have shown that tutoring by computers can be more effective than class room teaching (Anderson *et al.*, 1989; Reiser *et al.*, 1991). However, it appears that human tutors still outperform machine tutors (Merrill *et al.*, 1992). These findings raise the following questions for the ITS community: Why are human tutors so effective, and how can we make machine tutors better? Also why are only a few of the tutors built so far in use (Galdes, 1990)?

The development of an ITS is a complex task (Woolf, 1988b) and requires a multidisciplinary approach (Kearsley, 1987). As Kearsley (1987) noted, the design and development of ITS "lie at the intersection of computer science, cognitive psychology, and educational research" (p. 3). In order to make this design and development process clearer, we will describe ITS from three different viewpoints: the conceptual view, the system view, and the physical view.

Conceptual View of ITSs

This view of ITS is concerned only with the conceptual issues underlying the target tutoring expertise. Two main issues dominate here: the nature of tutoring expertise and the variables influencing tutoring expertise. Galdes (1990) claims that the goal of ITS research is "to build computer-based systems which emulate skilled human tutors" (p. 2). Although all researchers may not agree with this view of ITS development, studies have shown that human tutoring provides the best educational delivery method so far known (Bloom, 1984). Does this mean that tutoring by humans always provides the most effective method of instruction? Anania (1983), in a review of three studies of tutoring vs. group instruction, found that tutoring is not always better. Her review showed that group instruction is better than tutoring when the teachers are trained and the tutors are untrained. In a review of thirteen studies of tutoring vs. group instruction, Ellson (1976) found that only five of these studies clearly showed that tutoring was effective in improving cognitive skills.

Figure 11.1: Active Learning with Machine Tutor

The success of tutoring cannot be attributed to individual attention. If individual attention were the critical operating factor then all tutoring should be successful, but as the review has shown, only some is successful, perhaps less than half ...There is no magic in individual attention.

These studies raise the question of what makes human tutors effective? One explanation for the effectiveness of human tutoring is that it is the "skilled tutoring that provides the magic" (Galdes, 1990, p. 2). Skilled tutoring requires expertise in both the domain and in the process of tutoring (Khuwaja *et al.* (1993), in preparation (a)). A human tutor lacking either of these skills will not be able to perform optimally in a tutoring situation. Breuker (1988) has concluded that experienced users (domain experts) are not necessarily good tutors. This conclusion has also been drawn by Fletcher (1984). On the other hand, expert tutors lacking expertise in the domain are also not optimally effective because, as Jones *et al.* (1979) observed in their study, "no amount of (teaching) strategies can make up for the lack of knowledge in a subject matter."

As mentioned above, a skilled human tutor acts as an expert in the domain

(domain expert) and in the process of tutoring (expert tutor) while communicating with the student. The expert tutor is a composite role. In this capacity the human tutor *diagnoses* the student's problems, *plans* the feedback and *communicates* it to the student.

These three roles of the tutor have been identified since the early days of ITS research (Wenger, 1987; Barr & Feigenbaum, 1982). But as Wenger (1987) observed, most of these early efforts "concentrate on some of these issues (roles) at the expense of others" (p. 14). The research methodology used in early studies was correct but those systems only began to investigate the tutor's expertise in different domains (Galdes, 1990). Also it is relatively easy to isolate a role of the tutor for investigation and tempting to generalize findings over domains and tutoring situations. Almost all research efforts, so far, have ignored the question of *integration* between roles of the tutor or adopted a primitive view based on speculation.

If we want ITSs to be as effective as skilled human tutors then we must not only investigate the different roles of the skilled human tutor but also the processes integrating these roles. Stevens *et al.* (1982) have also emphasized this theme as

In much of psychology, there has been a bias towards emphasizing highly general, domain-independent mechanisms that are supposedly central to the instructional process. Our work demonstrates that such a perspective is incomplete without a detailed consideration of domain-specific knowledge, its representation and its interaction with more general aspects of cognition (p. 13).

It is now well established that people use multiple representations of the physical world when interacting with it (Collins, 1985; Gentner & Stevens, 1983). A mental model in this context can be defined as "an internal representation of a physical system\ used by a person or a programme to reason about processes involving that system" (Wenger, 1987, pp. 45-46). Although research on mental models is an active area in artificial intelligence (AI) and cognitive psychology, only recently have a few efforts been geared to emphasize its utility from a pedagogical standpoint. Most of these research efforts are concerned only with the learner's viewpoint, i.e., what models the learner possesses and how these models can be tuned to yield the desired responses (Collins, 1985). An alternative to this educational approach is the question: How does the tutor use his/her multiple conceptual/mental models of the domain to remedy student misconceptions and to help learners build correct mental models of the domain?

Another variable only briefly considered in ITS research is the *environment* in which the tutor and the student communicate. This variable is of central importance to the researchers involved in the development of learning environments. It is true that in some human tutoring situations this variable is of little importance. For example, in one form of face-to-face tutoring the tutor and the student mainly use verbal means for communication. In this case only simple rules of verbal communication need to be followed.

But this is not the case in all tutoring situations. In some tutoring situations the tutor and the student need to follow a complicated set of rules which, for example, determine the way different objects (e.g., charts, tables) are used while tutoring. These environments can also convey, implicitly, part of the problem-solving methodology that the tutor wants the students to discover. In these situations it is valuable to investigate how these environments are created by the tutor and how they impact on the various roles of the tutor.

The proper conceptual view of an ITS is literally incomplete without the consideration of appropriate variables influencing the *tutoring* expertise of the tutor. Ignorance of this aspect of the conceptual view of ITS is clear in the literature (e.g., see Galdes, 1990). Researchers are tempted by the "generality hypothesis" (White & Frederiksen, 1990) to generalize their findings, ignoring crucial variables (e.g., type of domain, educational setting, tutoring situation, goals of the tutor, knowledge level of students) affecting tutoring expertise. The result of this ignorance is theories having holes that can not be filled when these variables change! This is also one reason that after almost two decades of research, human tutors still out perform machine tutors (Merrill *et al.*, 1992) and the majority of ITSs are inapplicable in real educational settings! It is true that we are still in the exploratory phase of ITS development and as Galdes (1990) noted, "currently, we are still building an empirical base of knowledge and descriptive theories of what skilled human tutors do" (p. 80). But if we ignore the true context of our research, by ignoring the variables making up the context, our knowledge base will be inconsistent and incomplete and retard the development of a unified theory of ITS development, if such a theory is possible.

Studies like these are essential in understanding the processes underlying the target tutoring expertise. The conceptual view allows us to concentrate on the theoretical aspects underlying tutoring expertise without getting bogged down in the system and physical views that are required to implement conceptual views in machine executable form on a computer. It would be incorrect to totally reject the influence of the system and the physical view on the conceptual view of ITS because ultimately we want a theory of tutoring expertise whose prescriptions can be implemented in a machine form.

System View of ITSs

An ITS is a programme, a piece of software, and its purpose is to engage the student in an instructional activity. Unlike the conceptual view, which is concerned with natural tutoring expertise, the system view is concerned with the organization of tutoring expertise as a computational system. Here the behaviour of the ITS results from the coordination of its components. The system view is influenced by the conceptual view. The characteristics of the system view, in turn, influence the physical view. The system view of the ITS can be conveniently divided into two subviews explained as follows.

System View 1–System Model. Through this view an ITS can be seen as an instructional system. Here the tutoring theory of the conceptual view is realized as a computational model, but still this view is not related to the actual implementation formalism needed to realize the system as a computer programme.

An ITS viewed from this perspective deals with two major issues: curriculum and instruction (Halff, 1988). The curriculum issues involve the representation, selection, and sequencing of material to be presented to students, whereas instructional issues involve the presentation of that material to students. Halff (1988) noted that

For teaching methods such as lectures, which are less dynamic than tutoring, both curriculum and instruction can be developed prior to delivery, with as much or as little accountability to instructional principles as the developers feel is needed. Tutoring systems afford no such luxury because a tutor, human or machine, is bound to tailor the selection, sequencing, and methods of delivering instruction to meet the ever-changing needs of individual students (p. 80).

Lesgold (1988) claims that "intelligent instructional systems developed to date have explicit representation of the target (domain) knowledge but at best only implicit representations of the curriculum knowledge, the scope and sequencing of lessons" (p. 118). A lack of this explicit representation of curriculum is one of the causes of suboptimal performance of ITS.

Empirical studies have shown that human tutors perform a number of tasks that are hierarchically arranged (Goodyear, 1991). A proper execution of these tasks produces a successful management of an effective tutoring session. These tutorial tasks are usually classified at different levels of abstraction. One such classification comprises the major (core) objective level, exercise (or problem selection) level, unit level, lesson level, and discourse level. An ITS not only needs to explicitly represent its curriculum, but also needs to arrange it so that it can support a complete hierarchy of tutorial tasks.

The selection, sequencing and presentation of the curriculum to students by an ITS requires a sophisticated planning mechanism. The need for explicit representation of the curriculum adds further complications to this planning mechanism. This planning mechanism, regardless of the particular theory of tutoring on which it is based, should meet the ever changing needs of individual students. One of the currently popular opportunistic instructional planning mechanisms, which plans at the local discourse level, is MENO-TUTOR (Woolf, 1984). On the other hand, the IDE-INTERPRETER (Russell, 1988) attempts to represent plans at higher levels of abstraction, but this system lacks power at the local discourse level (Woo *et al.*, 1991). Currently there have been attempts to combine local discourse planning with global (or higher level) planning (Woo *et al.*, 1991). But again these systems lack explicit representation of the curriculum and fail to plan tutorial tasks at sufficiently high levels. At this point there is a need for a system model that uses a sophisticated planning mechanism (fueled by the tutoring prescriptions at the conceptual level) and also makes use of explicit curriculum and domain knowledge.

System View 2–System Architecture. This view brings the ITS a step closer to its realization in a machine executable form. Through this view an ITS can be seen as a software system. Software engineering principles shape this view of an ITS. But this view is still independent of the actual implementation formalism. Major concerns here include: the design of different modules and the communication between the modules.

Physical View of ITSs: An ITS seen through this view is a machine coded programme. Here each module of the system view is transformed into a chunk of code that executes on a machine. Major concerns here are the selection of a hardware platform and the implementation formalism to realize the ITS as an executable software programme.

Intelligent Tutoring System–Some Examples

Some developed ITS examples with their clear functioning are given below:

PAT: Algebra Tutor

PUMP (Pittsburgh Urban Mathematics Project) Algebra Tutor (PAT) [Koedinger, K.R., and Anderson, J.R. (1997)] was developed for use in High-School setting following the ACT theory. The main purpose of the system is teaching to apply mathematics learned at school to real world problem. Students work through PAT problem situations by reading its textual description and a number of questions about it. They investigate the situation by representing it in tables, graphs, and symbols and using these representations to answer the questions. The major focus of the tutor is helping students to understand and use multiple representations of information.

Students are presented with a screen divided in four windows each containing a tool for solving the problem (in addition to the window showing the current text of problem). While students work on a problem, tutor traces their activities and if something goes wrong (student makes error), the system shows the relative feedback in various form, depending on the type of error. An experiment was conducted on 470 students using this system and the experimental classes outperformed students in comparison classes by 15 per cent on standardized tests and 100 per cent on tests targeting the PUMP objectives (real life problems).

LISP Tutor

The LISP tutor [Anderson, J.R., and Reiser, B. (1985)] was an early attempt at a Cognitive tutor. The student is given a description of a small programme to encode in LISP, which she then writes with the system's help. In the LISP Tutor the expert model was created as a series of correct production rules for creating LISP programmes and a learner model was built as a subset of these correct production rules along with common incorrect ones. The tutor acts as a problem solving guide but never states the productions to be learned.

Students interact with a language editor that shows the structure of programme to be coded. As the user builds her solution, the system inserts tags that describe the general form of the programme, for example (user input in bold):

```
(defun fact (n)
(cond ((equalp) <ACTION>)
<RECURSIVE-CASE>))
```

In the above case the student was asked to code the programme that compute the factorial of a given number. At this point the system interrupts the student and asks for the use of ZEROP function, that tests a number against zero, instead of the general EQUALP. Then the tutor interacts with the student in similar manner until the final solution is reached. Note that, even if the use of EQUALP is valid, this would lead to a solution that is off the path specified in the LISP tutor, because the authors have deemed it undesirable. This is a design decision, rather than a characteristic of the modelling method.

The LISP tutor performs very well. In an initial mini-course at CMU, students using it solved a series of exercises in 30 per cent less time than those in a standard LISP environment, and performed one standard deviation better on their final test. However, later evaluations failed to conclusively prove that the style of teaching used (notably comprehensive, immediate help) improved performance per se. Anderson *et al.* concluded that the main reason for improved performance in post tests previously was probably because the LISP tutor enabled students to cover more exercises in the same amount of time, which subsequently gave them an advantage. However, this is, in itself, considered a worthwhile outcome, since enabling students to achieve their learning in less time gives them more time to learn additional material, or to do other things.

Constraint-Based Tutor

This kind of ITS is based on Ohlsson's theory of learning from performance errors. Constraint Based Modelling (CBM) focuses on faulty knowledge, realizing that it is not sufficient to describe what the student knows correctly. The basic assumption is that diagnostic information is not hidden in the sequence of student's actions, but in the problem state the student arrived at. This assumption is supported by the fact that there can be no correct solution of a problem that traverses a problem state, which violates fundamental ideas, or concepts of the domain.

The constraint-based model proposed by Ohlsson represents both domain and student knowledge in the form of constraints, where the constraints represent the basic principles underlying the domain. A constraint is characterised by a relevance clause, and a satisfaction clause. The relevance

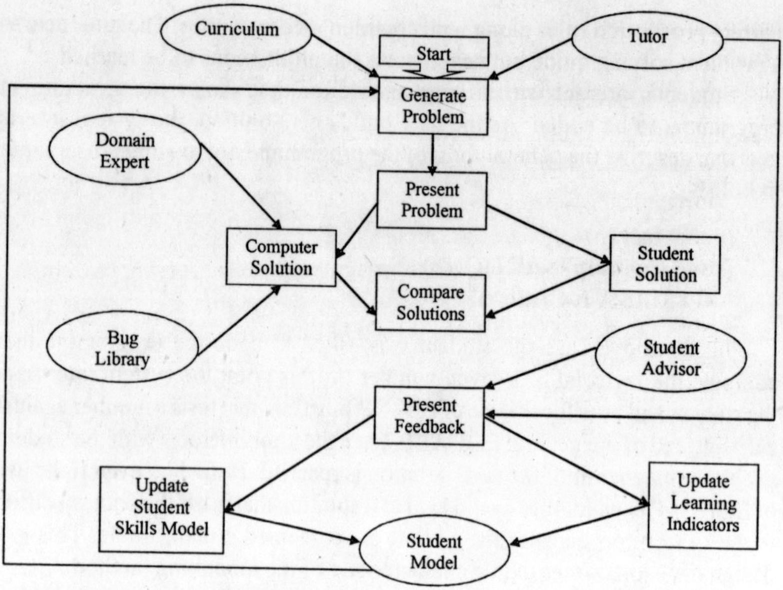

Figure 11.2: General Structure and Flow of an Intelligent Tutoring System

clause is a condition that must be true before the constraint is relevant to the current solution. Once the relevance clause has been met, the satisfaction clause must be true for the solution to be correct.

For example we can consider a student learning to code with a programming language. When she has to manipulate array inside an iterative statement one of such rules can be that the index used in the array must not exceed the array dimension. A constraint for the situation might be:

F array dimension is N
AND array index is I
THEN the guard is I < N
SQL-Tutor

SQL-Tutor is a knowledge-based teaching system which supports students learning SQL. The intention was to provide an easy-to-use system that will adapt to the needs and learning abilities of individual students. The tailoring of instruction is done in two ways: by adapting the level of complexity of problems and by generating informative feedback messages.

It consists of definitions of several databases, and a set of problems and the ideal solutions to them. The student are presented a question asking to write an SQL statement, a description of the database schema and the structure of the query (currently only SELECT query are addressed) consisting of all clause Select, From, Where, Order By, Group By, Having. When the student submits the solution, it is passed to the system that corrects errors, updates the student model and selects the next action (i.e. feedback or another question). In the early version the system had several limitations:

- the domain admits more than one solution to a given problem but the system was unable to recognize a different solution. This translates in misleading feedback that can confuse the student. This problem has been resolved changing the representation of constraints reducing it to simple pattern matching and developing a problem solving procedure able to produce a piece of solution from a constraint ([Martin, B., and Mitrovic, A. (2000), [Martin, B., and Mitrovic, A. (2002a)]). The partial solution replaces a piece of the student solution that violates the constraint and the procedure is iterated until no more errors exist.
- system had a limited problem set. Authoring a set of questions that cover all the defined constraint (over 500) is a very difficult task. In [Martin, B., and Mitrovic, A. (2002a)] have been developed a method, based on problem solving capability described in the previous point that generates a set of problem starting from the constraint set defined in the system. The author has to manually transform the generated solutions into natural language for presentation to the student.

Authoring a constraint based tutor is a task reserved to ITS engineers or expert with a necessary knowledge to represent constraints. In [Martin, B., and Mitrovic, A. (2002b)] a system called WETAS was developed to help the process of system authoring. In [Suraweera, P., Mitrovic, A., and Martin, B. (2004)] WETAS was augmented with the capabilities of extracting constraints from ontology.

Classification of ITS Technologies

One way to organize tutoring systems is around what role they are intended to play. At one end of the spectrum, some systems are intended to replace a textbook or classroom instruction to deliver domain content for the first time to a student (e.g., intelligent hypermedia systems). At the other end are systems designed to directly support *practice* (sometimes described as "homework helpers"). These usually complement an existing instructional component such as lectures. Although very few systems sit on the edge of this spectrum, ITS research tends to lean to the practice end. Indeed, practice is when "the rubber hits the road" in learning: it represents a volatile time when knowledge gaps are revealed and skills are automatized. Modern theories of learning stress the critical role of practice and most highlight the importance of feedback because of the risks of unguided learning (Kirschner *et al.*, 2006; Clark, 2004).

Tutoring systems typically support practice in one of two ways. *Product* tutors evaluate final outcomes, such as an essay or a mission plan. Typically, a student works on a solution until it is deemed complete, then submits it for feedback. The ITS analyzes the solution by looking for flaws, omissions, or sub-optimal elements. Some advanced product tutors are able to reverse engineer solutions using techniques such as *plan recognition* to identify the reasoning that likely underlies the solution. An inherent weakness of product tutors is that students might become stuck before they are able generate a solution. More interactive and pro-active systems that provide support while the student is working towards a solution are best described as *process* tutors. This is perhaps the most familiar category because most human tutors operate in this mode—the student is observed step-by-step, feedback and hints are given, questions are asked and answered, and so on. Figure 11.2 shows the general structure and flow of an intelligent tutoring system.

Recurring ITS Research Areas

A core collection of "good old fashioned" ITS research areas has managed to stay in favour throughout the years. Broad surveys of the field conducted roughly 10 years ago (Youngblut, 1994; Shute & Psotka, 1996) and more recently (Loftin, 2004) highlight several recurring themes, many that date back to the earliest years of ITS research:

- *Learner or student modeling:* General problems in this area include diagnosis of misconceptions, tracking of learning over time, representation of faulty (i.e., "buggy") reasoning, "open" learner modeling, and affective/emotional modeling. Learner models can provide assessments to instructors, used to generate appropriate problems, and be the basis for individualized, adaptive instruction (although this remains an unrealized goal).
- *Natural language dialogue:* Some of the earliest tutoring systems attempted to use techniques of natural language processing to simulate human-human tutorial dialogues. Even with intermittent periods of low activity, this stream of research has not gone away. Recent support from ONR and NSF helped produce some modernized systems shown to enhance learning as a direct result of improved dialogue quality.
- *Cognitive modeling:* Research in this area generally involves creation of plausible symbolic representations of the rules and strategic thinking needed to solve problems in a domain. Resulting models are used to evaluate student actions, generate feedback, and provide a basis for learner modeling (Anderson *et al.*, 1995). Tutoring itself can be treated as a task, and so researchers have also built cognitive models of expert tutoring.
- *Complete systems and evaluations:* ITS research overlaps significantly with the learning sciences, and so thousands of systems have been built and many hundreds evaluated to answer research questions. This trend should snowball in the coming years resulting in more effective tutors and continued contributions to the science of learning.

- *Authoring tools, knowledge acquisition, and development tools:* The burden of creating an ITS was quickly realized, and thus approaches to reducing ITS development time (e.g., encoding expertise, teaching strategies, and domain models) began to surface in the early 80's.

Researches Related to ITS

Many studies have shown that learning can often be aided by computers in the classroom with varying effect sizes depending on the system and the metrics used to measure learning. It has been shown that traditional computer-assisted instructional systems (CAI) can lead to better learning when compared to traditional classroom instruction (Kulik 1983, 1994, 2003; Bangert-Drowns *et al.* 1985). Kulik's (1985, 1994) studies indicate that CAI systems can lead to about 0.3 to 0.5 standard deviation effect sizes over classroom instruction suggesting that classrooms using CAI systems can learn more and learn faster than classrooms using traditional classroom instruction alone.

Evidence of the benefits of newer intelligent tutoring systems (ITS) over classroom instruction exists (Koedinger & Anderson, 1993; Koedinger *et al.* 1997; Anderson *et al.* 1995) as well. The Koedinger *et al.* (1997) study compared a commercially available ITS (Cognitive Tutor) to a classroom control and suggested a 1.0 standard-deviation effect size for experiment-designed metrics, while for external metrics (The Iowa Algebra Aptitude test and a subset of the Math SAT) the study found an effect size of 0.3. This study may suffer from a confound of the effect of the ITS with a new textbook prepared to go along with the curriculum. It is unclear how to compare these effect sizes with the Kulik and Kulik (1985) effect size of about 0.4 as we don't know if the metrics in the Kulik and Kulik studies are more generally like externally designed measures or experiment defined measures. In another study, VanLehn *et al.* (2005) compared an ITS not to classroom instruction, but to doing homework in a traditional paper-and-pencil manner. They found results similar to the Cognitive Tutor results mentioned above with effect sizes of about 1.0 standard deviation for their own measures, and about 0.4 for what they consider analogue to "externally designed measures."

Additionally, ITS have been shown to produce superior results when compared to CAI systems (Carroll & Kay, 1988; Schooler, & Anderson, 1990; Corbett, & Anderson, 2001; Mohan, 2003). One might conclude that the best learning results can be obtained first from ITS, secondly from CAI systems and finally from traditional classroom instruction alone. However, we are not aware of a study that compares an ITS to both classroom instruction and CAI.

Human Tutoring

Studies indicate that experienced human tutors provide the most effective form of instruction known. For example, Cohen *et al.* (1982) performed a meta-analysis on the findings of 65 independent evaluations of school tutoring programmes and found that tutoring raised performance on student achievement as measured on examinations with an effect size of 0.4 standard deviation units. The authors did not state whether the outcome measures were externally designed or experimenter designed. Bloom (1984), however, found significantly better results. In his study, tutors produced effect sizes of 2 sigmas, or standard deviations, over students receiving standard classroom instruction. Human tutors also enhanced learning with an effect size of 1 standard deviation over students in a mastery learning condition.

Other studies have been conducted to determine what behaviours make human tutoring effective and how these behaviours can be incorporated into computer-based tutoring systems (McArthur *et al.* 1990; Merrill *et al.* 1992; Graesser & Person 1994; Chi *et al.* 2001;). For example, Merrill, *et al.* (1992) concluded that a major reason human tutors are effective is that they let students do most of the work in overcoming impasses, while providing only as much assistance as necessary and keeping students from following "garden paths" of reasoning that are unlikely to lead to learning. VanLehn *et al.* (2003) also found that allowing students to reach impasses correlated with learning gains. Finally, numerous studies (Swanson 1992; Grasser *et al.* 1995; Chi *et al.*, 2001; Katz *et al.* 2003) hypothesized that it is the interactive nature of the tutorial dialog (i.e., interaction hypothesis) that accelerates learning.

Computer-Assisted Instruction

Computer-based tutoring systems appear to hold promise for improving mathematics instruction. The first computer-based tutoring systems appeared over thirty years ago with the goal of approaching the effectiveness of human tutors. According to Corbett & Trask (2000) these systems, called computer-assisted instruction (CAI) offered one advantage of human tutors: individualized interactive learning support. While these systems were interactive and provided explicit instruction in the form of long web pages or lectures they offered no dialog.

Studies demonstrated the effectiveness of CAI in mathematics at the elementary level (Burns & Bozeman 1981) secondary level (Kulik *et al.* 1983) and college level (Kulik *et al.* 1980). In a meta-analysis of 28 studies involving CAI, Kulik *et al.* (1985) found that CAI improved student achievement by an average effect size of 0.47 over students receiving conventional instruction. In another meta-analysis Kulik (1994) summarized 97 studies from the 1980's that compared classroom instruction to computer-based instruction and found an average effect size of 0.32 in favour of computer-based instruction. Kulik claimed that students learned more and learned faster in courses that involved computer-based instruction. Finally, Kulik (2003) summarized the findings of eight meta-analyses covering 61 studies published after 1990. The median effect size for studies using computer tutorials was 0.59, meaning that students who received computer tutorials performed in the 72nd percentile while students receiving conventional instruction performed in the 59th percentile. While these studies suggest that CAI can be an effective instructional aid in both elementary and secondary schools, CAI does not address the main concern of McArthur *et al.* (1990) who claim that teaching tactics and strategies are the least well developed components of most intelligent tutors.

Model-tracing ITS

With advances in computer science research on artificial intelligence and in cognitive psychology research on human learning and performance, the next generation of computer-based tutoring systems moved beyond the simple presentation of pages of text or graphics. These new intelligent tutoring systems (ITS), called cognitive tutors, incorporated model-tracing technology that is a cognitive model of student problem solving that captures students' multiple strategies and common misconceptions. The cognitive tutor uses model-tracing to understand students' input and to indicate when they have made a mistake. With model-tracing, cognitive tutors provide students individualized assistance that is just-in-time and sensitive to the students' particular approach to a problem (Anderson *et al.* 1995). They also provide canned explanations and hint messages that get more explicit as students continue asking for help until the tutor is telling the student exactly what to do. The feedback is immediate and step-wise and is structured so as to lead students toward expert-like performance. The tutor intervenes as soon as students deviate from the solution path, but the cognitive tutor does not engage students in dialog by asking new questions. Cognitive tutors also use knowledge tracing technology that traces students' knowledge growth across problem solving activities and uses this information to select problems and to adjust the pacing to adapt to individual student needs.

Although cognitive tutors do not engage students in dialog, they nonetheless have had a significant impact on student learning in a variety of domains. For example, Koedinger *et al.* (1997) compared a cognitive tutor, "Cognitive Tutor Algebra" to traditional algebra instruction. "Cognitive Tutor" was built to support the Pittsburgh Urban Mathematics Project (PUMP) algebra curriculum that is centrally focused on mathematical analysis of real world situations and the use of computational tools. The study evaluated the effect of the PUMP curriculum and "Cognitive Tutor" use and found that students in the experimental classes outperformed control classes by 100 per cent on assessments of the targeted problem solving and multiple representations. These results also translated into a one standard deviation effect size. Recent studies comparing "Cognitive Tutor" and traditional algebra instruction, have found improvements in the 50-100 per cent range thus replicating the above results (Koedinger *et al.* 2000). Approximately 375,000 students in over 1000 schools currently use this cognitive tutor.

Morgan and Ritter (2002) conducted a study comparing the Cognitive Tutor Algebra I course and a Traditional Algebra I Course that used a different text with students in their junior high school system. Dependent measures included the Education Testing Service (ETS) Algebra I end-of-course exam, course grades and a survey of attitudes towards mathematics. These measures certainly seem to have the benefit of not being defined by the experimenters themselves. When restricting the analysis to only those teachers who taught both curricula, the researchers found statistically significant differences on all dependent measures in favour of the cognitive tutor. Morgan and Ritter state that the strongest components of teacher effects have to do with teacher education and professional development and only indirectly with practices. In their study the curriculum effect that they were examining had to do with teacher practices that would be expected to be relatively small. Therefore, they conclude that the effect size of 0.29 is impressive taken in this context.

Finally, VanLehn *et al.* (2004) evaluated Andes, an ITS developed to replace paper-and-pencil homework and to increase student learning in introductory college physics courses. Andes provides immediate feedback to student responses and also provides three kinds of help including: 1) pop up error messages when the error is probably due to lack of attention rather than lack of knowledge, 2) *What's Wrong Help* when the student is essentially asking what is wrong with that, and 3) *Next Step Help* if students are not sure what to do next. The *What's Wrong* and *Next Step Help* selections generate a hint sequence that includes a pointing hint, a teaching hint, and a bottom-out hint that tells students exactly what to do.

Andes was evaluated from 1999 to 2003 and in all years Andes students scored higher than control students with effect sizes ranging from 0.21 to 0.92. VanLehn *et al.* (2005) compared their results to the results of the Koedinger *et al.* (1995) study that they suggest is the benchmark study with respect to tutoring systems. The Koedinger *et al.* study evaluated the "Cognitive Tutor" intelligent tutoring system and a novel curriculum (PUMP), which Carnegie Learning distributes as the Algebra I Cognitive Tutor. Koedinger *et al.* used both experimenter-designed questions and standardized tests. While analyzing the experimenter-designed tests, they found effect sizes of 1.2 and 0.7 and effect sizes of 0.3 while analyzing multiple-choice standardized tests. VanLehn *et al.* (2005) found very similar effect sizes (1.21 and 0.69) for their conceptual experimenter-written tests and similar effect sizes (0.29) for their multiple-choice standardized tests. Thus, both evaluations have similar tests and effect sizes. They both have impressive 1.2 and 0.7 effect sizes for conceptual, experimenter-designed tests, and lower effect sizes on standardized, answer only tests. Given the large difference between experimenter-designed tests versus externally designed tests, it makes one wonder how to interpret the Kulik (1994) studies that argue that CAI, when compared to classroom instruction, gives between 0.3 and 0.7 effect sizes.

The authors of the Andes study stated, that their evaluation differed from the Koedinger *et al.* (1997) evaluation in a crucial way. The Andes evaluations manipulated only the way that students did their homework: on Andes vs. on paper. The evaluation of "Cognitive Tutor" was also an evaluation of the Pittsburgh Urban Mathematics Project curriculum (PUMP), which focused on analysis of real world situations and the use of computational tools such as spreadsheets and graphers. Therefore, how much gain was due to the tutoring system and how much was due to the new curriculum is not clear. Finally, VanLehn *et al.* (2005) stated that in their study, the curriculum was not reformed; therefore, the gains in their evaluation may be a better measure of the power of intelligent tutoring systems *per se.*

Dialog-based Intelligent Tutors

Both CAI and cognitive tutors have proved to be more effective than traditional classroom instruction, yet neither has approached the effectiveness of human tutors. Perhaps they have not captured the features of human tutoring that account for its effectiveness. Researchers have recently developed ITSs that incorporate dialog that is based on human tutors in specific domains. Preliminary results are promising. We mention two related projects before focusing on Heffernan's system used in this evaluation.

The Tutoring Research Group at the University of Memphis has developed Auto Tutor (Graesser *et al.* 2001), an ITS that helps students construct answers to computer literacy questions and qualitative physics problems by holding a conversation in natural language thus taking advantage of the interaction hypothesis. AutoTutor attempts to imitate a human tutor by reproducing the dialog patterns and strategies that were likely to be used by a human tutor. AutoTutor presents questions and problems from a curriculum script, attempts to comprehend learner contributions that are entered by keyboard, formulates dialog moves that are sensitive to the learner's contributions and delivers the dialog moves with a talking head that simulates facial expressions and speech to give the impression of a discussion between the tutor and student (Graesser *et al.* 1999) AutoTutor has produced gains of 0.4 to 1.5 standard deviations depending on the learning performance measure, the comparison condition, the subject matter, and the version of AutoTutor (Graesser *et al.* 2003).

Rosé *et al.* (2001) integrated Atlas and the Andes system to compare a model-tracing ITS with an ITS incorporating dialog. Atlas facilitates incorporating tutorial dialog while Andes is a model-tracing ITS for quantitative physics that provides immediate feedback by highlighting each step attempted in either red or green to indicate a right or wrong answer. Andes also provides a hint sequence for students asking for help. The researchers were able to compare student learning between the original Andes and the integrated Atlas-Andes with dialog. Atlas-Andes students scored significantly higher on posttest measures with a difference of 0.9 standard deviations.

Heffernan and Koedinger (2002) and Heffernan (2001) developed an intelligent tutoring system (ITS) that uses dialog to help students write algebra expressions. It models both student behaviour and tutorial behaviour by combining a cognitive model of student behaviour in the domain of *symbolization* with a tutorial model of strategies observed in human tutors. The cognitive student model has a set of production rules that models the problem solving skills needed to write algebraic expressions. The tutorial model is based on the observation of an experienced human tutor during an hour-long tutoring session and thus captures tutorial strategies that were observed to be effective for human tutors in the domain of *symbolization.* It was the first intelligent tutor that had both a model of student thinking and a model of tutorial planning. The system is of the "coached practice" variety that is meant to scaffold "learning by doing" while students practice their problem solving skills. It is different from typical Cognitive Tutors in that it takes its cues more from the dialogs that human tutors have with students and is more flexible in the interactions it has with students. For example, it can acknowledge that part of an answer is correct and then engage a student in a "sub dialog" to help him or her to improve the incorrect path. It "breaks" problems down for students by asking questions and re-phrasing questions, but does not give students answers. Whereas Cognitive Tutors typically cover a full-year of algebra, Heffernan's ITS deals only with *symbolization* problems. The following is a sample tutorial dialog:

Heffernan (2001) investigated the impact on learning of two versions of his ITS. In the control version, if students answered incorrectly the tutor told them the answer to type then moved on to another problem. This approximates a common homework situation in which students can look up correct solutions in the back of the book. In the experimental version, the ITS engaged students in tutorial dialog specific to student errors in an attempt to help students construct the correct answer. Students in the experimental condition performed better on posttest measures showing evidence of learning form dialogs. Heffernan only controlled for the number of problems in this experiment and not for time, therefore, he did not determine if the extra time spent in the dialogs was worth the effort.

Heffernan (2002) reported on a web-based experiment in which he controlled for time in an attempt to see if the learning gains students acquired were worth the extra time students spent in dialog. Heffernan found students in the experimental condition completed only half as many problems as students in the control condition, but still showed learning gains over the control condition with an effect size of 0.5. Heffernan also reported a possible motivation benefit to dialog. In summary, Heffernan's ITS seems like one example that supports the hypothesis that incorporating dialog into an ITS can lead to increases in student learning. Heffernan & Croteau (2004) replicated some of the findings that the ITS seems to show some benefit over CAI for some lessons.

12

Classification of Intelligent Computer-Based Educational Systems

During the past one hundred years, three types of learning have evolved [Clark and Mayer 2002], and each of them can be seen in courses available in software tutoring systems: (1) *receptive learning*: information acquisition, used in lessons including lots of information with limited practice opportunities in order to satisfy "inform" goals, (2) *directive learning*: response strengthening, used in courses that require frequent responses from learners with immediate feedback in order to satisfy "perform-procedure" goals, and (3) *guided discovery*: knowledge construction, used in lessons that provide specific problems and supporting resources in order to satisfy "performprinciple" goals. These three learning types reflect a learning procedure from knowledge acquisition and review to the improvement of learners' problem solving abilities. In a specific course, they can be used in different lessons oriented to different learning phases.

Human being's Learning Mechanism

Cognitive learning theory explains how mental processes transform information received by the sensory organs into knowledge and skills in human memory. In general, the human being has a three-level memory structure: sensory memory, working memory, and long-term memory. Cognitive learning theory explains the human being's cognitive process of learning with several key ideas [Clark and Mayer 2002]: (1) human memory has two channels, visual and auditory, and a limited capacity for processing information, (2) learning occurs by active processing in the memory system, and (3) new knowledge and skills must be retrieved from long-term memory for transfer to the job. When a learner interacts with a software tutoring system, a lesson's visual and auditory information enters the learner's eyes and ears. This information is briefly stored in the sensory memory. It then enters working memory and is finally stored in long-term memory. The working memory is the center of cognition where all active thinking takes place but its capacity is very limited. Learning requires new knowledge and skills stored in working memory to be integrated with existing knowledge in long-term memory. The integration process is an *encoding* procedure, which requires active processing of the information in working memory. The active processing in working memory is called *rehearsal*. Later, the learner must be able to *retrieve* those skills from long term memory back into working memory for solving problems.

It is obvious that the human being's learning is an active information processing procedure. Thus, it is very natural to use learner control strategies to optimize the learning outcome and increase the involvement and autonomy of learners in learning.

Learning Processes and Requirements

Due to the human being's learning mechanism, learning in software tutoring systems relies on four key processes [Clark and Mayer 2002]:

- The learner must focus on key graphics or words in the lesson to select what will be processed.
- The learner must rehearse the information in working memory to organize and integrate it with existing knowledge in long-term memory.
- New knowledge stored in long-term memory must be retrieved back on the job.
- Metacognitive skills manage and adjust these processes.

Because the learner's cognitive system has limited capacity competed by many sources of information, the learner must select those that best match his/her goals. Thus the software tutoring systems should provide learners with information selection opportunities as well as selection guidance. The integration work requires that the limited working memory capacity be not overloaded, so the systems should enable learners to reduce their cognitive loads. To support the knowledge retrieval process, the systems must provide a job context during learning that will contain the needed retrieval links for learners' use. In addition, just as a computer has an operating system to manage data transfer, the human processor has metacognition to manage the learning processes. *Metacognition* refers to the mental management processes that monitor those information processing. A learner with effective metacognitive skills is able to set learning goals, decide in effective ways to reach those goals, oversee the progress, and make necessary adjustments. A good software tutoring system should provide some of the management processes to enable high metacognitive learners to take advantage of them and also help learners with low metacognitive skills for successful learning.

Learner Control vs. Programme Control

Learner control is a feature of tutoring systems where the learner can direct the tutoring flow provided by the system, thus guiding the system to respond to his/ her own needs and interests [Steinberg 1977, Duchastel 1986, Clark and Mayer 2002]. Learner control strategy (LC) is contrasted with programme control strategy (PC, also called system control or software control). LC allows each learner to control content sequencing and pacing, select learning contents, learning examples, the amount of practice exercises, and so forth, while PC lets a computer programme make such decisions for each learner in a lockstep manner. LC and PC may coexist in a tutoring system but more LC means less PC and vice versa.

It is commonly assumed that LC functions as a means of accommodating individual differences of learners. Many studies have concluded that learners are the best judges of their learning needs and performance strategies. Some researchers comparing LC with the traditional PC reported the superiority of the former over the latter (e.g., [Park and Tennyson 1980, Ross *et al.* 1980, Gray 1987]), while other studies demonstrated the superiority of PC strategies (e.g., adaptive PC strategy with elaborate advisement [Tennyson *et al.* 1985], and linear control of the learning task [Goetzfried and Hannafin 1985]).

To assess the effectiveness and efficiency of LC strategies relative to PC strategies, Lee and Lee examined the previous studies on the comparison of LC with PC [Lee and Lee 1991]. They focused on two learning phases: knowledge acquisition and knowledge review, in conjunction with learners' generic metacognitive skills and previous domain knowledge. The results indicate that the effectiveness and efficiency of the LC strategy cannot be taken for granted. Learners' specific knowledge base affords a more reliable source for learning management decision and action than the generic type of metacognitive skills. For both knowledge acquisition and review, LC is superior to PC for the low level of domain knowledge, whereas this difference diminishes as the level of domain knowledge increases. It means LC strategy may work better for tasks of simple content structure, in which minimal domain knowledge is required.

Young [Young 1996] also compared outcomes of learners with high or low metacognitive skills in either LC or PC. The experimental results showed that the learners with low metacognitive skills learned less in LC than the learners in PC, whereas the learners with high metacognitive skills learned more in both LC and PC than the learners with low metacognitive skills.

Other similar studies have compared LC with PC through complex evaluation work on experimental results. In summary, the appropriate application of learner control strategies largely depends on learners' metacognitive skills, content structure, and the quality of system-provided lessons. The learner must exactly know *when* and *how* to control the learning progress. A learner with high metacognitive skills and greater prerequisite knowledge may do better with LC. But a poorly designed lesson with LC is far worse than a good lesson with PC.

Although there are varieties of controversies on learner control in software tutoring systems, it is obvious from the learners' learning processes and the society's needs that the application of learner control strategies in software tutoring systems is not only important but also necessary. In the earlier studies, learner control strategies were mostly used to improve the efficiency of learners' learning. With the emergence of web-based learning and interactive learning, and the increasing amount of adults accepting skills training in companies, the pure programme control strategy cannot predict each learner's needs precisely, utilize learner's own resources maximally, or stimulate learners' motivations effectively. Especially in the context of microworlds—small modeling environments, learner control strategies have been not only more worthy but also necessary.

Learner Control Options

Although the term learner control is generally used, the actual control strategies vary. In general, there are four options regarding learner control:

- *Content and content sequencing.* Learners can select instructional goals and contents, and control the display order of the courses, topics, and screens within a lesson.
- *Pacing.* Learners can control the time spent on each lesson. Except for short video or audio sequences, learners can allocate different time periods to lessons for mastery according to their own needs.
- *Access to learning support.* Learners can control when to access which instructional components of lessons such as helps, examples, practice items, and coaches.
- *Instructional interaction method.* Learners can decide whether to learn individually or collaboratively, select peers as learning partners, and negotiate with systems on instructional goals and course contents.

In [Clark and Mayer 2002], only the first three options are given. The option of instructional interaction method is generated with the emergence of collaborative learning and constructive learning. All these control options represent the different tutoring and learning needs. In software tutoring systems, they can be controlled by learners to different degrees through corresponding software mechanisms. Note that although learners can control tutoring and learning, the learner control strategies are eventually implemented by software tutoring systems.

Software Tutoring Systems

The software tutoring systems are generally specific to situations where learners and tutors no longer have to meet like in the traditional classroom-based instruction. Similar to the definition of e-learning [Clark and Mayer 2002], a software tutoring system can be defined as a teaching and learning environment built on computers by way of CDROM, Internet, or Intranet with the following features: (1) include content relevant to the learning objective; (2) use instructional methods such as examples and practice to help learning; (3) use media elements such as words and pictures to deliver the content and methods; and (4) build new knowledge and skills to achieve individual learning goals or improve organizational performance.

The courses in software tutoring systems include both content (i.e., information) and instructional methods (i.e., techniques) helping people learn the content. They are digitized so they can be stored in electronic form, and delivered via computer using words in the form of spoken or printed text and pictures such as illustrations, photos, animation, or video. The purpose is to help individuals achieve educational goals or to help organizations build skills linked to improved job performance through training. The development of software tutoring systems has experienced three generations in rough and a variety of learner control strategies have been applied into each generation in different measures.

Computer-Assisted Instruction Systems

During the 1960s, educators were under considerable pressure to improve the quality of education as well as to educate a broader segment of society [Steinberg 1977]. Holt deplored the limitations of the widespread used lockstep instruction [Holt 1967]. Rapidly expanding community colleges had to accommodate increasingly numerous heterogeneous students. Teaching alternatives were sought at all levels and individualized instruction became a likely alternative. The application of computers to education made individualization even more feasible in terms of computer-assisted instruction (CAI, or computer-aided instruction). CAI systems were the first generation software tutoring systems. A CAI system presents a page of text or graphics, and puts up a different page depending upon the student's answer [Hefferman and Koedinger 2002]. Although the implementation approaches of CAI vary significantly, in which the computer plays the role of the tutor and communicates with the learner through human-computer interface in the form of text, graphics, multimedia, etc.

Inquiry-Based Intelligent Tutoring Systems

Although CAI systems and model-tracing ITS permit learner control, most of interactions between learners and systems are tightly controlled by the software. The system selects the next task or problem, decides when the learner needs support and feedback in problem solving, and determines the information the learners receive. The learners can tailor information, for example, they may request more detailed explanations, but their behaviours are usually highly limited. Essentially, these systems focus on knowledge acquisition and knowledge review more than on knowledge construction, and are employing computer technologies to implement traditional tutor-centered teaching and learning such as one-on-one and drill-and-practice methods.

Another teaching and learning method, *inquiry-based* method (also described as student-centered, constructionist, constructivist, or discovery-based), has been deeply explored over the recent years and a transition towards inquiry-based instruction has begun. In [McArthur *et al*. 1993], systems that implement inquiry-based learning are collectively referred as *interactive learning environments* (ILEs). The ILEs have the following common characteristics:

- *Construction.* Students learn by constructing their own knowledge, not through lecture or organized drill and-practice.
- *Learner control.* The tutor is viewed only as a guide.
- *Individualization determined by the learner*. Learners receive unique feedback and information as a function of their interaction with the environment built into the system instead of the tutor.
- *Rich feedback generated by the learner's interaction with the learning environment.* Fine-grained feedback arises from the learner's choices and actions rather than from discourse of the tutor.

Model-tracing ITS generally lack a good sense of interaction between learners and systems that may lie in the human tutoring as a dialog format. Based on model-tracing ITS and the features of ILEs, the third generation software tutoring systems have emerged which help learners to construct knowledge and tutor metacognitive processes. These inquiry-based ITS engage in *dialogs* with learners using multiple strategies. A learner's problem solving behaviour is the objective while the model tracing is the tool. The main difference between the first two generations and the third generation software tutoring systems is that the former is based on an "*instructionist*" approach to learning while the latter on a "*constructionist*" or "*constructivist*" approach to learning.

The classification of different generations of tutoring systems is not very strict. In fact, they have developed nearly in parallel. With the introduction of more complex tutoring and learning environments such as *collaborative learning*—a structured instructional interaction method among two or more learners to achieve a learning goal or complete an assignment [Panitz 1996], and *agent-based* tutoring systems—an agent is a computer system situated in some environment and capable of autonomous actions in this environment in order to meet its design objectives [Wooldridge 1999] which is often used in distributed tutoring systems, some researchers also classify the development of software tutoring systems into two generations, *solo-learning* (in form of individual) and *collaborative learning* (in form of small-group), from the perspective of learning. Thus the classification is becoming overlapped and obscured. Nevertheless, the most obvious fact is that more control is being given to the learner instead of the tutor in these systems. Therefore, the following discussion will focus on the learner control strategies in generic software tutoring systems.

It is now commonly accepted that research on Intelligent Tutoring Systems (ITS), also sometimes called Intelligent Computer Aided Instructional (ICAI) systems, started as a distinct approach with a dissertation by Carbonell (1970a) and with his system SCHOLAR (Collins *et al.*, 1975; Carbonell, 1970b; Barr & Feigenbaum, 1982; Clancey, 1987a). Since this beginning, this research has developed in many directions (Kearsley, 1987; Galdes, 1990). Broadly speaking, two major schools of thought have evolved and produced two different types of system: learning environments and active teaching systems (Goodyear, 1991; Galdes, 1990). As Goodyear (1991) noted, the builders of learning environments have adopted "models which favour learner-directed exploration, negotiation of purpose or the acquisition of higher-level cognitive skills" (p. 9), whereas the builders of active teaching systems "have adopted pedagogical models which could be described as instructional, goal-directed, system-led or content-driven" (pp. 8-9).

Learning Environment

At one extreme of this continuum lie the learning environments that support free exploratory (or discovery) learning, e.g., the LOGO system (Papert, 1980). The fundamental epistemological concept underlying LOGO is "it is more important to help children learn how to develop and debug their own theories than it is to teach them theories we consider correct" (Wenger, 1987, p. 125). A repeated conclusion from experience with these environments in practice is that students tend to require some additional assistance or guidance to take full advantage of their exposure. Another type of learning environment is called a reactive learning environment (Barr & Feigenbaum, 1982). These systems are designed to improve on the discovery learning approach by making more of the underlying domain and its structure visible to the student (Brown, 1983). With discovery learning, the student is on his own to discover any structure inherent in the learning environment but, as Brown (1983) noted, "much of the time he (the student) will appear to be wandering aimlessly down the garden path in search of some insight." In contrast, reactive learning environments are designed to prevent too much wandering by the student.

Active Teaching Systems

The second major category of ITS is active teaching systems. These systems deliver instruction and monitor guided practice. In other words these systems make the structure of the domain visible and accessible and also help to lead the student through his/her domain knowledge. Active teaching systems are sub-classified as: coaching systems (Breuker, 1988; Barr & Feigenbaum, 1982), mixed-initiative tutors (Barr & Feigenbaum, 1982; Wenger, 1987) and diagnostic tutors (Kearsley, 1987).

Coaching Systems

As the name suggests, coaching systems view the instructional system as a coach. Here the system's main task is "to look over the student's shoulder and decide whether to help the student around a particular pitfall or let him succumb to the pitfall so that he can learn to detect when he is on the wrong path" (Galdes, 1990, pp. 20-21). In other words a coaching system observes the student's performance quietly and provides advice that will help the student to perform better (Kearsley, 1987).

Mixed-initiative Tutors

Mixed-initiative tutors engage the student in a two-way conversation and attempt to teach the student via the Socratic method of guided discovery (Kearsley, 1987). As Galdes (1990) noted, the Socratic method here "refers more to a basic question-answering and dialogue approach (Resnick, 1977) than to the original method developed by Socrates (Jordan, 1963; Hayman, 1974; Plato, 1974)" (p. 20).

Diagnostic Tutors

According to Galdes (1990) "Diagnostic tutors debug a student's work once the student has completed the problem or reach an impasse". These programmes are driven by a bug library that identifies the misconceptions that students may have in solving a problem (Kearsley, 1987).

Research Approaches to the Design of Active Teaching Systems:

Why Study Human Tutors?

Tutoring is a *method* of educational delivery. In order to use this method one needs to make many decisions given below:

(1) What type of knowledge needs to be tutored? Here possibilities are:
- factual knowledge
- procedural knowledge
- conceptual knowledge
- basic principles
- or a combination of these

(2) What is the nature of the educational setting? For example, will tutoring be a part of or peripheral to the course under consideration. If it is a part of the course then how much of the curriculum will it cover? On the other hand, if it is peripheral to the course then on what aspects of the curriculum will it concentrate?

(3) What is the educational level for which this tutoring method needs to be used? This could range from primary to professional education. These decisions, in a way, are variables determining the nature of tutoring used in an educational system.

Tutoring studies performed by, for example, Bloom (1984), Collins *et al.* (1975), Fox (1993), Putnam (1987), Littman *et al.* (1985), and Galdes (1990), have used different variables and there are no systematic criteria yet available to compare these studies. In such a situation it is difficult to generalize the effectiveness of a study under one set of conditions to a similar study having a different set of conditions.

A survey of literature indicates that many of the researchers agree that tutoring is the most effective educational delivery method. One reason for this general agreement is that certain studies (for example, performed by Bloom (1984)) have clearly demonstrated the effectiveness of tutoring compared to other methods of educational delivery. These studies have provided a basis for the first-order generalization that tutoring as a method of educational delivery, without regards to the variables on which it depends, is most effective. It is true that the field of ITS is now sufficiently mature to strive for a more detailed classification of variables on which tutoring depends.

Studies have shown that tutoring by *humans* is more effective than currently known educational delivery methods (Bloom, 1984; Cohen *et al.*, 1982). One goal of ITS research is to make machine tutors at least as effective as human tutors (Galdes, 1990). However it appears that human tutors still outperform machine tutors (Merrill *et al.*, 1992). In light of these findings, the obvious approach to improving ITS design is to study the behaviour of the human tutors.

Multiple Expert Metaphor

Research on tutoring has shown that human tutors, while in the process of tutoring, perform a number of tasks (Collins *et al.*, 1975; Woolf & Cunningham, 1987; Littman, 1991; McArthur *et al.*, 1990). These tasks can be grouped into the following major activities:

- act as an expert in the domain
- act as an expert in the process of tutoring
- act as an expert in the process of diagnosing the student's problems and
- act as an expert in the process of communicating his/her responses to the student.

The most widely accepted model for the design of the ITS is based upon the multiple expert metaphor (Breuker, 1990; Self, 1988; Wenger, 1987; Polson & Richardson, 1988). According to this metaphor, an ITS consists of a set of experts that communicate with each other and coordinate their activities to create effective tutoring behaviour. The most commonly used components that take part in this process are the domain expert, student expert (or student modeler), pedagogical expert, and communication expert.

Domain Expert: The domain expert characterizes the knowledge and strategies needed for expert performance in a domain (Bonar, 1984).

Student Expert: The student expert is also called a student modeler because it represents the tutor's estimate of the student's understanding of the material to be taught (Barr & Feigenbaum, 1982). In other words, his expert "uncovers a hidden cognitive state (the student's knowledge of the subject matter) from observable behaviour" (VanLehn, 1988, p. 55).

Pedagogical Expert: The pedagogy or tutoring expert, using a theory of tutoring, provides assistance to the student, monitors and criticizes the student and selects problems and remedial material for the student (Halff, 1988; Wenger, 1987; Clancey, 1987a).

Communication Expert: The communication expert processes the flow of communication in and out of the system.

Wenger (1987) noted that "whereas the pedagogical module (expert) decides the timeliness and content of didactic actions, the ... (communication expert) takes care of their final form".

Criticism of Multiple Expert Metaphors

According to Breuker (1990), "In the ITS literature (e.g., Wenger, 1987) a confusion of functions, types of knowledge and agents is very persistent. In general it is explained that an ITS consist of a "classical" triad (Self, 1988) of a domain, student and didactic expert. In fact the roles of these "agents" overlap: in particular in diagnosing. This overlap is not a serious problem, unless it is preserved in the functional decomposition and worse: in the architecture of an ITS. Because, this metaphor is used over and over again, it may have been the cause for so many unarticulated ITS architectures.

This criticism of the multiple expert metaphor raises a very fundamental issue for ITS research. This metaphor is helpful at the conceptual level but according to Breuker that this metaphor should not be carried over to the implementation level.

Interactivity between the Components of Multiple Expert Metaphor: The Real Strength of an ITS

The multiple expert paradigm is the one most popularly used in the design of the ITS. But as Park *et al.* (1987) noted, because of the size and complexity of most ITS, researchers typically focus on only one or two components of the ITS at a time and ignore the others. For example, SCHOLAR (Carbonell, 1970b) and WHY (Collins *et al.*, 1975) emphasize knowledge representation (domain expert) and tutorial dialogues (pedagogy expert). BUGGY (Brown & Burton, 1978), DEBUGGY (Burton, 1982), and PROUST (Johnson & Soloway, 1984a) emphasize student modeling issues (student expert). MENO-TUTOR (Woolf & McDonald, 1985) emphasizes tutorial discourse strategies (pedagogy expert and communication expert). This partial and isolated approach was justifiable in these early systems because these research efforts only started to unfold the nature of the processes underlying effective but complex tutoring behaviour.

The multiple expert metaphor is a powerful modularization tool which breaks a complex behaviour into its components to facilitate understanding.

But one drawback of this approach is that it puts too much emphasis on the notion that sum of the components makes up the whole. This idea is nicely explained by Burns & Parlett (1991), "It is difficult to separate the dancer from the dance; nevertheless in Foundations of Intelligent Tutoring Systems (Polson & Richardson, 1988), the fundamental anatomy was used to discuss research issues within each of the separate components ... Because designing intelligent tutors is such an interdisciplinary activity, attending to the anatomy piece by piece often ignores the synergy that a wholly integrated system could achieve" (p. 2).

Approaches to the Inquiry of Tutoring Behaviour

A number of approaches have been used to develop the individual "experts" of an ITS. For the sake of clarity, we will discuss these approaches only in the context of developing the pedagogy expert of the ITS. The pedagogy expert of an ITS using a model/theory of tutoring, provides assistance to the student, monitors and criticizes the student and selects problems and remedial material for the student (Halff, 1988; Clancey, 1987a; Wenger, 1987). Broadly speaking three approaches have been used to develop a model/theory of tutoring for the pedagogy expert of the ITS (VanLehn, 1993).

Approach Based on Experience and Common Sense

In this approach the model/theory of tutoring is based on the author's experience (VanLehn, 1993) or observations of tutors (Galdes, 1990). These theories consist of heuristics, such as "Do not interrupt too often," and "Follow up an abstract definition with several examples and at least one negative example" (VanLehn, 1993, p. 3). One of the major objections to this approach is, since these theories are not based on careful empirical work, these theories are probably incomplete and possibly incorrect. Examples of systems that used this approach are WEST (Burton & Brown, 1979), which teaches arithmetic skills, WUSOR (Goldstein, 1982), which teaches logic and probability and GUIDON (Clancey, 1987b), which teaches diagnosis and therapy prescription for infectious diseases. Galdes (1990) has given two more reasons for not using this approach.

1. This approach can contradict facts: The initial version of PROUST (Johnson & Soloway, 1984b) was developed using this approach. An evaluation of this early version indicated that the system was a total failure (Johnson & Soloway, 1984b). One reason for this failure was that the method of diagnosis used by the system was not able to handle real student input. The new version of this system used a theory of programming bugs based on empirical studies of the kinds of programming errors real students make (Spohrer & Soloway, 1986). This example shows that theories based upon experience or common sense may not always be right.

2. This approach may not give us the right context: According to Galdes (1990) "A second problem with intuitions is that the "rightness" or "wrongness" often depends on the *context* where we want to apply it." (p. 30). For example in WEST (Burton & Brown, 1979) twelve pedagogical principles are used. One of these principles states "Do not tutor on two consecutive moves no matter what" (Burton & Brown, 1979). The purpose of this principle is "to keep the student's interest from being destroyed" (Galdes, 1990, p. 32). Here Galdes (1990) argues that this principle is fine for a game situation where students may not be highly motivated. But, is this principle also equally applicable for a system which teaches students how to deal with life threatening issues? The fact is that the right context for applying such principles can not be defined without empirical evidence.

Approach Based on Rigorous Experimentation

In this approach a careful experimentation is conducted to build a prescriptive theory of tutoring. This approach deals with simple hypotheses, which when, proven yield lists of heuristics such as "Immediate feedback is better than delayed feedback" (VanLehn, 1993). This is a slow approach but probably the best one in the long run to understand the process of tutoring (VanLehn, 1993). But, as VanLehn (1993) noted, this approach tends "not to produce a unified theory of how to tutor, at least not very quickly".

Approach Based on Studies of Human Tutors

In this approach, researchers study human tutors to develop a model/theory of tutoring. This is the best approach to develop an ITS. Research has shown that tutoring by humans is the best method of educational delivery (Bloom, 1984). Hence basing the design of the ITS on these empirical studies will increase our chance of building a system that is as effective as human tutors. Some ITSs that were based upon the study of human tutors are SCHOLAR (Carbonell, 1970b), WHY (Collins *et al.*, 1975), MENO-Tutor (Woolf & McDonald, 1985), PROUST (Johnson & Soloway, 1984a), EUROHELP (Breuker, 1990), and TP (Littman, 1991).

How "Expert" should the Human Tutor be?

Although studying human tutors is the best approach to the design of the ITS, one important question one still needs to ask is: how expert should the human tutor be to participate in the experiment?

Goodyear (1991) states that "the pressing need in the ITS field is not for knowledge about optimal ways of teaching but for knowledge about how to do any kind of teaching". A survey of the literature on tutoring systems indicates that most of the researchers would agree with Goodyear. The tutors in most of the empirical studies performed either lacked expertise in the process of tutoring or in the domain knowledge.

Collins *et al.* (1975) performed an empirical study of human tutoring to improve the performance of the SCHOLAR system. Four tutors and six students participated in this study. Collins *et al.* (1975) reported that the two of the tutors who participated in the experiment "have extensive teaching experience at the college level, though neither has taught geography (the domain of SCHOLAR system). The third and fourth tutors each taught only one session, and did not prepare nearly as extensively as the first two tutors.

Most of the human tutoring studies reported in the literature, also, do not explicitly state the level of expertise of their subjects. Admittedly "it is certainly true that it is very difficult to get universal agreement on the quality of a teaching performance, even harder to get agreement on the validity of the knowledge on which that performance may be based" (Goodyear, 1991, p. 13). But, for example, studies performed by Anania (1983) and Ellson (1976) concluded that tutoring by humans is not always better than group instruction! Galdes (1990) proposed that the effectiveness of human tutors lies in the skills they have in the domain and in the process of tutoring. A human tutor lacking either of these skills will not be able to perform optimally in a tutoring situation (Anderson, 1988; Breuker, 1988; Fletcher, 1984; Jones *et al.*, 1979). In the light of these findings it is imperative that human tutoring studies should explicitly state the level of expertise of their subjects and the standards by which this expertise are measured. This will help ITS research move towards a long term goal of making ITS's at least as effective as the best human tutors.

The literature on studies of differences between novice and expert teachers (e.g., Berliner, 1986; Leinhardt & Greeno, 1991) also have shown that expert teachers, compared to the novices, possess a variety of skills that make the process of teaching much more effective. Berliner (1986) provided a list of reasons for studying expert teachers. He further states that "the design of an intelligent tutoring system requires versatile output. That is, expert tutoring systems need a wide range of instructional options to choose from and some decision rules about when to use these options. Expert teachers are likely to have more of that kind of knowledge than ordinary teachers".

Problems in Studying Human Tutors

(i) *Methods are Not Well-Defined*: Galdes (1990) argues that human experts possess tactical knowledge and since this knowledge can not be easily articulated, researchers involved in the study need to rely on other methods of getting this knowledge. According to her—"previous studies of human tutors demonstrated that no standard methods exist for uncovering this tacit knowledge". Analyses of data obtained\ through some methods also vary for two reasons. "First, the analysis method used depends on which specific variables the researcher wants to study ... Second, the analysis method varies according to the level of detail desired in the result." As a result each new study of human tutors needs to develop its own methodology.

(ii) *Methods are Time Consuming*: The knowledge acquisition is usually regarded as the most time consuming process in the design of an AI system (Wielinga *et al.*, 1987). An ITS, being an AI system, is not an exception here.

(iii) *No Definite Criteria are Available for the Identification of Expert Tutors:* According to Berliner (1986) there are no definite and objective criteria available to identify an expert human tutor. This situation exists at all levels of educational practice.

(iv) *The Confounding of Experience and Expertise*: Berliner (1986) states that: "Another problem we encountered occurred because mere experience is simply not believed by most people to correlate highly with expertise in pedagogy. Perhaps this is because our problems are so ill structured. Perhaps it is due to the lack of external criteria. But for whatever reasons, the problems of studying expertise in pedagogy are harder than in some other fields because of the widespread belief that we need to separate expertise from experience and to study how experience".

(v) *What Knowledge Systems are used in Pedagogy*?: According to Berliner (1986), another problem in studying human teachers is in "understanding what domains of knowledge are used by expert teachers in accomplishing their tasks" (p. 9). Some researchers argue that the subject matter knowledge is important. Others argue that the teacher's personal knowledge of self is important (e.g., Lampert, 1984).

The Teacher as a Facilitator for Knowledge Integration:

The Current Theoretical Standpoint

Now we discuss about teaching philosophy used in ITS research. This discussion is based upon the ideas of Ohlsson (1991) who described three theories of teaching that are relevant for ITS research and "form a sequence, in the sense that each theory is a response to an inherent problem in the preceding theory". These theories are described briefly as follows:

(1) The Facilitation of Knowledge Transfer

Ohlsson (1991) called the "facilitation of knowledge transfer" theory as the first-order theory of teaching. This theory "views teaching as the communication of subject matter" and paints the traditional view of pedagogy. Although current ITS research does not subscribe to this point of view, much of the school practice still rests on this theory of pedagogy (Wheatley, 1991). From this viewpoint ideas and thoughts are communicated in the sense that meaning is packaged into words and sent to another who unpacks the meaning from the sentences. Here the learner is like a sponge (Wheatley, 1991). According to Ohlsson (1991) "this theory of teaching is radically inadequate".

A teacher using this theory needs to make two types of decisions: what to say and how to say it. These decisions require the teacher to have "a codification of the subject matter and he or she needs to know effective methods for the presentation of each unit of the subject matter" (Ohlsson, 1991).

The first-order theory of teaching is that "implicitly assumes that the teacher knows the extent of the student's previous knowledge" (Ohlsson, 1991). Current educational practice does not rest on individualization of instruction. Also from Lesgold's (1988) two fundamental laws of instruction we know that "not everyone who passes a test on a topic knows what appears to have been tested," and "not everyone who fails a test on a topic lacks the knowledge that appears to have been tested". It follows that in order for the teacher to have an accurate estimate of previous knowledge, he or she must diagnose the knowledge state of the individual student. This requirement gives rise to the need for the second-order theory of teaching.

(2) The Facilitation of Knowledge Integration

According to Ohlsson (1991), the second-order theory of teaching says that "to teach is to correct the learner's mental representation of the subject matter". According to this theory the learner possesses some representation of the subject matter but this representation is either incomplete or incorrect or both. "The job of the teacher is to provide remediation for the discrepancies between the learner's representation and the complete and correct representation" (Ohlsson, 1991). In other words, the goal of teaching is that the learner ultimately integrates his/her view of the domain into a correct, coherent, and desired model of the domain. This theory makes up the current view on which almost all ITS are based (Ohlsson, 1991). The major theme of this theory is the process of cognitive diagnosis, which can be described as the process of "inferring what the student does and does not know on the basis of his or her performance on some diagnostic task" (Ohlsson, 1991).

In accordance with this theory, the instruction generated by the teacher should be tailored to the knowledge state of the learner. A presentation of the subject matter about a particular misconception, for example, is not enough because different students need different presentations for the same misconception. The problem with this theory is that "the description of a deviation between the student's mental representation of the subject matter and the correct representation does not entail any conclusion about which tutorial message might cause the learner to correct that deviation" (Ohlsson, 1991). Ohlsson (1991) concluded that a learning theory can only drive the content of a needed tutorial message. This conclusion gives rise to the third-order theory of teaching.

(3) The Facilitation of Knowledge Construction

The third-order theory, according to Ohlsson (1991), paints a future view of teaching theory. According to this theory, teaching is the process of facilitating knowledge construction. In other words "to teach is to help the learner improve his or her current world view". This theory, although most promising, is not yet sufficiently fully developed to help in building ITSs. Ohlsson (1991) defined productive learning sequences as a sequence of learning events (e.g., to replace a vague idea with a clearer one, to generalize an idea) which leads to a better view of the subject matter. "To teach is, in this theory, neither to communicate the subject matter, nor to remedy cognitive errors, but to arrange situations in which productive learning sequences are likely to occur" (Ohlsson, 1991).

(4) Jigsaw-Puzzle Metaphor

The goal of the teacher, in the second-order theory, is to correct the learner's mental representation of the subject matter. Here the teacher provides remedial material so that the discrepancies between the learner's representation and the complete and correct representation can be removed. The teacher using this theory needs to know how the subject matter knowledge is encoded in the learner (at some particular moment in time)? Ohlsson (1991) listed a set of four types of actions that a teacher needs to make:

(1) "Which subject matter topic is to be taught?"
(2) "How does an expert represent that topic?"
(3) "Which deficiency does the mental representation of this student suffer from at this moment in time?" and
(4) "How can that deficiency be remediated?"

The activities of the teacher using this theory can be visualized as if he/she is solving a jigsaw-puzzle. This puzzle is analogous to the learner's mental representation of the subject matter. The puzzle solving process starts with a partially completed puzzle, representing the learner's mental representation at that point in time. This process is partially guided by the teacher's knowledge of the domain. The job of the tutor is to identify (i.e., perform cognitive diagnosis) on pieces of the puzzle (chunks of knowledge), which are missing or/and correctly and incorrectly placed.

After this piece by piece identification process, the teacher needs to put all the pieces together correctly (integrate them into a model of the domain) to complete this process of puzzle solving. Unlike a person solving a jigsaw puzzle, the teacher in real life does not have physical access to the student's mental state of the subject matter knowledge. He/she can only, using various teaching actions (e.g., asking questions, providing a summary), help the student integrate his/her knowledge into a coherent, correct and desired mental model of the domain. Although second-order teaching theory is more sophisticated than any metaphor of it can portray, the jigsaw-puzzle metaphor captures the essential ingredients of this theory.

13

Intelligent Tutoring System and Bloom's Challenge

Why should be care about tailoring training to individual students? Why should we care about individualized instruction? Benjamin Bloom and his students attempted to answer these questions by comparing the achievement of individually tutored students (one human teacher per one student) with that of classroom students (one human teacher per 28-32students) (Bloom, 1984). They found the difference in achievement to be about two standard deviations, which means, roughly, that tutoring improved the achievement of 50th percentile students to that of 98th percentile students.

Intelligent Tutoring System May Answer Bloom's Challenge

Intelligent tutoring system technology can increase the achievement of students because it offers several advantages to the students which are never found in traditional teaching-learning process. These advantages of ITS are discussed below:

Advantages of Using Intelligent Tutoring System for Teaching and Learning

ICAL Systems can involve Multiple Senses

A computer can provide a multi-sensory learning environment for the student. Most computers in use today are capable of stimulating the senses of seeing, hearing and touching. The student sees what is displayed on the screen, hears the sounds reproduced by the speaker and touches the mouse, the keyboard and on some computers, the touch screen.

Sound is often used in the classroom to enhance the learning process. Children with powerful musical intelligences can be kept focused on the lesson with use of rhythmic sounds. It is relatively easy to add basic sounds to a programme on most computer systems. Different sounds can be used to help the student remember sequence or just help keep the other intelligences focused on the lesson long enough to master the material. If a stereophonic system is used the spatial intelligence can be involved. Sound can help the child with a strong linguistic intelligence who can not yet read.

The linguistic person loves stories and playing word games. They may become very frustrated if they can not read. The computer can "read" stories and play word games using voice synthesis. For example, if a child is to match one of three lower case letters to a displayed uppercase letter, he will remember each displayed letter more easily if it is visually highlighted in some way and it is verbalized by the system. The final sense used when interacting with computers is touch. Touch is generally not used as much as seeing and hearing. In addition to touching the keyboard or a mouse for input, a touch screen can be used. A touch screen, as the name implies, allows a user to make choices by reaching out and actually touching the screen. If for example the child has to touch the lower case letter that matches the uppercase letter "B", he will be seeing the letter, hearing it pronounced and touching the area of the screen where the letter is. When a child with strong spatial intelligence tries to remember the shape of a lower case "b" he will have a better chance of choosing the "'b" instead of a "d" because ehe can feel. or remember a spatial difference between the "b" and the 'd'—on the screen. He may also hear it being said in his mind. With multiple senses being used the chances of the student correctly remembering the information is increased.

ICAL Systems can be Highly Adapted to Individual Students

One of the key advantages of using a computer to present instructional material is the ease of varying the visual presentation. All children are not equally stimulated by any one graphic image or theme. The computer programme can be designed to present the same lesson in several different ways and automatically select the screens that are most likely to capture the attention of the student. For instance, a student that has trouble reading will not be attracted to a screen filled with text, but a highly graphic screen with simple instructions may keep his attention long enough for him to read and follow the instructions. Thus he will have a confidence building success instead of being intimidated. On the other end of the scale this highly graphic screen may be overwhelming for a child that has trouble focusing. This person may well respond better to a simple, soothing screen with very little information to process and straight-forward choices. An interpersonal child will probably respond well to some kind of character that acts as a guide or mentor, while an intrapersonal child is more likely to think that the character is a silly affectation and quickly become bored with the programme. A well-written programme can determine the students' preferences, based on how they react to sample choices in a front-end diagnostic test, that may be disguised as a short game and present them with screens that are optimized for that individual's dominant intelligences and learning styles.

Providing information in a multi-intelligence format increases the chances one of them will be a strong intelligence for the user. This is of particular importance for the "learning-disabled" child whose learning "disability" is having dominant intelligences other than linguistic or mathematical/logical. As an added benefit, the brain will process the information in two or more different ways, increasing the number of neural paths that are developed which in turn, increases the chances that it will be remembered. Every additional facet of the students intelligences that can be employed increases the attention that the student will focus on learning the assigned task, since it is harder to ignore stimuli that engage multiple senses.

With effective programming employing recent developments in object oriented programming and expert system engines, a powerful programme can be written that is self tailoring. The expert system will diagnose both the student's ability and learning preferences. From the learning preferences, the expert system will deduce the dominant intelligences and select lessons and styles to most effectively present the material to the student. The inheritance characteristic of object-oriented programming and the ability of the programme to build links and calls on the fly greatly reduce the programming efforts and allow for the vast number of dynamic changes that are necessary to take advantage of both the gross and subtle differences between learning styles.

A less powerful programme requires the teacher or the student to set default settings and to modify the programme as the student accomplishes the tasks. This will be easy to do using menus and help screens. In between these two extremes are many possible approaches that may use techniques such as strings of "if then" statements to automatically increase the difficulty as the student's performance improves.

While it is true that a computer system is limited by its hardware and programmes, the fact is that it can be very versatile. A good intermediate programme can be tailored to the needs and abilities of the individual student. This can be done most easily by setting defaults for the user that are used each time the programme is used. The programme can have many ways of presenting the lesson, selected by the student or teacher through software switches. The defaults can be set by selecting choices from a menu. This menu can be locked, or invisible to the user. More advanced students may use a programme with pull down menus which change the difficulty level or even which intelligences the programme addresses.

ICAL Systems can be Patient Tutors

One of the biggest advantages to using a computer is that it has the capacity for great patience. It can allow the student to repeat the same task over and over without getting upset, bored or distracted. A student can repeat the same thing until he understands it or gets tired of it. The computer will give consistent responses. It will not snap at the user because the "teacher" is having a bad day. It may not count the number of times the user did the same problem. A properly-programmed computer can be infinitely patient and consistent when it is appropriate. The value of this to a slow learner cannot be over emphasized.

Many children, especially those who are not linguistically oriented or who are intrapersonal, do not like being called by the teacher. They freeze up and can't think because of the intense pressure they feel. As a result, they often fail to answer the teacher's question and are more tense the next time they are called on. It becomes a never-win situation for the student. Many of these children love using a computer. They do not feel the pressure to answer and provide the correct answer. They do not have the intense fear of failure that they feel in an open classroom. They are one-on-one with the computer and feel more relaxed and are thus more able to learn. The computer, when properly programmed, will provide positive feedback. Using a computer thus helps give non-linguistic and intrapersonal students a chance to maximize their potential in a way they are comfortable with. As a result, their self-confidence grows and they are better able to interact with the class. With their growing self-confidence, they can learn to translate the information they learned on the computer to the open classroom and begin to overcome their fear of failure.

A computer can provide immediate, positive feedback. Studies have shown that feedback enhances learning. They also show that it is important for the feedback to be given immediately with an explanation if necessary, instead of just the correct answer. (Crawford, 81). The feedback can be more consistent, more often and more repetitive, if necessary, than that provided by a teacher. A teacher generally has 20-30 students to respond to and physically can't provide the one-on-one feedback a computer can. There are times when this immediate feedback is essential for learning. Because the computer's responses are immediate, the chances of increasing learning is greater than when a student gets back a corrected worksheet (some children even look at the corrections) several days after they did the work. A child who is learning a new word may need to hear it over and over. Using a programme such as Kidworks by Davidson & Associates, Inc. (Kid Works, 92), the child can have the computer say it to them as many times as necessary. The child knows he has to hear it over and over. The computer can satisfy that need. In most cases, the teacher won't be able to.

A computer doesn't give unintended negative feedback either directly or indirectly *(if* programmed properly) like teachers frequently do with comments such as. "that's incorrect" and their nonverbal signals. A fellow classmate or teacher may roll their eyes, sigh or just have a look of disappointment on their face when Rohit misses the same word for the fifth time. A computer can give the same response the fifth or even 100th time as it did the first time. There won't be any negative human emotion added because of the number of times the word was missed. The computer doesn't give non verbal to discourage the student.

As mentioned briefly above, the computer can provide multiple learning styles for the child to learn from. There can be thirty children at thirty different computers studying the same new math problems or reading words in many different ways. The computer is not limited, as a teacher is, to providing only one teaching style to an entire class at one time. With multiple computers, each child can be learning the material in a way that best suits them. As a result, they will learn it faster, enjoy it more and remember it longer. They will want to learn more because they enjoy learning using a computer. A computer can be as flexible as the hardware and software allows.

Recent Trends and Developments in ITS Research

Now, we summarized several traditional areas of ITS research that continue to receive attention from the community. In this section, we unpack the most prominently represented of these research themes and describe several other areas of interest that have emerged recently.

Learner Modeling

In the last five years, a great deal of attention has been given to the modeling of the *affective state* of learners. Most of this effort has targeted *motivation* since there is evidence form the learning sciences that (1) expert human tutors *do* manage the motivational and emotional states of learners, and (2) instruction can be adjusted according to motivation in ways that improve learning. Often using the highly detailed measurements a computer environment can provide (e.g., time between keystrokes), researchers have built algorithms that translate these patterns into evidence about affective states. In some cases, motivation has been tied to ability and help-seeking tendencies while in others feedback frequency has been adjusted based on the system's motivational state estimate of the student.

Open learner modeling is an extension of traditional learner modeling that makes the model a visible and interactive part of the learning environment. In other words, the display includes a representation of the system's internal belief of the student's knowledge state. A common visualization used is the progress bar. As a student solves problems in a domain, each action is tracked and treated as positive or negative evidence towards a belief domain elements are understood (or not). The progress bars move in one direction or the other, all for the student to see. It is often argued that this inherently motivating because students are usually given the chance to "challenge" the model, essentially telling the ITS "I want a problem to solve to prove I possess skill X." Open learner models are often argued to support reflection and active learning because in order to challenge the model, students must assess their own understanding and decide how to work through the curriculum.

Authoring Systems

As discussed previously, if ITS technology is to make its way out of the lab on a large scale, authoring tools will need to be available for end users who want to build new tutors or tweak the system's behaviours based on what they find in the field. A recent book on state of the art authoring tools (Murray, Blessing, &

Ainsworth, 2003) makes it clear that although the many existing systems have been successful, all remain research prototypes. This is not true for authoring systems that focus solely on creating and modifying domain *content*, but rather in the case of authoring tutorial and expert *knowledge*, significant hurdles remain.

A particularly promising approach to authoring is based on the idea of *authoring by example*. The basic idea is that rather than encoding domain expertise and tutoring knowledge in an AI programming language, the author instead *demonstrates* ideal solutions. To create feedback messages, the user specifies what the system should say to a student at various points of the demonstration. To handle mistakes, the author simply labels parts of the demonstration as errors, then again authors appropriate feedback messages. This is the approach taken by the Cognitive Tutoring Authoring Tools (CTAT) project. Preliminary testing has shown an authoring speedup of between 1.4 and 2 times over a "reduced" version of the tool lacking the demonstration capability (Aleven *et al.*, 2006). Because the demonstrated models tend to be overly rigid, researchers are also exploring the use of machine learning techniques in attempts to infer cognitive models from series of demonstrations.

Group, Collaborative and Online Learning

The advent of the internet and relative ease of networking computers together has radically advanced the state of the art in collaborative learning. ITS work in this area, including intelligent support for team training, has historically been quite limited (Loftin *et al.*, 2004), but has seen dramatic increases in the last few years thanks in part to the successes of the Computer Supported Collaborative Learning (CSCL) community. Jermann, Soller, & Muehlenbrock (2001) point out that early CSCL systems were essentially networked work environments that performed "mirroring" of actions so all participants could be aware of actions taken in some community workspace.

Advanced CSCL systems go beyond mirroring to provide deeper supports, such as *rate* data (showing how fast collaborators are at completing tasks), social networking tools (to reveal level of communication between participants, for example), and problem solving monitoring with feedback (to offer guidance to individual team members). Because robust free-form natural language understanding is an unsolved problem, advice-giving CSCL systems tend to use other techniques to monitor communicative activities. One approach is to require the use of *sentence openers* (such as "I agree, but..." or "Do you know...") which can provide a deep enough level of intentional information to track collaboration patterns.

Evaluations of CSCL systems have shown that many of the expected benefits, such as increased motivation and participation, have not been realized. Studies repeatedly reveal problems such as low participation and communication rates, satisfaction, and limited learning. To deal with some of these problems, ITS researchers have recently focused on a variety of approaches, such as improving team visualization, support for peer and reciprocal tutoring, and intelligent "matching" of group members. In general, automatic assessment of individual performance in a team environment is limited because of the complex nature of doing plan recognition on groups of human participants. However, in some cases it is feasible to provide one-on-one style tutoring to individuals in a team environment. One example appears in Livak (2004) in the form of a cognitive tutor that supports tactical operations in a 3D first-person "shooter" game.

Natural Language Dialogue

In face-to-face situations, human tutors use a variety of communicative techniques such as body language, gesture, hesitation, intonation, and, of course, dialogue. Because many intelligent tutoring systems avoid the use of natural language (often called "2nd generation systems"), researchers have suggested that improved natural language dialogue may help "close the gap" between human and computer tutors. This is also motivation for research into *pedagogical agents* that attempt to also leverage non-verbal modes of communication such as facial expressions, body language, and so on.

The pedagogical power of dialogue lies in the increased opportunity for interaction it affords for tutoring systems. Dialogue-capable tutoring systems are now showing learning gains over read-only control groups in support of an *interactivity* hypothesis for learning with tutoring systems. Improved natural language understanding techniques and authoring tools are making it possible to understand student utterances well enough to allow systems to respond in productive and realistic ways. Beginners, who have yet to refine their domain vocabularies but are surprisingly consistent in their language patterns, are ideal targets for modern dialogue-based tutoring technology (Lane & VanLehn, 2005).

ITS as a Catalyst in the Development of a Science of Learning

An often overlooked benefit of automated tutors is that their behaviour can be "dialed" to test specific hypotheses about learning and tutoring effectiveness. This is difficult to do consistently with human tutors. An area where this strength is quite evident is in the study of feedback. Given a "good" ITS, it is usually a straightforward matter to experimentally adjust the frequency, form, and content of feedback messages and test for difference in learning. For example, McKendree (1990) conducted a study comparing feedback types in a geometry proof tutor. The study showed that goal-directed feedback (i.e., forward-looking hints) led to better performance than backward-looking feedback that flagged errors or explained why steps were incorrect. Studies like this one play an important role in the search for methods of effective instruction and guided learning. At the Pittsburgh Science of Learning Center (PSLC), intelligent tutoring technology is being leveraged (alongside a host of traditional learning science approaches) to address a broad range learning issues and develop a robust theory of learning.

14

Mobile Learning and Intelligent Tutoring System

Learning is an active process of building knowledge and skills through practice within a supportive community. It comprises not only a process of continual personal development and enrichment, but also the possibility of rapid and radical conceptual change (Mike Sharples, Josie Taylor, Giasemi Vavoula; 2005). A first step in postulating the theory of M-learning is to distinguish what is special about mobile learning compared to other types of learning activities. An obvious, yet essential, difference is that it starts from the assumption that learners are continually on the move. We learn across space as we take ideas and learning resources gained in one location and apply or develop them in another. We learn across time, by revisiting knowledge that was gained earlier in different context, and more broadly, through ideas and strategies gained in earlier years providing a framework for a life time of learning. The need to re-conceptualize learning in the mobile age has given rise to intensive research work on Mobile learning. In recent times, this need has also propelled researchers to recognize the essential role of mobility and communication in the process of learning. That is to say, the role communication and interaction play in the learning process is a critical success factor. Within this context M-learning can contribute to the overall quality and accessibility of learning.

Mobile learning is an emerging discipline in the area of education. The field of mobile learning is approximately a decade old and has grown rapidly. As personal computer integration predicated computer-enhanced learning, a primary factor in the growth of mobile learning is the increasingly ubiquitous integration of cell phones into society. For example, the second quarter of 2005 saw more than 190 million mobile devices and smart phones sold worldwide (Raiciu, 2005) and it is expected that by 2015 more than five billion people will utilize services via mobile devices (GSM Association). In addition to cellular phones, there has recently been an increase in the use of non-phone wireless devices such as MP3 players (such as the iPod™) and personal digital assistants (PDA). While these devices do not perform voice services, they do have many of the same services as today's smart phones including basic word processing and Internet access. This increase in wireless connectivity has led educators and researchers to investigate methods of integrating mobile devices into education. As the field continues to grow, researchers are increasingly investigating how mobile learning can benefit education for students and teachers alike.

Researchers have described mobile learning as an e-learning analog that uses mobile devices in place of desktop computers. This definition views m-learning as having the potential to serve in contexts similar to e-learning. A different perspective on m-learning, however, views the discipline as being able to provide support in contexts not previously available such as allowing students use mobile devices to dynamically update a wiki with their impressions of museum artifacts while on a class trip (Pierroux, 2007). The integration of mobile devices with other technologies such as Bluetooth and GPS, enable mobile learning applications to provide context-aware applications to learners in a manner not previously realized. For example, students visiting museums have been able collaborate using mobile devices to play a scavenger hunt game. As students transition through the museum the location aware devices receive information relating to the exhibit within their proximity and allows students to share this information with each other (Cabrera *et al.*, 2005).

Recognizing that there is potential for learning anywhere and anytime, some researchers define mobile learning as including any environment that supports scenarios in which the learner's mobility is germane to the educational environment. For example in an open field learners can freely travel with the devices to explore the natural surroundings and then relay the information to classmates in the classroom (Silander *et al.*, 2004). This definition also supports scenarios in which the learner is performing typical stationary tasks but the learning environment is mobile. For instance, Aderinoye's description of a project supporting the learning of nomadic populations in Nigeria (Aderinoye, *et al.*, 2007): The nomads were provided with classrooms that could be constructed in 30 minutes and used mobile phones as a means of communicating between course facilitators and nomadic learners that did not disrupt their nomadic lifestyle.

In contrast, Keegan proposed a more rigid definition of mobile learning requiring that the devices be restricted to the size "a lady can carry in her handbag or a gentleman can carry in his pocket" (Keegan, 2005). The devices are further described as those that users are likely to carry everywhere with them and are cheap and easy to use, e.g. cell phones, smart phones or PDAs. This stricter definition would prohibit the use of laptops, microcomputers or other portable wireless devices. In this dissertation, Keegan's rigid of mobile learning is adopted.

Although there may be a lack of a common definition for mobile learning, all these definitions center on the use of a mobile device. Researchers have used a variety of approaches to integrate the mobile device and/or learning applications into existing learning environments.

M-Learning

The term m-learning is coined to describe the convergence of mobile technologies with e-learning (Chen, C.-M., & Hsu, S.-H.; 2008). Unlike the traditional teaching and learning environments, in which learners follow a fixed sequence to instructional resources, such as textbooks in classroom settings, M-learning as an extension of E-learning has the potential to make learning even widely available and more accessible than we are used to in the existing E-learning environments. While mobile devices are approaching ubiquity today, the m-learning industry is still in its infancy (Kinshuk, Taiyu Lin; 2004). M-learning, like E-learning has no standard model per se; only enhancements of models of learning (*Terry Mayes & Sara de Freitas* JISC). Different authors and researchers have made attempts at developing models which are reviewed in this paper. The MOBILearn project (Taylor, J., Sharples, M., O'Malley, C., Vavoula, G. & Waycott, J.; 2006) is an attempt at developing a framework for M-learning.

Features of Mobile Learning Systems

The mobile learning system described by the following features:

- Allows users to have access to course resources independent of time and place.
- Allows authenticated users to have access to the system.
- Allows users to have access to the resources in different formats (voice, text, picture and video).
- Allows the reuse of material.
- Allows users to carry out the functions defined as an education component.
- Offers flexible environment in which other services and components can be added.

Where is Mobile Learning Used?

When new technologies are introduced into education, researchers typically seek to capitalize on affordances of these technologies to improve existing learning environments or to create new ones. A review of the mobile learning literature yields three common strands of implementation, each seeking to enhance learning environments in some unique way. The first strand uses mobile learning applications to support communications between instructors and students as well as between peers (Tater *et al.*, 2003 and Yatani *et al.*, 2004). The second strand uses mobile learning to improve learning environments by providing a platform for the implementation of learning theories as well as support for learner collaboration (Yatani *et al.*, 2004 and Danesh *et al.*, 2001). The third uses mobile learning to deliver educational material to learners (Aderinoye *et al.*, 2007 and Song, Y. & Fox, R., 2005).

Mobile learning has been implemented successfully in science classrooms enabling students to use a constructivist approach towards learning. K-12 students conducting science field explorations have been able to gather and organize information while exploring an environment, such as a wooded forest, and transfer the information to desktop systems once they return to school (Tater *et al.*, 2003). Lai *et al.* (Lai *et al.*, 2007) describe a m-learning application that facilitates students' science knowledge acquisition. Their system uses the mobility afforded by the device to support learning in a natural environment, namely a garden. For example, students are able to record questions, orally or written, about the studied environment during their field visit or receive prompts from the PDA to direct them to make deeper observations while providing them with background material when necessary. In this and similar instances, the use of m-learning provides students with real time technology to support their science learning outside of the formal classroom setting.

Researchers also design mobile learning applications to support students in mathematics learning. Handheld math games have been shown to improve student performance as well as maintain students' motivation and engagement with the technology (Shin *et al.*, 2006). Capitalizing on technology such as infrared and Bluetooth integrated into mobile devices researchers have been able to create ad-hoc networks enabling collaborative usage of mobile devices (Tater *et al.*, 2003). Such networks have been utilized to enable mathematics learners to collaborate on graphing activities (Tater *et al.*, 2003). In addition, educators use mobile learning applications for language learning and job training for learners in K-12, higher education, and adult education both formally and informally (Attewell *et al.*, 2002; Lonsdale *et al.*, 2004; Pierroux, P., 2007; Song, Y. & Fox, R., 2005 and Chen *et al.*, 2004). Adults learning English as a second language (ESL) have been shown to benefit from Short Message System (SMS) text messages containing vocabulary words (Song, Y. and Fox, R., 2005).

One of the critical aspects of mobile systems is their ability to exploit context. As one example, mobile devices have been used to create context-aware interactive user experiences in museum settings (Lonsdale *et al.*, 2004 and Chen *et al.*, 2004). The integration of mobile devices with technology such as GPS, infrared, and Bluetooth enables mobile devices and applications to interact with other artifacts to provide individual experiences users. In the museum example, museum patrons are able to receive information regarding the artist or exhibit they are viewing in real time. As patrons move between exhibits, available information changes to correspond with their location, thereby providing a unique experience that is fine-tuned to each patron's personal tour of the museum space.

Mobile learning research has been focused on understanding the space of possible applications for mobile devices in education. Some researchers are guided primarily by the ability of the devices to provide adaptive environments, and others by the light weight of the devices themselves. Therefore, there are many possible characterizations of mobile learning, and pinning down one characterization has proven to be elusive. In the context of this research, the major affordances of mobile learning are low cost and portability: The low cost increases accessibility to the intelligent tutors, and portability increases the range and flexibility with which these tutors may be used.

Challenges in Developing Mobile Applications for Education

It is often difficult for educators, administrators, and even parents to view mobile devices as being useful for educational purposes because they have been predominately used for social purposes including phone communication and text messaging. The current educational system produces lesson plans, learning activities, and assessments based upon traditional educational models. However, the introduction of mobile devices enables students to interact and collaborate with one another in ways not previously realized. Therefore, educators must now determine how to design lessons and activities structured around this mobility and accurately quantify the results of the use of the technology.

The use of mobile devices also raises questions that relate to the implementation of the technology, namely the hardware and software. Previous trials of mobile learning applications reveal that concerns regarding device ownership, battery life, and network connectivity can greatly affect the learning outcomes of students (Facer *et al.*, 2005).

Interestingly, researchers implementing and testing mobile learning applications have noted that there is potential for mobile learning applications to exist alongside traditional instructional tools (Vahey *et al.*, 2004). While the use of mobile learning applications can be transformative, it is necessary to understand and consider the existing learning environment in which it is intended. While there are certainly instances in which a mobile learning application can provide an experience not possible without the technology (Chen *et al.*, 2003), it seems plausible and even likely, that this technology can co-exist and support traditional paper-based methods.

Mobile Learning Theories and Principles

While there are no widely adopted theories for mobile learning, a few researchers have put forth frameworks and principled guidelines for their development. For example, Sharples (Sharples *et al.*, 2005) puts forth a theory of four mobile learning based principles: (1) mobile learning can be distinguished from other types of learning activities; (2) mobile learning recognizes the learning that takes place outside of formal classroom settings to be valuable; (3) mobile learning should promote practices that enable successful learning; and (4) mobile learning considers the ubiquity of mobile devices in society. Others have proposed principles based on shaping the content of the mobile applications (Grasso, A. and Roselli, T., 2005). For example, a user-centered approach to designing m-learning interfaces should take into consideration the manner is which mobile learning differs from other types of activities. Another principle that is important in the development of m-learning applications is the understanding of how students' mobility will either be constrained by or supported by the device.

Intelligent Tutoring Systems and Cognitive Tutors

Intelligent tutoring systems have their foundation in the artificial intelligence and computer assisted instruction disciplines. Burns and Capps (Burns, H.L. and Capps, C.G., 1988) describe the "intelligence" of this software as the collection of the five subsystems shown in Figure 14.1. The first is an expert model that represents the domain knowledge. This knowledge constitutes the understanding of the subject matter that an expert has in the tutored area. The second is the student diagnosis model. This model represents the knowledge and behaviour of a student learning the domain. The third is the instruction module, which is responsible for recognizing student input and responding to student actions. The fourth is the instructional environment that provides support to the learner. It can consist of the activity, the situation, and tools provided by the system to facilitate learning. The fifth component is the interface, an essential component that provides the means by which the user can communicate with the system. With respect to intelligent tutoring systems, it is the integration of the models that separate ITS technology from other forms of computer aided instruction (Heffernan, *et al.*, 2003).

Intelligent Tutoring Systems assist students in mathematics, science, and language learning domains for learners in high school and higher education courses (VanLehn, K. *et al.*, 2005 and Heilman, M. and Eskenazi, M., 2006). When integrated into school curricula students use the tutors during school hours in computer labs and classrooms. However, in K-12 environments interaction typically takes place on desktop computers in school computer labs. Students using tutors have been proven to have learning gains greater than peers not utilizing the tutor and receiving more typical instruction (Koedinger *et al.*, 997 and Corbett, A. 2001).

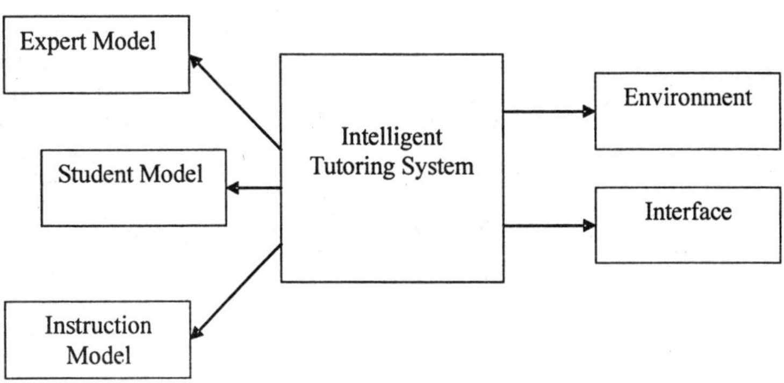

Figure 14.1: Intelligent Tutoring System Model

Traditionally, tutoring systems are developed for use on desktop-sized computers. The interfaces are often complex and but share common components, identified by Brown, *et al.* (Brown *et al.*, 2008) as Problem Description, Student Workspace, and Student Status. With respect to the tutor, each of these regions serves a specific purpose in the tutor's efficacy. In the Problem Description area, users are provided with given information, a context for the problem, and a description of what students are solving. Workspaces provide students with charts, tables, or other space to organize data, or thoughts, and place problem answers. The Student Status provides feedback to the user regarding their performance in the tutor sequence as well as information regarding their performance on skills they are learning.

Cognitive Tutors are one specific class of intelligent tutoring system based upon computational theories of cognition (Koedinger *et al.*, 1997 and Carnegie Learning, 2009). In Cognitive Tutors, cognition is programmed through the creation of cognitive models in the form of production rules. The production rules consist of a series of if-then statements describing the goals and sub-goals required to complete specific problem solving tasks. These tutors utilize cognitive models of learners and domain experts to provide individualized instruction to learners.

The Cognitive Tutor was developed in part as a response to the "2-Sigma Problem," in which Bloom challenged researchers to develop methods providing individual tutoring to large numbers of students (Corbett, A., 2001 and Bloom, B., 1984). Cognitive Tutors have been extensively researched and proven to improve student achievement of between one and 1.6 standard deviations greater than peers receiving traditional group instruction (Corbett, A., 200). They are used as part of a curriculum that integrates classroom instruction with the use of the tutors. Student use the tutors approximately two days per week (40% of the total course time), and spend the remaining three days (60% of course time) receiving traditional group instruction in the classroom.

Examining the history of the development of Educational Psychology, be it Behaviourism, Constructivism or Cognitivism, the emphasis is always on the importance of information feedback, which basically has two meanings. The first is that a teacher should know the learning progress of their students. Through information feedback, they are them able to make appropriate adjustments to their teaching material or methods. The second one is that the teacher releases information on the teaching material to the students, who are then to make the necessary adjustments and improvements to their learning process.

In teaching, instructors often adjust their method according to feedback, but with conventional teaching techniques, this feedback is rather poor. It is often difficult for a teacher to monitor the learning progress of all the students due to the large class size. Interaction between students and teachers is thus superficial (e.g. answering questions by raising hands), impersonal (e.g. answering question together with others) and delayed (e.g. doing bring-home assignments, having exams and so on). A teacher spends a lot of time on grading students' work, who then will have to wait at least one day to know how they perform. Worse still, such delayed feedback may not have much impact on students' learning. Being aware of this problem, teachers have attempted to make students' feedback more instantaneous and scientific. However, the results have not been satisfactory. In most cases, only some students may have the chance to interact with their teacher and their interaction tend to be limited to, for example, the teacher asking students to raise their hands in agreement, or naming a particular student to answer a question. Asking questions rarely, a teacher may not be able to have a thorough understanding of students' learning progress. In other words, a teacher cannot adjust their approach to see to students' needs and they, too, due to a lack of participation, will lose interest in the class. The efficiency of the teaching is thus further lowered, and students may even stop coming to the class.

In the conventional classroom setting, various obstacles limit the interaction between students and teachers. There are obstacles like limited class hours, fixed seating and inadequate time for after class discussion. So far, most teaching methods have been concerned with either teaching or learning, and few have focused on improving classroom interaction. Since the amount of information that is involved in teaching has been increasing, a corrective method is urgently needed, and with the introduction of multimedia feedback techniques it is possible to receive instant feedback from every student in the class. Moreover, such techniques facilitate precise and scientific data analysis and allow recording of the entire teaching process. The multimedia mobile classroom feedback system in this paper is developed using a client-server model. Handheld devices (like a mobile phone or PDA) use a wireless network (GPRS, 3G or WiFi) to transmit students' immediate responses, for example, questions that they raise in the class, answers to quizzes (multiple choice, short answer, fill-in the blank types of question), and the like. The feedback from students can be displayed instantaneously on the teacher's notebook computer. The teacher can then use this system with pre-designed materials and then modify the content according to the feedback. In preparing for courses, a teacher can always include this system as a piece of auxiliary teaching equipment. Using this tool, the interaction between teachers and students is enhanced, improving the efficiency of learning. To sum up, there are several advantages with this system:

1. *Automated attendance checking mechanism:* It replaces the conventional method by which attendance is checked manually by instructor. With the system, students need to key in their ID number on a handheld device. The teacher will then know immediately which students are absent from the class.
2. *In-class instant evaluation:* In a class, the teacher can give a quiz at any time (multiple choice, short questions and answers, and fill-in

the blank types of question) to examine whether students really understand what has been taught. With an instant feedback mechanism like this, students are required to be attentive to the class. In addition, the teacher is able to understand and monitor the effect of their teaching on the students.

3. *Improving the willingness to ask questions:* It is often the case that students may wish to ask questions, but they are unable to do so due to shyness or thinking that their question is not appropriate. By using this system, questions can be asked upon without registering who has made them. In so doing, the teacher becomes aware of the problems in students' learning, and thus able to devise ways to assist them and raise the quality of teaching.
4. *Instant results checking:* Students are able to check their own results at any time through a handheld device, with which their privacy is better protected. With such an arrangement, it is also easier for teacher to publish students' results.
5. *Multi-platform system:* The construction of this system does not need to be tied to any particular platform, as Java is used. All that a student needs is a handheld device which supports J2ME. Server-side implementation can either be with Microsoft or Unix-like platforms.
6. *Virtual Mobile Classroom:* Since a wireless network is used as the transmitting media, students are able to use this system whenever they like (be it in or out of the class). When students are reviewing their lessons without a computer, they can still use this system to fire question to their instructor.
7. *Comprehensiveness of the collected data:* This system employs a database to store student-related information. Through the use of the transaction and locking mechanisms of database, asking questions and sending answers simultaneously will not cause any problem, and thus data is properly collected.
8. *Low construction cost:* The client-side equipment, i.e. mobile devices that students will use, do not need to be redesigned. It can be a mobile phone, a PDA or a notebook computer, something which students may already possess. As to the server-side machine, it requires only a web-server.
9. *Group learning:* Very often, a group discussion in class only allows students to present the result of their discussion. It may not be easy to tell whether all of the students have really learned something from the person who is presenting the work. In this case, an instructor can pass the system to students who are presenting their work and they can set a quiz for other students or receive questions from them, while the instructor can make observations without interrupting the students.
10. *Recording learning process:* The discussion and interaction between

the teacher and students can be stored in the database which is in the back-end of the system. By reproducing learning process, it allows the teacher to investigate any problems that might hinder students' learning. Consequently, in preparing the teaching materials, adjustments can be made for future classes.

Mobile Interaction Framework in a Conventional Classroom

Thus framework includes three levels. The first is about in-class interaction, the second presents the advantages of mobile telecommunication, and the third is the e-learning environment, as shown in Figure 14.2.

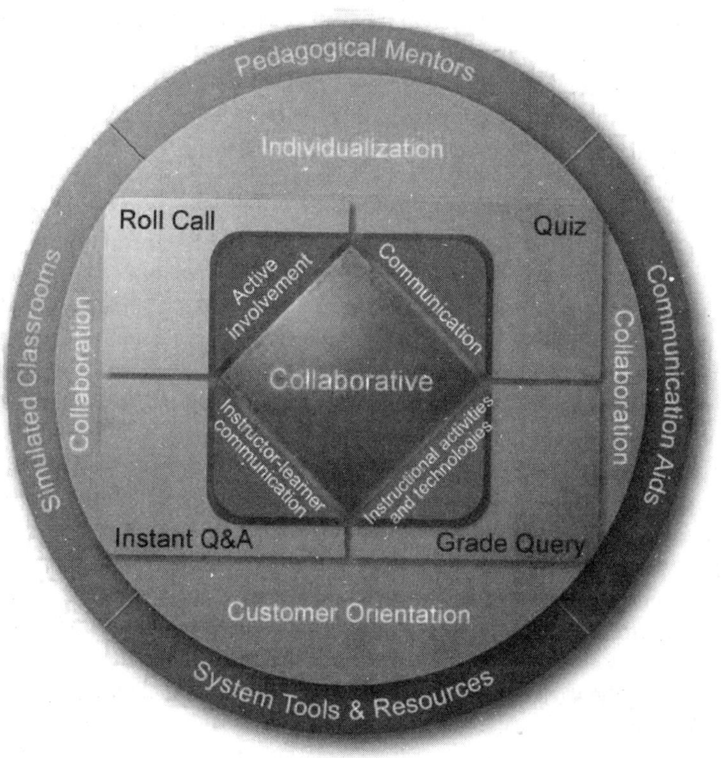

Figure 14.2: Mobile Interaction Framework in Conventional Classroom

The multimedia mobile classroom feedback system has four different functions, which are shown in green. They are Roll Call, Quiz, Instant Q&A and Grade Query. The correspondent behaviour in the classroom will be as follows: 1. making students actively participate in the class: Before class is started, the teacher often checks the attendance of students. Therefore, the sense of participation of students starts with checking themselves into the class, with logging themselves into the system. After registering their attendance, students are able to use the system to ask or answer questions as they wish. 2. Providing one-to-many interaction between the teacher and students: students and teacher should begin to interact instantly to maintain the sense of participation. By conducting an instant quiz, the teacher is able to have some idea of whether students really understand what has been taught. Since information is sent instantly and anonymously, students are able to freely pick answers without embarrassment, while the teacher is able to adjust the class according to the responses. 3. Facilitating one-to-one interaction between teacher and student: if a teacher does not know his or her students' learning problems, can only answer a small number of students' queries, or if some of the students are shy or scared of asking questions directly, their learning will be impeded. Through this system, students can ask questions instantly and anonymously. In this way, the teacher is aware of every student's problem and can address their questions right away. This will heighten students' sense of participation in the class, increase their interaction with the teacher and other students, and finally improve their learning. 4. Applying technologies to class activities. The activities include attendance taking, assigning quizzes, asking questions and grade enquiries, which can all be done through student's mobile devices. The centre of the graph, which is in purple, is the result of a series of in-class activities. Teachers and students can use this system to propose and discuss questions to enhance in-class interaction. The part in orange is about the advantages of mobile networking. In-class activities and mobile networking can be combined to get a better result. When a student asks or answers questions, it is transmitted anonymously, and thus they can do it on their own without any interference from others. As the information received by teacher in class arrives instantly, explanations can be made straight away. Lastly, the blue part is the strategies used in mobile classroom interaction. In a class, a tutor is the main actor while mobile devices are the subsidiary system tools, but interaction between students and the teacher can continue after class, in a virtual mobile classroom. As the attitude toward learning and the results of students are positively affected by improved in-class interaction, this framework is able to support the concepts proposed in the three educational psychology theories described previously, Behaviourism, Constructivism and Cognitivism.

Model of Web-based Intelligent Learning Environment

In the works (Sabbir Ahmed Kazi; 2005), (Kassim, A.A., Kazi, S.A. and Ranganath, S; 2004) the author (Colling *et al.*) proposed a model of an ideal Intelligent Tutoring System (ITS), a product of Artificial Intelligence (AI) research. The model was based on *Computer Aided Learning* (CAL), which he said has been used in learning and teaching since the 1950s. Traditional CAL resources primarily consisted of tutorials, which are essentially computer-based forms of "programmed instructions". He described the ITS as a new type of CAL system. The Intelligent Tutoring Systems (ITS) typically consist of an internal model of the expert knowledge, the learner's current knowledge and the pedagogical principles. As the learner proceeds, the model of the learner's knowledge and the model of the expert's knowledge are compared, and using AI, the sequence of instructions is dynamically generated to suit the needs of the learner. Figure 14.3 shows the functional model of an ideal ITS.

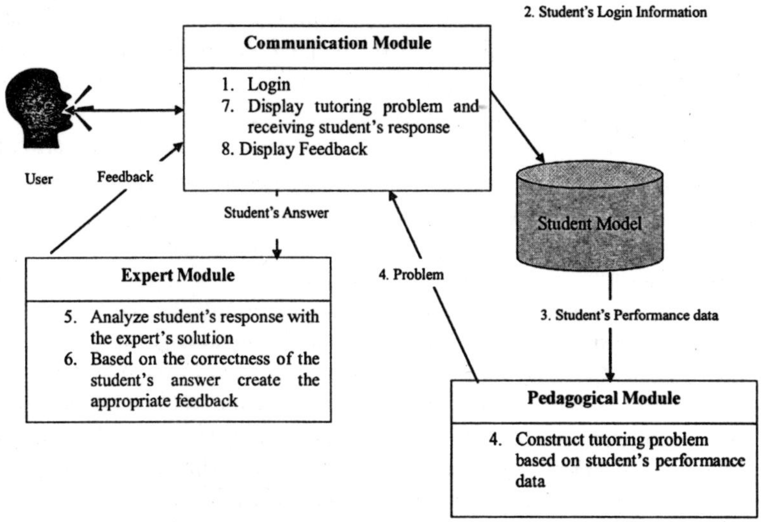

Figure 14.3: Functional Model of an Ideal ITS
(Adapted from: Colling N. Udanor *et al.*)

15

Collaborative Inquiry Tutors

In traditional classrooms, students often passively absorb topics from teachers, books and fixed curricula. Concepts are covered briefly and stripped of their contextualizing complexity (Eylon and Linn, 1988; Koschmann *et al.*, 1994). Teachers ask 95 per cent of the questions, most requiring short phrase answers (Graesser and Person, 1994; Hmelo-Silver, 2002). In a worst-case scenario, teachers reformulate concepts into digestible bits, students absorb these bits and exhibit their understanding on multiple choice tests. Such teaching approaches are ineffective and produce inert knowledge (Waterman *et al.*, 1993). However, student-centered teaching methods, such as inquiry and collaborative-based instruction, differ from traditional teacher-centered approaches. This chapter discusses advantages, limitations, and possibilities afforded by approaches that invite students to ask questions, work collaboratively, judge their own input, and tackle difficult problems. Collaboration and inquiry are closely intertwined because inquiry often requires that students discuss their ideas and work cooperatively (Kluger-Bell, 2000). Collaboration and inquiry strategies both train students to articulate and reflect on their own knowledge and to transfer their knowledge to teammates (Goldman, 1992; Kuhn, 1991; Newman *et al.*, 1989; Scardamalia and Bereiter, 1991; Slavin, 1990a; Wan and Johnson, 1994).

Motivation and Research Issues

Educational institutions are revising their teaching approaches as a result of the needs of a global information society based on knowledge. A society built on knowledge requires its members to acquire skills, form new learning communities, and engage in new learning approaches in rapid sequence. For educators, this implies rapidly revising *what* is taught and *how* it is taught, based on evolving knowledge including teaching about *ill-defined* domains, e.g., medical diagnosis, geological features, which lack formal theories or clear and unambiguous problems. Many tutors taught only in well-defined domains (e.g., mathematics, physics, equipment operation), characterized by either formal theory or clear-cut domain models that supported clear pedagogical strategies; answers were unambiguous and classified as either correct or incorrect. On the other hand, ill-defined domains are particularly difficult to teach using traditional quantitative pedagogy in which instructors deliver digestible bits. For this reason, they are ripe for teaching through new student-centered techniques. Revising *how* domains are taught means helping students to reason about processes and strategies rather than simply delivering facts for memorization (Dewey, 1938). History students should reason about source documents (personal letters, news stories), do history, and make inferences about historical relationships. Scientists should understand rules and principles of their domain and know not only the key facts and concepts of their field but also the processes by which claims were generated, evaluated, and revised (Suthers and Weiner, 1995). Then learning can be transferred to new contexts and adopted to real-world problems (White *et al.*, 1999).

The need for people to develop inquiry reasoning and to collaborate is more pressing than ever as citizenship in a high-technology world requires scientific reasoning and disciplined thinking. Broad agreement exists that students must understand how science works (AAAS, 1994; NRC, 1996) and how to become engaged in long-term investigations and team problem solving. People need to reason, think like scientists, and solve messy problems without nearby authoritative help (answers supplied by instructors). Inquiry and collaborative learning strategies are ideal for helping students to articulate and reflect on their own knowledge and to transfer that learning to new contexts (Kuhn, 1991; Wan and Johnson, 1994). These methods invite students to work on parts of a problem and to discover things for themselves.

Inquiry Learning

Inquiry is an approach to learning in which students actively construct their own knowledge. Students ask questions and gather data to support and refute hypotheses. Inquiry activities ask why dinosaurs became extinct, where the next earthquake will occur, and how to make soap bubbles firm enough to make a foam tower. Inquiry invites students to make discoveries, rigorously test them in the search for new understanding, and explore new knowledge (Kluger-Bell, 2000). It closely mirrors the enterprise of doing real science or history. Students learn which questions to ask and how to make predictions from theories, test theories, and derive theories from data.

In inquiry students *apply* and *transfer* knowledge in addition to just acquiring it. In the classroom, inquiry often begins with a case or problem rather than with content to be memorized. This encourages student-initiated learning and investigations as an outgrowth of case analysis (Suthers and Weiner, 1995). There is no "correct" method of investigation, and frequently several appropriate hypotheses and arguments are possible. Performing authentic hands-on activities helps students see their work as relevant (Wenk, 2000). This section describes benefits and challenges of inquiry learning, provides several examples, and discusses a classification framework to organize technology support options.

> Humans are born inquirers. You can see it from the moment of birth: Babies use all of their senses to make connections with their environment and through those connections they begin to make sense of their world. As children discover objects and situations that are puzzling or intriguing—things that provoke their curiosity—they begin asking questions and looking for ways to find answers, all in an effort to understand the world around them. This is the essence of the inquiry process. —*Kluger-Bell* (2000)

Benefits and Challenges of Inquiry-Based Learning

Inquiry learning has many pedagogical benefits, including improved student reasoning ability, self-directedness, and understanding the scientific process (D'Avanzo and McNeal, 1997). Inquiry-based methods help students remain active and develop an integrated understanding of concepts in their field (Edelson *et al.*, 1999). The importance of active and authentic contexts for learning has been established (Greeno *et al.*, 1996). In inquiry learning, students learn to plan and manage investigations and to analyze and communicate results (Blumenfeld *et al.*, 1991; Welch *et al.*, 1981).

> Inquiry is central to science learning. When engaging in inquiry, students describe objects and events, ask questions, construct explanations, test those explanations against current scientific knowledge, and communicate their ideas to others. They identify their assumptions, use critical and logical thinking, and consider alternative explanations. —*National Research Council* (1996)

Inquiry skills improve student ability to acquire knowledge (White and Fredrickson, 1995). When students manipulate artifacts themselves and think freely about problems, they become more actively involved and generally more systematic and scientific in their discovery of laws (Shute and Glaser, 1990). The increased interactivity alone has been shown to increase learning (White and Fredrickson, 1995). Inquiry also provides a deeper and more lasting understanding of phenomena (Slotta, 2006a). It engages students in reflection. Reflection, the ability to monitor and evaluate past and ongoing actions in order to help plan next steps, is an essential element of human reasoning. Reflective inquiry can be seen as a set of practices that helps students adopt a critical orientation, which includes planning, monitoring, and evaluating (Kyza and Edelson, 2003; Loh *et al.*, 1997). Different disciplines use different inquiry methods and standards of evidence; for example, students might use controlled experimentation (Schauble *et al.*, 1995), modeling (Resnick, 1994; Wilensky, 1995), synthesis of primary sources (Wallace *et al.*, 1998), or exploration of quantitative data (Hancock *et al.*, 1992).

Challenges of Inquiry Teaching

However, teaching with inquiry methods presents many challenges, especially in classrooms. Teachers have to monitor the progress of teams and individuals who articulate different hypotheses and pursue unique experiments. They have to intervene appropriately and encourage students to articulate questions, refine existing hypotheses, and gather evidence (Derry *et al.*, 2000). Teaching with inquiry is time and labour intensive and difficult to manage. Smallcollege settings have sponsored excellent undergraduate inquiry projects (D'Avanzo and McNeal, 1997; Stillings *et al.*, 1999). However, moving such activities to large classrooms is challenging.

Software Support for Inquiry Learning

Software supports inquiry methods by facilitating storage and manipulation of large quantities of information (Edelson *et al.*, 1999). Tools help students model phenomena and processes for gathering, organizing, visualizing, and analyzing data (Aleven and Ashley, 1997; Alloway *et al.*, 1996; Krajcik *et al.*, 1998; Lajoie *et al.*, 1995; Suthers and Weiner, 1995; van Joolingen and de Jong, 1996; White *et al.*, 1999). Some rich simulation environments present authentic cases in their contextual complexity to support students ' active participation, investigation, and ability to generate hypotheses. Networking technologies provide access to information and adaptable representations, structuring diagnosis, correcting errors, and enhancing interest and motivation (Edelson *et al.*, 1999). Just working interactively with simulated objects and events may improve the student's understanding of scientific models. Inquiry software often enables students to explore new representations and create personal representations to express their own ideas (Slotta, 2006a). Simulated environments help students understand what models are and how they are used (Shute and Glaser, 1990). However, inquiry learning is not dependent on simulations and can work with real data, either historical or created at the time of use. Inquiry tutors have focused on a single domain; for example, Smithtown taught microeconomics (Shute and Glaser, 1990) and ThinkerTools taught force and motion (White and Frederickson, 1995). They provided in-depth knowledge about the content of the domain. On the other hand, *domain independent* inquiry tutors, Belvedere and Rashi, supported a variety of domains and provided generalized environments in which students made observations, formed hypotheses, and structured arguments (Paolucci *et al.*, 1996).

Technology allows students to control time and other factors while they carry out experiments and collect data that would otherwise be impossible for many reasons such as money, time, and the danger involved in situations involving complicated or dangerous experiments (Slotta, 2006a). Students are often able to move opportunistically within such environments from one phase to another, to plan and conduct experiments, support individual difference, and discover their individual approaches (Bransford *et al.*, 2000a). One important function of a computer is to take on some roles of instructors. Software provides examples, suggests strategies for accomplishing tasks, helps students get back on track when they are lost (Shute and Glaser, 1990), and provides levels of computational support as discussed next.

Three Levels of Inquiry Support

Tools, classified into a computational framework of support, aid students working with inquiry software. The framework, adapted from Soller *et al.* (2005), focuses on the locus of control for inquiry—that is, who is in control of the inquiry process, designs the investigation, and decides what is an acceptable answer (Kluger-Bell, 2000; Soller *et al.*, 2005). For example, in classroom inquiry, guided worksheet activities often direct students through several steps and leave little room for student exploration or innovation, except for their actual answers on the worksheets. Another classroom activity invites students to compete to solve inquiry cases; however, this activity determines a student's path toward solution and tends to provide a narrow focus to that path. On the other hand, in open exploration activities, students have control over questions and the means and practice of the investigation; a wide range of results might be acceptable, giving students more control.

The three support levels have arisen as computers assume greater responsibility for various phases of the inquiry process (Soller *et al.*, 2005). The locus of processing is a continuum that suggests where decisions are made. It identifies teachers as the focus for tools that organize inquiry. Teachers observe students as they respond to structured inquiry materials, and teachers propose additional evidence or arguments to be explored. At the other end of the continuum, the focus is on students and tools that advise about arguments and evidence. These tools diagnose students' reasoning and provide comments and automatic coaching. This framework, presented below the next, does not focus on the phases of inquiry, which are shown in Table 15.1, nor does it focus on leading students to the correct answer, because inquiry cases do not always have a clear correct answer. Rather the framework emphasizes who is teaching. In inquiry software, the three categories of tools are designed to *structure* inquiry (the teacher is in control as the system displays inquiry steps), *monitor* inquiry (both students and system are in control using *cognitive* and *metacognitive* supports to compare a model of student inquiry behaviour to the desired behaviour), or *advise* students (system can fully support learning by providing remedial help).

Tools That Structure Inquiry

Inquiry tools in the first classification *structure* the inquiry process or identify the phases of inquiry and invite students to input their reasoning (Slotta, 2006a).

The most basic level of structural support involves visualizing the inquiry cycle. The phases of inquiry are outlined to increase student awareness and create favourable learning conditions. The structure provides space for students to propose hypotheses or offer evidence that supports arguments. These tools organize materials to support arguments and clarify the components of inquiry. Tools ask students to explain what they see, help them reflect on their observations and provide evidence for their arguments (Slotta, 2006a). They raise students' awareness about their own missing steps and behaviours (Linn 2006; Linn *et al.*, 2004). Graphical organizers or other notations help students plan and organize problem solving and representations help students track what steps they have taken (Collins and Brown, 1988). Structural tools do not typically understand a student's input, nor the text typed. Rather they note whether a space is filled in and which resources were used. Teachers are responsible for assessing the quality of student inquiry (comparing their own model of desired knowledge to that of the student) and determining if remedial action is needed.

The web-based Inquiry Science Environment (WISE) was an example of an inquiry structural tool used with children from 12 to 17 years old (Linn and Hsi, 2000; Linn *et al.*, 2004). Students worked collaboratively on inquiry science projects on the web. WISE cases were based on relevant science topics (e.g., global warming, climate change, genetically modified foods, biodiversity, malaria control, or HIV worldwide). In one project, students designed a house for the desert climate by critiquing web-based energy-efficient house designs (Slotta, 2006a). In another, they compared competing theories about global climate change. They employed "inquiry maps" for procedural guidance, online discussions, reflection notes, journals, whiteboards, modeling, and visualizations. Scripts were used to structure inquiry, left menu of each screen). Scripts asked questions (Can you identify X?), or led students to activities (Learn about X; Write an evidence note about X). Teachers worked with students as they developed criteria, discussed topics with peers online, wrote reflection notes, or prepared for a debate. WISE was designed to make science accessible by connecting students to personally relevant questions, helping them learn from each other, and showing them how to perform investigations (Slotta, 2006b). More than 100,000 students and 25,000 teachers used WISE in several countries. The system was freely available as a platform for the development and delivery of inquiry science curriculum and provided a wealth of questions and hints for each case. Students examined real-world evidence and analyzed current scientific controversies. They worked in pairs in the classroom while teachers circulated and sometimes regrouped students to discuss findings and questions (Slotta, 2006b).

Other software inquiry systems modeled objects that students manipulated. For example, the Young Scientist Project involved problem-based learning objects (e.g., animation of the problem situation, theoretical information, personalized feedback notes, and scaffolding from the teacher) (Pedaste and Sarapuu, 2006). Students opened learning objects, received technical help for using the model, and used worksheets with inquiry tasks. The general design of tasks involved becoming acquainted with a situation, carrying out a theoretic inquiry experiment, and moving back to the initial situation to solve the problem according to the findings of the experiment. Students were encouraged to formulate research questions, select virtual equipment, and apply an electronic tool for collecting data, analyzing data, and making inferences.

Another structured inquiry system, STOCHASMOS, focused on reflective inquiry or a student's ability to monitor and evaluate past and ongoing actions to help plan the next steps (Kyza *et al.*, 2006). Reflective inquiry helped students adopt a critical orientation, which included planning, monitoring and evaluating (Edelson, 1992; Kyza and Edelson, 2003; Loh *et al.*, 1997). The system used scaffolding to help students reason about rich-data learning in science. It provided opportunities for reflection, helped focus and organize investigations, and supported the explanation building process.

Tools That Monitor Inquiry

Inquiry tools in the second classification monitor student learning, or collect data about students 'interactions, develop indicators of the quality of the interactions, and display indicators to students (Jermann *et al.*, 2004). These tools compare student behaviour with that encoded by the expert, both cognitive behaviour (e.g., correct and incorrect hypotheses) and metacognitive behaviour (e.g., how often a student asks for help) (van Joolingen, 1999). Monitoring inquiry involves first assessing student data (e.g., evidence and hypotheses) and then reasoning about solutions or arguments. The goal for these tools is to offer guidance to students in a way similar to how teachers do it: consider the context (learning situation, arguments being made) and the activities of the inquiry team. The computational monitor tool accounts for similar complex variables and recommends actions for students to take; it identifies incomplete arguments or missing evidence to explore. These tools may be domain independent or specific.

LeCS was an example of a domain specific tutor that monitored inquiry and provided real-time support to learners who collaborated around case studies of production engineering (Rosatelli and Self, 2002; Rosatelli *et al.*, 2000). It was based on a model of teaching inquiry (Christensen and Hansen, 1987) and used with open-ended problems about design, analysis, selection, and planning of a large engineering project. The tutor presented complex, realistic situations, and agents guided students through analyses of each case; they monitored students ' levels of participation, tracked progression through the task, and brought students to each inquiry step (Table 15.1). The tutor used a textual representation of the solution path taken by learners and identified the time spent by students on each step, the degree of participation

Table 15.1: Inquiry Case Solution Steps in LeCS

Inquiry Steps	Student Activities	Questions
1. *Understand* the situation	Relate the initial statements in the case.	What do you think are the relevant pieces of information presented by the case?
2. *Diagnose* problem areas.	List problems.	What are the problems that come up for you in this case?
3. *Generate alternative* solution.	List solutions.	Would you please list the alternative solutions?
4. *Predict* outcome.	List outcomes.	Can you tell me what can happen as a result of each action?
5. *Evaluate* alternatives.	List pros and cons.	Can you list the pros and cons of each outcome?
6. *Round out* the analysis.	Choose.	What is your choice among the alternative solutions?
7. *Communicate* the result.	Present salient features of the case.	What is your answer to the question posed by the case?

of each learner, misunderstandings learners might have, coordination of the group, and accomplishment of the step activities. The interface included a participant's list, browser, solution, graphical representation, collaborative text editor, and chat system. The collaborative framework, written in Java, enabled the browser to access web pages presenting the case study, the text editor to answer questions posed in the steps, and the chat system to facilitate case discussion.

Questions associated with each step were chosen from examples modeled on approaches used by case study instructors in the traditional classroom (Meyers and Jones, 1993). Questions were elaborated according to a classification that took into account the case instructor's purpose (Rosatelli and Self, 2002) and included categories of questions such as discussion starters, challenging questions, analytical and evaluative questions, summary questions, and so on. Hyperlinks of web pages were followed sequentially, according to the nature of the approach: step-by-step. In each step learners were supposed to individually answer the question posed. Inquiry and collaboration are often intertwined as the application of the case method often demands collaboration. In LeCS, collaboration was a main concern in the empirical study. The collaborative text editor was used to edit, present, and register both individual and group answers. The text-based chat environment was where the discussion reached an agreement about both each step answer and the case solution.

Tools That Offer Advice

Inquiry tools in the third classification *advise* or coach students about their reasoning and propose remedial actions. These tools represent the structure of inquiry, monitor student activities, and model all phases in the inquiry process. The system's assessment of the current student state may be used to decide how to provide advice and is typically hidden from the student. One of the greatest challenges for developing advising tools is to build tutors that understand student reasoning. This is not trivial. Computers do not understand free fl owing natural language. They can only understand limited text input. Additionally, students' answers are not judged right or wrong in inquiry tutors, thus tutors must reason about student exploration of spaces and arguments. One approach to understanding student reasoning is to focus on the structure of their argument, not try to understand their words. Tutors are built to recognize the type of related data collected and then to offer help (Dragon and Woolf, 2007). This is what Belvedere did (Suthers *et al.*, 2001). The coach asked if evidence refuted a student's hypothesis, even if it did not understand the student's hypothesis. Another approach is to invite students to select preexisting knowledge statements. Rather than type a hypothesis ("the patient has mononucleosis"), students select from a list of diseases and receive feedback comparing their selection to that in the expert knowledge base (Suebnukarn and Haddawy, 2004).

After "understanding" student input, advising inquiry tutors monitor student activity (e.g., data collection) to gain insight about whether students are engaged in good inquiry behaviour. However, tutors should not interrupt students' train of thought. Students need to drive the inquiry process and not be disturbed. Most inquiry systems do not interrupt students. Smithtown monitored student activity for what it considered "buggy" behaviour (Shute and Glaser, 1990), such as changing multiple variables in the same experiment or collecting data in a haphazard fashion. On the other hand, Belvedere offered advice only when requested to maintain student initiative, which is crucial to good inquiry.

After monitoring student activity, the tutor reasons about the *type* of feedback to offer (Dragon and Woolf, 2007). Effective techniques include helping students to create hypotheses, considering multiple hypotheses, selecting counterexamples, and tracing consequences to contradiction (Collins and Stevens, 1983). The coach might expand student arguments and help correct errors in logic. It might have knowledge only about the structure of an argument, not the semantics of it. While it may not know the meaning, or substance of the argument, it can recognize logical flaws, such as circular arguments or incorrect relationships (observations supporting observations) and can ask students to create multiple hypotheses and/or consider whether data supporting one hypothesis could also support another.

Advising tools are *knowledge-centered* or represent domain knowledge and track a student's mastery of that knowledge (Brandsford *et al.*, 2000). They are *learner*-and *assessment*-centered, or respond in the context of the student's reasoning and indicate whether student reasoning is consistent with that of the expert. Advisory tools guide students toward effective inquiry and learning.

Because inquiry learning includes both learning critical inquiry skills (e.g., generating hypotheses, providing supportive evidence) and learning a topic (e.g., diagnosing a patient), advisor tools must address both sets of issues. The next two sections describe two inquiry tutors that provided advice to students based on reasoning about the cognitive and pedagogical nature of their inquiry.

Belvedere Inquiry Model

The first inquiry tutor discussed here taught inquiry in the context of science for secondary school children, ages 12 to 17. *Belvedere* taught students to engage in critical discussions of competing scientific theories (Suthers *et al.*, 2001; Suthers *et al.*, 1997). Belvedere was a collaborative inquiry system since it supported students to both reason about hypotheses and work in teams. A diagrammatic representation helped students identify the overall structure of their arguments (Figures 15.1 through 15.3). Students assembled graphical shapes, connected them with links, and constructed "inquiry diagrams" through shared workspaces, and the tutor provided recommendations concerning ways in which arguments could be extended or revised (Figure 15.2).

Belvedere presented cases such as why dinosaurs became extinct or how animals traveled to the Galapagos Islands (Suthers *et al.*, 1997, 2001). These cases hinged on conflicts between scientific theories and discrepant data. In one experiment, pairs of students sat side-by-side working on individual monitors, close enough to see and point to each other's displays. Students used a modest collection of text-based information (Figure 15.1,

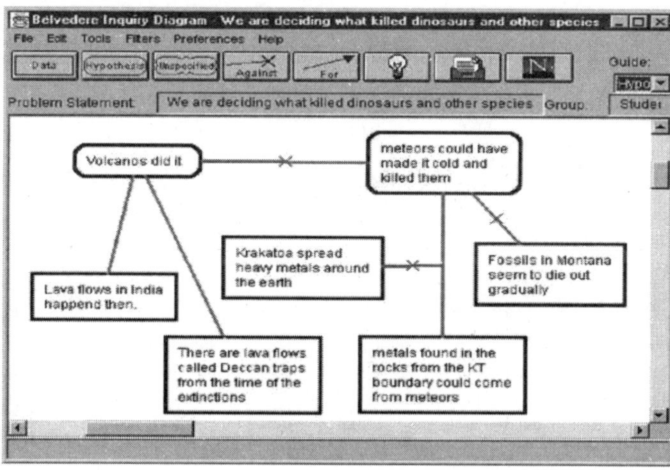

Figure 15.1: Students reasoned about why dinosaurs became extinct in Belvedere. Students entered new hypotheses and evidence through the top menu. Data were selected from a modest collection of information supplied by the system.

nodes) to argue about competing theories and worked together to solve any anomalies. The simple interface reduced students' need to learn new graphics, enabling them to focus on their cognitive effort. The symbol environment expressed logical and rhetorical relations between *propositions* (Figure 15.3). Command and icon layouts were similar to a typical drawing programme.

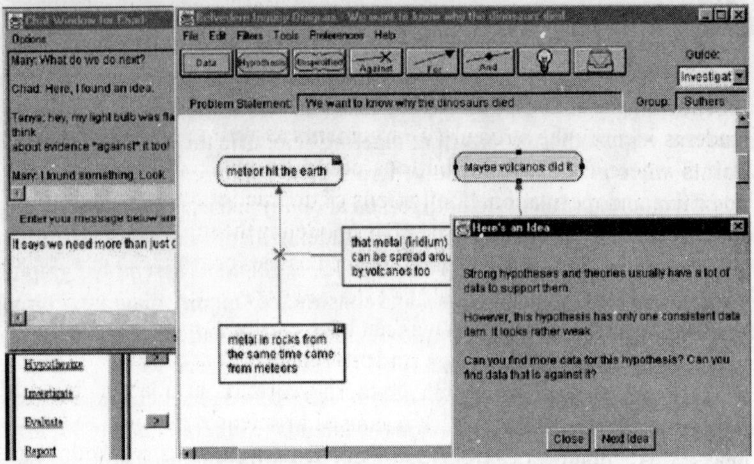

Figure 15.2: Belvedere Provided Advice. The Coach Suggested how an Argument could be Extended or Revised

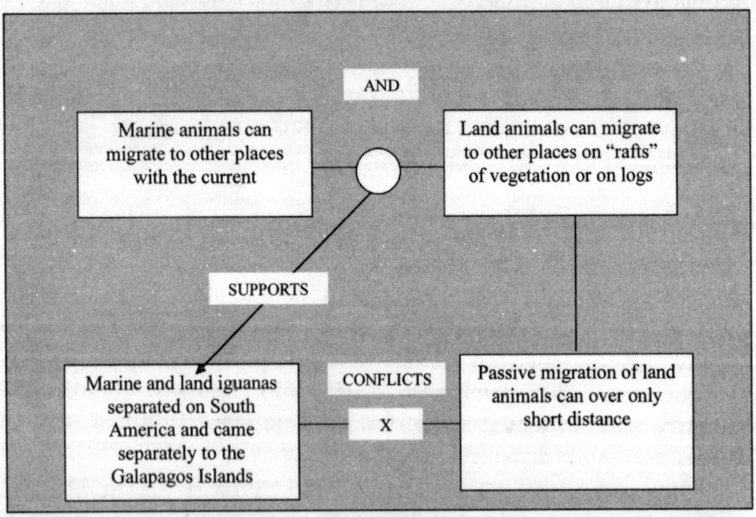

Figure 15.3: Contradictory Evidence is Represented in Belvedere While a Student Discusses how Animals Traveled to the Galapagos Islands. Students Added Additional Supporting or Conflicting Evidence to their Arguments

Students generated inquiry diagrams and were supported in acquiring the critical distinctions required to conduct scientific inquiry. The argumentation palette (Figures 15.1 and 15.2, top), supported theories and justifications. Students used icons such as "Data" (empirical statements), "Hypotheses" (theoretical statements), and "unspecified" (for disagreements), along with links representing "against" and "for" evidential relations and a link for conjunction. The goal was to stimulate critical discussion that otherwise might not take place. Diagrammatic representations provided concrete forms for showing the abstract structure of a theory and related arguments and helped students identify the structure of arguments as well as their weaknesses and points where further contributions could be made. Belvedere addressed cognitive and motivational limitations of unpracticed beginners.

The tutor provided advice based on modeling the student's argument (Figure 15.2, bottom right). Artificial intelligence coaches provided advice concerning ways in which an argument could be extended or revised. Students were exposed to standards of evaluation that may not have existed in their peer group and that stimulated further inquiry when students reached an impasse.

Belvedere was tested with 12-to 15-year-olds in a lab study and in an inner city public high school. It was used in science, physics, and chemistry classes. An independent evaluator noted that students worked in groups, organized and reviewed arguments, and integrated their work with applications (Word or Excel). Cooperatively, students stayed focused. Some of the most productive discussions were not captured by the interface yet were stimulated by the diagramming activity. Several social impediments to learning were noted, including management struggles when one student wished to pursue a line of argument and others preferred to make a large list of hypotheses. Another issue was that cooperative pairs of students may not make the most of an individual's knowledge if they stopped to listen to all members.

Rashi Inquiry Tutor

The second inquiry tutor discussed here addressed issues about *when* and *how* to advise students and *what* type of help to offer. There are no right or wrong answers to these questions. Rashi provided case descriptions for students to investigate, along with information about how to approach each problem (Murray *et al.*, 2005; Woolf *et al.*, 2002, 2005). Rashi was also a collaborative inquiry tutor in that it supported both collaboration and inquiry. The infrastructure was domain independent and presented cases in forestry, geology, biology, and art history (Figure 15.4). Various data collection methods (interactive images, interview interfaces, video, and dynamic maps) provided open-ended spaces for student exploration and acquainted students with methods commonly used by professionals to access and organize information.

In the *Forestry Tutor*, students took on the role of ecologists and uncovered historical disturbances (forest fires, flooding, acid rain, or global warming) that impacted the current landscape through observation of features (downed trees, snag trees, stumps, and basal scars) based on maps, photos, videos, and data. Students suggested, for instance, why there was a discontinuity between hardwoods and softwoods in an old forest and were encouraged to reason about a variety of disturbances both natural (wind storms) and unnatural (logging). They explained how a fire that took place perhaps 100 years ago affected development of the forest as it looked today.

In the *Geology Tutor*, students took on the role of geologists in the earthquake zones of San Andreas, California. They reasoned about future events (e.g., predicting where the next earthquake might occur). They were invited to locate a new road and were provided with three possible routes. Each route passed through a combination of suspicious recurring earthquakes. Students evaluated each area, measured offsets from previous earthquakes, made observations, reasoned from data, and recommended a route.

As an example of Rashi functionality, we describe the *Human Biology Tutor*, in which students evaluated patients and generated hypotheses about their medical condition. Patients' complaints formed an initial set of data from which students began the diagnostic process; virtual patients were interviewed about symptoms (Figure 15.4, B). Data were made visible by student action (e.g., asking for chest x-rays, prescribing a certain drug, or using a measurement

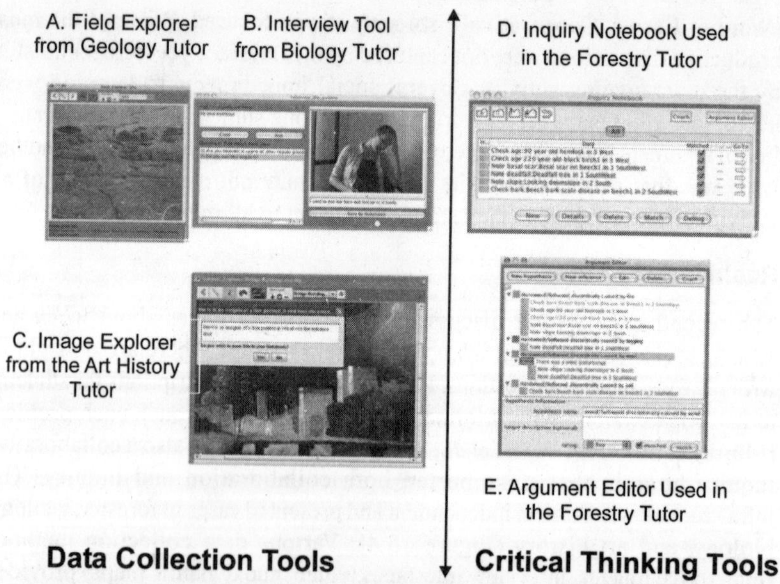

Figure 15.4: Rashi provided a variety of data collection (left) and critical thinking tools (right). The Notebook and Argument Editor (right) were available in every domain

tool) (Figure 15.5, left). Some data were interpreted for students ("x-ray normal"); other data provided raw material, which students interpreted and then drew conclusions. Medical cases included patients with hyperthyroidism, lactose intolerance, food poisoning, diarrhea, mold allergy, and iron deficiency anemia. Students moved opportunistically from one inquiry phase to another as they sorted, filtered, and categorized data according to predefined categories or ones they invented.

Structured prompts, reminders, and help motivated students during each inquiry phase. Data recorded in the *Notebook* (Figure 15.5, top right), revealed flaws in student hypotheses, recorded in the Argument Editor. Students revised their hypotheses, changed their belief, and generated new hypotheses. The student in the example postulated at least three hypotheses, suggesting that the patient had mononucleosis, diabetes, or was pregnant (Figure 15.5, bottom right). Students dragged data from the *Inquiry Notebook* (top right) into the *Argument Editor* (bottom right) to support or refute each claim.

Patient Examination Inquiry Notebook

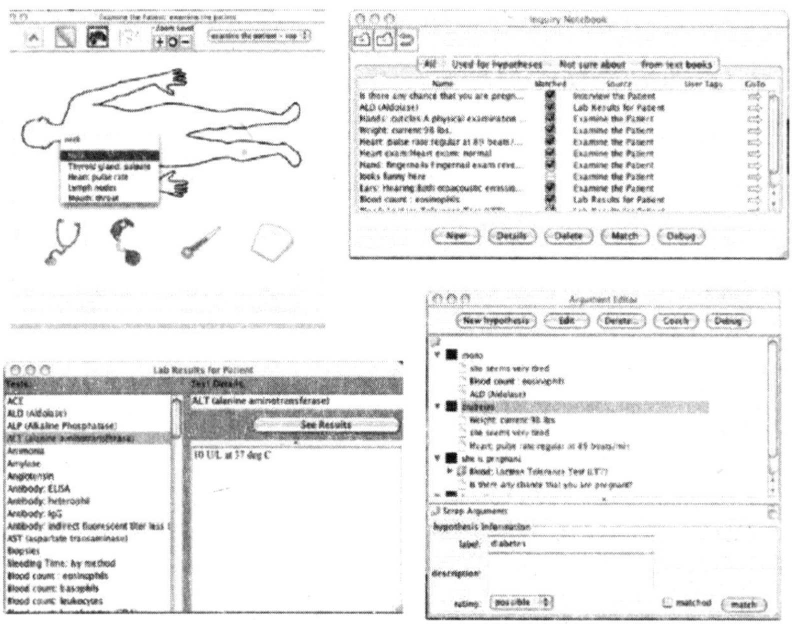

Laboratory Tests Argument Editor

Figure 15.5: Rashi Human Biology Inquiry Tutor. Student observations from physical exams, lab tests, and interviews were automatically recorded in the Inquiry Notebook (top right). Students indicated the type of proposition entered (e.g., observations, inferences, and hypothesis), the importance of each observation, and their confidence in their observations

Students used tools to collect data and reason about evidence and arguments. Some tools were domain independent or available in every domain. *Cognitive* tools organized pieces of evidence (e.g., the Notebook recorded data) and *metacognitive* tools reasoned about student learning (e.g., the Argument Editor advised students when more evidence was needed). Other tools were domain specific and guided students to collect data, enter simulations, or access repositories to extract information needed to support or refute arguments.

Tools organized complex and ill-structured knowledge and did not disconnect it from context. They helped students search the web for diagnostic material, definitions, and interpretations of laboratory results, preparing students to operate in real-world scenarios and to consult material outside of the system (e.g., Internet). This is especially important in ill-defined domains because no tutor can represent all the necessary or useful knowledge in an ill-defined domain. Critical thinking tools helped students structure their thoughts and create well-defined arguments supported by evidence. They served as a repository of all information and recorded student data, inferences, and hypotheses.

Advising Students: Rashi generated advice after reasoning about student input. The first and most straightforward strategy was to match student statements to statements contained in the knowledge base. Students typed in their own observations, inferences, and hypotheses, and the tutor matched these with phrases stored in the expert knowledge base, a collection of propositions about the case formulated into a directed graph. For each node in the graph, the author defined an importance number, or the amount of support/refutation to be supplied by the student. Rashi also reasoned about students' knowledge based on their navigation through the environment (Dragon and Woolf, 2007). As long as students used the environment, the Coach had an understanding of evidence the student compiled and knew which arguments were supported or refuted.

A student argument was similar in structure to the expert argument and represented as a directed graph of propositions. The tutor coached students by comparing these two graphs. A rule-based system accomplished much of the coaching, consisting of creating a set of rules about the student argument, such as "an argument can be supported by more than one support link."

Rashi first traversed the student graph to count the number of support and refutation links and identify those properly connected to nodes. After this preprocessing step, the Coach knew for each node how much support the student found, how much was properly connected, and the same for refutation. As students moved through the inquiry cycle, the tutor provided several types of feedback (Dragon *et al.*, 2006):

Hypothesis Feedback: promoted consideration of multiple hypotheses and offered a list of hypotheses from the expert knowledge base.

Support/refutation Feedback: encouraged students to supply more supporting or refuting data for their arguments (top-down arguments).

Argument Feedback: encouraged students to consider higher-level arguments, offering arguments students might have missed (bottom-up argument) Advice included contextual information about cases being solved. The tutor might bring students to a location where additional support/refutation links could be found. It might directly address and correct a student's misconceptions, when correcting a student's relationship. Teachers adapted the Coach to their teaching styles; they specified the order in which domain knowledge was presented/ promoted for discussing arguments and the number of required support/refutation links to be supplied by the student (Dragon *et al.*, 2006).

Phases of the Inquiry Cycle

The previous section described three levels of tools that supported inquiry reasoning and helped students proceed through the phases of inquiry. Although inquiry learning is described in many ways, it is often referred to as a cycle and generally characterized by phases. Students do not move through the phases in sequence, and it is not uncommon to find people moving opportunistically from one phase to a nonadjacent phase. Five phases of inquiry learning are described in this section.

Inquiry reasoning follows a simple process, illustrated in the first two columns of Table 15.2. Because the result of the inquiry task is ambiguous, may not result in a single correct answer, and may change during the course of inquiry, the framework provides a general description of the involved activities rather than a guide for predicting inquiry outcomes (Soller *et al.*, 2005). The last two columns represent the computer's actions as it compares the current state of student inquiry with a desired state. The tutor might intervene whenever an opportunity arises to improve the quality of the investigation or further engage students.

Phase 1: Orientation: Students are first invited to observe what is ostensibly present without making an interpretation and are often presented with a goal or problem to solve. Students extract whatever information is salient in the initial case description and should recognize the difference between pure observation and inference, but both may take place.

Phase 2: Formulate Hypotheses: Forming a hypothesis is similar to forming a skeleton plan: an initial hypothesis might be vague, such as "I think the weather caused the bridge to fail. "Hypotheses of this sort require further refinement.

Phase 3: Gather Information: Collecting data, perhaps by searching printed and graphical resources, is germane to producing open questions and hypotheses. *Structuring, cognitive* (e.g., data collection tools), and *advising* tools are useful here. The difference in tutor behaviour between phases 1 and 2 to 3 describes the difference between a system that structures activities (phase 1) providing a space for inquiry and a system that prepares case data (phases 2 to 3) to be assessed by computer models (Soller *et al.*, 2005).

Table 15.2: Phases in the Inquiry Cycle and Computer Tools Supporting

Inquiry Cycle	Student Activity	System Activity	Computer Tools
Phase I: Orientation ⇓	Read and analyze problem, observe environment	Question students	Structuring tools (scripts)
Phase 2: Formulate hypotheses ⇓ ⇓	Generate hypotheses	Observe and record student activities, log and store hypotheses	Structuring tools Cognitive tools
Phase 3: Gather information ⇓ here and 4 return⇓	Collect data, investigate, perform experiments/ laboratory tests, search printed resources		Structuring tools Data collection tools Cognitive tools Advising tools
Phase 4 : Generate argument ⇓ ⇓	Predict outcome of investigation, draw conclusions, analyze arguments, support/ refute data with each argument	Observe and record student activities, model arguments, log and store arguments	Advising tools
Phase 5: Advise student ⇐⇐⇐⇐ ⇓		Diagnose missing data or arguments, coach student to strengthen case analysis	Advising tools Guidance system
Evaluation ⇓ ⇓	Interpret findings, communicate results, submit case solution		Report generation tools

Phase 4: Generate Arguments: Students collect additional evidence until one argument becomes stronger than the others. They might predict the outcome of an investigation and draw conclusions. *Advising* tools are used here based on modeling a student's argument and comparing it with alternative desired ones.

Phase 5: Advising Students: These final tools help students strengthen the support or refutation evidence for each hypothesis. The coach might diagnose missing data or hypotheses and advise students where to look for further evidence. If discrepancies appear, remedial actions might be suggested. Then students might propose new hypotheses and evidence to support or refute their own arguments.

Collaborative Learning

Knowledge has become complex (e.g., global data are processed by multidisciplinary teams in real-time 24 hours a day). Individuals can no longer single-handedly solve major problems. Teamwork is vital and students need to be taught skills to understand the processes by which teams of people generate, evaluate, and revise knowledge (Johnson and Johnson, 1989; Kuhn, 1991; Slavin, 1990a; Webb, 1982). Collaboration itself has its own set of unique benefits for education. Nearly 700 studies clearly indicate that cooperation results in higher achievement and greater productivity; more caring, supportive, and committed relationships; and greater psychological health, social competence, and self-esteem for students (Johnson and Johnson, 1989).

This section describes approaches for building computational models of collaborative learning. We describe the benefits and challenges of collaboration, both as taught in the classroom and as supported computationally. A classification framework (Soller *et al.*, 2005) helps to organize available technology similar to that for inquiry phases of collaboration. Four levels of computational support, based on the five phases of collaboration, help to *structure* collaboration, *mirror* or visualize it, provide *metacognitive* support, and *advise* teams about their participation (Jermann *et al.*, 2004). Example computational collaborative systems are described and classified by the four types of technology support.

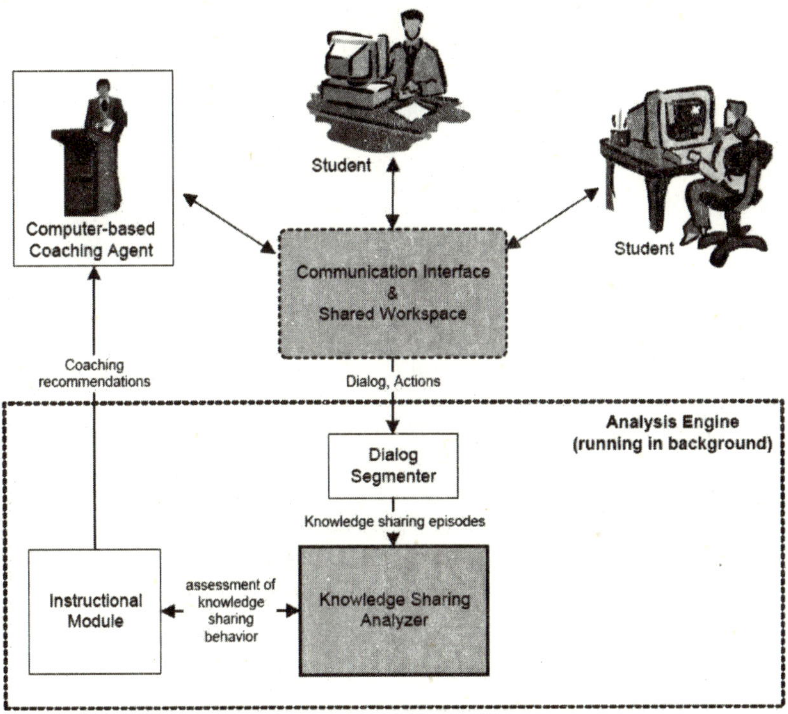

Figure 15.6: Sharing knowledge by Collaborative Learning

Benefits and Challenges of Collaboration

Collaborative projects encourage students to work in teams to articulate and reflect on knowledge, engage in active learning, and envision how knowledge is shared and extended (Johnson and Johnson, 1994; Slavin, 1990b; Smith *et al.*, 2005). Students question processes, make mistakes, and monitor each other's reasoning. In *competitive* environments (the opposite of collaborative environments), students perceive that they can obtain their goals if and only if other students *fail* to obtain their goals (i.e., there is a negative interdependence among goal achievements) (Deutsch, 1962; Johnson and Johnson, 1989). When competition is used, some students (often the under-represented, women, low achievers) stop trying because they do not believe they can win. On the other hand, collaborative learning is one of the most valuable educational approaches in terms of improved learning outcome.

Collaboration in classrooms has proven to be successful and powerful (Brown and Palincsar, 1989). It invites students to work on parts of problems with teammates and to discover things for themselves. Collaborative student discourse (i.e., reflective discussions among students about content) promotes deep and meaningful learning and enhances students' reasoning skills (Johnson and Johnson, 1989). It often results in learning that outperforms the ability of the best individuals in the group, produces knowledge that none of its members would have produced by themselves, and leads to the generation of new ideas (Ellis *et al.*, 1994; Fischer and Granoo, 1995; Johnson and Johnson, 2005; Smith, 1996; Smith *et al.*, 2005). It emphasizes structured or formal collaborative work, positive interdependence (of task, identity, role, and goals), individual and group accountability (challenging and motivating every student), and authentic interaction (brainstorming, planning, social and team building skills, and solidarity). Peer-to-peer interactions and social learning are vital parts of both activities (Kuhn, 1991; Slavin, 1990 b; Webb, 1982).

Collaboration enhances a teacher's role as advisor and, when successful, supports structural and institutional changes that move classroom activities from teacher-centered didactic instruction to student-centered inquiry (O'Neil and Gomez, 1994; Slavin, 1990b; Suthers and Weiner, 1995; Suthers *et al.*, 1997, 2001). Cognitive learning occurs through interaction between students, as well as among students and teachers (Scardamalia *et al.*, 1989; Wasson *et al.*, 1999). This type of collaborative learning has been connected with notions of "socially shared cognition" (Resnick *et al.*, 1991), "distributed cognition" (Solomon and Perkins, 1998), and jointly accomplished performance (Pea, 1994).

Teaching Collaboration Skills

Teaching students to collaborate requires teaching them communication skills (how to discuss alternative approaches, engage in reflection, jointly collect data, explore and construct knowledge, and reach consensus). Organization and management skills are needed for students to share and assume ownership of knowledge. Teaching such skills in a classroom is time and labour intensive. Teachers need to know how and when to intervene appropriately (Derry *et al.*, 2000). Not all groups make progress in similar settings, and teachers must help decide which groups are productive and should remain together and which are not making progress (Howe *et al.*, 1992, Tedesco and Rosatelli, 2004). Traditional classrooms teachers cannot easily track the progress of multiple teams articulating different approaches and pursuing individual experiments. Factors such as motivation, behaviour, and group dynamics interact with each other in unpredictable ways, making measuring and understanding learning effects difficult (Soller *et al.*, 2005).

Computational Support of Inquiry

Traditional collaborative tools, e.g., support for groups to share, organize, analyze, and critique documents, websites, and other forms of information, and chat mechanisms that enable group discourse (Stahl, 2006), help students to reach out and communicate with others. However, they do not understand the knowledge being communicated by students, nor do they support communicative activities, such as knowledge acquisition and negotiation. Computational support for inquiry and collaborative learning presents a number of unique challenges, including the need to develop *intelligent interfaces* that allow students to respond spontaneously (with little restriction) and yet enable the tutor to understand and analyze student actions. Student models need to accommodate the uncertainty involved in collaborative formation of a solution. Systems should model both student and domain knowledge and accommodate uncertainty in that knowledge. Where natural language dialogue is supported, argumentation theory provides an analytic framework for assessing the quality of student discussions in terms of depth of reasoning, amount of backing for claims, and consideration of counterarguments.

Computer-Based Collaborative Learning (CSCL)

Several successful classroom models of collaboration have been developed through the computer supported collaborative learning (CSCL) community. In some cases, persistence of the system helps support teams, reason about activities, and intervene. The nature of the computational support varies along a continuum from a persistent discussion forum (typed and threaded nodes) to supporting students to process ideas in shared discussion and helping them to select, edit, arrange, link, and summarize notes freely. Environments organize and manage teamwork and collaboration artifacts (Soller, 2004; Stahl, 2003). They help students to explain their reasoning to others and facilitate the receipt of feedback.

Collaboration tools support synchronous, symmetric cooperation through the Internet and encourage students to question processes and monitor each other's reasoning (Soller, 2004). To an increasing degree, software transparently supports the exchange and sharing of information among students and provides artifacts or tools and services. Technology might direct students to interact with teammates or indicate how and when to communicate, or when to question, inform, and motivate one's teammate. Other technologies represent collaboration as a dialogue grammar, maintain a relational and hierarchical representation of dialogue, or ask participants to refine their beliefs (Baker and Lund, 1997). Intelligent analysis facilitates structured collaboration (Barros and Verdejo, 1999; Constantino-Gonzalez *et al.*, 2003; Jermann *et al.*, 2001; Muehlenbrock, 2001; Soller, 2004).

Unfortunately, though many electronic tools exist to support collaboration, the expected benefits of teamwork (high motivation, deep involvement in learning, and substantial knowledge gains) often do not materialize (Kay *et al.*, 2006). An increasing number of studies report low participation rates, low levels of communication and collaboration (both in terms of quantity and quality of contributions), small knowledge gains, and little satisfaction with the group learning situation (e.g., Heath, 1998; Zumbach *et al.*, 2005). Social interaction does not occur automatically once an environment makes it possible. The social and psychological dimension of collaborative learning must not be forgotten (Kreijns *et al.*, 2003). Computational methods help mediate and support collaborative learners and are fundamentally grounded in our understanding of the group activity described by models of collaborative learning interaction (Soller *et al.*, 2005). Online collaboration is not as effective as face-to-face learning, in part because technology does not yet provide sufficient constructive guidance or direction.

Four Levels of Collaboration Support

This section describes four levels of collaboration support used before, during, and after collaboration. Soller and colleagues (2005) developed this framework to describe the process of collaboration management, building on the work of Jermann *et al.* (2001) and Barros and Verdejo (1999). They described levels that *structure*, *mirror*, *metacognitively support*, and *coach* collaboration. The locus of processing suggests locations at which decisions are made about the quality of the collaboration and how to facilitate it (Soller *et al.*, 2005). Processing is located anywhere on a continuum that includes student, teacher, and system. *Mirror* tools raise students ' awareness about team activities and place the locus of control with students, providing them information to reason about their own interactions. *Metacognitive* tools help students to understand collaboration by comparing a model of the teams' participation to the desired behaviour, and they place the locus with students and researchers. C*oaching* tools explain why students may not be working together effectively, and they place the locus of processing with the system. These tools model a team's current state and compare it to implicitly or explicitly agreed upon collaborative referents. They diagnose progress made, target difficulties, and provide appropriate coaching or remedial advice.

Tools That Structure Collaboration

Several tools help design collaborative teams and the situation *before* collaboration begins (Jermann *et al.*, 2004; Soller, 2006). They *structure* the collaboration and focus on features, such as choosing a *partner*, *reciprocal tutoring*, and *learning companions*. Choosing a *partner* is critical to collaboration. In the classroom, teams might be pre-selected by teachers or groups dynamically formed on the fl y. However, placing students in groups and telling them to work together does not always result in cooperation. Some students prefer to work with strong partners, others with weak or shy partners. In studies where students choose the type of artificial partner to work with, they chose partners with a variety of personalities and abilities (Hietala and Niemirepo, 1998; Baylor, 2005). Another issue involves the characteristics of the partner; a competitive and aggressive partner might motivate some people and intimidate others. Software helps form groups by creating favourable conditions for learning (Brusilovsky and Cooper, 1999; Dillenbourg, 1999; Soller *et al.*, 2005).

One system identified the most competent peer to assist students complete their computer programming assignments (Greer *et al.*, 1998). Intelligent Helpdesk proposed students who would work with others at the University of Saskatchewan. Student models are often used to help select teammates because the algorithms and parameters needed to customize problems for an individual student (traditional use of a student model) might overlap those needed to select team members for collaboration. Polling after collaboration might determine whether each team member was productive and this information used to further improve the student model. Software helps assign roles to team members (e.g., task manager, skeptic, accuracy checker, social facilitator, and record keeper). Assigning a role to a student has been an essential part of successful classroom case base learning methods (Bruno, 2000), and students should experience each different role (Smith, 1996). Software triggered by intelligent rules might remind students to discharge their alternative roles and to use tools to accomplish each role (e.g., the skeptic uses a critique tool, and the task manager a planning tool). All students are expected to work collaboratively to solve problems; roles are extra duties or "hats" that students assume periodically.

Reciprocal tutoring tools enable students to take on the role of either teacher or student; partners might be real or virtual and might organize the physical structure of the collaboration. For example, Belvedere was initially built for multi-users on a single computer, with collaboration taking place by either student moving icons on the screen. Multi-users and multi-systems (several remote users) require hierarchical control structures.

Learning companions are roles taken on by educational software to provide individual helpers for students. This approach began with software that enabled a student to learn as would a "prince" (Chan and Baskin, 1988) and has evolved to include students studying with animated pets, computer-based toys (Liu *et al.*, 2003), intelligent 3-D humanoid creatures, multiple learning companions, troublemakers (Aïmeur and Frasson, 1996), teachable agents (Biswas *et al.*, 2005a, 2005b), and affective learning companions (Burleson, 2006; Burleson and Picard, 2004; Picard *et al.*, 2004). Learning companions have been defined for all stages of life (e.g., learning cribs for babies, toys for small children, pets for pupils, peer tutors for teenagers, mentors for adults, and pets for elders) (Chan, 2002; Chan *et al.*, 2007; Chan, 2007). A variety of learning companions have been used in classrooms, assisted by computers and coordinated by teachers (Chan *et al.*, 2006), including individual human-computer, computer-mediated face-to-face (f2f), inter team, and one-to-class interactions.

Companions take on a variety of social roles such as collaborator or challenger (opponent, critic, or troublemaker) (Aïmeur and Frasson, 1996; Frasson and Aïmeur, 1996; Frasson *et al.*, 1998). Learning by disturbing makes the tutor into a troublemaker who sometimes provides good advice to the learner but also can provide wrong recommendations. The troublemaker provokes a reaction from the learner, who evaluates his own opinions to resolve the conflict. This demonstrates the usefulness of intentional conflicts in various cooperative learning strategies, showing that social interaction is basic to the development of cognition. Peer strategy is a technique by which agents produce cognitive conflict, expose the conflict, and then resolve the conflict through discussion for a common outcome. Other software agents cooperate with humans to design and deliver courses and advise students on teamwork and learning strategies. The architecture includes a cooperative task and knowledge management model that describes subject knowledge, learning tasks, and tutoring tasks.

Teachable agents are another form of learning companion where students learn by teaching an intelligent agent who initially knows nothing about the domain (Biswas *et al.*, 2005a, 2005b). Students teach the agent by developing causal diagrams or concept maps with binary links indicating cause-and-effect relationships (e.g., increase (+) or decrease (-) a variable). Students use this teachable agent to make decisions, perform actions, explore qualitative interactions between concepts, and answer questions.

Tools that Mirror Collaboration

The second level of computational support for collaboration includes *mirror* tools that show students and teachers a representation of each participant's activities in the space (Soller, *et al.*, 2006). *Mirror* tools visualize processes, indicate components of teamwork, and display how participants contribute to team effort. Dimensions such as average participation levels, quantity of interactions, and timelines for team members track student interaction. They automatically collect and aggregate data and enable students and teachers, who compare the reflected information to their own model of desired interaction, to determine what remedial actions are needed. This information is mirrored back to the group with the intent that students and teachers react to its non-interpretative feedback and regulate their own activity, placing the locus of processing in the hands of students and teachers. Visualization encourages students to participate, make their work transparent, collaborate, and share documents.

Tools that Provide Metacognitive Support

The third level of computational support for collaboration includes metacognitive tools that monitor general trends in student work, diagnose interactions, and deduce or infer problems in student reasoning (Jermann *et al.*, 2004; Soller *et al.*, 2005). Metacognitive tools display high-level indicators to support students' collaboration, teachers' monitoring, and researchers' analysis. They might indicate that certain activities have not been performed and that certain interactions should be changed. They facilitate accountability within groups and make visible the general level of work a student has accomplished without revealing the solution in progress.

Metacognitive tools display what the desired interaction might look like alongside a visualization of the current state of indicators. They provide the referents needed by learners or human coaches to diagnose the interaction. Like mirror tools, learners using metacognitive support tools are responsible for making decisions regarding diagnosis and remediation. They evaluate both social and task-oriented aspects of collaboration. Several perspectives on task-oriented issues are helpful to ground this discussion. Collaboration might be viewed as a collection of perspectives based on principles of interpersonal interaction that emphasize an understanding of language, culture, and other aspects of the social setting (Scott *et al.*, 1992; Sorensen, 1994, 1999; Wasson *et al.*, 1999). Each computer collaborative environment places emphasis on a variety of activities, such as joint construction of knowledge and joint negotiation of alternatives (Fjulk, 1998). We discuss a knowledge construction perspective in this section and knowledge negotiation perspective in the next.

Knowledge construction. Participants in collaboration jointly construct knowledge or engage in problem solving by mutual refinement (Brown and Palincsar, 1989; Dillenbourg, 1999; Soller, 2004; Stahl, 2006). A knowledge construction episode is a segment of an interaction (including student utterances and workspace actions) in which one student presents or develops a new piece of knowledge (Soller, 2004). Each student exchanges knowledge that he or she brings to bear on the problem. The resultant knowledge is a unique synthesis of knowledge, grounded in individual experience. The combination of these experiences, the ontological reconciliation of each participant's understanding of them, and the personality and behaviour of each member determine how the collaboration proceeds and whether or not group members can effectively learn from and with each other (Soller, 2004). Early systems, such as CoVis (Edelson *et al.*, 1996; Pea, 1994, 2004; Pea and Gomez, 1992) and CSILE (Scardamalia and Bereiter, 1994; Scardamalia *et al.*, 1989), provided simple email applications plus database connections to enable students to jointly construct knowledge.

Computational support of knowledge construction focuses on scaffolding its distinct tasks, including brainstorming, organizing, analyzing, and generalizing. Virtual workspaces help students formulate ideas and view each other's ideas. Both a personal and a group workspace are required so that the team as a whole can agree on expressions of negotiated knowledge. An editing window is often provided to set tentative ideas and provide a discussion area to respond to a flow of interchanged ideas.

Some collaboration environments provide simple threaded discussion to enable participants to interchange ideas (e.g., Rosatelli and Self, 2002). However, threaded discussion does not suffice as the tree structure imposed by standard threaded discussion is inadequate. In threaded discussions, each participant submits an idea, with one contribution or note leading to another (Figure 15.7) (Stahl, 1999). Discussions proceed along ever diverging lines as ideas branch out, and there is no systematic.

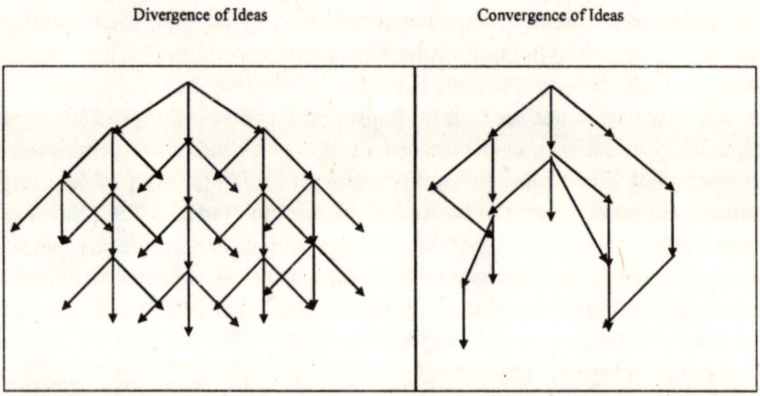

Figure 15.7: Divergent and convergent structures in collaborative discussion. Supplementary linking (*right*) supports convergence

Tools that Coach Students in Collaboration

The fourth level of computational support for collaboration includes tools that coach students. Students frequently comment on and critique each other's work while collaborating, and teachers also critique work at the individual, team, or class level. Teachers often mediate social interaction by observing and analyzing a team's conversation (e.g., noting the degree of conflict between group members' roles or the quality of the conversation) (Soller *et al.*, 2005). Comments and reviews of this type are important for cooperative learning and are essential in distant and asynchronous learning.

This section describes tools that offer automated *coaching* to increase the effectiveness of collaboration and learning (Soller *et al.*, 2005). Computational support might evaluate the topic of collaboration or the *social* aspects of collaboration—distribution of roles among students (critic, mediator, idea generator), equality of participation, or the group's ability to reach a common understanding (Teasley and Roschelle, 1993). The *coach* might analyze the state of collaboration or alternatively provide an expert solution to support task-oriented issues that involve student understanding and application of key domain concepts.

Knowledge Negotiation

One perspective on collaboration is that participants must manage joint *knowledge negotiation* of alternatives (Stahl, 2006; Roschelle and Teasley, 1995). A knowledge negotiation episode is a segment of an interaction (e.g., student utterances and workspace actions) in which one member attempts to present, explain, or illustrate new knowledge to his peers, while his peers attempt to understand and assimilate other new information (Stahl, 2006; Roschelle and Teasley, 1995). This is in contrast to a "knowledge construction" episode, discussed in Section 8.3.2.3, in which one student presents or develops a new piece of knowledge (Soller, 2004).

During negotiation, participants are involved in discussions, argumentations, debate, and dialogue. Collaboration systems can model these alternatives, reason about them, support students to resolve differences, and agree on a summary or conclusion. Once students provide their views and knowledge, and view the arguments of others, they are ready for joint negotiation (Suthers, 2001). They need the opportunity to reach a consensus, to bring all issues together and agree on whose ideas will be accepted as the group's position. In this way negotiation leads to knowledge that exceeds what any one member had expressed individually and individuals build upon knowledge they inherited from their social context.

Negotiation is far more difficult to support than is knowledge construction. Even given technical support, students often prefer to argue and negotiate face to face rather than through the computer (Stahl, 2003; Suthers *et al.*, 2001). Technology support for argumentation involves providing an interface or artifact around which users can interact. Clearly, negotiation support requires an environment that makes argumentation an enjoyable social experience and a flexible consensual process (Stahl, 2002, 2003; Suthers and Weiner, 1995).

One possibility for negotiation is that all participants bring proposals from their personal file to be voted on by the group. A promoted note then represents knowledge accepted by the group. Research issues in negotiation include representation and the nature of a representational aid (graphic, matrix, text). Each representation has its own strengths and weaknesses, restricting some interactions and making some information more salient than other information (Suthers *et al.*, 2001). The issue is to identify and enhance a particular representation and guide the dynamics of that type of collaboration. Another issue includes constructing active media that provide a natural way for students to record their activities and emerging knowledge. The form of this representation has been shown to have a significant effect on the discourse process of collaborating students (Baker and Lund, 1997; Suthers, 1999).

One example system that supported task-oriented issues in collaboration was the *Argumentation Inquiry* system (Paolucci *et al.*, 1996). Students explored problematic situations and manipulated inquiry diagrams. Advice was phrased as suggestions and questions and supported reciprocal tutoring, mutual evidence, cognitive scaffolding, self-reflection, and exploration of multiple perspectives.

Another example was COLER, which taught Entity-Relationship modeling, a formalism for conceptual database design (Constantino-Gonzales *et al.*, 2003). The system focused on both individual and collaborative learning and supported agreement by the group of a joint solution of a collaborative task. It monitored student participation and encouraged students to discuss their differences. COLER used decision trees to coach students and might recommend that a student take an action to invite other students to participate in his suggestion if it noticed that other members did not offer their opinions. The system compared students' private workspaces to the group's shared workspace and recommended discussion items based on the differences it found. It monitored the personal and shared workspaces to detect opportunities for group-learning interactions. COLER drew on the socio-cognitive conflict theory (Doise and Mugny, 1984) that states that disagreements can be opportunities for learning (Constantino-González *et al.*, 2003). COLER identified three coaching opportunities: differences between individual and group diagrams, differences in the levels of participation of the learners, and difficulties in the quality of the group diagram. It generated a set of potential advisory comments for each situation.

Advising students about both the social and task-oriented aspects of collaboration is difficult. Separating these two aspects is even more difficult and is described as the "Berlin Wall" of collaborative learning (Dillenbourg, 1999; Soller *et al.*, 2005). Students cannot effectively learn how to collaborate outside the context of a concrete task, and they cannot effectively learn how to perform a task collaboratively without attention to social and socio-cognitive factors that influence the group. A few systems have taken advantage of this idea by monitoring and analyzing both students' task-based and social actions to gain a better understanding of collaboration as a whole. COLER responded to both task and social aspects of interaction. One approach to supporting the social aspects of collaboration was to analyze students' dialogue (Baker and Lund, 1997; Dillenbourg, 1999; Soller and Lesgold, 2000). Such systems placed the analysis focus on the communicative acts and few considered domain knowledge in addition to the verbal interaction, although some did exemplify action-based analysis (e.g., Bravo *et al.*, 2006; Constantino-

González *et al.*, 2003; Mühlenbrock, 2001). The analysis of dialogue and actions generally takes into account the process carried out by the students.

One example of a system that used dialogue to provide advice about the social aspects of interaction was DEGREE, an asynchronous news group-type system that began to understand dialogue between group members (Barros and Verdejo, 1999; Soller *et al.*, 2005). The system required users to select the type of contribution (e.g., proposal, question, or comment) from a list each time users contributed to the discussion. The possible contribution types were provided by a conversational graph, defined differently for each collaborative scenario.

Another system that supported the social aspects of collaboration was OXEnTCHÊ (Soller *et al.*, 2005; Vieira *et al.*, 2004). A chat tool monitored interactions for teachers and learners and was coupled with an automatic dialogue classifier that analyzed online interactions and provided just-in-time feedback through reports, either user-specific or about the whole dialogue. Researchers identified conversational moves that they believed were necessary for effective learning dialogue and implemented these moves as mandatory sentence openers (or complete utterances) in a "semi-structured interface." The tool used a chatterbot as a coach to maintain dialogue focus. It interrupted group chat when it detected an unproductive change of subject and attempted to motivate less participative students to engage in conversation. Qualitative evaluation of the tool's usability and the quality of the feedback provided was encouraging. The main limitations included the reliance on sentence openers and an unclear theoretical justification for the chosen collaboration skills (Soller *et al.*, 2005).

Other systems addressed both social and task-oriented aspects of group learning. HabiPro was a programming environment that used two databases—one with words related to the domain (computer programming) and the other with potential off-topic terms (Vizcaino *et al.*, 2000). A simulated peer agent detected off-topic words in the students' utterances and intervened as necessary to bring students back on task. Another system that offered both social and task-oriented advice used machine learning methods to train agents to recognize when students experienced trouble related to specific aspects of the interaction (Goodman *et al.*, 2006; Soller *et al.*, 2005). Neural networks were trained with segmented, coded (speech act) student dialogue, and surface features (question marks and keywords) to recognize when students were having difficulty.

Phases of Collaboration

The previous section described four levels of tools that supported collaboration and helped students with both the tasks and the social aspects of collaboration. In this section, we present five phases of collaboration management, which follow a simple "homeostatic process that continuously compares the current state of the interaction..." with a target configuration (the desired state) (Soller *et al.*, 2005). The tutor intervenes whenever a perturbation arises with the intention of bringing the system back to equilibrium (Table 15.3).

The difference between Table 15.3, which described inquiry phases and this table, is found primarily in the first column, which for inquiry describes five different student *behaviours* while engaged in inquiry, whereas collaboration describes five phases of computer *observation* of student collaboration behaviour.

Table 15.3: The Phases of a Computational Model for Supporting Collaborative Learning

System Observation and Modeling	Student Activity	System Activity	Computer Tools
Phase 1: Collect interaction data	Team members interact with each other to solve problem/ case	Computer stores interaction activities through activityor state-based analysis; logs and snapshots of collaboration are stored	Mirror tools Metacognitive tools Coaching tools
Phase 2: Model the interaction		System selects and computes high-level indicators (e.g., verbosity, participation, reciprocity)	Mirror tools Metacognitive tools Coaching tools
Phase 3: Compare interaction to desired state		System diagnoses student interaction; prepares interaction data to be assessed by computer model or researchers	Metacognitive tools Coaching tools
Phase 4: Coach students	Student responds to system feedback	System performs remedial activities; suggests changing control; asks students to explain a concept	Coaching tools
Phase 5: Evaluate, assess; and diagnose		System assesses collaboration "What is the final objective?" Online or offline evaluation (human or machine)	

The collaboration framework does not focus on predicting collaborative learning outcomes, because the definition of the desired state may not be fully known and may change during the course of group activity. The framework is represented by a "feedback loop, in which the metacognitive or behavioural change resulting from each cycle is evaluated in the cycle that follows" (Soller *et al.*, 2005):

Phase 1: Collect Interaction Data: Data collection involves observing and recording student interaction. "Typically student actions (e.g., "student1 clicked on I agree,""student1 changed a parameter,""student1 created a text node")" are logged and stored for later processing (Soller *et al.*, 2005).

Phase 2: Construct a Model of Interaction: Modeling the interaction involves selecting and computing one or more higher-level variables, termed *indicators*, to represent the current state of the interaction (e.g., an *agreement* indicator for comparing the problem-solving actions of two or more students or a *symmetry* indicator for computing participation indicators).

Phase 3: Compare Interaction to the Desired State: The system diagnoses the interaction comparing the current state to a desired model of interaction, differentiating between productive and nonproductive interaction states. "A productive state... typically corresponds to a representation of interaction that might positively influence learning" (Soller *et al.*, 2005). For example, prefer that learners be verbose, thus attain a high verbosity indicator, interact frequently, thus maintain a high reciprocity indicator, and participate equally, thus minimize an asymmetry indicator. From a theoretical perspective, the difference between phases 2 and 3 describes the difference between a system that reflects the group's activities back to the members (phase 2) and a system that prepares interaction data (phase 3) to be assessed by computer models in preparation for understanding student behaviour and explaining the interaction (Soller *et al.*, 2005). This is a prelude to coaching.

Phase 4: Coach the Interaction: Finally, some remedial actions might be proposed to users. Simple remedial actions (e.g., "Try letting your partner have control for a while") might result from analyzing a model containing only one indicator (e.g., word or action count), which can be directly computed from the data, whereas more complex remedial actions (e.g., "Try explaining the concept of generalization to your partner using a common analogy ") requires more sophisticated computational analysis.

Phase 5: Evaluate the Interaction, Assess and Diagnose: The system reevaluates the impact of its remedial feedback to ensure that it produced the desired effects. During this evaluation phase, the system assesses how well it has met its goals. In some cases, evaluation may be performed offline, taking complete courses of interaction as the units of analysis.

16

Intelligent Tutoring System and Online Learning

Starting in the 1970s, early computer-mediated communication (CMC) technologies, such as email and computer conferencing, were employed to support efforts in online education. Although development was performed in a piecemeal fashion and early systems had definite shortcomings, online education offered important potential benefits (Harasim, 1999). Communication, interaction, and collaboration among students and faculty were encouraged and supported despite the limitations of systems built with early networking tools.

Starting in the early 1980s, efforts focused on developing asynchronous, place-independent approaches, providing text and multimedia content via many-to-many computer-mediated learning systems. This educational approach is sometimes referred to as network-mediated collaborative learning (Harasim, 1999). In collaborative learning environments, students actively construct knowledge through a highly interactive group process, a very different approach from the one-to-many transmission model of education via instructor-delivered lectures. Although technology advances in networking during the 1980s initially supported this new form of collaborative learning, users soon encountered the limitations of systems built with generic networking tools (Harasim, Hiltz, Teles, & Turoff, 1995).

Weaknesses of Generic Tools

Early online learning systems were built using generic networking tools, such as email, conferencing, and newsgroups. However, these tools were applied to online education rather than designed for online education (Harasim, 1999). Thus, instructors were forced to redesign their classroom lectures and activities to conform to online learning systems. In addition, models and tools were not available to support and shape the virtual learning environment, thereby increasing the administrative, organizational, and pedagogical tasks, difficulties, and costs to deliver education online (Harasim, 1999).

Analysis of shortcomings of these early online learning systems indicated that problems arose from the facilities lacking in these generic online learning environments. Such generic online learning environments were found to be limited in the following ways (Harasim, 1999):

- No standard organizational scheme for course material.
- Not tested or proven to be effective for instructional purposes.
- Lack tools and require significant development effort and technical support.
- Lack underlying models that support collaborative learning, knowledge building, and learning strategies with multiple representations of concepts and knowledge.

Technology Facilities for Online Learning

In order to address the shortcomings of online learning systems built with earlier generic tools, let us now consider technology facilities used to build current online learning systems (sometimes referred to as e-learning systems).

Multimedia Technologies

There are a number of different media-based technologies that provide delivery services for e-learning solutions (Cisco, 2001). These technologies include:

- Broadcast Video—live, streaming video, audio and slides.
- Video on Demand—on demand pre-recorded video and/or audio with accompanying graphics that can be accessed by a learner.
- Virtual Classroom.
- Combination of a browser-based Web conferencing tool and audio conferencing.
- Interactive graphics, slide shows, audio and video clips, and Web pages.

Interactive graphics and sophisticated audio and video capabilities increase the interest level in some online learning environments though some still rely on Microsoft PowerPoint (or similar presentation software) slides for presentation of content. Other systems combine PowerPoint slides with an audio or video lecture, simulating the delivery of a lecture-based in-person course. However, it is important to keep in mind that multimedia features should support learning objectives rather than detract from the presentation of Web-based learning content.

Computer-Mediated Communication (CMC) and Collaboration

Computer-Mediated Communication (CMC) includes such facilities as email, computer conferencing, informational Web sites, network news, bulletin boards with asynchronous postings, synchronous discussion forums, and chatrooms. Saunders, Sigmon, and Bull define Internet collaboration tools as: "protocols, hardware, and software which allow individuals to exchange information in real time, in particular, using audio, video, file transfer, chat (typing), application sharing (e.g. spreadsheets), and white boards (drawing)" (Saunder,

Sigmon, & Bull, 1998). Rheingold (1993/2000), a pioneer in the development of virtual communities, builds online social networks for organizations using a variety of CMC and collaboration tools. These tools allow users to incorporate text, graphics, streaming media, and/or HTML into their message board posts through a Web browser interface. In addition, Rheingold suggests using group calendaring, threaded discussion forums and online chat facilities to facilitate collaboration and learning among virtual community members. Some collaboration software provides facilities to handle personal to-do lists, calendar functions, and photo albums in addition to the more typical facilities of file sharing, and threaded discussion groups (Collabrio, 2001).

Classroom Management and Assessment

Classroom management and assessment tools are typically found in Web-based learning environments such as Learning Management Systems (LMS), Course Management Systems (CMS), and Total e-Learning solutions. Besheārs (1999) divides these types of tools into those that are intended for instructor use, those that support student work, and those that perform administrative functions.

The faculty tool set may include:

- Online grade book and grade reporting tool (i.e. to allow students to view grades)
- Quiz/Survey development tool
- Course Web site backup, download, upload facilities, Web-based file management
- Student account, student group, and grader account administration tools
- Student access tracking (how many articles posted/read, which pages accessed)
- Page access tracking (number who accessed a page and when) and page counters
- Course Web site glossary building tool
- Course Web site indexing, course announcements, calendar administration tool
- The student tool set includes such facilities as the following:
- Student self-evaluations
- Student accounts and group work areas for Web page publishing
- Course content annotation facility and bookmarks
- Web-based email and discussion groups, real-time chat rooms and whiteboards
- Individual grade and progress status reports and grade distribution status report

The administrator tool set may include the following:

- Course Web site creation, duplication, and deletion and course Web site backups

- Course Web site downloading and uploading
- Course Web site statistics, including number of students in course, file space used, number of hits on site, first and last access date
- Course Web site student account administration—batch mode account and course roster management

Learning Objects

Learning objects can be defined as "any entities, digital or non-digital, which can be used or referenced in technology-supported learning" (Innes, McGreal, & Roberts, 2000). Learning objects may be components, lessons, modules, courses, or programmes. Learning objects can be described as: "adaptable, affordable, accessible, discoverable, durable, interchangeable, interoperable, manageable, reliable, and re-usable" (Innes, McGreal, & Roberts, 2000). According to Dan Daniel, the Chief Information Officer (CIO) for NYUonline, the term in its current usage has several meanings. A learning object should be limited to objects with the following characteristics:

- *Instructional*—acquiring a new skill or gaining proficiency in a new concept.
- *Discrete and focused*—smaller than a lesson, module, or course, teaching a focused concept through a fairly small unit of instruction.
- *Self-sufficient*—each object can stand on its own without relying on other content.
- *Targeted*—appropriate to learner's skill level, not too easy and not beyond skill level.
- *Interactive*—offering opportunities for the learner to interact with the material.
- *Reusable*—learning objects should be constructed so that they can be assembled into larger courses and mixed and matched in various ways to create new courses.
- *Searchable*—to be able to reuse a learning object, must be easy to identify and access. Objects can be stored in online searchable repositories or libraries.
- *Valid*—concepts presented should have practical, real-world application.
- *Standards compliant*—learning objects should run on standard Web platforms and require no special plug-ins or additional applications to run. Learning objects should adhere to applicable standards. (NYUonline, 2001).

Categorization Schemes for Online Learning

Harasim, Hiltz, Teles, and Turoff (1995) describe seven models or learning approaches used for educational computer networks. The categorization into seven different learning approaches is depicted by Yuen and So (1999) as in Table 16.1.

Table 16.1: Online Learning Approaches

E-Lectures	Electronic Lectures, presenting instructional materials online.
Ask-an-expert	Interaction between an expert and a group of students in a question-and-answer communication model.
Mentorship	To facilitate Mentor-apprentice interaction online.
Tutor support	To implement face-to-face tutor-student interaction online.
Access to Network Resources	Making the information on the Internet and other electronic media available to students.
Informal Peer Interaction	To facilitate communication on the network in an informal manner.
Structured Group Activity	Curriculum-based group learning activities online.

The top four categories: e-lectures, ask-an-expert, mentorship, and tutor support are based on the use of instructors, mentors, and experts to serve as online resource personnel and provide support to students (Harasim et al., 1995). The lower three categories are student-centered, involving the student or learner in accessing relevant information, interacting with peers, and participating in structured group activities.

Yuen and So (1999) indicate that there is significant overlap among these learning approaches and propose categorizing the seven models in terms of their approaches to information as follows: Information Transmission, Information Discovery, and Information Construction. In their classification, Yuen and So (1999) view E-lectures as a form of Information Transmission and Access to Network Resources as a form of Information Discovery. However, Yuen and So (1999) do not distinguish among the other five approaches of Ask-an-expert, Mentorship, Tutor support, Informal Peer Interaction, and Structured Group Activity, choosing to group them all under the category of Information Construction. Yuen and So (1999) note that the amount of user control increases from Information Transmission, the first category, to Information Construction, the third category.

Khan (2000) lists various names used for e-learning activities: "Web-Based Instruction (WBI), Web-Based Training (WBT), Web-Based Learning (WBL), and Internet-Based Training (IBT)" (Khan, 2000). According to C. Smith, Murphy, and Teng (2001), a study conducted by the Distributed Centre (sic) for Learning Technologies at Mount Allison University for TeleEducation in New Brunswick, Canada categorizes online learning environments into three categories: self-paced, group-learning, or Learning Management Systems (C. Smith *et al.*, 2001).

A survey conducted for Industry Canada by Gram, Mark, and McGreal (1998) classified new media development and delivery tools into the following categories. However, many of the tools have disappeared through market consolidation, while others have added new functionality.

- Media Creation Tools—HTML, PDF, various text formats, and graphics tools
- Web Publishing tools—HTML editors, Macromedia Dreamweaver
- Conferencing tools—chat, Internet telephony, videoconferencing, collaboration tools
- Internet Enabled Authoring Systems
- Integrated Distributed Learning Environments

Jackson (2001) suggests categorizing online learning systems by format or function. Categorizing by format, Jackson lists the following types of online learning systems:

- Directed study (or Asynchronous "Self study")
- Instructor-led Events (or synchronous "live, real-time" learning)
- Small Group Collaboration

Categorizing by function, Jackson (2001) lists these types of online learning systems:

- Authoring tools—multimedia creation tools.
- Course Management Systems (CMS)—content delivery, assessment, administration.
- Educational Delivery Systems—real-time "virtual classrooms" or "collaboration tools."
- Learning Management Systems (LMS)—similar to course management systems with an integrated view of all active courses, with assessment and goals tracking facilities.
- Learning Content Management Systems (LCMS)—integrates standard Learning Management System features, authoring tools, and knowledge management tools.

In the Consortium for Information Technology in Education (CITE) study, C. Smith *et al.* (2001) organize online learning systems into synchronous environments, course management systems, learning management systems, total e-learning solutions, and related e-learning tools. Figure 16.1 depicts the elements of an online learning experience.

The Web

In 1991, *Tim Berners-Lee* demonstrated the *World Wide Web* (WWW, W3) at CERN, inventing the Web's core independently from Nelson's and

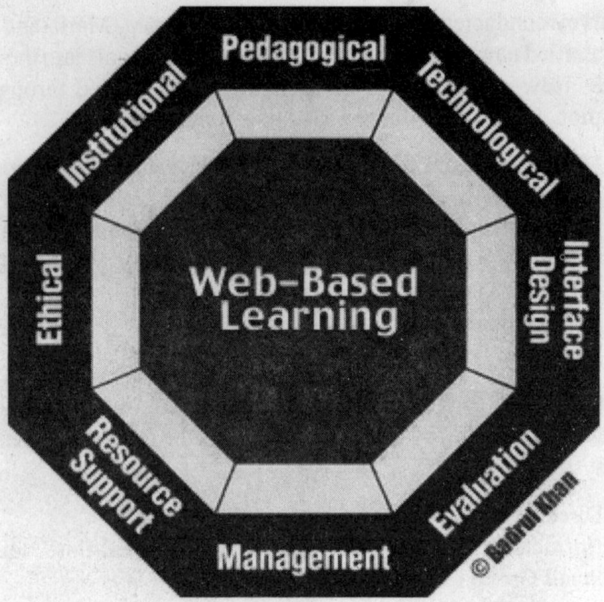

Figure 16.1: WBL (Web-Based Learning) Framework

Maurer's work. An URL (Uniform Resource Locator) mechanism incorporates other Internet protocols such as FTP, Gopher, or Newsgroups; by this, "'the Web' has embraced and become almost synonymous with 'the Net'" (Andrews, 1996). The Web uses *HTTP* (Hypertext Transfer Protocol based on TCP/IP) to transfer network data and *HTML* (Hypertext Markup Language) to separate content from design and structure. Two years later, NCSA (National Center for Supercomputer Applications at the University of Illinois) presented the graphical *Mosaic* browser rendering the World Wide Web the most popular web. From that time on, the browser client has driven Web technology.

The more mature Hyperwave system could not turn around the Web's steady growth in popularity; in particularly, its browsers (Harmony, Amadeus) could not keep up with standard Web browsers in terms of functionality. (Later, Hyperwave compensated this drawback by a Web gateway (Hyperwave Information Management, Inc., 1999) transforming protocols and delivering HTML to ordinary Web browsers). The limitations of the Web would lead to many ambiguities. An URL contains the physical document location, so it may produce broken links. HTTP is stateless; in contrast to Hyperwave's protocol, it supports neither subsequent connections, nor user sessions. Lastly, with Mosaic many details of Berners-Lee initial proposal (Berners Lee, 1999)—such as typed links, multiple linking options (embed, jump to, show in separate window, etc.), scripting, and full integration of browsing and editing—are lost.

In 1994, ex-members of NCSA developed *Netscape Navigator* to seize Mosaic's commercial role. Microsoft released Windows 95 with built-in connectivity to their Microsoft Network (MSN) hoping it will replace the Web. Yet, they soon turned to a Web-based strategy, making MSN a Web site and developing *Internet Explorer*. This was the beginning of the browser war. Microsoft integrated the browser into its operating systems; Netscape in turn created the open source *Mozilla* browser. More than 100 browsers evolved (see e.g. the browser archive at http://browsers.evolt.org). Only a few could withstand Microsoft and Netscape's market role, e.g. *Opera*, which started as a research project run by Norway's telecommunication company Telenor, and would consistently manage to gain innovative features.

Also in 1994, Berners-Lee founded the World Wide Web Consortium (*W3C*), intended to lead the Web to its full potential by developing common protocols ensuring interoperability. Currently, W3C recommends 53 specifications targeting for example Web publishing (*HTML*, *XML*), linking (XLink, XPointer), 2D vector graphics (*SVG*), or multimedia synchronization (*SMIL*). The open source W3C *Amaya* browser seamlessly integrates editing and remote access, and serves as framework for other W3C technologies. Likewise, standards initiatives of the Internet Engineering Task Force (IETF) address Web issues such as the HTTP extension *WebDAV* (Distributed Authoring and Versioning, (Whitehead, 1998).

Despite of Kay's *Dynabook* vision, the Web still provides little interactivity, i.e. opportunities for learners to compose or construct their own ideas (Roschelle, 1998]. Web browsers render content "read-only" and bring with them a "Web mode" incompatible to the Desktop (hyperlink paradigm vs. direct manipulation and WIMP). Missing dynamics features are compensated for either by server extensions (CGI—Common Gateway Interface), or, client-side, by browser plug-ins and scripting (DHTML). VRML (Bell, 1995) introduced interactive simulations (virtual worlds) in 1995. At about the same time, Macromedia presented the *Shockwave* and *Flash* plug-ins for (pixel-oriented, respectively vector-oriented) interactive Web graphics; both are very popular today. Founded in 1992 to create interactive multimedia CD-ROMs, Macromedia provided authoring tools such as Authorware, Director, and Dreamweaver for creating Web and Flash/Shockwave content (with extensions for learning content). Flash is also integrated into two other widespread browser plug-ins for multimedia content, Apple *Quicktime* and RealNetworks *RealPlayer*. While focusing on audio/video, Quicktime further supports sprite animations and mouse interactions.

In 1996, the HTML 3.2 specification finally included Sun's *Java* programming language. Initially part of browser functionality (Java 1.0/1.1), it has now become a standard browser plug-in (Java 2). The Java core is enriched with optional packages such as Java Advanced Imaging (JAI), Java Media Framework (JMF), Java 3D, and others (Sun Microsystems, Inc. (1995). While providing high-level design concepts, they delegate rendering to low-level (native) libraries and hardware, e.g. Java 3D relies on OpenGL and

Direct3D. Note that Java still provides access to low-level structures by encapsulating them into objects.

Web-based Education

Web-based education is currently a hot research and development area (Khan, 1997). Benefits of Web-based education are clear: classroom independence and platform independence. An application installed and supported in one place can be used by thousands of learners all over the world who are equipped with any kind of Internet-connected computer. Thousands of Web based courses and other educational applications have been made available on the Web within the last five years. The problem is that most of them are nothing more than a network of static hypertext pages. A challenging reset goal is the development of advanced Web-based educational applications which can offer some amount of interactivity and adaptivity. Adaptation is especially important for Web-based education for at least two general reasons. First, most Web based applications are to be used by a much wider variety of users than any standalone application. A Web application which is designed with a particular class of users in mind may not suit other users. Second, in many cases the user is "alone" working with a Web "tutor" or "course" (probably from home). That is why assistance that a colleague or a teacher typically provides adaptively in a normal classroom situation, is not available.

Web-based Learning

The internet is more frequently becoming a part of our daily lives, and its presence in education is unmistakable. Web-based courses seem to dominate the attention of educators and students. If presentations at international conferences are any indication, the interest in this new instructional medium is indeed commanding. Web-based learning encompasses all educational interventions that make use of the internet (or a local intranet). There are currently three broad classifications or configurations within WBL: tutorials, online discussion groups, and virtual patients. The distinctions between these configurations are often blurred, and in fact a given WBL intervention might use a combination of two or three, but the implications for teaching warrant a conceptual, albeit at times arbitrary, separation.

Online tutorials are similar to face-to-face lectures. They generally consist of information structured by the teacher in a way that will (hopefully) facilitate learning. Tutorials are often enhanced by features such as multimedia (sound, pictures, movies, and animations), links to online resources (full-text journal articles or related websites) and other areas within the course, and self-assessment tools.

Online discussion is similar to the face-to-face small group session. As with any small group, there may be an element of didactic teaching from the instructor (e.g a brief tutorial) but the heart of the teaching lies in group discussion. Teachers take on the role of facilitators—defining the scope of the discussion, monitoring and guiding the discussion as needed, and providing or helping students to find additional resources. Communication among group members can be asynchronous (delay between sending a message and receiving the response) or synchronous (live).

Virtual patients are computer-based simulations of patient encounters. Depending on the scenario students might query the computerised 'patient' to obtain a history, request information about the findings of physical examinations, order and interpret laboratory results and other tests, and/or institute therapy.

It is also worth noting what WBL is *not*. The internet has found many functions in education in which the primary intent is not an educational intervention designed for web-based delivery. These include archives of face-to-face lectures (eg. Power-Point slides or videotaped lectures) and course syllabi, online administration of tests and course evaluations, and administrative communications. While certainly useful, these functions do not constitute WBL.

Advantages of Web-based Learning

Any advantages and disadvantages of WBL are contingent upon at least two conditions: the nature of the WBL intervention, and the intended setting including the prospective learners. The advantages of a pencil depend on the kind of pencil (wood or mechanical, black lead or coloured, etc) and the use to which the pencil is applied (writing a test, marking a piece of wood, drawing a poster, etc). It is also important (but unfortunately not always considered) that the WBL intervention must be well designed.

Distance Learning, Economies of Scale and Consistent Message: Perhaps the most obvious advantage of WBL is that it overcomes physical distances. This is the cardinal feature separating WBL from other computer-assisted instructional methods, and enables WBL to facilitate the teaching of students scattered across different practice sites in the same city, different cities, and even different countries. The result of distance independence is that learners have the opportunity to participate in the same instructional activities regardless of physical location. For teaching settings in which faculty expertise varies across sites this can be an important advantage.

Distance learning also permits the possibility of economies of scale. Once a WBL tutorial or virtual patient has been developed, class size is limited only by server capacity and bandwidth. Viewed another way, it is possible for schools to share resources and thus avoid redundancy in developing course materials. Individual components of a course (for example, a paragraph of text, an animation, or a video clip) can be indexed and made available for use in other courses (reusable learning objects). Note that economy of scale is less apparent in online discussion settings, where demands on faculty facilitator time usually increase with each additional learner.

Flexible Scheduling: Along with flexibility in physical location, WBL offers flexibility in timing of participation. In contrast to lectures given at a fixed time, learners can access a WBL tutorial or virtual patient at any time day or night. Participating in an asynchronous online discussion group also offers flexibility, but it is tempered by the need to respond to communications from other group members in a timely manner and adhere to agreed schedules.

Easily Updated Perpetual Resource: Changes in practice and feedback from students often prompt teachers to update or alter their course. With WBL, such changes can be made quickly and easily, and avoid the expense of reprinting the course syllabus. Other faculty, and even students, can also be involved in the process of updating the course. Web-based learning products persist long after the course ends. Learners may thus return to access the tutorial as a reference when seeing patients or studying for a test, the text of a rich online discussion when writing a final paper, or the virtual patient simulator for additional practice.

Individualised Learning: Web-based learning offers the promise of individualized learning. Learners can be given greater control over the learning environment by allowing them to select from among multiple different learning opportunities within a given course and move at their own pace. Learners struggling to learn a topic can pursue remedial work, those interested in learning more can do so, and those already familiar with the topic can move quickly to the next. Likewise, asynchronous communication in an online discussion group allows learners to tailor participation to their needs; those desiring or requiring more time for study and reflection can use it.

Another way to individualise instruction involves adaptive instruction in which the computer uses information about the learner to alter and thus optimise the learning experience. Adaptation has been suggested in response to various individual differences including baseline knowledge of the subject matter, motivation, attitudes toward computers, and learning and cognitive styles.

Novel Instructional Methods: Web-based learning facilitates several instructional methods that would be infeasible or at least difficult in traditional settings. For example, virtual patient simulators can present medical students with a wide variety of patients and medical contexts to supplement classroom learning. This provides the opportunity to 'experience' uncommon scenarios, facilitates the repetition and temporal spacing (distributed practice) required for enduring learning, and allows communication of detailed performance-based feedback. Other learning exercises, such as interactive models and games, or using the internet to search for and assimilate information from multiple sources, can engage learners. Multimedia (colour, sound, video, photographs, graphics, and animations) can enrich a course in ways that would be difficult, if not impossible, using a textbook. The asynchronous nature of many online discussion groups allows time to think deeply about the issues at hand and spend time constructing a thoughtful response. This is in contrast to a face-to-face setting where the conversation may move on before a learner has had time to grasp the concepts let alone formulate a question or comment.

Assessment and Documentation: Finally, WBL facilitates assessment and documentation of educational objectives. Online assessment has the same flexibility in distance and timing as the WBL intervention, and also allows immediate customised feedback. Furthermore, in an age when documentation of learning tasks and competence is increasingly expected, WBL can serve a useful administrative purpose. Automated record-keeping can verify exactly what content learners reviewed and can also document successful completion of a summative assessment.

Disadvantages of Web-based Learning

The main disadvantages of web-based learning are given below:

Social Isolation: Flexibility in time and location means that the learner using WBL tutorials and virtual patients is often studying alone, which over time may lead to a perception of social isolation. Online discussion groups have a distinct social organisation which differs to that of a face-to-face small group. In an era when teamwork and team learning is increasingly valued, will WBL build or detract from critical interpersonal relationships and communication skills?

De-Individualised Instruction: Despite the promise of individualised instruction noted above, it has yet to be clearly shown that these theoretical promises bear fruit as hoped. On the contrary, more often WBL fails to respond to the individual needs of the learner. Whereas a good teacher can monitor the group and adapt instruction to accommodate various learning needs, adaptive WBL interventions must be explicitly programmed to monitor, recognise, and respond appropriately to individual needs. This is not as easy as it sounds, and only a handful of WBL interventions have done this successfully—and only at a very rudimentary level. It remains to be seen whether the potential advantage of individualised instruction can be realised, but for the moment adaptive WBL appears to be more vision than reality, and instruction is more often predetermined than personalised.

Cost: Offsetting the potential economies of scale are the large up-front costs associated with developing WBL. While it is a simple matter to convert an existing textbook, syllabus, or lecture to a web-based format, such conversions rarely if ever constitute effective instruction. In contrast, the development of an effective online tutorial or virtual patient can be very expensive—ranging from thousands to hundreds of thousands of dollars when time and opportunity costs are accounted. Also, ongoing faculty time commitments to an online discussion group can be significant. Finally, each WBL experience comes at the expense of learner time that might have been devoted to other purposes. Educators often capitalise on the flexible scheduling of WBL activities without taking into account the cumulative time required to complete all assignments.

Technical Problems: Despite best intentions, technical problems are inevitable with virtually all instructional media (for example, running out of chalk when teaching with a blackboard). However, as instructional media become more dependent upon technology the impact of technical problems becomes greater. In the absence of chalk a good teacher could improvise and teach, but serious computer problems will completely disrupt a WBL course. Even minor problems (which in my experience are far too common) can be a serious impediment, decreasing satisfaction and course participation while increasing cognitive load, which in turn impede learning.

Poor Instructional Design: The quality of instructional design varies in all teaching settings. However, in WBL this is more obvious because once complete a website can be viewed and critiqued by all users. Furthermore, in contrast to a face-to-face course in which a talented instructor can teach with minimal preparation, instruction in WBL must be explicitly planned and implemented. Research shows that many—perhaps most—WBL courses have an inferior instructional design. A classic example is the 'textbook on the web'—publishing the text of an existing syllabus or book on the internet and calling it a course. Such courses offer little if any advantage over the previous format while incurring the disadvantages listed here, and hardly qualify as 'instruction'. While poor instructional design is certainly not unique to WBL, the challenge of implementing effective designs on the internet and the absence of an instructor for needed clarification may make WBL more sensitive to flawed designs.

Technology for Technology's Sake: Perhaps not so much a disadvantage as a potential error, many educators and administrators are seeking out WBL and other education technologies for the sake of technology, rather than to achieve an educational goal. It is as though the technology train is leaving the station and no one wants to be left behind. Unfortunately, this has often led to poor instructional design (as noted above) or, worse yet, the use of WBL in situations in which other instructional methods or media would be more effective. For example, using WBL to teach medical interviewing may be less effective than other modalities. It is important to remember that, like chalk, PowerPoint slides, and calculators, WBL is just a tool—a powerful tool, perhaps, but one that may not be appropriate in all situations.

Web-based Adaptive Educational Systems in a Broader Context

Web-based Adaptive Educational Systems (AES) are not an entirely new or unique kind of systems. Historically, Web-based AES inherit from two earlier kinds of AES: *intelligent tutoring systems* (ITS) and *adaptive hypermedia systems*. Traditionally, problems of developing AES were investigated in the area of intelligent tutoring systems (Burns & Capps, 1988). ITS use the knowledge about the domain, the student, and about teaching strategies to support flexible individualized learning and tutoring. Adaptivity was one of the goal features of any ITS. Adaptive hypermedia is a much newer research domain (Brusilovsky, 1996). Adaptive hypermedia systems apply different forms of user models to adapt the content and the links of hypermedia pages to the user. Education is one of the main application areas for adaptive hypermedia and a number of adaptive educational hypermedia systems was built before "Web Rush". From a systemic point of view current Web-based AES can be considered simply as ITS or adaptive hypermedia systems implemented on the Web. However, WWW context provides serious impact on design and implementation of these system and let us treat them as a special subclass. For example, very few standalone ITS use adaptive hypermedia, while almost all Web based AES can be classified as both ITS and adaptive hypermedia systems. It is the impact of a "hypertext" nature of the Web.

In another context, Web-based AES is one of existing kinds of adaptive Web-based systems. WWW appears to be a nice platform for developing and testing various adaptive applications. From one side, it is challenging: Web-based systems really need adaptivity because they have to work with a much greater variety of users than earlier standalone systems. From another side, it is attractive: The Web gives complex AI-based adaptive systems a nice chance to reach many real users. While an adaptive system is installed on a powerful server which is serviced and updated by knowledgeable personnel, thousands of users can connect to it from cheap computers or kiosks. Web users can also help to solve a painful evaluation problem because all data about user interaction with an adaptive Web-based system can be recorded on the central server and used for comprehensive analysis.

What can be Adapted in Web-based Educational Systems

This section provides a brief review of current research on adaptive Web-based educational systems. The goal of the review is to demonstrate what can be adapted in this kind of systems. To provide compatibility with earlier papers on adaptive hypermedia (Brusilovsky, 1996) and Webbased ITS (Brusilovsky, 1995) we call essentially different ways of adaptation as *adaptation technologies.* Currently, all adaptation technologies applied in Web-based AES are adopted from either the ITS area (curriculum sequencing, intelligent analysis of student's solutions, interactive problem solving support, example-based problem solving support, and collaboration support) or the adaptive hypermedia area (adaptive presentation and adaptive navigation support). In a near future, we expect the appearance of newer adaptation technologies, for example, adaptive collaboration support, specially designed for the context of Web-based education.

The goal of the *curriculum sequencing* technology (also referred to as instructional planning technology) is to provide the student with the most suitable individually planned sequence of knowledge units to learn and sequence of learning tasks (examples, questions, problems, etc.) to work with. In other words, it helps the student to find an "optimal path" through the learning material. The classic example from the domain of teaching programming is the BIP system (Barr, Beard & Atkinson, 1976), recent examples are ITEM-IP (Brusilovsky, 1992b) and SCENT-3 (Brecht, McCalla & Greer, 1989). It make sense to distinguish two kinds of curriculum sequencing techniques. High-level sequencing or *knowledge sequencing* determines next concept or topic to be taught. Low-level sequencing or *task sequencing* determines next learning task (problem, example, test) within current topic (Brusilovsky, 1992a). In the context of Web-based education, curriculum sequencing technology becomes very important to guide the student through the hyperspace of available information. Currently, it is the oldest and the most popular.

Web-Based Courseware

"But the problems that remain [...] are how to make sufficient room for two fundamental elements of scientific education in the training of the young. These elements are: (a) the genuine "activity" of the students, who will be required to reconstruct, or in part rediscover, the facts to be learned; and (b) above all, individual experience in experimentation and related methods." (Piaget, 1973)

Educational Software

The idea to support the learning process by the use of computers (computer-based teaching, CBT) and the Web (WBT) has lead to many variants and acronyms (Schulmeister, 1997, Blumstenge, 1999, Maurer, 2001] such as CBE, CBI, CAT, CAI, CAL, CBL, CML, CMT, ICAI, or ITS. They accentuate respectively the base (B) of a computer (C) or an intelligent (I), interactive (I) system (S) to aid (A), assist (A), manage (M), or support (S) education (E), instruction (I), learning (L), teaching (T), training (T), or tutoring (T).

Learning Theory	Behaviorism	Cognitivism	Constructivism
Mind is...	passive	interactive	autarkic
Knowledge is...	stored	processed	constructed
We learn...	"what", facts	"how", understanding	"how we come to know", discover solutions
Strategy	teach, instruct	observe, help	cooperate, do not teach
Interactivity	hard-wired	dynamic	autonomous
Educational Software	tutoring system, drill & practice	adaptive system, intelligent tutoring system	microworld, simulation, hypermedia

Let us go back to the first attempts of CBT in the 1950s, the time when behaviourism had significant impact on education. A behaviourist concentrates on observable, evaluable behaviour, and avoids referring to the learner's internal states such as feelings or cognitive processes (Kearsley, 2003). *Edward Thorndike (*Thorndike, 1922) characterized learning as the result of associations forming between stimuli and responses. Behaviourism forms the base of today's classroom setting. Further, as a single teacher cannot appropriately assist 30 students simultaneously, *Burrhus Frederic Skinner (*Skinner, 1954) suggested a teaching machine for individual use that could present and reinforce information, and choose the level of difficulty according to the learner's performance. Due to technological constraints, Skinner's theory of programmed instruction produced only gap-filling tests (Schulmeister, 1997) or linear "page-turning" programmes. Behaviourism became associated with tutoring systems, trial and error, and drill and practice; typically, interactivity is hard-wired (Baumgartner, 1992; Blumstenge, l999].

In the 1960s, *Jerome Bruner (*Bruner, 1966) focused on mental processes and put down the theoretical foundation for cognitivism, which deals with the question of how we achieve, structure, conceptualize, and transfer information. Learning occurs by interactions between internal and external models. At first, efforts to optimize these interactions led to instructional design models. *David Merrill* for example developed the component display theory specifying ingredients necessary for efficient learning for a given objective and learner: rules, examples, recall, and exercise with feedback. He implemented his theory in the course structure of his *TICCIT* project (Time-shared Interactive Computer Controlled Information Television, (Merrill, 1980; Schulmeister, 1997) at the University of Texas and Brigham Young University. Many future authoring tools for instructional design would follow his principles. Adaptive systems and intelligent tutoring systems continue the search for a representation producing the most effective learning experience for a given individual and subject. (In some ways, reusable learning objects have the same intention.) TICCIT received funding of the *DoD* to determine whether CBT may reduce cost and time for training. The same initiative supported *Donald Bitzer*'s group at the University of Illinois in developing the more technical *PLATO* (Programmed Logic for Automated Teaching Operation, (Bitzer, 1970; Schulmeister, 1997). PLATO introduced networking to CBT by offering a central computer with courseware and permitting to use it from terminals, communicate and include statistics and feedback (Maurer, 2002). Again, this corresponds with a principle of Bruner, namely the ability to verbalize to one and others.

Bruner	enactive	iconic	symbolic
Piaget	Sensory motor	concrete	formal
Kay	doing	with images	makes symbols
GUI	mouse	icons/windows	programming

Following the principle of "learning without being taught", Papert introduced the concept of microworlds (Papert, 1980]. A microworld such as the Logo world of turtle-geometry represents an explorative learning environment that does not formulate concepts to be learned explicitly. Authoring tools offering visual programming implicitly establish associations between software components and provide the ability to manipulate the structure and behaviour of microworlds at a high conceptual level (Birbilis, 2000]. Discovery learning further provided a solid base for simulations, which expose the underlying dynamic model, and for educational hypermedia, which supports self-controlled exploration per se (Blumstenge, 1999).

Following van Dam (vanDam, 1987), Nelson was the first one to point out the importance of hypermedia in teaching. In the 1970s, van Dam applied *FRESS* in schools. Students of an English poetry course had to analyze and critique a poem; the context included word glosses, references to other poems, and some professional analyses. In a second phase, they reviewed other students' writings together with the teacher's comments, and, in turn, reworked their analysis accordingly.

"Electronic graffiti, as I though of them. The reason I encouraged such annotations was that I remembered that when I was in college with Ted, I would always grab the dirtiest copy of a book in the library, rather than the cleanest one, because the dirtiest ones had the most marginalia, which I found very helpful." (vanDam, 1987}

Consequently, the subsequent *Intermedia* system was meant to prototype a future hypermedia system providing "a user-level framework for creating exploratory contexts of educational and research materials for students and faculty" (Meyrowitz, 1989). Apple's *Hypercard* enabled educators to create dynamic educational hypermedia. Maurer (Maurer, 2002] reflects on the era of authoring systems and underlying technology (e.g. interactive videodisks) before the advent of the Web in the 1990s. During the time the Web appeared, advanced authoring facilities were competing with the continuous discussion of learning models. This was not only a battle between authoring systems and browsers, but also between cognitivism and constructivism. The importance of communication and collaborative work grew steadily, as did the spread of large educational environments. The educational community started standardizing protocols and metadata. In the new millennium, the trend moved towards learning technology standards to provide a common platform for future educational software. Maurer states:

"To use electronic educational material on a large scale it is necessary to be able to locate and re-use material created elsewhere. It is with satisfaction that we can observe a continued harmonization between North-American and European efforts in this important area. It is also gratifying to see that the necessity for communication, collaboration, and large digital libraries accessible via the Web is now universally accepted as basis for viable learning systems. [...] It has also become clear that a substantial learning system needs a huge array of administrative features and that the authoring of material is just a small part of what is necessary to make e-Learning work." (Maurer, 2002]

E-Learning

E-learning is identified as one of the emerging areas as shown by means of concrete numbers in [Brennan 2003] and has turned out to be important for educational institutions as well as for companies as highlighted by concrete application scenarios in [Dietinger 2003]. Nevertheless, various problematic aspects such as higher costs and political influences [Noble 2001], the focusing on technology and the negligence of pedagogical principles [Park *et al.* 1987], usability problems of e-learning systems, etc. were reported. According to [Gunawardena & McIsaac 2004], a shift from technology-to pedagogy-based research can be observed within the field of distance learning. Educators have become more interested in examining pedagogical themes and strategies within online courses instead of experimenting with new technologies.

Defining e-Learning

Electronic learning (or E-learning or E-learning) is a type of Technology supported education/learning (TSL) where the medium of instruction is through computer technology, particularly involving digital technologies. E-learning has been defined as "pedagogy empowered by digital technology". In some instances, no face-to-face interaction takes place. E-learning is used interchangeably in a wide variety of contexts. E-learning means that you no longer need to spend long periods travelling to a location to attend a course. You can now have access to learning when you want it, at the time you want it day or night, wherever you want it at home, at work, in your local library. For many students this has opened up a new, much more flexible and accessible world of learning that was previously closed to them due to disability or family circumstances, or perhaps due to the fact that the course they wanted was on the other side of the world. In other words, there are now no longer any geographical constraints to learning; E-learning brings learning to people, not people to learning. E-learning empowers learners to manage their own learning and in the most appropriate way for each learner. We all learn in different ways—reading, watching, exploring, researching, interacting, doing, communicating, collaborating, discussing, sharing knowledge and experiences. E-learning learners can have access to a wide range of learning resources: both materials and people, and in this way each learner can have an individualized, personalized experience, where they access the learning that is best for them.

Goals of E-learning

E-learning lessons are generally designed to guide students through information or to help students perform in specific tasks. Information based E-learning content communicates information to the student. Examples include content that distributes the history or facts related to a service, company, or product. In information-based content, there is no specific skill to be learned. In performance-based content, the lessons build off of a procedural skill in which the student is expected to increase proficiency.

E-Learning Theories

Implementing e-learning courses can be seen as a complex process going beyond systematically executing steps within an instructional design model. Among a large number of critical aspects, [McLeod 2003] suggests instructors to consider principles of learning by means of historically grown learning theories. Thus, it is possible to reuse certain procedures, for instance pre-defined instructional components as stated in [Merrill 2001]. Within the e-learning situation, three learning theories—the Behaviourism, the Cognitivism, and the Constructivism—are of importance as shown in [Cooper 1993], [Dietinger 2003], etc. In the following, these three theories are described in short, and implications for realising online courses are derived.

Behaviourism

The behaviourist school of thought, influenced by researchers like Watson, Thorndike, Pavlov, and Skinner who postulates that "*learning is a chance in observable behaviour caused by external stimuli in environment*" [Skinner 1974]. Behaviourists see the mind as a "black box", in the sense that a response to a stimulus can be observed quantitatively, totally ignoring the effect of thought processes occurring in mind. [Atkins 1993] highlights four aspects relevant for realising online courses with respect to the behaviourist school:

- The learning material should be broken down into small instructional steps being presented in a deductive way by means of starting with a rule, category, principle, formula or definition, giving positive examples to reinforce understanding, and showing negative examples to establish conceptual boundaries;
- Course designers have to define sequences of instructions using conditional or unconditional branching to other instructional units and pre-determining choices within the course. Normally, activities are sequenced for increasing difficulty or complexity. The sequence and pacing through the materials are usually beyond learner control;
- To maximise learning efficiency, learners may be routed to miss or repeat certain sections based on the performance on diagnostic tests, or on tests within the sequence of learning activities. Nevertheless, the instructional designer may also allow a learner to choose the next instruction out of a set of activities, giving the learner more control over the learning process;

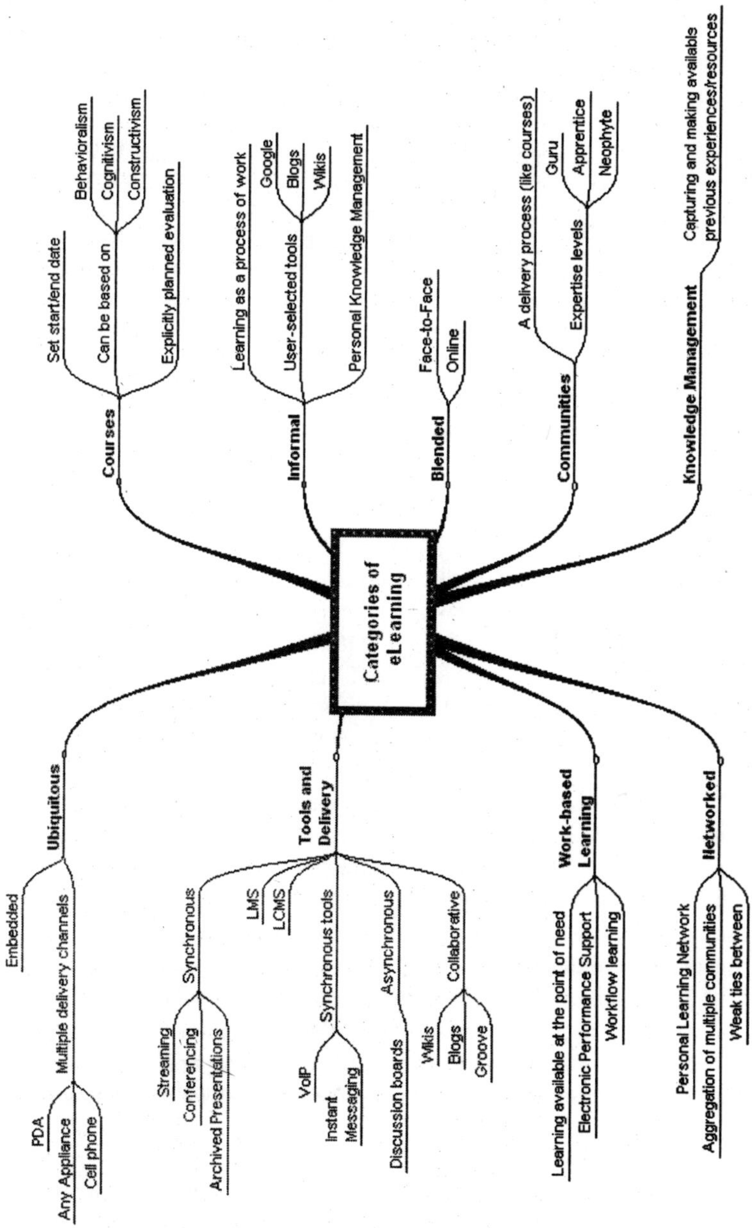

Figure 16.2: Mindmap of Categories of E-Learning

- The behaviouristic approach for learning suggests to demonstrate the required operation, procedure or skill, and to break it down into its parts with appropriate explanation before learners are expected to copy the desired behaviour. Learners are supposed to build proficiency from frequent review or revision with check tests at strategic points or repeat practice with feedback. Instructional design emphasises low error rate and the usage of remedial loops back through material if necessary. Furthermore, reinforcement messages should be used to maintain motivation.

Overall, behaviourists recommend a structured, deductive approach to design an online course, so that basic concepts, skills, and factual information can rapidly be acquired by the learners. Further implications on online learning can be summarized by the concept of drill and practice, portioning materials and assessing learner's achievement levels, and giving external feedback. However, the effectiveness of behavioural design approaches for higher-order learning tasks or for transfer of learning is as yet unproven.

Cognitivism

Cognitivists consider learning as an internal process that involves memory, thinking, reflection, abstraction, motivation, and meta-cognition as outlined by [Ally 2004]. Cognitive psychology comprises the learning process from an information processing point of view, where information is received in the sensory store through different senses and, further, transferred to the short-term and the long-term memory through different cognitive processes.

Furthermore, the cognitive school recognises the importance of individual differences and of including a variety of learning strategies to accommodate those differences. Thus, different learning styles [Kolb 1984], [Myers 1978], etc. refer to how a learner perceives, interacts with, and responds to learning material. In addition, cognitive styles as addressed e.g. in [Witkin *et al.* 1977] describe learner's preferred way of processing information, that is a person's typical mode of thinking, remembering, or problem solving.

Besides, the individual cognitive trend derived from Piaget's theory, [Deubel 2003] states that the learning process also includes socio-cultural perspectives emphasizing socially and culturally situated contexts of cognition as expressed by Vygotsky (see [Duffy & Cunningham 1996]). Instructional designers have to consider the following aspects for realising online courses:

- The teaching strategy should enhance the learning process by facilitating all sensors, focussing the learner's attention by highlighting important and critical information, reasoning each instruction, and matching the cognitive level of the learner;
- The instructional designer should tie up to new information with existing information from long-term memory using advanced

organisers to activate exiting cognitive structures or to incorporate the details of the lesson, providing conceptual models to enable the learner to retrieve existing mental models, using pre-instructional questions to set expectations and to activate the learner's existing knowledge structure, and using prerequisite test questions to activate the prerequisite knowledge structure required for new materials;

- The learning content should be chunked to prevent cognitive overload. Exceeding a number of five to nine items to learn, linear, hierarchical, or spider-shaped information maps should be provided;
- Strategies requiring the learner to apply, analyse, synthesise, and evaluate should be used to promote deep processing of information and higher-level learning;
- Online learning materials should include activities for the different learning and cognitive styles. Furthermore, it is necessary to provide adequate and the right type of support for students with different types of learners;
- With respect to dual-coding theory [Paivio 1990], information should be presented in different modes to accommodate individual differences in processing and to facilitate transfer to long-term memory;
- Students need to be motivated to learn by means of learning strategies addressing the intrinsic motivation (driven from within the learner) and the extrinsic motivation (instructor or performance driven). Therefore, methods such as Keller's ARCS model—the abbreviation for attention, relevance, confidence, and satisfaction [Keller & Suzuki 1988]—could be applied by the instructor;
- With respect to [Meyer 1998], the teaching strategy should enforce learners to use their meta-cognitive skills by reflecting on what they learn, collaborating with other learners or checking their progress;
- Finally, the teaching strategy should connect learning content with different real-life situations, so that the learners can tie up to own experiences and, therefore, memorise things better. Furthermore, a transfer to real-life situations could support the development of personal meaning and contextualisation of the information.

To sum up, cognitive psychology focuses on learners' receiving and processing of information to transfer it into long-term memory for storage. Therefore, instructional designers have to consider different aspects beginning from chunking the learning content into smaller parts and supporting different learning styles up to higher concepts such as motivation, collaboration or meta-cognition. Although the cognitive-focused approach is well suited for reaching higher-level objectives, a major weakness can be identified, if a learner lacks of relevant prerequisite knowledge. To account this, a course designer has to ensure that the instructions are appropriate for all skill levels and experiences, which is evidently costly and timeconsuming.

Constructivism

The constructivist school of learning suggests that learners construct personal knowledge from the learning experience itself as stated in [McLeod 2003]. Thus, learning can be seen as an active process, and knowledge cannot be received from outside or from someone else. According to [Duffy & Cunningham 1996], learners should be allowed to construct knowledge rather than being given knowledge through instructions. Furthermore, constructivists emphasise situated learning, which sees learning as contextual and suggests strategies promoting multi-contextual learning to make sure that learners can apply the information broadly.

With respect to [Boethel & Dimock 1999], the following assumptions can be made up on this learning theory: Learning is an adaptive activity and situated in the context where it occurs. Knowledge is constructed by the learner who also deals with resistance to change. Experiences and social interactions play a role in the learning process. By deriving implications for creating instructions for online learning, the following statements have to be made up:

- Learning should be an active process by means of keeping learners active doing high-level activities such as asking learners to apply information in practical situations, facilitating personal interpretation of learning content, discussing topics within a group, and so forth;
- To enforce learners constructing their own knowledge, instructors have to provide good interactive online instructions, since the students have to take the initiative to learn and interact with other students and the instructor and since the learning agenda is controlled by students [Murphy & Cifuentes 2001]. In contrary to traditional lecture where instructors contextualise and personalise information to meet their own needs, students have to experience the learning content at first-hand;
- As stated e.g. in [Hooper & Hannafin 1991], collaborative and cooperative learning should be encouraged to facilitate constructivist learning. Working with other learners gives students real-life experience and allows them to use and improve their meta-cognitive skills. When assigning learners for a group work, membership should be based on the expertise level and learning style, so that team members can benefit from one another's strengths;
- Learners should be given control of the learning process. Besides, there should be a form of guided discovery where learners can make their decision on learning goals, but can also use some guidance from the instructor;
- When learning online, students should be given time and opportunity to reflect the learning content. Embedded questions on the content

can be used throughout the lesson to encourage reflection and processing of the information;

- Learning should be made meaningful and illustrative for learners by including examples and use cases for theoretical information. Besides, activities should enforce learners to apply and personalise the learning content offered;
- Instructors should focus on interactive learning activities to promote higher-level learning and social presence and to help develop personal meaning. As learning focuses on developing new knowledge, skills, and attitudes, e-learning faces the problem that psychomotor, affective and higher-level objectives are hard to reach within virtual learning phases. Therefore, [Mödritscher & Sindler 2005] suggest providing other ways—such as social or interactive activities, context-based learning, assessment through open-ended questions, etc.—to realise such didactical aspects.

Examples of constructivist learning can be found within the scope of experiential learning, self-directed learning, context-aware learning, and reflective practice. Despite a variety of advantages of Constructivism, like the presentation of content from multiple perspectives, the active knowledge construction, the development of meta-cognitive strategies, this learning theory also faces a few disadvantages, such as problems in adequately evaluating the learning process, lack of instructional resources to respond to the multitude of student interests or higher effort to create context-based learning content, restrictions on driving the learning process to a certain direction given e.g. by science, higher drop-out rate due to a lack of extrinsic motivation for students with low capabilities on self-directed learning, etc.

E-learning companies tend to fall into one of the following categories:

Providers of content—often corporate and IT training: Within this category there are three subcategories: companies that develop content and sell to all who choose to enroll; those that aggregate content developed by others; and those that custom design content for the specific needs of an organization.

Providers of learning platforms: These companies provide a range of hard-and software technologies that facilitate the development and delivery of online courses, ranging from content creation to learner registration and course record keeping.

Learning hubs: *Learning hubs* or portal companies offer learners or organizations consolidated access to learning and training resources from multiple sources.

A complete package: Some e-learning companies are attempting to do all of the above.

The Future of E-Learning

Increased access to the Internet and greater bandwidth are both expected to increase the number of individuals moving into online learning. International Data Corporation (IDC) forecasts that there will be 320 million Internet users worldwide by the end of 2002, up from 97 million at the end of 1998. And broadband connectivity is expected to grow from approximately one million households in 2000 to almost 26 million by 2003 (Close *et al.* 2000). Broadband access increases the speed of Internet access and does away with the frustrating tedium of waiting for Web pages to download—a disincentive for the e-learning process. A study conducted by MediaOne found that households with broadband cable Internet connections averaged 22.5 hours of usage per week as compared with just 4.7 hours for households with dial-up connections.

Benefits of E-learning versus Traditional Classroom Settings

E-learning can provide for major benefits for the organizations and individuals involved.

- Reducing environmental impact: E-learning allows people to avoid travel, thus reducing the overall carbon output. The fact that it takes place in a virtual environment also allows some reduction of paper usage. With virtual notes instead of paper notes and online assessments instead of paper assessments, E-learning is a more environmentally friendly solution.
- Quality education, made affordable: The fact that instructors of the highest caliber can share their knowledge across borders allows students to attend courses across physical, political, and economic boundaries. Recognized experts have the opportunity of making information available internationally, to anyone interested at minimum costs. This can drastically reduce the costs of higher education, making it much more affordable and accessible to the masses. An internet connection, a computer, and a projector would allow an entire classroom in a third world university to benefit from the knowledge of an opinion leader.
- Convenience and flexibility to learners: in many contexts, E-learning is self-paced and the learning sessions are available 24x7. Learners are not bound to a specific day/time to physically attend classes. They can also pause learning sessions at their convenience.

The Advantages of E-Learning

There are a number of benefits to learning online that are unique to the medium:

- *Any time.* A participant can access the learning programme at any time that is convenient—not just during the specific 1-3-hour period that is set for a conventional course. The episodes can be quick snatches at odd times or long late-night sessions. Cross-time-zone communication, difficult to arrange in real time, is as easy as talking to someone across town when using the Internet.

- *Any place.* The participants do not have to meet. That means they can be anywhere. International sharing is feasible. Individuals can log on at work, home, the library, in a community learning center or from their hotel when traveling.
- *Asynchronous interaction.* Unlike face-to-face or telephone conversations, electronic mail does not require participants to respond immediately. As a result, interactions can be more succinct and to-the-point, discussion can stay more on-track, and people can get a chance to craft their responses. This can lead to more thoughtful and creative conversations.
- *Group collaboration.* Electronic messaging creates new opportunities for groups to work together, creating shared electronic conversations that can be thoughtful and more permanent than voice conversations. Sometimes aided by on-line moderators, these net seminars can be powerful for learning and problem-solving.
- *New educational approaches.* Many new options and learning strategies become economically feasible through online courses. For instance, the technology makes it feasible to utilize faculty anywhere in the world and to put together faculty teams that include master teachers, researchers, scientists, and experienced professional developers. Online courses also can provide unique opportunities for teachers to share innovations in their own work with the immediate support of electronic groups and expert faculty.
- *Integration of computers.* The online learner has access to a computer, so computer applications can be used without excluding some participants. This means, for instance, that a mathematical model implemented in a spreadsheet can easily be incorporated into a lesson and downloaded so all participants can run, explore, and refine the model and then share their findings and improvements.

Does E-Learning Work?

The individualized interactivity provided by an Internet connected computer is believed to contribute significantly to the effectiveness of the online learning environment. And even without the Internet connectivity, computer-based learning programmes have shown compelling results in both effectiveness and efficiency. While no machine can come close to the quality of instruction that can be provided by a good human teacher working with a student one-on-one, teachers typically have 25 to 35 students to deal with at one time—and often many times that number. A well-designed computer-based or online learning programme can offer much more opportunity for individualized interactivity than is available in most classrooms. Studies have shown that individualized learning environments are considerably more interactive.

References

A.N., K. (2002). Model-based reasoning for domain modeling in a web-based intelligent tutoring system to help students learn to debug c++ programs. In *Intelligent Tutoring Systems*, Vol. 2363 of LNCS, pp. 792 801.

Aberek, B., Popov, V. (2004). Intelligent tutoring system for training in design and manufacturing. *Advances in Engineering Software* 35(7), 461-471.

ACOT (1996). "Changing the Conversation about Teaching and Learning and Technology." A Report on 10 years of ACOT Research, Apple Computer, Inc. http://www.info.apple.com.education.

Acquiring and Maintaining Group Models. ITS 2004 Workshop on Computational Models of Collaborative Learning, Maceio-Algoas, Brazil, Springer.

Aderinoye, R.A.; Ojokheta, K.O. and Olojede, A.A. (2007). "Integrating Mobile Learning into Nomadic Education Programmes in Nigeria: Issues and perspectives," *International Review of Research in Open and Distance* Learning, Vol. 8.

Advanced Technology Program (ATP) (1998a). Project Brief: Real Adaptive Intelligent Learning Systems. http://jazz.nist.gov/atpcf/prjbrie…brief.cfm?Project Number=98-09-0012

——, (1998b). Project Brief: Courseware Conversion Factory: Re-Engineering Objects for Web-Based Instruction on Demand. http://jazz.nist.gov/atpcf/prjbrie…brief.cfm?ProjectNumber=98-09-0038

——, (1998c). White Paper: Adaptive Learning Systems. http://www.atp.nist.gov/atp/97wp-lt.htm

Aimeur, E. and Frasson, C. (1996). Analyzing a new learning strategy according to different knowledge levels. *Computers and Education* 27 (2): pp. 115-127.

Albacete, P.L., VanLehn, K. (2000). The conceptual helper: an intelligent tutoring system for teaching fundamental physics concepts. In: Gauthier, G., VanLehn, K., Frasson, C. (eds.). *ITS 2000. LNCS*, Vol. 1839, pp. 564-573. Springer, Heidelberg.

Alessi, S. and Trollip, S. (2000). *Multimedia for Learning: Methods and Development*. Allyn and Bacon.

Aleven, V. *et al.* (2006). Rapid authoring of intelligent tutors for real-world and experimental use. In Proceedings of the Sixth IEEE International Conference on Advanced Learning Technologies, pages 847{851 IEEE, Computer Society.

——, McLaren, B., Sewall, J., Koedinger, K.R. (2006). The Cognitive Tutor Authoring Tools (CTAT): Preliminary evaluation of efficiency gains. In M. Ikeda,

K. Ashley, and T.W. Chan (Eds.), Intelligent Tutoring Systems 2006, LNCS 4053 (pp. 61-70). Berlin: Springer-Verlag.

Alexandra C. and Toshio O. (2000). An adaptive distance learning environment for language teaching. In Proceedings of the International Workshop on Advanced Learning Technologies.

Ally, M. (2004). "Foundations of educational theory for online learning." In Anderson, T. and Elloumi, F. (Eds.): "*Theory and practice of online learning*", Athabasca University, Athabasca, pp. 3-31.

American Association for the Advancement of Science (AAAS) (1993). Benchmarks for Science Literacy: Project 2061. Oxford Press, New York.

Anania, J. (1983). The influence of instructional conditions on student learning and achievement. *Evaluation in Education*, 7, 1-92.

Anderson, J. and Reiser, B. (1985). The LISP Tutor. Byte, 10, 4, pp. 159-175.

——, (1993). *Rules of the Mind.* New Jersey, Lawrence Erlbaum Associates.

Anderson, J.A., Corbett, A.T., Koedinger, K., and Pelletier, R. (1995). Cognitive Tutors: Lessons Learned. *The Journal of the Learning Sciences*, 4(2), 167-207.

Anderson, J.R. (1980). Cognitive psychology and its implications. San Francisco, CA: W.H. Freeman and Company.

——, (1983). *The architecture of cognition.* Cambridge, MA: Harvard University Press.

——, (1987). Production systems, learning and tutoring. In *Production System Models of Learning and Development* (eds. D. Klahr, P. Langley and R. Neches). MIT Press, London, pp. 437-458.

Anderson, R.C. (1984). Some reflections on the acquisition of knowledge. *Educational Researcher*, 5-10.

Andrews, K. (1996). Browsing, Building, and Beholding Cyberspace, New Approaches to the Navigation, Construction, and Visualisation of Hypermedia on the Internet, Ph.D. thesis, Graz University of Technology. http://www2.iicm.edu/keith-phd

Atkins, M.J. (1993). "Theories of learning and multimedia applications: An overview", *Research Papers in Education*, 8(2), pp. 251-271.

Atkinson, R.C., Wilson, H.A. (eds.) (1969). *Computer-Assisted Instructions*. Academic Press, New York.

Attisha, M.G and Yazdani, M. (1984). An expert system for diagnosing children's multiplication errors. *Instructional Science*, 13, 79-92.

Audi, R. (Ed.) (1995). *The Cambridge Dictionary of Philosophy*. Cambridge, UK: Cambridge University Press.

Ausubel, D.P. (1963). *The psychology of meaningful verbal learning: An introduction to school learning*. New York: Grune and Stratton.

Barr, A. and Feigenbaum, E.A. (1982). (Eds.). Applications-oriented AI research: Education. *Handbook of artificial intelligence*, vol. II. Reading, MA: Addison-Wesley.

Beard, M., and Atkinson, R.C. (1976). The computer as tutorial laboratory: the Stanford BIP project. *International Journal on the Man-Machine Studies* 8 (5), 567-596.

Barretto, S.F.A., Piazzalunga, R., Ribeiro, V.G., Dalla, M.B.C., Filho, R.M.L. (2003). Combining interactivity and improvement layout while creating educational software for the Web. *Computers and Education* 40(3), 271-284.

Barzilay, A. (1985). SPIRIT: a flexible tutoring style in an intelligent tutoring system. In *Artificial Intelligence Applications: The Engineering of Knowledge-Based Systems* (ed. R.C. Weisbin). IEE Computer Society, North Holland.

Baumgartner, p., Payr, S. (1992). *Lernen mit Software*, 2nd ed., Innsbruck, StudienVerlag.

Berliner, D. (1986). In pursuit of the expert pedagogy, *Educational Researcher*, 15, 5-13.

Berners-Lee, T. (1999). Weaving the Web, HarperCollins.

K., Belynne, K., Viswanath, K., Schwartz, D. and Davis, J. (2004). Developing learning by teaching environments that support self-regulated learning. International Conference on Intelligent Tutoring Systems. Berlin, *Springer. Lecture Notes in Computer Science*, Vol. 3220: 730-740.

Bitzer, D.L. and Easley, J.A. (1965). Plato: A computer-controlled teaching system. In Sass and Wilkinson, editor, Symposium on Computer Augmentation of Human Reason-

Bitzer, D.L., Skaperdas, D. (1970). The Economics of a Large Scale Computer Based Educational System: Plato IV, in: Holtzman, W., Computer Assisted Instruction, Testing and Guidance, pp. 17-29, New York, Harper and Row.

Blaine, L.H. (1982). EXCHECK. *Handbook of Artificial Intelligence*, Vol. 2 (eds. A. Barr and E.A. Feigenbaum). Addison-Wesley, Reading, MA.

Bloom, B. (ed.) (1956). *Taxonomy of Educational Objectives*. New York, NY, Mackay Publishing.

Bobrow, D.G., Mittal, S. and Steffik, M. (1986). Expert systems: perils and promise. *Communications of the ACM*, 29, 880-893.

Boethel, M. and Dimock, K.V. (1999). "Constructing Knowledge with Technology", Southwest Educational Development Laboratory, Austin.

Bonar, J. (1985). Understanding the Bugs of Novice Programmers. PhD Thesis, Dept of Computer and Information Science, University of Pittsburgh, Pittsburgh, PA.

Bonar, J.G. (1984). Cognition based intelligent tutoring systems. In Salvendy, G. (Ed.), *Human-computer interaction*. Elsevier Science Publishers.

Bonnet, A. (1985). *Artificial Intelligence: Promise and Performance*. Prentice Hall, London.

Bransford, J.D., Brophy, S. and Williams, S. (2000 a). When computer technologies meet the learning sciences: Issues and opportunities. *Journal of Applied Developmental Psychology* 21 (1): pp. 59-84.

Brecht, B.J., McCalla, G.I., and Greer, J.E. (1989). Planning the content of instruction. In: D. Bierman, J. Breuker and J. Sandberg (eds.) Proceedings of 4-th International Conference on AI and Education, Amsterdam, 24-26 May 1989, Amsterdam, IOS, pp. 32-41.

Breuker, J. (1987). Coaching in help systems. In *Artificial Intelligence and Human Learning: Intelligent Computer-aided Instruction* (ed. J. A. Seft). Chapman and Hall, London.

——, (1988). Coaching in help systems. In Self, J. (Ed.), *Artificial intelligence and human learning* (pp. 310-337). London: Chapman and Hall Computing.

——, (1990). Conceptual model of intelligent help system. In Breuker, J. (ed.), *EUROHELP: developing intelligent help systems* (pp. 41-67). Copenhagen: EC.

Brown, A.L., and Palincsar, A.S. (1989). Guided, cooperative learning and individual knowledge acquisition. In L.B. Resnick (Ed.), Knowing, learning, and instruction: Essays in honor of Robert Glaser (pp. 393-451). Hillsdale, NJ: Erlbaum.

Brown, J.S. (1983). Learning by doing revisited for electronic learning environments. In White, M.A. (Ed.), The future of electronic learning. Hillsdale, NJ: Lawrence Erlbaum Associates Publishers.

——, (1985). Process versus product: a perspective on tools for communal and informal electronic learning, lournal of Educational Computing Research 1,179-201.

——, Burton, R.R. and Bell, A.G (1975). SOPHIE: a step towards a reactive learning environment. International/ournal of Man-Machine Studies, 7, 675-696.

——, and de Kleer, J. (1982). Pedagogical, natural language, and knowledge engineering techniques in SOPHIE I, II and II1. In *Intelligent Tutoring Systems* (eds D.H. Sleeman and J.S. Brown). Academic Press, London, pp. 227-282.

——, and Zydel, F. (1973] A model-driven question-answering system for mixed-initiative CAI. IEEE Transactions on Systems, Man, and Cybernetics, 3, 248-257.

Brown, Q.; Lee, F.; Aleven, V. and Salvucci, D. (2008). "Interface Challenges for Mobile Intelligent Tutoring Systems," in International Conference on Intelligent Tutoring Systems, pp. 693-695.

Bruner, J. (1986). *Actual Minds, Possible Worlds*. Harvard University Press, Cambridge, MA.

——, (1990). *Acts of Meaning*. Harvard University Press, Cambridge, MA.

——, (1992). Science Education and Teachers: A Karplus Lecture. *Journal of Science Education and Technology*, 1, March, pp. 5-12.

Bruner, J.S. (1961). The act of discovery. *Harvard Educational Review*, 31, 21-32.

——, (1966). *Towards a theory of instruction*, Cambridge, Harvard University Press.

Bruno, M. (2000). Student-Active Learning in a Large Classroom. Project Kaleidoscope 2000 Summer Institute, Keystone, Colorado.

Brusilovsky, P. (1995). Intelligent tutoring systems for World-Wide Web. In: R. Holzapfel (ed.) Proceedings of Third International WWW Conference, Darmstadt, Darmstadt, April 10-14, 1995, Fraunhofer Institute for Computer Graphics, pp. 42-45.

——, (1996). Methods and techniques of adaptive hypermedia. In P. Brusilovsky and J. Vassileva (eds.), Spec. Iss. on Adaptive Hypertext and Hypermedia, User Modeling and User-Adapted Interaction 6 (2-3), 87-129.

——, (1998). Methods and Techniques of Adaptive Hypermedia. In P. Brusilovsky, A. Kobsa, and J. Vassileva, editors, *Adaptive Hypertext and Hypermedia*, Chapter 1, pp. 1-44, Kluwer Academic Publishers, The Netherlands, 1998.

——, (2004). Knowledge tree: A distributed architecture for adaptive e-learning.

——, and Pesin, L. (1998). Adaptive navigation support in educational hypermedia: An evaluation of thesis-tutor. *Journal of Computing and Information Technology*.

——, *et al.* (1998). Web-based education for all: A tool for development adaptive courseware. In *Computer Networks and ISDN Systems*, Volume 30, pages 291(300).

Burns, H. and Parlett, J.W. (1991). The evolution of intelligent tutoring systems: Dimensions of design. In Burns, H.,

——, and Capps, C. (1998). Foundations of Intelligent Tutoring Systems. Lawrence Erlbaum Associates, 1988.

Burns, H.L. and Capps, C.G. (1988). "Foundations of Intelligent Tutoring Systems: An Introduction," in *Foundations of Intelligent Tutoring Systems*, M.C. Polson, J.J. Richardson, and E. Soloway, Eds. London: Lawrence Erlbaum Associates, pp. 1-19.

Burns, P.K. and Bozeman, W.C. (1981). Computer-Assisted Instruction and Mathematics Achievement: Is There a Relationship? *Educational Technology* 21, 32-39.

Burton, R. and Brown, J.S. (1977). A tutoring and student modelling paradigm for gaming environments. *SIGCSE Bulletin*, 8, 236-246.

——, (1982). An investigation of computer coaching for informal learning activities. In *Intelligent Tutoring Systems* (eds. D.H. Sleeman and]. S. Brown). Academic Press, London, pp. 79-98.

Burton, R.R. (1982). Diagnosing bugs in a simple procedural skill. In D.H. Sleeman, and J.S. Brown (Eds.), Intelligent tutoring systems (pp. 157-183). New York: Academic Press.

——, and Brown, J.S. (1979). An investigation of computer coaching for informal learning activities. *International Journal of Man-Machine Studies*, 11, 5-24.

——, (1976). A tutoring and student modeling paradigm for gaming environments. In R. Colman and P. Lorton, Jr. (Eds.), Computer Science and Education. ACM SIGCSE Bulletin, 8(1), 236-246.

Cabrera, J.S.; Frutos, H.M.; Stocia, A.G.; Avouris, N.; Dimitriadis, Y.; Fiotakis, G. and Liveri, K.D. (2005). "Mystery in the Museum: Collaborative Learning Activities using Handheld Devices," in 7th International Conference on Human Computer Interaction with Mobile Devices and Services, pp. 315-318.

Calderhead, J. (1988). Teachers' professional learning. London: The Falmer Press.

Carbonell, J.R. (1970). AI in CAI: An artificial intelligence approach to computer-assisted instruction. *IEEE Transactions on Man-Machine Systems*, 11(4), 190-202.

——, (1970a). Mixed-initiative man-computer instructional dialogues. Doctoral Dissertation, Massachusetts Institute of Technology, Cambridge, Massachusetts.

——, (1971). Artificial intelligence and large interactive man computer systems. Proceedings of the Joint National Conference on Major Systems, Anahein, CA, pp. 167-173.

Carr, B., and Goldstein, I.P. (1977). Overlays: A theory of modeling for computer-aided instruction. AI Lab Memo 406 MIT, Cambridge, Massachusetts.

Carroll, J.M., and Kay, D.S. (1988). Prompting, feedback and error correction in the design of a scenario machine. *International Journal of Man-Machine Studies* 28, 11-27.

Chan, T.W. (2002). Social design of network learning society. International Conference on Computers in Education (ICCE). Aukland, New Zealand, IEEE Computer Society. 1: 1-5.

Chan, T.W. and Baskin, B. (1988). Studying with the prince, the computer as a learning companion. First International Conference on Intelligent Tutoring Systems. Montreal, Canada, Springer.

Chan, T.W., Paiva, A., Shaffer, D.W., Kinshuk and Yang, J.C. (2007). Digital 2007. The first IEEE international workshop on digital game and intelligent toy enhanced learning, Jhongli, Taiwan, IEEE Computer Society.

Chan, T.W., Roschelle, J., Hsi, S., Kinshuk, Sharples, M. and Brown, T. (2006). One-to-one technology-enhanced learning: An opportunity for global research collaboration. Research and Practice in Technology Enhanced Learning 1 (1): pp. 3-29.

Chang, T., Hung, D. (2000). Web-based distance experiments: design and implementation. In: IEEE International Conference on Engineering Education, Taipei, Taiwan http://www.ineer.org/Events/ICEE2000/Proceedings/papers/WA4-4.pdf

Chen, C.-M., and Hsu, S.-H. (2008). Personalized Intelligent Mobile Learning System for Supporting Effective English Learning. *Educational Technology and Society*, 11 (3), 153-180.

Chen, Y.S.; Kao, T.C. and Sheu, J.P. (2003) "A mobile learning system of scaffolding bird watching learning," *Journal of Computer Assisted Learning*, Vol. 19, pp. 347-359.

Chen, Y.S.; Kao, T.C.; Yu, G.J. and Sheu, J.P. (2004) "A mobile butterfly-watching learning system for supporting independent learning," in *Wireless and Mobile Technologies in Education*, pp. 11-18.

Chi, M.T.H., Siler, S.A., Jeong, H., Yamaguchi, T., and Hausmann, R.G. (2001). Learning from human tutoring. *Cognitive Science* 25, 471-533. http://www.pitt.edu/~chi/papers/image3.pdf

Chomsky, N. (1957). *Syntactic Structures*. The Hague: Mouton.

Circsim-tutor project. http://www.cs.iit.edu/~ circsim/.

Clancey, W. (1987). *Knowledge-Based Tutoring: The Guidon Program*. MIT Press, Cambridge, MA.

Clancey, W. and Letsinger, R. (1981). Tutoring Rules for Guiding a Case Method Dialog. In Proceedings of the Sixth IJCAI, Vancouver, B.C., Morgan-Kaufmann, San Mateo, California, pp. 829-835.

Clancey, W. and Letsinger, R. (1981). NEOMYCIN: Reconfiguring a Rule-Based Expert System for Application to Teaching. Proceedings of the Seventh International Joint Conference on Artificial Intelligence Vancouver, BC: 829-835.

Clancey, W.J. (1979). Transfer of Rule-Based Expertise through a Tutorial Dialogue. Computer Science Stanford, CA, Stanford University. Ph.D.

Clancey, W.J. (1979). Tutoring rules for guiding a case method dialogue. *International Journal of Man-Machine Studies*, 11 (9), 25-49.

Clark, R.C. and Mayer, R.E. (2002). *e-Learning and the Science of Instruction: Proven Guidelines for Consumers and Designers of Multimedia Learning*. Jossy-Bass Publishers, 2002.

Cohen, P.A., Kulik, J.A. and Kulik, C. (1982). Educational outcomes of tutoring: A meta-analysis of findings. *American Educational Research Journal*, 19, 237-248.

Cohen, P.A., Kulik, J.A., and Kulik, C.C. (1982). Educational outcomes of tutoring: A Meta-analysis of findings. American Educational Research Journal 19, 237-248.

Collabrio (2001). Collabrio Technologies home page. http://www.myevents.com/Login.asp

Colling N. Udanor et. al. A Review of M-Learning Models, *Indian Journal of Computer Science and Engineering*, Vol. 1 No. 4 426-435.

Collins, A. and Brown, J.S. (1988). The computer as a tool for learning through reflection. In H. Mandl and A. Lesgold (Eds.), Learning issues for intelligent tutoring systems (pp. 1-18). New York, NY: Springer-Verlag.

Collins, A. and Stevens, A.L. (1982). Goals and strategies for inquiry teachers. In *Advances in Instructional Psychology*, Vol. 2 (ed. R. Glaser). Lawrence Erlbaum, Hillsdale, NJ.

Collins, A. (1977). Processes in acquiring knowledge. In R.C. Anderson, R.J. Spiro, and W.E. Montague (Eds.), *Schooling and the acquisition of knowledge* (pp. 339-363). Hillsdale, NJ: Erlbaum.

Collins, A. (1985). Component models of physical systems. In Proceedings of the seventh cognitive science society conference. Irvine, CA.

Collins, A., Warnock, E.H. and Passafiume, J.J. (1975). Analysis and synthesis of tutorial dialogues. In Bower, G.H. (Ed.), *The psychology of learning and motivation*, 9, (pp. 49-87). Academic Press.

Constantino-Gonzalez, M.A., Suthers, D.D. and Escamilla delos Santos, J.G. (2003). Coaching web-based collaborative learning based on problem solution differences and participation. *International Journal of Artificial Intelligence in Education* 13 (2-4): pp. 263-299.

Cooper, P.A. (1993). "Paradigm shifts in designing instruction: From behaviorism to cognitivism", *Educational Technology*, 33(5), pp. 12-19.

Corbett, A. (2001). "Cognitive Computer Tutors: Solving the Two-Sigma Problem," in *User Modeling*. Vol. 2109-2008, M. Bauer, P.J. Gmytrasiewica, and J. Vassileva, Eds.: Springer Berlin/Heidelberg, 2001, pp. 137-147.

Corbett, A., and Anderson, J.R. (2001). Locus of feedback control in computer-based tutoring: Impact on learning rate, achievement and attitudes. In Proceedings of ACM CHI 2001 Conference on Human Factors in Computing Systems (J. Jacko, A. Sears, M. Beaudouin-Lafon and R. Jacob, eds.), pp. 245-252, ACM Press, New York.

Corbett, A.T., and Anderson, J.R. (1989). Feedback timing and student control in the LISP intelligent tutoring system. In D. Bierman, J. Brueker, and J. Sandberg (Eds.), *Artificial intelligence and education: Synthesis and reflection* (pp. 64-72). Springfield, VA: IOS.

Costa, E. de B. and A. Perkusich (1996). Modelling the co-operative interactions in a teaching/learning situation. In C. Frasson, G. Gauthier and A. Lesgold (Eds.) Lecture notes in computer science: intelligent tutoring systems, Proceedings of ITS'96, third international conference on intelligent tutoring systems, Montreal: Springer-Verlag.

Crawford, C. (1981). Joint Educational Management Research Report. A Standard's Guide for the Authoring of Instructional Software. Reference Manual, Vol. II.

Crowder, N.A. (1959). Automatic tutoring by means of intrinsic programming. In Automatic Teaching: The State of the Art, Wiley, New York, pp. 109-116.

Crowley, R., Medvedeva, O. and Jukic D. (2003). SlideTutor: A Model-Tracing Intelligent Tutoring System for Teaching Microscopic Diagnosis. International Conference on AI and Education. Sydney, Australia.

Danesh, A.; Inkpen, K.; Lau, F.; Shu, K. and Booth, K. (2001). "Geney: Designing a Collaborative Activity for the Palm Handheld Computer," in *Human Factors in Computing Systems*, CHI 2001, pp. 388-395.

Daniel, D. (2001). iAuthor Object-Oriented Publishing. Retrieved June 5, 2001, from the World Wide Web: http://www.nyuonline.com/PDF/ObjectOriented.pdf

D'Avanzo, C. McNeal, A.P. (1997). Inquiry teaching in two freshman level course: Same core principles but different approaches. Student-active science: Models of innovation in college science teaching. C. D'Avanzo and A.P. McNeal. Philadelphia, PA, Saunders Press.

Davies, N.G., Dickens, S.L. and Ford, L. (1985). Tutor — a prototype ICAI system. In *Research and Development in Expert Systems* (ed. M.A. Bramer). Cambridge University Press, Cambridge.

Dear, B.L. (1991). Artificial Intelligence Techniques: Applications for Courseware Development. In: *Expert Systems and Intelligent Computer-Aided Instructions*, pp. 91-99. Educational Technology Publications, Englewood Cliffs.

Dede, C. (1986). A review and synthesis of recent research in intelligent computer-assisted instruction. *International man-machine studies*, 24, 329-353.

Derry, S.J., Levin, J.R., Osana, H., Jones, M.S. and Peterson, M. (2000). Fostering students' statistical and scientific thinking: Lessons learned from an innovative college course. *American Educational Research Journal* 37: pp. 747-773.

Derry, S.J., Hawkes, L.W. and U. Ziegler (1988). A plan-based opportunistic architecture for intelligent tutoring. In Proceedings of ITS-88, first international conference in intelligent tutoring systems, Montreal: University of Montreal.

Deubel, P. (2003). "An Investigation of Behaviorist and Cognitive Approaches to Instructional Multimedia Design", *Journal of Educational Multimedia and Hypermedia*, 12(1), pp. 63-90.

Deutsch, M. (1962). Cooperation and trust: Some theoretical notes. Nebraska symposium on motivation. M.R. Jones. Lincon NE, University of Nebraska Press: 275-319.

Dewey, J. (1938). *Experience and Education.* Macmillan Publishing Company, New York.

Dietinger, T. (2003). "Aspects of E-Learning Environments", dissertation, Graz University of Technology, Graz.

Dillenbourg, P. (1999). Introduction; What do you mean by Collaborative Learning? Collaborative Learning. Cognitive and Computational Approaches. Dillenbourg, P. (ed.), Oxford, UK, Elsevier Science Ltd.: pp. 1-19.

Dix, A., Finlay, J., Abowd, G. and R. Beale (1993). *Human-computer interaction.* Hemel, Hampstead: Prentice-Hall.

Dreyfus, H. (1999). The Primacy of Phenomenology over Logical Analysis. http://ist-socrates.berkeley.edu/~hdreyfus/

Duchastel, P. (1986). Intelligent Computer Assisted Instruction Systems: The Nature of Learner Control. *Journal of Educational Computing Research*, 2(3): 379-393.

Duffy, T.M. and Cunningham, D.J. (1996). "Constructivism: Implications for the design and delivery of instruction." In Jonassen, D.H. (Ed.): "*Handbook of Research for Educational Communications and Technology*", Simon and Schuster Macmillan, New York, pp. 170-198.

Eliasmith, C. (Ed.) (1998). Dictionary of philosophy of mind. Department of

Philosophy, Washington University in St. Louis. http://www.artsci.wustl.edu/~philos/MindDict/

Eliot, C. and Woolf, B. (1995). An Adaptive Student Centered Curriculum for an Intelligent Training System. User Modeling and User-Adapted Interaction, 5, 1, pp. 67-86.

Ellis, S., Klahr, D. and Sieglar, R. (1994). The birth, life and sometimes death of good ideas in collaborative problem solving. Annual meeting of the American Educational Research Assocation. New Orleans.

Ellson, D.G. (1976). Tutoring. In Gage, N.L. (Ed.). *The psychology of teaching methods*. Chicago, IL: University of Chicago Press.

Elsom-Cook, M. (1987). Intelligent Computer-aided instruction research at the Open University. Technical Report No: 63. Computer-Assisted Learning Research Group, The Open University, Milton Keynes.

Elsom-Cook, M. (1989). Guided Discovery Tutoring and Bounded User Modeling. In *Artificial Intelligence and Human Learning*, J. Self (Ed.), pp. 165-170.

Ertugrul, N. (2000). Towards virtual laboratories: a survey of LabVIEW-based teaching/ learning tools and future trends. *International Journal of Engineering Education* 16 (3), 171-180.

Eylon, B.S. and Linn, M.C. (1988). Learning and instruction: An examination of four research perspectives in science education. *Review of Educational Research* 58 (3): pp. 251-301.

Feigenbaum, E.A. and McCorduck, P. (1983). *The fifth generation*. New York: Addison-Wesley.

Feng, M. and Heffernan, N.T. (2007). Towards live informing and automatic analyzing of student learning: Reporting in the Assessment system. *Journal of Interactive Learning Research* (JILR) 18 (2): pp. 207-230., Chesapeake, VA: AACE.

Fischer, K. and Granoo, N. (1995). Beyond one-dimensional change: Parallel, concurrent, socially distributed processes in learning and development. *Human Development* 1995 (38): pp. 302-314.

Fletcher, J.D. (1984). Intelligent instructional systems in training. In Andriole, S.J. (Ed.). *Applications in artificial intelligence*. Petrocelli Books.

Fletcher, J.D. (1995). Meta-Analyses of the Benefit Analysis of Educational Technology,. The Costs and Effectiveness of Educational Technology. A. Melmed, RAND DRU-1205-CTI.

Fox, B.A. (1993). *The human tutorial dialogue project*. Hillsdale, NJ: Lawrence Erlbaum Associates Publishers.

Frasson, C. and Aimeur, E. (1996). A comparison of three learning strategies in intelligent tutoring systems. *Journal of Educational Computing Research* 14 (4): pp. 371-383.

Frederiksen, J.R., White, B.Y., Collins, A., and Eggan, G. (1988). Intelligent tutoring systems for electronic troubleshooting. In J. Psotka, L.D. Massey, and S.A. Mutter (Eds.), *Intelligent tutoring systems: Lessons learned* (pp. 351-368). Hillsdale, NJ: Erlbaum.

Freedman, R. and Evens, M. (1997). The Use of Multiple Knowledge Types in an Intelligent Tutoring System. Proceedings of Cognitive Science 97. Stanford, CA: 920.

Fuller, R.B. (1962). *Education automation: Freeing the scholar to return to his studies*. Carbondale, Ill: Southern Illinois University Press.

Gagne, R. (1985). *The Conditions of Learning and Theory of Instruction*. New York: Holt, Rinehard, and Winston.

Gagné, R.M. and Briggs, L.J. (1974). *Principles of Instructional Design*. Holt, Rinehart and Winston, New York.

Gardner, H. (1985). *The Mind's New Science: A History of the Cognitive Revolution*. NY: Basic Books.

Gardner, H. (1995). *Reflections on Multiple Intelligences: Myths and messages*. Phi Delta Kappan, 77, 200-209.

Garito, M.A. (1991). Artificial intelligence in education: evolution of the teaching-learning relationship. *British journal of educational technology*, 22(1), 41-47.

Genesereth, M.R. (1982). The role of plans in intelligent teaching systems. In *Intelligent Tutoring Systems* (eds. D.H. Sleeman and J.S. Brown). Academic Press, London, pp. 137-155.

Genter, D.R. (1977). The FLOW tutor: a schema-based tutorial system. Proceedings of the Fifth International Joint Conference on Artificial Intelligence, Cambridge, MA 787-790.

Gentner, D. and Stevens, A.L. (1983). (Eds.). *Mental models*. Hillsdale, NJ: Lawrence Erlbaum Associates Publishers.

Gilmore, D. and Self, J.A. (1988). The application of machine learning to intelligent tutoring systems. In *Artificial Intelligence and Human Learning: Intelligent Computer-Aided Instruction* (ed. J.A. Self). Chapman and Hall, London, pp. 179-196.

Godwin-Jones, B. (1998). Emerging technologies, dynamic Web page creation. *Language, Learning and Technology Journal* 1(2), 7-13 http://polyglot.cal.msu.edu/llt/vol1num2/emerging/default.htm

Gold, S.C. (1998). The design of an ITS-based business simulation: A new epistemology for learning. Simulation and Gaming. 29(4).

Goldman, S. (1992). Computer Resources for Supporting Student Conversations about Science Concepts. SIGCUE Outlook 21 (3): pp. 4-7.

Goldstein, I.P. and Miller, M.L. (1976). AI-based personal learning environments: directions far long term research. AI lab Memo 384. Massachussetts Institute of Technology, Cambridge, MA.

Goldstein, I.P. (1979). The genetic graph: A representation for the evolution of procedural knowledge. *International Journal of Man-Machine Studies*, 11, pp. 51-77.

Gomez, L.M., Fishman, B.J. and Pea, R.D. (1998). The CoVis Project: Building a large scale science education test bed. *Interactive Learning Environments* 6 (1-2): pp. 59-92.

Goodyear, P. and Johnson, R. (1990). Knowledge-based authoring of knowledge-based courseware. In Proc. of ICTE-7, Brussels: CEP Consultants LTD.

Goodyear, P. (1991). Research on teaching and the design of intelligent tutoring systems. In Goodyear, P. (Ed.), *Teaching knowledge and intelligent tutoring* (pp. 3-23). Norwood, NJ: Ablex Publishing Corporation.

Graesser, A.C. and Person, N.K. (1994). Question asking during tutoring. *American Educational Research Journal* 31: pp. 104-137.

Graesser, A.C., Person, N.K. and Magliano, J.P. (1995). Collaborative dialogue patterns in Naturalistic One-to-One Tutoring. *Applied Cognitive Psychology* 9, 495-522.

Graesser, A. *et al.* (2001). Intelligent tutoring systems with conversational dialogue. *AI Magazine*, pages 39(51).

Graham, D.T., McNeil, J., Pettiford, L. (2000). *Untangled Web: Developing Teaching on the Internet*. Pearson Education, Harlow.

Gram, T., Mark, T., and McGreal, R. (1998). A survey of new media development and delivery software for internet-based learning. http://teleeducation.nb.ca/content/slideshows/newmedia.ppt

Grandbastien, M. (1999). Teaching expertise is at the core of ITS research. *International journal of artificial intelligence in education*, 10, 335-349.

Greeno, J., Collins, A. and Resnick, L.B. (1996). *Cognition and Learning. Handbook of Educational Psychology*, R. Calfee and D. Berliner (Eds.), New York, MacMillan.

Greer, J.E., McCalla, G.I., Collins, J.A., Kumar, V.S., Meagher, P. and Vassileva, J.I. (1998). Supporting peer help and collaboration in distributed workplace environments. *International Journal of Artificial Intelligence in Education* 9: pp. 159-177.

GrignettL M., Hausman, C.L. and Gould, L. (1975). An intelligent on-line assistant and tutor: NLS-SCHOLAR. Proceedings of the National Computer Conference, 775-781.

Haddad, Wadi D. (1998). Education for All in the Age of Globalization-The Role of Information Technology. In Claudio de Moura Castro (ed.). *Education in the Information Age*. Washington: Inter-American Development Bank.

Hafkin, Nancy, and Taggart, Nancy. (2001). Gender, Information Technology, and Developing Countries. Washington: Learn Link, Academy for Educational Development.

Hai Zhuge and Yanyan Li. (2004). Active e-course for constructivist learning. In Proceedings WWW, 2004.

Halff, H.M. (1988). Curriculum and instruction in automated tutors. In Polson, M. C. and Richardson, J. J. (Eds.). *Foundations of intelligent tutoring systems* (pp. 79-108). Hillsdale, NJ: Lawrence Erlbaum Associates Publishers.

Han, S.G., Lee, S.G., Jo, G.S. (2005). Case-based tutoring systems for procedural problem solving on the www. *Expert Systems with Applications* 29(3), 73-582.

Hancock, C., Kaput, J.J. and Goldsmith, L.T. (1992). Authentic inquiry with data: Critical bariers to classroom implementation. *Educational Psychologist* 27 (3): pp. 337-364.

Harasim, L. (1999). A Framework for Online Learning: The Virtual-U. IEEE Computer. http://www.telelearn.ca/g_access/news/r9044.pdf

Harasim, L.M., Hiltz, S.R., Teles, L., and Turoff, M. (1995). *Learning Networks: A Field Guide to Teaching and Learning Online*. Cambridge, MA: MIT Press.

Hartley, J.R. and Sleeman, D.H. (1973). Towards more intelligent teaching systems. *International Journal of Man-Machine Studies*, 5, 215-236.

Hartley, J.R. (1993). Interacting with Multimedia. University Computing, No. 15, pp. 129-136.

Hartley, J.R. (1973). The design and evaluation of an adaptive teaching system. *International Journal of Man-Machine Studies*, 5, 421-436.

Hasemann, K. (1981). On difficulties with fractions. Educational Studies in Mathematics, 12, 71-287.

Hayman, R.T. (1974). Ways of teaching, 2nd edition. J.B. Lippincott Company.

Heath, E.F. (1998). Two cheers and a pint of worry: An on-line course in political and social philosophy. *Journal of Asynchronous Learning Networks* 2: pp. 15-33.

Heffernan, N.T., and Koedinger, K.R. (1997). The composition effect in symbolizing: the role of symbol production versus text comprehension. In Proceeding of the Nineteenth Annual Conference of the Cognitive Science Society, pp. 307-312, Lawrence Erlbaum Associates, Hillsdale, NJ.

Heffernan, N.; Koedinger, K.R. and Aleven, V. (2003) "Tools towards Reducing the Costs of Designing, Building, and Testing Cognitive Models," in *Behavior Representation in Modeling and Simulation*, BRIMS 2003.

Hietala, P. and Niemirepo, T. (1998). The Competence of Learning Companion Agents. International Journal of Artificial Intelligence in Education 9: pp. 178-192.

Hmelo-Silver, C.E. (2002). Collaborative ways of knowing: Issues in facilitation. Computer Support of Collaborative Learning. Stahl, G. (ed.), Hilldale, NJ, Erlbaum: pp. 199-208.

Hollan, J.D. Hutchins, E.L. and Weitzman, L. (1984). STEAMER: an interactive inspectable simulation-based training system. *AI Magazine*, 5, 15-27.

Holt, J. (1967). How Children Fail. New York: Pitman Publishing.

Hong, J. (2004). Guided programming and automated error analysis in an intelligent prolog tutor. *Int. J. Hum.-Comput. Stud.* 61, 4, 505-534.

Hooper, S. and Hannafin, M.J. (1991). "The effects of group composition on achievement, interaction, and learning efficiency during computer-based cooperative instruction". *Educational Technology Research and Development*, 39(3), pp. 27-40.

Howe, C., Tolmie, A., Anderson, A. and MacKenzie, M (1992). C onceptual knowledge in physics: The role of group interaction in computer-supported teaching. *Learning and Instruction* 2: pp. 161-183.

Hunt, E. and Minstrell, J. (1994). A cognitive approach to the teaching of physics. Classroom lessons: Integrating cognitive theory and classroom practice. McGilly, K. (ed.), Cambridge, MA, MIT Press.

Hyperwave Information Management, Inc. (1999). Hyperwave Administrator's Guide, Hyperwave Information Server, Version 5.1, Westford, USA, September. http://www.hyperwave.com

Iowa Public Television (1997). Earth Trails.

Jackson, R.H. (2001). Web Based Learning Resources Library. http://www.outreach.utk.edu/weblearning/

Jameson, A. (1995). Numerical uncertainty management in user and student modeling: An overview of systems and issues. User Model. User-Adapt. Interact. 5, 4, 193-251.

Jaques, P.A., Vicari, R.M. (2006). A BDI approach to infer student's emotions in an intelligent learning environment. Computers and Education http://dx.doi.org/10.1016/j.compedu.2005.09.002

Jensen, A.R. (1998). *The g factor: the science of mental ability*. Westport, CT: Praeger.

Johnson, W.L. and Soloway, E. Proust (1985). Knowledge-based program understanding. *IEEE Transactions on Software Engineering* 11, 3, 267-275.

Jonas, S. (1978). Medical mystery. New York: W.W. Norton and Company.

Jones, A.A., Bagford, L.W. and Wallen, E.A. (1979). Strategies for teaching. The Scarecrow Press.

Justen, J.E., Waldrop, T.M., and Adams, T.M. (1990). Effects of paired versus individual user computer-assisted instruction and type of feedback on student achievement. *Educational Technology*, 30(7), 51-53.

Kalkowski, P. (2001). Peer and cross-age tutoring. www.nwrel.org/scpd/sirs/9/c018.html

Kanflo, T.J., Sagert, P.A. (1994). Teaching the design of manufacturing systems using simulation. *European Journal of Engineering Education* 19(1), 117-123.

Kashihara, A., A. Sugano, K. Matsumura, T. Hirashima and J. Toyoda. (1994). A Cognitive Load Application Approach to Tutoring. In Proceedings of the Fourth International Conference on User Modeling, pp. 163-168.

Kassim, A.A., Kazi, S.A. and Ranganath, S. (2004), "A Webbased Intelligent Learning Environment for Digital Systems". *International Journal for Engineering Education*, Vol 20, No 1, pp 13-23, 2004.

Katz, S., and Lesgold, A. (1993). The role of the tutor in computer-based collaborative learning situations. In S.P. Lajoie and S.J. Derry (Eds.), Computers as cognitive tools (pp. 289-318). Hillsdale, NJ: Erlbaum.

Kay, J. (1995). T he UM Toolkit for Cooperative User Modeling. User Modeling and User Adapted Interaction 4 (3): pp. 149-196.

Kearsley, G. (1987). Overview. In Kearsley, G. (Ed.). Artificial intelligence and instruction: Applications and methods (pp. 3-10). Reading, MA: Addison-Wesley Publishing Company.

Kearsley, G. (2003). Explorations in Learning and Instruction: The Theory Into Practice Database. http://tip.psychology.org

Kearsley, G. Learning and Instruction: The TIP Database. http://gwis2.circ.gwu.edu/~kearsley/.

Keegan, D. (2005). "The Incorporation of Mobile Learning into Mainstream Education and Training," in 4th World Conference on MLearning.

Keller, J.M. and Suzuki, K. (1988). "Use of the ARCS motivation model in courseware design." In Jonassen, D.H. (Ed.): "Instructional design for microcomputer courseware", Lawrence Erlbaum Associates, Hillsdale, pp. 401-434.

Khan, B.H. (ed.) (1997), *Web Based Instruction*. Englewood Cliffs, New Jersey: Educational Technology Publications.

Khan, B.H. (2000). A Framework for Web-Based Learning. http://bookstoread.com/framework/

Khuwaja, R.A., Evens, M.W., Rovick, A.A. and Michael, J.A. (1992). Knowledge representation for an intelligent tutoring system based on a multilevel causal model. Proceedings of the ITS'92 (pp. 217-224). New York: Springer-Verlag.

Khuwaja, R.A., Evens, M.W., Rovick, A.A. and Michael, J.A. (1993). Building the domain expert for a cardiovascular physiology tutor. Proceedings of the 6th Annual IEEE Computer-Based Medical Systems Symposium (pp. 165-170). Ann Arbor, MI: IEEE Computer Society.

Kibby, M. and Mayer, T. (1990). Learning About Learning from Hypertext. In Hypermedia for Learning, D. Jonassen (Ed.), pp. 135-143, Springer-Verlag.

Kid Works 2 (1992). Davidson and Associates, Inc., P.O. Box 2961 Torrance CA 90509.

Kimball, R.A. (1982). A self-improving tutor for symbolic integration. In *Intelligent*

Tutoring Systems (eds D.H. Sleeman and J.S. Brown). Academic Press, London, pp. 283-307.

Kinshuk, Patel, A. (1997). A Conceptual Framework for Internet Based Intelligent Tutoring Systems. In: Behrooz, A. (ed.) *Knowledge Transfer*, vol. 2, pp. 117-124. pAce, London

Kirschner, P., Sweller, J., and Clark, R.E. (2006). Why minimally guided learning does not work: An analysis of the failure of discovery learning, problem-based learning, experiential learning and inquiry-based learning. Educational Psychologist, 41(2), 75-86.

Kiser, L. "Spatial-visual Ability: Can Computer Visualization Facilitate Achievement?" Educational Technology, 27(5):36-40, 1987.

Koffman, E.B. and Blount, S.E. (1975). Artificial intelligence and automatic programming in CA1. *Artificial Intelligence*, 6, 215-234.

Kohl, Herbert. (1996). Foreword In Andrea R. Gooden. *Computers in the Classroom: How Teachers and Students Are Using Technology to Transform Learning.* Josse-Bass.

Kolb, D.A. (1984): "Experiential learning: Experience as the source of learning and development", Prentice-Hall, Englewood Cliffs.

Kolodner, J.L. (Ed.). (1988). Proceedings of the First Case-Based Reasoning Workshop. Los Altos, CA: Morgan Kaufmann Publishers, Inc.

Koschmann, T.D., Myers, A.C., Feltovich, P.J. and Barrows, H.S. (1994). Using technology to assist in realizing effective learning and instruction: A principled approach to the use of computers in collaborative learning. *Journal of the Learning Sciences* 3 (3): pp. 225-262.

Krajcik, J., Blumenfeld, P.C., Marx, R.W., Bass, K.M., Fredricks, J. and Soloway, E. (1998). Inquiry in project-based science classrooms: initial attempts by middle school students. *The Journal of the Learning Sciences* 7 (3 and 4): pp. 313-350.

Kreijns, K., Kirschner, P. and Jochems, W. (2003). Identifying the pitfalls for social interaction in computer-supported collaborative learning environments: A review of the research. Computers in Human Behavior 1[a] (3): pp. 335-353.

Kuhn, D. (1970). The structure of scientific revolutions, (Original work published 1962)., Rev. ed. University of Chicago Press, Chicago.

Kuhn, D. (1991). T he skills of argument. Cambridge, New York.

Kulik, C.C. and Kulik, J.A. (1991). Effectiveness of Computer-Based Instruction: An Updated Analysis. Computers in Human Behavior 7, 75-94.

Kulik, J.A. (1994). Meta-Analytic Studies of Findings on Computer-Based Instruction. In Technology Assessment in Education and Training, (E.L. Baker and H.F. O'Neil, Jr., eds.), pp. 9-33, Erlbaum Associates, Hillsdale, NJ.

Kulik, J.A., Bangert, Robert, L., and Williams, G.W. (1983). Effects of Computer-Based Teaching on Secondary School Students. *Journal of Educational Psychology* 75(1), 19-26.

Kulik, J.A., Kulik, C.C. and Bangert-Drowns, R.L. (1985). Effectiveness of Computer-Based Education in Elementary Schools. *Computers in Human Behavior* 1(1), 59-74.

Kyza, E.A. and Edelson, D.C. (2003). Reflective inquiry: What is it and how can software scaffolds help? Annual Meeting of the American Educational Research Association, Chicago, IL.

Kyza, E.A., Zacharia, Z. and Constantinou, C.P. (2006). Stochasmos: A web-based learning environment for supporting reflective inquiry. Workshop on Inquiry Learning, Building Bridge to Practice. University of Twent Conference, The Netherlands.

Lai, C.H.; Yang, J.C.; Chen, F.C.; Ho, C.W. and Chan, T.W. (2007). "Affordances of mobile technologies for experiential learning: the interplay of technology and pedagogical practices," *Journal of Computer Assisted Learning*, vol. 23, pp. 326-337.

Lajoie, S. and A. Lesgold. (1992). Apprenticeship Training in the Workplace: Computer-Coached Practice Environment as a New Form of Apprenticeship. In *Intelligent Instruction by Computer*, Farr and Psotka, eds., Taylor and Francis, Washington, DC, pp. 15-36.

Lajoie, S.P. (1993). Computer Environments as Cognitive Tools for Enhancing Learning. Computers as Cognitive Tools, Lajoie, S. and Derry, S., eds., Lawrence Erlbaum Associates, NJ, pp. 261-288.

Lajoie, S.P., Greer, J.E., Munsie, S.D., Wilkie, T.V., Guerrera, C., and Aleong P. (1995). Establishing an argumentation environment to foster scientific reasoning with BioWorld. International Conference on Computers in Education D. Jonassen, and G. McCalla, (eds.) Association for the Advancement of Computing in Education: 89-96.

Lampert, M. (1984). Teaching about thinking and thinking about teaching. *Journal of Curriculum Studies*, 6, 1-18.

Lampert, M. (1986). Knowing, doing, and teaching multiplication. Cognition and Instruction, 3(4), 305-342.

Lane, H.C. and VanLehn, K. (2005). Teaching the tacit knowledge of programming to novices with natural language tutoring. Computer Science Education, 15(3), 183-201. http://people.ict.usc.edu/~lane/papers/lane05-CSE-NLT.pdf

Larkin, J.H., Chabay, R.W. (eds.) (1992). Computer-Assisted Instruction and Intelligent Tutoring Systems: Shared Goals and Complementary Approaches, pp. 151-186. Lawrence Erlbaum and Assoc., Hillsdale.

Larkin, J.H., Chabay, R.W. (eds.) (1992). Computer-Assisted Instruction and Intelligent Tutoring Systems: Shared Goals and Complementary Approaches, pp. 151-186. Lawrence Erlbaum and Assoc., Hillsdale.

Lave, J. and Wenger, E. (1991). Situated Learning: Legitimate Peripheral Participation. Cambridge University Press, Cambridge.

Lawler, R., and Yazdani, M. (Eds.). (1987). *Artificial Intelligence and Education*, Volume 1. Norwood, NJ: Ablex.

Lee, S. and Lee, Y.H.K. (1991). Effects of Learner-Control Versus Program-Control Strategies on Computer-Aided Learning of Chemistry Problems: For Acquisition of Review? *Journal of Educational Psychology*, 83(4): 491-498.

Leinhardt, G. and Greeno, J.G. (1991). The cognitive skill of teaching. In Goodyear, P. (Ed.), *Teaching knowledge and intelligent tutoring* (pp. 233-268). Norwood, NJ: Ablex Publishing Corporation.

Lelouche, R. (1998). The successive contributions of computers to education: A survey. *European Journal of Engineering Education*, 23(3):297{308.

Lesgold, A. (1988). Towards a theory of curriculum for use in designing intelligent instructional systems. In Mandl, H. and Lesgold, A. (Eds.), Learning issues for intelligent tutoring systems (pp. 114 137). New York: Springer-Verlag.

Libbrecht, P. *et al.* (2001). The active math learning environment system description. In Calculemus Workshop at IJCAR, pages 173(177).

Linn, M.C. (2006). WISE teachers: Using technology and inquiry for science instruction. Meaningful Learning Using Technology: What Educators Need to Know. E.A.A. and and R.E. Floden. New York, Teachers College Press: 45-69.

Littman, D. (1991). Tutorial planning schemas. In Goodyear, P. (Ed.), *Teaching knowledge and intelligent tutoring* (pp. 107-122). Norwood, NJ: Ablex Publishing Corporation.

Liu, T.C., Wang, H.Y., Liang, J.K., Chan, T.W., Yang, J.C. and Ko, H.W. (2003). Wireless and mobile technologies to enhance teaching and learning. *Journal of Computer Assisted Learning* 19 (3): pp. 371-382.

Lonsdale, P.; Byrne, W.; Beale, R.; Sharples, M. and Baber, C. (2004) "Spatial and context awareness for mobile learning in a museum," in Computer Supported Collaborative Learning Workshop on Spatial Awareness and Collaboration.

Maedche, A., and Staab, S. (2000). Semi-automatic engineering of ontologies from text. In 12th International Conference on Software Engineering and Knowledge Engineering, pp. 231-239.

Major, N. and H. Reichgelt. (1992). COCA-A Shell for Intelligent Tutoring Systems. In Proceedings of Intelligent Tutoring Systems, Frasson, C., Gautheir, G. and McCalla, G., eds., Springer Verlag, Berlin.

Major, N. (1995). REDEEM: Creating Reusable Intelligent Courseware. In Proceedings of the International Conference on Artificial Intelligence in Education., Greer, J., ed., AACE, Charlottesville, VA, pp. 75-82.

Mandl, H. and Lesgold, A. (eds.) (1988). *Learning Issues for Intelligent Tutoring Systems*. Springer-Verlag~ London.

Martin, B., and Mitrovic, A. (2002a). Automatic problem generation in constraint-based tutors. In *Intelligent Tutoring Systems*, pp. 388-398.

Martin, B., and Mitrovic, A. (2002b). Wetas: A web-based authoring system for constraint-based its. In Adaptive Hypermedia and Adaptive Web-Based Systems, Second International Conference, pp. 543-546.

Martin, J. and VanLehn, K. (in press) Student assessment using Bayesian nets. *International Journal of Human-Computer Studies*, Vol. 42.

Mathan, S. (2003). Recasting the feedback debate: Benefits of tutoring error detection and correction skills. Carnegie-Mellon University, Pittsburgh, PA.

McArthur, D., Stasz, C. and Zmuidzinas, M. (1990). Tutoring techniques in algebra. *Cognition and Instruction*, 7, 197-244.

McCalla, G.I., Greer, J.E. and SCENT Team (1988). Intelligent advising in problem solving domains: the SCENT-3 architecture. In Proceedings of the International Conference on Intelligent Tutoring Systems, Montreal, Canada, pp. 124-131.

McCarthy, J. (1959). Programs with Common Sense. In Mechanization of Thought Processes, Proceedings of the Symposium of the National Physics laboratory, pages 77-84, London, U.K.

——, (1959). Programs With Common Sense. Proceedings of the Teddington Conference on the Mechanization of Thought Processes. http://www-formal.stanford.edu/jmc/mcc59/mcc59.html

——, (1989). Artificial Intelligence, Logic and Formalizing Common Sense. In *Philosophical Logic and Artificial Intelligence*, Richmond Thomason (Ed.), Kluver Academic.

——, (1996). Defining AI Research: a Collection of Essays and Reviews. CSLI lecture notes: no. 49. Centre for the Study of Language and Information. Cambridge University Press.

McGuire, C.H., Foley, R.P., Gorr, A., Richards, R.W. and Associates (1983). *Handbook of health professions education.* San Francisco, CA: Jossey-Bass Publishers.

McKendree, J. (1990). Effective feedback content for tutoring complex skills. *Human Computer Interaction*, 5, 381-413.

McLeod, G. (2003). "Learning Theory and Instructional Design", Learning Matters, 2, pp. 35-43.

McMillan, S., Emme, D., and Berkowitz, M. (1980). Instructional Planners: Lessons Learned. In Psotka, Massey, and Mutter (Eds.), Intelligent Tutoring Systems, Lessons Learned. Hillsdale, NJ: Lawrence Erlbaum, pp. 229-256.

Merrill, D.C., Reiser, B.J. Merrill, S.K., and Landes, S. (1995). Tutoring: guided learning by doing. Cognition and Instruction 13(3), 315-372.

Merrill, D.C., Reiser, B.J., Ranney, M. and Trafton, J.G. (1992). Effective tutoring techniques: A comparison of human tutors and intelligent tutoring systems. *Journal of the Learning Sciences*, 2, 277-305.

Merrill, M.D. (1980). Learner control in computer based learning, Computers and Education, 4:77-95.

Merrill, M.D. (1983). Component Display Theory. In Instructional-design theories and models: An overview of their current status,. C.M. Reigeluth. (ed.). Hillsdale, NJ: Lawrence Erlbaum, pp. 279-333.

Merrill, M.D. (2001). "Components of Instruction Toward a Theoretical Tool for Instructional Design", *Instructional Science*, 29(4), pp. 291-310.

Michael, J.A. (1993). Teaching problem solving in small groups. Ann. NY Acad. Sci., 701, 37-48.

——, and Modell, H. (1993). Life science education: Reflections on some of the challenges facing us. Ann. NY Acad. Sci., 701, 83-90.

Mike Sharples, Josie Taylor, Giasemi Vavoula (2005). Towards a Theory of Mobile Learning. *International Journal of Continuing Engineering Education and Life Long Learning*, 12(5/6), 504-520.

Miller, M.L., and Lucado, S.R. (1992). Integrating intelligent tutoring, computer-based training, and interactive video in a prototype maintenance trainer. In M.J. Farr and J. Psotka (Eds.), *Intelligent instruction by computer*: Theory and practice (pp. 127-150). Washington, D.C.: Taylor and Francis.

Mitchell, T. (1997). *Machine Learning*. McGraw Hill.

Mitrovic, A., Mayo, M., Suraweera, P., and Martin, B. (2001). Constraint-based tutors: A success story. In *Industrial and Engineering Applications of Artificial Intelligence and Expert Systems*, pp. 931-940.

MEDIA 2005), AACE, Montreal, pp. 3275-3278.

Molnar, A.R. (1990). Computers in Education: A Historical Perspective of the Unfinished Task. *T.H.E. Journal* 18 (4): pp. 80-83.

Muehlenbrock, M. (2001). Action-based Collaboration Analysis for Group Learning. IOS Press, Amsterdam.

Munro, A., Johnson, M.C., Pizzini, Q.A., D.S. Surmon, d. M.T., and Wogulis, J.L. (1997). Authoring simulation-centred tutors with rides. *International Journal of Artificial Intelligence in Education* 8, 284-316.

Murphy, K.L. and Cifuentes, L. (2001). "Using Web tools, collaborating, and learning online", Distance Education, 22(2), pp. 285-305.

Murray, T. and B. Woolf. (1992). Results of Encoding Knowledge with Tutor Construction Tools. In Proceedings of the Tenth National Conference on Artificial Intelligence, San Jose, CA, July, pp. 17 23.

Murray, T. (1996). Having It All, Maybe: Design Tradeoffs in ITS Authoring Tools. In Proceedings of the Third International Conference on Intelligent Tutoring Systems, Montreal.

Murray, T. (1997). Expanding the knowledge acquisition bottleneck for intelligent tutoring systems. *International J. of Artificial Intelligence in Education*. Vol. 8, No. 3-4, pp. 222-232.

Murray, W.R. (1987). Automatic program debugging for intelligent tutoring systems. *Computational Intelligence*, 3(1).

Murray, W.R. (1998). A Practical Approach to Bayesian Student Modeling. In B. Goettl, H. Halff, C.

Myers, I. (1978). "Myers-Briggs type indicator", Consulting Psychologists Press, Palo Alto.

Naisbitt, J. (1984). *Megatrends: Ten new directions transforming our lives*. New York: Warner Books.

National Research Council (1996). *National Science Education standards*. National Academy Press, Washington, DC.

National Science Foundation (1983). Educating America for the 21th century. Washington, D.C.

Navigli, R., Velardi, P., and Gangemi, A. (2003). Ontology learning and its application to automated terminology translation. *IEEE Intelligent Systems* 18, 1, 22-31.

Newman, D., Goldman, S.V., Brienne, D., Jackson, I. and Magzamen, S. (1989). Computer Mediation of Science Collaboative Investigations. *Educational Computing Research* 5: pp. 151-166.

Niemiec, R. and Walberg, H.J. (1987). Comparative effects of computer-assisted instruction: A synthesis of reviews. *Journal of Educational Computing Research*, 3, 19-37.

Noble, D. (2001). "Fool's gold: Digital diploma mills, Part V". http://communication.ucsd.edu/dl/ddm5.html (2005-10-22).

Nwana, H.S. (1989). An iterative-style approach to constructing intelligent tutoring systems in mathematics. PhD Thesis, Aston University, Birmingham.

Nwana, H.S. (1990). Intelligent Tutoring Systems: An Overview. *Artificial Intelligence*, 4, pp. 251-277.

Nwana, H.S.C. (1990). The anatomy of FITS: a mathematic tutor. *Intelligent Tutoring Media*, 1(2).

Ohlsson, S. (1987). Some Principles of Intelligent Tutoring. In Lawler and Yazdani (Eds.), *Artificial Intelligence and Education*, Volume 1. Ablex: Norwood, NJ, pp. 203-238.

Ok-choon, P., Ray, S.P. and Seidel, R.J. (19871 Intelligent CAI: old winein new bottles or a new vintage? In *Artificial Intelligence and Instruction: Instruction and Methods*, Addison-Wesley, Reading, MA, pp. 11-43.

Olsen, J.B. (1991). The Four Generations of Computerised Testing: toward Increased Use of AI and Expert Systems. In: *Expert Systems and Intelligent Computer-*

Aided Instructions, pp. 66-71. Educational Technology Publications, Englewood Cliffs.

O'Shea, R. and Self. (1983). *Learning and Teaching with Computers*. Harvester Press, Sussex.

O'Shea, T. (1982). A self-improving quadratic tutor. In *Intelligent Tutoring Systems* (eds. D.H. Sleeman and J.S. Brown). Academic Press, London, pp. 283-307.

O'Shea, T. Bornat, R., Du Boulay. B., EisenstadL M. (1984). Tools for creating intelligent computer tutors. In *Artificial and Human Intelligence* (eds ?. Elithorn and R. Beneiji). Elsevier, North Holland, pp. 181-199.

Osin, Luis (1998). Computers in Education in Developing Countries: Why and How? *Education and Technology Series*, Vol. 3, No. 1. Washington: The World Bank.

Paivio, A. (1990). "Mental representations: A dual coding approach", 2nd ed., Oxford University Press, Oxford.

Palincsar, A.S., and Brown, A.L. (1984). Reciprocal teaching of comprehension-fostering and comprehension-monitoring activities. *Cognition and Instruction*, 1, 117-175.

Papert, S. (1980). *Mindstorms: Children, Computers and Powerful Ideas*. Basic Books, New York.

Park, O.C. and Tennyson, R.D. (1980). Adaptive Design Strategies for Selecting Number and Presentation Order of Examples in Coordinate Concept Acquisition. *Journal of Educational Psychology*, 72: 362-370.

Park, O., Perez, R.S. and Seidel, R.J. (1987). Intelligent CAI: Old wine in new bottles, or a new vintage? In Kearsley, G. (Ed.). *Artificial intelligence and instruction: Applications and methods* (pp. 11 45). Reading, MA: Addison-Wesley Publishing Company.

Parlett, J.W. and Redfield, C.L. (Eds.), *Intelligent tutoring systems: Evolutions in design* (pp. 1-11). Hillsdale, NJ: Lawrence Erlbaum Associates Publishers.

Pask, G. (1976). *Conversation Theory: Applications in Education and Epistemology*. Elsevier Science.

Patel, A., Russell, D. (1998). An initial framework of contexts for designing usable intelligent tutoring systems. Information Services and Use, 18(1/2).

Patil, A.S. (2004). Issues in the design and development of Web-based computer-assisted tutorials and laboratory procedures in basic electrical engineering. Unpublished masters dissertation, Monash University, Melbourne.

Pea, R. (1994). Seeing what we build together: Distributed multimedia learning environments for transformative communications. *Journal of the Learning Sciences* 3 (3): pp. 285-299.

Peachey, D.R. and McCalla~ G.I. (1986). Using planning techniques in intelligent tutoring systems. International]ournal of Man-Machine Studies, 24, 77-98.

Piaget, J. (1954). The construction of reality in the child. New York: Ballentine Books.

——, and Inhelder, B. (1969). *The psychology of the child*. Basic Books, New York.

Picard, R.W., Papert, S., Bender, W., Blumberg, B., Breazeal, C., Cavallo, D., Machover, T., Resnick, M., Roy, D. and Strohecker, C. (2004). Affective Learning—A Manifesto. *B.T. Technical Journal* 22 (4): pp. 253-269.

Pierroux, P. (2007). "Mobility In Learning: Meaning Making Across Classroom and Museum Settings," in International Association For Development Of The Information Society Mobile Learning.

Plato (1924). Laches, Protagoras, Meno, and Euthydemus. (W.R.M. Lamb, trans.) Harvard University Press, Cambridge, Mass.

Polson, M.C. and Richardson, J.J. (1988). (Eds.). Foundation of intelligent tutoring systems. Hillsdale, NJ: Lawrence Erlbaum Associates Publishers.

Potashnik, Michael (1996). Chile's Learning Network. Education and Technology Series, Vol. 1, no. 2. Washington: World Bank.

——, and Adkins, Douglas. (1996). Cost Analysis of Information Technology Projects in Education: Experiences from Developing Countries. Education and Technology Series, vol. 1, no. 3. Washington: World Bank.

Potter, J., Blankenship, J., and Carlsmith, L.(1999). So that every child can read...America reads community tutoring partnerships. Portland, OR: NorthWest Regional Education Laboratories. www.nwrel.org/ecc/steccr/index.html

Powell, A.M. (1997). Academic tutoring and mentoring: A literature review. Retrieved November 6, 2002, from www.library.ca.gov/CRB/97/11/97011.pdf

Prentzas, J. *et al.* (2001). Architectural aspects of a web-based its for teaching new information technologies. In Proceedings of ED-MEDIA.

Psotka, J., Massey, L.D., and Mutter, S.A. (Eds.). (1988). *Intelligent tutoring systems: lessons learned.* Hillsdale, NJ: Lawrence Erlbaum.

Pudlowski, Z.J. (1995). Major Issues in Developing Computer-Aided Authoring Programs for Engineering Education. In: Pudlowski, Z.J., *et al.* (eds.) Computers in Electrical Engineering Education-Research, Development and Application, pp. 23-31. EEERG and USICEE, Melbourne.

Putnam, R.T. (1987). Structuring and adjusting contents for students: A study of live and simulated tutoring of addition. *American Educational Research Journal*, 24, 1, 13-48.

Qiu, L., and Riesbeck, C. (2004). An incremental model for developing computer-based learning environments for problem-based learning. In ICALT.

Raiciu, T. (2005). "190.5 Million Cell Phones Sold-In the second quarter of 2005".

Reed, J.A., Afjeh, A.A. (1998). Developing interactive educational software for the World Wide Web with Java. *Computers and Education* 30(3-4), 183-194.

Regian, J.W., Seidel, R.J., Schuler, J. and Radtke, P. (1996). Functional Area Analysis of Intelligent Computer-Assisted Instruction, Training and Personnel Systems Science and Technology Evaluation and Management Committee, USA.

Reigeluth, C. (1983). The Elaboration Theory of Instruction. In Reigeluth (Ed.), *Instructional Design Theories and Models*. Hillsdale, NJ: Lawrence Erlbaum.

Resnick, L.B. (1983). Mathematics and science learning: A new conception. *Science*, 220, 477-478.

Rheingold, H. (1993/2000). *The Virtual Community: Homesteading on the Electronic Frontier*. Cambridge, MA: MIT Press.

Rich, E. (1979). User modelling via stereotypes. *Cognitive Science*, 3, 329-354.

Richards, T.C. and Fukuzawa, J. (1989). "A Checklist for Evaluation of Courseware Authoring Systems." *Educational Technology*, 29(10):24-29.

Ridgway, J. (1988). Of course ICAI is impossible,. worse though, it might be seditious. In *Artificial Intelligence and Human Learning: Intelligent computer-aided instruction* (ed. J.A. Self). Chapman and Hall. London, pp. 28-48.

——, (1989). Of course ICAI is impossible...worse though it might be seditious. In Artificial Intelligence and Human Learning, J. Self (Ed.), pp. 28-48.

Riesbeck, C.K., and Schank, R.C. (1990). From training to teaching: Techniques for case-based ITS. In H. Burns, C. Luckhardt, and J. Parlett (Eds.), *Knowledge architectures in intelligent tutoring systems*. Orlando, FL: Academic Press.

Robotham, D. (1995). Self-Directed Learning: The Ultimate Learning Style. *Journal of European Industrial Training*, Vol. 19, No. 7, pp. 3-7.

Roorda, J., Cartwright, T. (1994). Engineering design simulation: a computer-based teaching environment. *European Journal of Engineering Education* 19(1), 105-115.

Rosatelli, M. and Self, J.A. (2002). A case study system for distance learning. *International Journal of Artificial Intelligence in Education* 12: pp. 1-25.

Rosatelli, M., Self, J.A. and Thirty, M. (2000). LeCS: A collaborative case study system. Fifth International Conference on Intelligent Tutoring Systems. Montreal, Canada: 242-251.

Roschelle, Jeremy, Jim Kaput, Walter Stroup, Ted M. Kahn (1998). Scaleable Integration of Educational Software: Exploring the Promise of Component Architectures, *Journal of Interactive Media in Education*. http://www-jime.open.ac.uk/98/6

Rosé, C.P., Jordan, P., Ringenberg, M., Siler, S., VanLehn, K., and Weinstein, A. (2001). Interactive conceptual tutoring in Atlas-Andes. In J.D. Moore, C.L. Redfield, and W.L. Johnson (Eds.), *Artificial Intelligence in Education: AI-ED in the Wired and Wireless Future* (pp. 256-266). Amsterdam: IOS Press.

Rosé, C.P., VanLehn, K. and NLT Group, (2003). Is Human Tutoring Always More Effective than Reading? Proceedings of AIED Workshop on Tutorial Dialogue Systems: With a View towards the Classroom: Vol. VI.

Ross, P. (1987). Intelligent tutoring systems, *Journal of Computer Assisted* Learning, 3, 194-203.

Ross, P., Jones, J. and Millington, P. (1987). User modelling in intelligent teaching and tutoring. In *Trends in Computer Assisted Instruction* (eds. R. Lewis and E.D. Tagg). Blackwell, London, pp. 32-44.

Ross, S.M., Rakow, E.A., and Bush, A.J. (1980). Instructional Adaptation for Self-Managed Learning Systems. *Journal of Educational Psychology*, 72: 312-320.

Rothstein, W.G. (1987). *American medical schools and the practice of medicine*. New York: Oxford University Press.

Rudenstine, Neil L. (1997). "The Internet and Education: A Close Fit." The Chronicle of Higher Education.

Russell, D.M. (1988). IDE: The interpreter. In Psotka, J., Massey, L.D. and Mutter, S.A. (Eds.), *Intelligent tutoring systems: Lessons learned* (pp. 323-349). Hillsdale, NJ: Lawrence Erlbaum Associates Publishers.

Scardamalia, M., Bereiter, C., McLean, R.S., Swallo, J. and Woodruff, E. (1989). Computer-supported intentional learning environments. *Journal of Educational Computing Research* 5 (1): pp. 51-68.

Scardamalia, M. and Bereiter, C. (1991). Higher levels of agency for children in knowledge building: A challenge for the design of new knowledge media. *Journal of the Learning Sciences* 1: pp. 37-68.

Schacter, J. (2003). The Impact of Education Technology on Student Achievement: What the Most Current Research has to Say, http://www.mff.org/publications/publications.taf?page=161

Schank, R. (1994). Active learning through multimedia. IEEE Multimedia 1 (1): pp. 69-78.

Schank, R.C. (1982). *Dynamic memory: A theory of learning in computers and people.* Cambridge, MA: Cambridge University Press.

Schauble, L., Glaser, R., Duschl, R.A., Schulze, S. and John, J. (1995). Students' understanding of the objectives and procedures of experimentation in the science classroom. *Journal of the Learning Sciences* 4 (2): pp. 131-166.

Schoenfeld, A.H. (1985). *Mathematical problem solving.* New York: Academic Press.

Self, J.A. (1985). A Perspective on Intelligent Computer-Aided Instruction. *Journal of Computer Assisted Learning* 1: pp. 159-166.

Self, J.A. (1987b). Realism in student modelling. Alvey-IKBS Research Workshop Tutoring Systems. University of Exeter.

Self, J. (1988). (Ed.). Artificial intelligence and human learning: Intelligent computeraided instruction. London: Chapman and Hall Computing.

Self, J. (1998). Hanging by Two Threads: The Evolution of Intelligent Tutoring Systems Research. (Abstract). In B. Goettl, H. Halff, C. Redfield, and V. Shute (Eds.), Intelligent Tutoring Systems. 4th International Conference, San Antonio, TX. Berlin, Germany: Springer-Verlag.

Self, J.A. (1987a). The application of machine learning to student modelling. In Artificial Intelligence and Education 1: Learning Environments and Tutoring Systems (eds. R. Lawler and M. Yazdani). Ablex, Norwood, pp. 267-280.

Self, J.A. (1999). The distinctive characteristics of intelligent tutoring systems research: ITSs care, precisely. *International journal of artificial intelligence in education*, 10, 350-364.

Sell J.A. (1974). Student models in computer-aided instruction. *International Journal of Man-Machine Studies*, 6, 261-276.

Shapiro, S. (1992). *Encyclopedia of Artificial Intelligence*, 2nd Ed. John Wiley and Sons.

Sharples, M.; Taylor, J. and Vavoula, G. (2005). "Towards a Theory of Mobile Learning," in 4th World Conference on Mobile Learning.

Shin, N.; Norris, C. and Soloway, E. (2006) "Effects of Handheld Games on Students Learning in Mathematics," in Proceedings of the 7th International Conference on Learning Sciences, pp. 702-708.

Shortliffe, E.H. (1976). Computer-based medical consultations: MYCIN. Amsterdam, Holland: Elsevier Science Publishers.

Shute, V.J. and Glaser, R. (1990). A Large-scale Evaluation of an Intelligent Discovery World: Smithtown. Interactive Learning Environments 1: pp. 51-57.

Shute, V. (1995). Smart: Student Modeling Approach for Responsive Tutoring. User Modeling and User-Adapted Interaction, 5, 1, pp. 1-44.

Shute, V.J. and Psotka, J. (1996). Intelligent tutoring systems: Past, present, and future. In D.H. Jonassen (Ed.), *Handbook of research for educational communications and technology* (pp. 570-600). New York: Simon and Schuster Macmillan.

Silverman, B.G. (1992). Survey of expert critiquing systems: Practical and theoretical frontiers. Commun. ACM 35, 4, 106-127.

Sison, R., and Shimura, M. (1998). Student modeling and machine learning. *International Journal of Artificial Intelligence in Education* 9, 128-158.

Skinner, B.F. (1958). Teaching Machines. Science, 128, 969-977.

Skinner, B.F. (1954). The science of learning and the art of teaching. Harvard Educational Review, 24, 86-97.

Skinner, B.F. (1974). "About behaviorism", Knopf, New York.

Slavin, R.E. (1990a). Research in Cooperative Learning: Consensus and Controversy. Educational Leadership 47 (4): pp. 52-55.

Slavin, R.E. (1990b). Cooperative learning: Theory, Research, and Practice. Prentice-Hall, Englewood Cliffs, NJ.

Sleeman, D.H. and Smith, M.I. (1981). Modelling students' problem solving. Artificial Intelligence, 16, 171-188.

Sleeman, D.H. (1975). A problem-solving monitor for a deductive reasoning task. *International Journal of Man-Machine Studies*, 7, 183-211.

Sleeman, D.H. (1983). Intelligent tutoring systems: a review. Proceedings of EdCompCon '83 meeting. IEEE Computer Society, pp. 95-101.

Sleeman, D.H. (1984). Intelligent tutoring systems: A review. (Report No. IR011683). Stanford, CA: Stanford University, School of Education and Department of Computer Science. (ERIC Document Reproduction Service No. ED 257 450).

Sleeman, D.H. (1985). UMFE: a user modelling front-end subsystem. *International Journal of Man-Machine Studies*, 23, 71-88.

Sleeman, D.H. (1987). PIXIE: a shell for developing intelligent tutoring systems. In Artificial Intelligence and Education (eds R. Lawler and M. Yazdani). Ablex, Norwood, pp. 239-265.

Sleeman, D.H. and Brown, J.S. (1982b). Introduction: intelligent tutoring systems. In *Intelligent Tutoring Systems*. (Eds.) D.H. Sleeman and J.S. Brown. Academic Press, London, pp. 1-11.

Sleeman, D.H. and Brown, J.S. (eds.) (1982a). *Intelligent Tutoring Systems*. Academic Press, London.

Sleeman, D.H., Kelly, A.E., Martinak, R., Ward, R.D., and Moore, J.L. (1989). Studies of diagnosis and remediation with high school algebra students. Cognitive Science, 13(4), 551-568.

Smith, K.A. (1996). Cooperative learning: Making "Groupwork" Work. New Directions for Teaching and Learning 67: pp. 71-82.

Smith, K.A., Sheppard, S.D., Johnson, D.W. and Johnson, R.T. (2005). Pedagogies of Engagement: Classroom based Practices. Journal of Engineering Education 94 (1): pp. 87-101.

Smith, C., Murphy, T., and Teng, T. (2001). The Perfect Fit: Selecting the Online Learning Environment of Tomorrow Today. http://cite.telecampus.com/LMS/Perfect%20Fit.PDF

Soller, A., Martinez-Monez, A., Jermann, P. and Muehlenbrock, M. (2005). F rom mirroring to guiding: A review of state of the art technology for supporting collaborative learning. *International Journal of Artificial Intelligence in Education* 15 (4): pp. 261-290.

Soloway, E. and Johnson, W. (1984). Remembrance of blunders past: a retrospective on the development of PROUST. Proceedings of the Sixth Cognitive Science Society Conference, Boulder, CO, p. 57.

Soloway, E., Rubin, E., Woolf, B., Johnson, W.L., and Bonar, J. (1983). Meno ii: An ai-based programming tutor. *Journal of Computer-Based Instruction* 10, 20-34.

Song, J.S., Hahn, S.H., Tak, K.Y., and Kim, J.H. (1997). An intelligent tutoring system for introductory c language course. *Computers and Education* 28, 2, 93-102.

Song, Y. and Fox, R. (2005). "Integrating m-technology into Web-based ESL vocabulary learning for working adult learners," in *Wireless and Mobile Technologies in Education*, pp. 154-163.

Sorensen, E.K. (1994). Dialogues in Networks. The Dynamic Nature of Asynchronous Linguistic Interaction in Computer-Mediated Communication Systems. The Computer as Medium. Anderson, P.B., Holmqvist, B. and Jenson, J.F. (eds.), Cambridge, MA, Cambridge University Press: pp. 389-421.

Sorensen, E.K. (1999). Intellectual amplification through reflection and didactic change in distributed collaborative learning. 1999 Conference on Computer Support for Collaborative Learning.

Spohrer, J.C. and Soloway, E. (1986). Novice mistakes: Are the folk wisdoms correct? Communications of the ACM, 29, 7, 624-632.

Stahl, G. (2003). Meaning and interpretation in collaboration. Conference on Computer Support for Collaborative Learning (CSCL 2003). Bergen, Norway.

Stansfield, J.C., Carr, B., and Goldstein, I.P. (1976). Wumpus advisor I: A first implementation of a program that tutors logical and probabilistic reasoning skills. AI Lab Memo 381. MIT, Cambridge, Massachusetts.

Stathacopoulou, R., Magoulas, G.D., Grigoriadou, M., Samarakou, M. (2005). Neuro-fuzzy knowledge processing in intelligent learning environments for improved student diagnosis. *Information Sciences* 170(2-4, 25), 273-307.

Steinberg, E.R. (1977). Review of Student Control in Computer-Assisted Instruction. *Journal of Computer-Based Instruction*, 3(3): 84-90, 1977.

Stern, M., J. Beck and B. Woolf. (1996). Adaptation of Presentation and Feedback in an Intelligent Mathematics Tutor. In Proceedings of the Third International Conference on Intelligent Tutoring Systems, Montreal.

Suebnukarn, S. and Haddawy, P. (2004). A collaborative intelligent tutoring system for medical problem-based learning. International Conference on Intelligent User Interfaces.

Sun Microsystems, Inc. (1995). Java 2 Platform, Standard Edition (J2SE), http://java.sun.com/j2se

Suppes, P. (19661 The uses of computers in education. Scientific American, 25, 206-221.

Suppes, P. (1967). Some theoretical models for mathematics learning. *Journal of Research and Development in Education*, 1, 5-22.

Suppes, P. (1981). Future educational uses of interactive theorem proving. University-Level Computer-Assisted Instruction at Stanford: 1968-1980, Stanford, Institute For Mathematical Studies In *The Social Sciences*: 399-430.

Suraweera, P., Mitrovic, A., and Martin, B. (2004). The role of domain ontology in knowledge acquisition for itss. In Intelligent Tutoring Systems, pp. 207-216.

Surber, J., Leeder, J. (1988). The effect of graphic feedback on students' motivation. *Journal of Computer-Based Education* 15(1), 14-17.

Suthers, D., Connelly, J., Lesgold, A., Paolucci, M., Toth, E. and Toth, J. (2001). Representational and advisory guidance for students learning scientifi c inquiry. Smart Machines in Education: The Coming Revolution in Educational Technology. Forbus, K.D. and Feltovich, P.J. (eds.), Menlo Park, CA, AAAI/MIT Press: pp. 7-35.

Suthers, D. (1992). Answering Student Queries: Functionality and Mechanisms. In Proceedings of the 2nd International Conference on ITS (ITS-92), Montreal, June.

Suthers, D. and Weiner, A. (1995). Groupware for developing critical discussion skills. Computer Supported Cooperative Learning (CSCL '95), Bloomington, IN.

Thagard, P. (1996). Cognitive Science. In E. Zalta (Ed.), Stanford Encyclopedia of Philosophy. http://plato.stanford.edu/entries/cognitive-science

The World Bank. (1999). *World Development Report Knowledge for Development*. New York: Oxford University Press.

Thomas, E. (2003). Intelligent Tutoring Systems, ITS http://coe.sdsu.edu/eet/Articles/tutoringsystem/start.htm

Thorisson, K.R. (1993). Dialogue control in social interface agents. Proceedings of INTERCHI (pp. 139-140). Amsterdam, Holland.

Thorndike, E. (1922). *The Psychology of Arithmetic*. Macmillan, New York,.

Tinker, B. (1997). "Thinking About Science." Concord Consortium, from http://www.concord. org/publications/fi les/ThAbSci.pdf.

Tobias, S. (1985). Computer assisted instruction. In Adapting Instruction to Individual Differences (eds. M.C. Wang and H.J. Waldberg), McCutchan, Berkeley, CA, pp. 139-159.

Tom Snyder Production (1995). Geography Search [Computer Software]. Watertown, MA.

Tom Snyder Production (1998). Rainforest Researchers [Computer Software]. Watertown, MA.

Toogood, R.W., Wong, D. (1993). An interactive fluid mechanics tutorial using authorware. In: 1993 ASME International Computers in Education Conference and Exhibition, pp. 539-545.

Uhr, L. (1969). Teaching machine programs that generate problems as a function of interaction with students. Proceedings of the 24th National Conference, ACM, 125-134.

Vahey, P., Tater, D. and Roschelle, J. (2004). "Leveraging Handhelds to Increase Student Learning: Engaging Middle School Students with the Mathematics of Change," in 6th International Conference on Learning Sciences.

Van Dam, A. (1988). Hypertext '87 Keynote Address, Communications of the ACM 31(7):887-895. http://www.cs.brown.edu/memex

Van Lehn, K. (1990). Mind bugs: The origins of procedural misconceptions. Cambridge, MA: MIT Press.

Vanlehn, K. (1987). Learning one subprocedure per lesson. Artificial Intelligence 31, 1-40.

VanLehn, K. (1988). Student modeling. In Polson, M.C. and Richardson, J.J. (Eds.). Foundations of intelligent tutoring systems. Hillsdale, NJ: Lawrence Erlbaum Associates Publishers.

VanLehn, K. (1993). How people learn from a tutor. Unplished research proposal, Learning Research and Development Center, University of Pittsburgh, Pittsburgh, PA.

VanLehn, K. *et al.* (2005), "The Andes Physics Tutoring System: Five Years of Evaluations," in Artificial Intelligence in Education.

VanLehn, K., Graesser, A.C., Jackson, G.T., Jordan, P., Olney, A., and Rose, C.P. (2007). When are tutorial dialogues more effective than reading? Cognitive Science 31(1), 3-62.

VanLehn, K., Lynch, C., Schulze, K. Shapiro, J.A., Shelby, R., Taylor, L., Treacy, D.,

Weinstein, A., and Wintersgill, M. (2005). The Andes physics tutoring system: Lessons Learned. In *International Journal of Artificial Intelligence and Education*, 15 (3), 1-47.

Veith, T.L., Kobza, J.E., Koelling, C.P. (1998). World Wide Web-based simulations. *International Journal of Engineering Education* 14(5), 316-321.

Vizcaino, A., Contreras, J., Favela, J. and Prieto, M. (2000). An adaptive, collaborative environment to develop good habits in programming. International Conference on Intelligent Tutoring Systems, Montreal, Canada.

Vygotsky, L.S. (1978). Mind in Society: The development of higher psychological processes. Harvard University Press, Cambridge, MA.

Wachsmuth, I. (1988). Modelling the knowledge base of mathematical learners: situation-specific and situation-nonspecific knowledge. In Learning Issues for Intelligent Tutoring Systems (eds. H. Mandl and A. Lesgold). Springer-Verlag, London, pp. 63-79.

Wan, D. and Johnson, P.M. (1994). Experiences with Clare: A computer-supported collaborative learning environment. *International Journal of Human-Computer Studies* 41 (6): pp. 851-879.

Wankat, P.C., Oreovicz, F.S. (1993). Teaching Engineering. McGraw-Hill, New York.

Webb, N. (1982). Student Interaction and Learning in Small Group. *Review of Educational Research*, 52, pp. 421-445.

Weber, G., and Mllenberg, A. (1995). Elm-programming-environment: A tutoring system for lisp beginners. In Cognition and Computer Programming, Ablex, Ed. Norwood, NJ, pp. 373-408.

Weber, G., and Specht, M. (1997). User modeling and adaptive navigation support in www based tutoring systems. In 6th International Conference on User Modeling, pp. 289-300.

Wedekind, J. (1988). Computer-Aided Model Building. In: Mandl, H., Lesgold, A. (eds.) *Learning Issues for Intelligent Tutoring Systems*, pp. 287-294. Springer, New York.

Weischedel, R.M., Voge, W.M. and Ames, M. (1978). An artificial intelligence approach to language instruction. Artificial Intelligence 10, 225-240.

Welch, W.W., Klopfer, L.E., Aikenhead, G.S. and Robinson, J.T. (1981). T he role of inquiry in science education: Analysis and recommendations. *Science Education* 65 (1): pp. 33-50.

Wenger, E. (1987). Artificial Intelligence and Tutoring Systems. Morgan Kaufmann, Los Altos, CA.

Wenk, L. (2000). Improving science learning: Inquiry-based and traditional first-year college science curricula. School of Education, University of Massachusetts, Amherst.

Wexler, J.D. 11970). Information networks in generative computer-assisted instruction. IEEE Transactions on Man-Machine Systems 11, 181-190.

Wheatley, G.H. (1991). Constructivist perspectives on science and mathematical learning. *Science Education*, 75, 9-21.

White, B.Y. and Frederiksen, J.R. (1990). Causal model progressions as a foundation for intelligent learning environments. In Clancey, W.J. and Soloway, E. (Eds.), *Artificial intelligence and learning environments* (pp. 99-157). Cambridge, MA: The MIT press.

White, B.Y. and Horowitz, P. (1987). Thinker tools: Enabling children to understand physical laws. (Report No. 6470). Cambridge, MA: Bolt, Beranek, and Newman.

Whitehead, E.J., JR., Wiggins, M. (1998). WebDAV: IETF Standard for Collaborative Authoring on the Web, IEEE Internet Computing 2(5):34-40.

Wilson, B.G., Welsh, J.R. (1991). Small Knowledge-Based Systems in Education and Training: Something New under the Sun. In: *Expert Systems and Intelligent Computer-Aided Instruction*, Vol. 2. Educational Technology Publications, Englewood Cliffs.

Winkels, R., J. Sandberg and J. Breuker. (1990). The Coach. In EUROHELP: Developing Intelligent Help Systems, Breuker, J., ed., EC: Copenhagen, pp. 119-146.

Witkin, H.A., Moore, C.A., Goodenough, D.R., and Cox, P.W. (1977). "Fielddependent and field-independent cognitive styles and their educational implications", *Review of Educational Research*, 47, pp. 1-64.

Woods, P., and Hartley, J.R. (1971). Some learning models for arithmetic tasks and their use in computer-based learning. *British Journal of Educational Psychology*, 41 (1), 35-48.

Wooldridge, M. (1999). Intelligent Agents. In Multiagent Systems: A Modern *Approach to Distributed Artificial Intelligence*, ed. Weiss, G., pages 27-77, The MIT Press.

Woolf, B. and Hall, W. (1995). Multimedia Pedagogues: Interactive Systems for Teaching and Learning. IEEE Computer, Special Issue on Multimedia 28 (5): pp. 74-80.

Woolf, B. and Cunningham, P.A. (1987). Multiple knowledge sources in intelligent tutoring systems. IEEE Expert, 2, 2, 41-54.

Woolf, B. and McDonald, D.D. (1985). Building a computer tutor: Design issues. AEDS Monitor, 23, 10-18.

Woolf, B. (1986). Intelligent tutoring systems: A survey. In Shrobe, H.E. and American Association for Artificial Intelligence (Eds.), Exploring artificial intelligence (pp. 1-43). San Mateo, CA: Morgan Kaufmann Publishers, Inc.

Woolf, B. (1988a). 20 years in the trenches: What have we learned? Proceedings of the 'lst international conference on intelligent tutoring systems (pp. 33-39). Montreal, Canada.

Woolf, B. (1992). AI in Education. *Encyclopedia of Artificial Intelligence*, Shapiro, S., ed., John Wiley and Sons, Inc., New York, pp. 434-444.

Woolf, B. (1998). Training and Development. 52 (11). University of Massachusetts.

Woolf, B.P. and McDonald, D.D. (1984). Context-dependent transitions in tutoring discourse. Proceedings of the National Conference on Artificial Intelligence. Austin, Texas, pp. 355-361.

Woolf, B.P. (1984). Context dependent planning in a machine tutor. Ph.D. Dissertation, University of Massachusetts, Amherst, Massachusetts.

Woolf, B.P. (1988). Representing complex knowledge in an intelligent machine tutors. In Self, J. (Ed.), *Artificial Intelligence and Human Learning* (pp. 3-27). London: Chapman and Hall Computing.

Woolf, B.P. (1992). Building knowledge based tutors. In: Tomek, I. (ed.) ICCAL 1992. LNCS, Vol. 602, pp. 46-60. Springer, Heidelberg.

Wu, H., Houben, G.J., and De Bra, P. (2000). Supporting User Adaptation in Adaptive

Hypermedia Applications. On-line Conference and Informatiewetenschap 2000. Rotterdam, NL. http://wwwis.win.tue.nl/~debra/infwet00/infwet00.ps

Yaakub, M.N. (2001). Effectiveness of Computer-Assisted Instruction in Technical Education: a Meta-Analysis http://voc.ed.psu.edu/projects/publications/books/Fall%202001/WEF2001.2.html

Yang, H., Lu, W.F. (1993). Procase: a prototype of intelligent case-based process planning system with simulation environment. In: 1993 ASME International Computers in Education Conference and Exhibition, pp. 571-577.

Yatani, K.; Sugimoto, M. and Kusunoki, F. (2004). "Musex: A System for Supporting Children's Collaborative Learning in a Museum with PDAs," in International Workshop on Wireless and Mobile Technologies in Education, p. 109.

Yazdani, M. (1983). Introduction: artificial intelligence and education. In New Horizons in Educational Computing led. M. Yazdani). Wiley, New York.

Yazdani, M. (1986). Intelligent tutoring systems survey. *Artificial Intelligence Review*, 1, 43-52.

Yazdani, M. (1987). Intelligence tutoring systems: an overview. In *Artificial Intelligence and Education* (eds R. Lawler and M. Yazdani). Ablex, Norwood, pp. 182-201,

Young, J.D. (1996). The Effect of Self-Regulated Learning Strategies on Performance in Learner Controlled Computer-Based Instruction. *Educational Technology Research and Development*, 44: 17-27.

Youngblut, C. (1994). Government sponsored research and development efforts in the area of intelligent tutoring systems. Institute for Defense Analyses (IDA Paper P-3003). https://www.spider.hpc.navy.mil/html-docs/its-ida/

Zissos, A.Y. and Witten, I.H. (1985). User modelling for a computer coach: a case study. *International Journal of Man-Machine Studies*, 23, 729-750.

Zumbach, J., Reimann, P. and Schoenemann, J. (2005). Effects of resource distribution and feedback on computer-mediated collaboration in dyads. Towards sustainable and scalable educational innovations informed by the learning sciences. C.K. Looi, D. Jonassen and M. Ikeda, (eds.), Amsterdam, IOS Press: pp. 587-596.

Index